TOY FORTS & CASTLES

European-Made Toys of the 19th & 20th Centuries

ALLEN HICKLING

Schiffer Publishing Ltd®

4880 Lower Valley Road • Atglen, PA 19310

For Judith

Designed by Molly Shields
Type set in Bulmer BT/Times New Roman

ISBN: 978-0-7643-4813-6
Printed in China

Published by Schiffer Publishing, Ltd.
4880 Lower Valley Road
Atglen, PA 19310
Phone: (610) 593-1777; Fax: (610) 593-2002
E-mail: Info@schifferbooks.com

For our complete selection of fine books on this and related subjects, please visit our website at www.schifferbooks.com. You may also write for a free catalog.

This book may be purchased from the publisher. Please try your bookstore first.

We are always looking for people to write books on new and related subjects. If you have an idea for a book, please contact us at proposals@schifferbooks.com.

Schiffer Publishing's titles are available at special discounts for bulk purchases for sales promotions or premiums. Special editions, including personalized covers, corporate imprints, and excerpts can be created in large quantities for special needs. For more information, contact the publisher.

This is a painting by my 15-year old granddaughter Madhuri. It captures the context in which toy forts and castles come to life in the imagination during play. Here the players involved in the game on the carpet go through its transition in the trees to the fantasy of the castle above.

CONTENTS

FOREWORD

It is my pleasure to write the foreword for Allen Hickling's reference book on *Toy Forts and Castles*.

Allen has been collecting, researching, photographing, and recording toy forts and their manufacturers for the past thirty years and has finally completed this comprehensive reference work.

A book on toy forts and castles has never before been published and this work is unique; it is a superb addition to the list of toy soldier-related books already published by Schiffer Publishing.

Allen Hickling combines his background as an architect with the subject of toy forts and castles, and this combination makes for a well-researched reference book. The book certainly fills a void in the literature and will be useful to museums, auctioneers, antique dealers, and others in the business, as well as academics and collectors.

Manufacturers, dimensions, dates, and detailed descriptions of toy forts, along with excellent photographs, are included, and, while no book is ever complete, this ground breaking reference work certainly goes a long way to documenting the subject in great detail.

Here is a work that begins to make it possible for others to follow the evolution of toy forts and castles. It is a major breakthrough. It is a starting place in an under-explored field, and will provide the basis for other collectors and researchers to add to Allen's knowledge and fill in some of the gaps in the record. We are grateful to Allen Hickling for beginning the work.

Norman Joplin
*Norman Joplin is an internationally
renowned collector, researcher, author,
dealer, and auctioneer*

This is a computer-generated picture by Judith Hickling. It uses two toy forts. The one on this side of the river is quite detailed, while that on the other side is quite small. The figures are German-made flats. Together they give a marvelous impression of the sort of scene that can be generated by the imaginations of the players.

Acknowledgments

It is difficult to know where to start when it comes to giving credit to those who have supported and helped me in the writing of this book.

I shall start with Norman Joplin, because it was he who got the whole idea off the ground by selling the idea to Peter Schiffer. Up to that time, I had been talking about writing a book for a while and getting nowhere with it. It was he that got it on track.

He had strong backup from my friend Rob Wilson, who has since proved a tower of strength, always in the background urging me on. But he was only one among many who have been very supportive throughout, not the least of whom was his wife Jack.

Those who proofread the whole or parts at various stages include: Marc Azzini; Richard Lines; André Raemdonck; Jack Wilson; Rob Wilson; and Bernd Zimmermann.

Jack Wilson translated the many documents, magazines, and books.

Those who gave me access to their collections include: Marc Azzini; Peter Clark; Swantje Kohler ; Arnold Mueller; André Raemdonck; and Bernd Zimmermann.

Finally, those who have given me permission to use their images were: Evelyn Ackerman; Lynn Amari; Noel Barrett Auctions, USA; François Beaumont; Brightwells Auctions, UK; Jeffrey Caufield; Peter Clark; James Dalgety (for The Puzzle Museum, UK); Gisbert Freber; Geoff Green; Hastings House/Daytrips Publishers, USA; Janet Kirk (for Peter Kirk); Lyon & Turnbull Fine Art Auctioneers, UK; Arnold Mueller; Peter Müller; Mike Murphy; James Opie (for Bonhams Auctions, UK); Marion Osborne; Jim Osborne; Andreas Petruschka (for *Figuren Magazin*, D); Ed Poole; Ron Rosenburg; Peter Stenning; Steve Sommers; Alain Thomas; Ann Timpson; Vectis Auctions Ltd, UK; and Rob Wilson.

There are, of course, those who have agreed to let me use their work, the artists Judith and Madhuri Hickling (aged 16). Their works illustrate the psychological value of toy forts as an essential aid in stimulating imagination during play.

My family have been amazingly supportive throughout; more than I had any right to expect. However there are two who had an important role – my daughter Genevieve Howe, and my son Fergus. Genevieve gave me terrific support in the endless administrative tasks of all types, while Fergus spent many long hours in front of a computer getting the images into shape for publication.

Finally there is Doug Congdon-Martin, editor-at-large with Schiffer Publishing, who really should be giving master classes on how to take a rambling, error-ridden original script, and, in the style of the author, to knock it into a shape fit for publication. Brilliant.

Thanks to you all. I have no doubt that I have missed a number of contributors. To those who I have missed, please do not think this was intended. All your input was gratefully received.

This is another computer-generated picture by Judith Hickling. The central feature of the background is a toy fort imaginatively used as the context for the action. It shows again how such castles, combined with a lively imagination, can provide the basis for many exciting play opportunities.

INTRODUCTION

Originally, a toy fort was a vital accessory to somebody's game of toy soldiers – after all, every toy army needed something to attack and defend, and somewhere to live! Now, if it survives, it may be seen from very different points of view.

One may see it as an essential display structure for a prized toy soldier collection. Someone else might see it as a large bit of dusty, worm-eaten old junk cluttering up the attic. In such a scenario, we can only hope that a dedicated collector, rather than the local waste tip, will be the recipient of such an unloved treasure.

This book is about those commercially manufactured toy forts on which toy soldiers came to life in a three-dimensional context. It does not include the early lead, "flat" type of toy forts that can only be used as scenery or for target practice, nor the build-it-yourself (e.g.: Lego, Exin) and the very few do-it-yourself home-made types. Nor does it include those based on the forts that were built against the native tribes in the "Wild West" on the frontier in America.

Unfortunately, it also does not include forts that were manufactured in the USA. It is not that there were so few, but I just could not get enough information for it to be a viable option. I am sure that this and the "Wild West" forts will be the subject of another book.

The work is further limited in at least two ways. First, it is incomplete in that, where the information was not available, manufacturers have been left out. This has led to the omission of many fine forts. Second, some of the explanation of why certain things happened in a given way is only my opinion.

The intended readership is anyone who has an interest in tracing the maker or the time and place of manufacture of a given fort or castle – particularly collectors, auctioneers, and museum curators. In fact, it is aimed at anyone who has an interest in the subject. It is also intended as a coffee table book, of interest to anyone who likes to browse through photographs of antiques.

It was based originally on my personal collection, but it soon became apparent that that was far too limited, so I have included images from many other sources. In this regard, I would like to mention in particular André Raemdonck, Bernd Zimmerman, Marc Azzini, and the many, many others who have cooperated by giving me access to their collections.

Here I must mention that the work has been going on for at least five years. In that time, some of my personal collection has been sold and is now in the possession of the SOFIA Foundation in Cyprus. Their aim is to set up a Castle and Fort Museum there, which will feature some of the wonderful collections of toy soldiers and other figures that they have, as well as toy forts.

The Structure of this Book

In this book, I describe the development of the toy fort industry as a series of phases, each following the one before in an orderly sequence. Of course, history is never as neat as that, and the styles and production methods were often operating in parallel and, sometimes, in reverse order. The sequence I describe, however, is generally right – related to the passage of time as it is way-marked by the invention of new materials, the changing world economic order, market trends, and the development of new industrial practices.

In this way, I have structured each of the main chapters, each manufacturer's contribution, and the sequence in which they came, one after the other. This has not been an easy task. In order that the reader can more easily grasp the content of the book at the beginning of each chapter, 2 to 7, there is an overview of that chapter.

There are two chapters dedicated to two of the best known manufacturers in Germany, Moritz Gottschalk and O. and M. Hausser (Elastolin), and a chapter dedicated to manufacturers in the rest of Germany. There are two chapters dedicated to the industry in Britain, one to Lines Bros. (Tri-ang) and the other to the rest in Britain. Finally, there is a chapter dedicated to the rest of Europe, including manufacturers from three main producing countries, France, Belgium, and Denmark.

There are matters that are of a more general nature and do not fit into a structure of chapters. They may have a relevance to the subject where they appear, but also elsewhere. They do not have a specific place in the story as a whole. These are identified by appearing in sidebars, and explored in detail there as a subject in their own right.

This is not to say that this is fully comprehensive or, indeed, the best way of structuring the material. In all probability it is not. But it is the best way I have come up with to convey my knowledge of the subject. In order that the reader may find specific manufacturers and other information, I have included an index.

These toys were made to represent various types of buildings that are commonly called forts, castles, palaces, and fortresses – amongst other things. To avoid having to mention them all each and every time, I have chosen to use the word "fort" generically. If, by so doing, the sense would have been lost, I have used the appropriate specific word or words.

Wherever money is mentioned, it is listed in the currency, at the time, of the country in question. For the vast majority of countries, who used a decimal system, this does not present too much of a problem. However, in England we have a different story. Only since 1972 have we had a decimal system. Prior to that, when most of the forts were on the market, a system of pounds, shillings, and pence was used. For readers who do not know the system, there were twelve pence to the shilling and twenty shillings to the pound.

Manufacturers' model numbers are available in some cases, but certainly not all of them. Where the forts are either missing a label, or where the number is indecipherable on the fort itself, I have used question marks for the relevant digit or digits.

Where the date of manufacture is concerned I have adopted the convention of stating the earliest date of manufacture. When they went out of production is not of concern. Needless to say, many of these are uncertain. In some of these cases, where it is more or less known, or unknown, I have used a "c" (for circa) before the year.

As far as the size of forts is concerned I have adopted the conventional order of breadth by depth by height for listing the dimensions, where indeed these are known. These dimensions are given in inches (no feet or yards), and in millimeters (no centimeters or meters). Where some of them are known but not others, those others are indicated with question marks.

As far as the structure of the book is concerned, I have identified three manufacturers who were the three best known (to me), prolific producers of toy forts. They are Moritz Gottschalk, O. and M. Hausser, and Lines Bros., all of whom have a chapter each. I reckoned that, as Germany ruled the world as far as toy manufacturing was concerned, they had to have a chapter to themselves. Then, as I live in Britain and, naturally, have much information about the industry there, the British forts should also have a chapter. Finally there was the rest of Europe, which, as far as my information went, meant, in the main, France, Belgium, and Denmark.

For all of these, where the information is completely unavailable and an intelligent guess cannot be made, I have stated that it is unknown.

Of course, there are other sources, not least of them being America. However, I do not have enough knowledge of their toy forts to warrant a chapter. Maybe this will have to be done by others some other time, a thought which applies to everything else here.

There are enormous gaps in my version of the story. Also, I am sure, many mistakes. I hope the book will give impetus to others to take up the story – to fill the gaps and correct the inaccuracies. I wish them all the best.

Another computer-generated picture by Judith Hickling featuring the image of a toy fort. It does not matter what the situation is – imagination can always feed on it.

ONE

A BRIEF HISTORY OF
TOY FORTS AND CASTLES

At the beginning of the nineteenth century, the first manufactured toy forts and castles appeared in Germany. They formed elements in the sets of small wood blocks cut into the shape of buildings, which were to be laid out as miniature towns and villages. This happened in Germany simply because, up to the First World War, Germany ruled the world in toy manufacturing. Their dominance waned after the war, as others, from other countries, took up the challenge.

Each of these sets contained a number of houses, usually in two sizes, and one or two special buildings. Most common among these special buildings – sometimes made out of more than one piece – were churches and gatehouses, but forts and castles (or the ruins of them) were also sometimes included. Georg Hieronymus Bestelmeier of Nuremberg was well known for this sort of production, and he was active about 1800. Of course, there were many others who were also involved at the time, but he was probably better known because he was also an author.

About the same time, the same basic technology was being applied to the production of building blocks – usually wood cubes that were to be stacked together to form quite large buildings. The idea was to provide blocks of a generic nature intended to be used in the creation of many different buildings. The more sophisticated sets had blocks cut as roofs, arches, and columns, and it was only a small step from there – usually by the provision of a few crenellated blocks – to sets specifically made for constructing forts and castles. Constructions built with them had the added advantage of falling down with splendid realism when bombarded by toy cannon. The Erzgebirge region, especially in Saxony, was full of small workshops that were busy making these sets. I am sure others can provide the details of who they were and when they were active. This type of set is still being produced today, albeit in slightly modified forms.

Many of the surviving early examples evolved away from this generic concept and were designed to represent specific, mostly real buildings. This meant that the blocks had to be assembled in one particular configuration, coincidently making them something more in the nature of a puzzle with a unique solution. I do not know who these manufacturers were, but I do know of their forts. They were usually associated with sieges in wars of the time, which provided them with a marketing base. Examples are The Siege of Sebastopol, The Attack on the Lion Tower, and Fort Ali Musjid.

Some building blocks became much more sophisticated, being made of reconstructed stone and employing more, smaller pieces. They were not specifically made for forts and castles, although they could be used in this way, and indeed instructions were provided for them to be so. This form of manufacture was continued up until the Second World War.

The leading exponent of this sort of building set was Dr. F. A. Richter, who produced them from about 1880 to about 1925. Of course, the method of production was copied by many others. Construction with blocks had much to commend it, and sets continue to be made to this day.

However, about 1850, toy fort manufacture evolved into a form that could be more easily and more quickly erected. Drawing on the design and technology used in the manufacture of dollhouses, which had existed for some time, toy forts and castles were assembled in the factory using relatively thin, flat pieces of wood held together with nails and glue.

The more-or-less standard approach, which became the norm for the best part of a hundred years, was to provide a box containing building components. These components were similar to, but generally somewhat larger than, those of the earlier wood block village and town building sets. The inverted box was used as the base – usually covered with tree bark to represent a rocky hill, but sometimes painted a stone-color to represent the solid foundations and lower levels of the fort itself. On top, the building components were placed in the form of houses, towers, and battlements – usually located by means of spikes protruding from the underside of the pieces slotted into corresponding holes in the base.

These components – usually three-dimensional, but sometimes flat – were made more interesting by the application of detail in the form of doors, windows, stonework, and even vegetation, such as ivy. This was usually achieved by pasting architectural façades directly to the wood; they were finely drawn and printed on paper using lithography. Later, hand painting using stencils became the standard way of providing detail.

Christian Hacker started to make forts about 1850. Moritz Gottschalk came onto the scene about 1870, closely followed by Emil Schubert. They led the way for wooden forts.

Before long, other materials were being used. For example, the use of pressed sheet metal made possible very large structures with water features, such as harbors, lakes, streams, and fountains that were only possible to a limited extent in wood, and then only with a metal lining.

This was happening at the end of the nineteenth century – about the same time as the introduction of tin toys. The same basic technology was adopted for forming forts, but a zinc alloy was used in place of tin, which would not have been strong enough for such large structures and would have rusted too easily. Also, unlike tin toys, which had a printed surface, the forts tended to be hand painted.

This was when manufacturers with expertise in metal came on the scene. Rock and Graner and, to a slightly lesser extent, the firms of Lutz and Märklin started their production.

The use of metal for toy forts waned dramatically during the first decade of the twentieth century, but it had something of a renaissance in Britain just before the Second World War and in America just after it. In Britain, metal forts were mostly in the form of building sets, which tended to be quite small and small in scale. In America, metal was also used, somewhat like the tinplate buildings for model railways, during the 1950s and 1960s.

Wood, however, remained the choice of most manufacturers. By 1890, several firms started producing wooden forts, with Carl Moritz Reichel, Emil Weise, Richter and Wittich, and Emil Rudolph leading the opposition to Moritz Gottschalk. Weise was taken over by Carl Krause, and he and Weber came on the scene about 1900. They were swiftly followed by many others, including Albin Schönherr and Emil Hinkelmann, who, together with Moritz Gottschalk, were the backbone of the German toy industry.

About 1900, there was the beginning of activity elsewhere. The French had the firm of Villard and Weill (or Bon Dufour?) and others, in Denmark there was the rise of forts made in the prisons, and in Britain there was Charterhouse.

After the First World War, the existing German manufacturers were joined by Emil Neubert, who came on strongly. They recovered some of their position, but their presence was not as great as it had been before. In 1929, when the world depression came, the British took their chance, and, led by Lines Bros. with their well-known Tri-ang trade name, developed a viable alternative.

Composition, in its broadest sense meaning some form of paste that can be molded and then left to harden, is usually taken to mean a mixture of wood dust, casein, kaolin, and animal glue. This was first used in the production of dolls about 1850. It was used considerably later in the manufacture of toy soldiers and then, in the 1920s and 1930s, for toy forts.

One of the problems with this material was its instability during the curing process, especially for larger pieces. Consequently, the forts tended to be rather small, unless the composition was used as a molded facing on a wood structure or was reinforced with sackcloth. About 1920, the firm of O & M Hausser was centrally involved as the prime mover in the use of this material. They invented the name Elastolin, which became common parlance for the material, and became a major force in the production of toy forts.

Another material (often combined with wood) was cardboard. A reasonably heavy gauge was used, especially in the form of tubes used for circular towers. It was also used as a substitute for very thin sheets of wood or plywood, and treated in the same way with applied paper or paint.

Masonite, or hardboard as it is known in Britain, invented about 1920, started to be used in a small way about 1935 in America. It did not, however, come into consideration for toy forts until the mid-1950s in Europe. Then, together with medium-density fiberboard (MDF), which came in various thicknesses, it was used extensively in place of cardboard. Tudor Toys in England was the first to use the materials extensively in toy forts, followed by Tri-ang and many manufacturers, including Starlux in France and VEB Holzspielwaren in Germany.

Finally, as far as this history is concerned, the last material to be used commercially was plastic. Of course, there were many types of plastic – celluloid, Bakelite, polystyrene, and polythene, to name but a few. These different types of plastic, combined with the different ways of molding them, led to the main categories of fort manufacture. Polystyrene was the first to make a big impact on the market for toy castles in about 1955. Molded it could reproduce almost any shape and provided a level of detail unthought-of before, although the parts still had to be relatively small. The first manufacturer in this field was Kleeware, who, in 1955, produced their Crusaders Castle. This design has traveled the world appearing under different names, even for the system to be copied by Timpo. Hausser was not far behind with some magnificent forts.

This continued until about 1965 and the advent of vacuum molding, which enabled very large models to be made that weighed very little and, thus, were very easy for shipping and handling. This proved to be the ideal material for the job, and replaced nearly all others. Two companies, Hausser and Eco, were the leaders, both of them German. They were followed a few years later by Britains in England, which was just getting into toy forts.

The coming of television and computers then gradually took over. Older children could now create their own environments, and the gaming aspects of it had a dynamic fascination. Big structures like forts could be depicted much better on the screen. The market for static three-dimensional toy forts and castles got younger and younger, until there was no longer a big demand for them, unless they were juvenile or associated with the world of fantasy. But that is a different story.

TWO

FROM DOLLHOUSE TO FORTRESS:
The More Military Side of Moritz Gottschalk's Toy World

Ludwig Moritz Gottschalk (1840–1905), a gifted artist, started his working life as a bookbinder. It was from this constructive craft that he gradually developed into one of the world's most influential toy manufacturers in the late 19th and early 20th centuries.

By the age of 25, using his bookbinding skills and knowledge, he had already branched out to create children's toys from paper and cardboard. This start, plus lithographic printing and wood easily available from the local forests around his native Marienberg in Saxony, Germany, provided the basis for his enormous success as a manufacturer of dollhouses and their related products (specific rooms such as kitchens, dollhouse furniture, etc.). The name of Gottschalk became well known at the Leipzig Toy Fair.

Operating under the simple name of "Moritz Gottschalk," he went through a preliminary stage of employing piece workers in a sort of "cottage industry," but, by 1875, he owned a "factory" employing twenty people. Logs were sawn into boards using their own water-powered sawmill, and the final production, which included full-scale lithography, was done in the factory proper.

It was only a short step from this to using the same combination of technologies for diversification into different markets, such as grocery stores, stables, warehouses, and "fortresses." So the company grew, quite extraordinarily fast, over the next thirty years.

They went through two major fires and rebuilt bigger and better each time. The railway came, they expanded their premises, and they converted from water to steam power. By the turn of the century, with over 200 employees, they were one of the foremost toy manufacturers in the world.

Then, in 1905, Moritz Gottschalk died. Perhaps it was the pressure of keeping the business going that led to the death of the man himself – toy-maker extraordinaire. He had been at the forefront of industrialization in the toy fort, dollhouse, shop, and stable industry for thirty-five years. But this was not the end of the Gottschalk name.

The world does not stand still – least of all in the German toy industry at that time – and things had to change radically if they were to stay in front. So, armed with the name, the organization, and the culture of the production of quality toys that went with them, Wilhelm Gottschalk – son of Moritz – was already waiting to lead the enterprise to new heights.

Major changes in production followed and the growth continued, even accelerated, until the First World War. Serving in the military, Wilhelm, who was nothing if not a patriot, was killed during the first few months. His wife Lina inherited the business and carried it on as if little had happened, except that things had to slow down because of the war.

After the war, Lina married Kurt Wagner, who had been with the company since 1881; between them they maintained the tradition of producing quality toys. They had no easy task. They had to survive the aftermath of the war, raging national inflation, world recession, and the coming of the Third Reich – all in the space of fifteen years.

In 1934, Kurt's son Alfred Wagner, who had been working for the company since 1913, took over the leadership. He led it up to the Second World War, and in 1942 the factory was given over to producing transport boxes for the armed services.

Immediately after the war, the factory was expropriated by the Soviet army and the grounds were used as soldiers' quarters. In 1947, Gottschalk toys and dollhouses were seen again at the Leipzig fair. However, control of their affairs eroded over the next few years. Their production was managed by the state throughout the 1950s, at which point, for all practical purposes, the name Moritz Gottschalk ceased to exist. Then, in 1972, it was nationalized.

The First Fortresses

It is known that Moritz Gottschalk was in the business of making toys from about 1865. He started making toys in quite a small way using paper, cardboard, and *papier mâché,* but progressed quickly. Within two years, he had created a cottage industry and, by about 1870, he started making larger toys using wood, tree bark, cardboard, and printed paper. This was about the time that he started his catalogue.

Little is known about his production until about 1875 – at least by me. I would say that there must have been forts, several series of them, in fact. Maybe some will come to light before too long.

There are three forts that may or may not have been made during this period, though they may have been made by someone else altogether. They were, however, all made by the same manufacturer and they bear a number of features that are known to be characteristics of Gottschalk.

There were at least two types. One type stood on two fairly traditional linked boxes (2-001 & 2-003) – one covered with lithographed paper and the other in bark. The other type was octagonal in shape (2-002). Both were covered in buildings. These provided a roofscape with a mass of ornamentation in the form of spires, lanterns, chimneys, and the like. The buildings had detail in three dimensions, which was only portrayed graphically on the later versions, of which we have examples.

There is evidence of Gottschalk production from 1876 in the form of a page from the factory records that has provision for items numbered from 576 to 611. Of these No.576 to No.587, and No.595 to No.599, are filled in with handwritten script, while No.606 to No.610 are not filled in at all. The rest are typeset.

The explanation of this is difficult to assess, but probably has something to do with the rate of growth of the company. The reporting of new lines may not have been even across the company, and they had to leave spaces to accommodate this.

There is another strange anomaly on this one sheet of the factory record. Of the first set of forts, No.588 to No.593, only four of the six were assigned a series number in addition to the model number. I have no idea how or why this should have occurred.

Of the items on the page, those numbered from 588 to 605 are all forts. This means that Moritz Gottschalk had at least eighteen forts in his catalogue at this time, and this does not include any carried over from previous series. By modern standards this is a very large number indeed. Maybe Gottschalk was still finding his feet in the world of industrialized toy-making, or perhaps that was just the fashion. In any case, it all got a bit out of hand.

These eighteen were of four types. Starting with the typeset Nos.588 to 593, they are described as being square. This, indeed, they were, as demonstrated in No.590, one of which is in my possession. At 14¼" x 14¼" (360 x 360mm) this was middle of the range, which went from 10¼" x 10¼" (260 x 260mm) to 20" x 20" (510 x 510mm). As far as height is concerned, the factory records only record a box height of 4" (100mm), and did not include the erected buildings on top. However the one I have is 15" (380mm), and we can assume the others were, in proportion, similar.

MORITZ GOTTSCHALK: 580 Series
c1874 to c1875

NO.	DESCRIPTION	DATE	DIMENSIONS	DISTINCTIVE FEATURES
588	**smallest of this series** (listed in Gottschalk factory record 1876) eg: no known example	c1875	10¼"x10¼"x4" 260x260x100mm	• square
589	**second of this series** (listed in Gottschalk factory record 1876) eg: no known example	c1875	12¼"x12¼"x4" 310x310x100mm	• square
590 (2-004)	**third of this series** (identified by an example in the ownership below) eg: Allen Hickling Toy Forts	c1875	14¼"x14¼"x15" 360x360x380mm	• square–separate single slope ramp • 3 houses & gatehouse w/towers • four self-standing circular towers • central 3-piece circular tower
591	**fourth of this series** (listed in Gottschalk factory record 1876) eg: no known example	c1875	14½"x14½"x4" 370x370x100mm	• square
592	**fifth of this series** (listed in Gottschalk factory record 1876) eg: no known example	c1875	16"x16"x4" 450x450x100mm	• square
593	**largest of this series** (listed in Gottschalk factory record 1876) eg: no known example	c1875	20"x20"x4" 510x510x100mm	• square

In terms of materials, the buildings were made almost entirely of wood, with just a few bits of cardboard. These were nearly all covered with lithographed papers – only the roofs of the towers and perimeter walls were painted. This allowed the depiction of windows, doors, and stone details.

When one comes to look at these objectively, one would have to say that they were extremely fanciful compared to more recent forts. For example, all the towers were different in that they had mostly different papers on them, even though they were the same shape. Examining one of the towers more closely, however, one can see that it had three levels, each with its own paper, all separated by some fancy wood turning, and that the whole tower was capped off by a curvilinear sort of conical roof with a ball on top – with a flag on top of that. And this is only one of the towers. The main one at the center of these fortresses had three separate levels, all surmounted by a more conventional conical roof.

2-001 **Moritz Gottschalk**: *probable early fort*
2-002 **Moritz Gottschalk**: *probable early octagonal fort*
(Courtesy Noel Barrett Auctions)
2-003 **Moritz Gottschalk**: *probable early fort (Courtesy Bernd Zimmermann)*

These are early forts, probably by Moritz Gottschalk. One has to be careful when making comparisons because, at least, the one top right (2-003) has been restored, and one cannot be certain things were put back correctly. However, apart from the overall "feel" of them, there are several features which are common to these and the ones we know. Looking, first of all, at the two forts at the top (2-001 & 2-003), the roofs on the circular towers are very similar.

This also goes for the various pinnacles, lanterns, etc. on the rooftops. There is the paper decoration around the towers, and the balcony on the central tower. The houses have similar proportions and detail, even though some of it is three-dimensional. The perimeter walls have remarkably similar detailing.

The octagonal fort to the left (2-002) is quite small, and there are one or two missing parts. Also, the main tower should be in the middle. However, the parts are by the same manufacturer as the two above, and their general disposition is characteristic of Gottschalk. The crenellation and general coloring indicate that it was made at a slightly different time, but not by much.

2-004

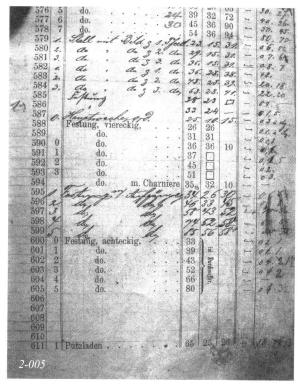

2-005

2-004 Moritz Gottschalk No.590
2-005 Moritz Gottschalk: *factory record*

This fort has suffered badly over the years. The roof on the larger building, three of the small lanterns on the lesser buildings, the ramp, and several perimeter wall pieces have all been replaced. Notice how the lithographed paper is coming off the base and some of the buildings. Despite this, it remains a fine example of the square format fortresses.

The paper on the building at the front in the photograph gives an excellent view of how detail was represented in two dimensions. Looking at one of the probable earlier fortresses on the previous page, even though the architectural style is different, one can see how the central vertical feature is projecting out from the building. In this case there is only a graphic representation of it.

The flags, of course, would have been German.

The page from the factory record above is the only one we have. It is fortuitous that these fortresses are on it.

The ornamental treatment of the structures on the roofs of the buildings were quite extraordinary, and when you get the roofs all bedecked with flags, the effect is stunning.

THE GOTTSCHALK NUMBERING SYSTEM

The Gottschalk numbering system, which is nothing if not eccentric at times, is not much of a help – but at least he had one, which is more than many of his contemporaries. Though nothing can be taken for granted, the only conclusion, which is generally agreed, is that the numbers reflect some sort of chronological order.

However, there is no hard evidence about when they started. It may have been right at the beginning, when Moritz Gottschalk first began in 1865, or it may have been anytime up to as late as 1870 or 1871. Nor is there any evidence of which number they started with – it may have been one but, equally, it might have been four hundred.

There was probably a logic that escapes us today. For example, based on the limited evidence to hand so far, it would appear that the numbering system shifted up, very roughly, about a hundred every year, and coincided with significant changes in the design, construction, and range available.

It seems that they numbered every product they made in the same sequence, regardless of what it was. So, for example, one might get dollhouses, followed by stables, followed by forts, followed by theatres, etc.

Each series of whatever product had a group of consecutive three or four figure numbers. These numbers were followed by an oblique and another number – starting at one, for example 3203/1. This stopped and started again for each product, and it seems as though this was no more than a check on the number of units in a series. By the time Moritz Gottschalk died in 1905, the practice of including the number after the oblique had been dropped.

They always started with the smallest, although this was sometimes difficult to differentiate, and they kept similar changes of style together in the sequence.

As an aid to stock-taking, and as a means of general communication within the works, items were given a number as they were made. Initially, and continuing well into the 1920s, this was handwritten in pencil on the underside of the item – presumably an instrument easily at hand in the workshop. It is quite rare, but certainly not unheard of, for this number to be missed, but it is quite often difficult to read. Only after the First World War did they mechanize the process with the introduction of rubber stamps in a few cases. As far as I can make out they never used paper labels.

Interestingly, this did not prevent them marketing forts from different ranges at the same time, as evidenced in Gamage's 1913 catalogue (where the 4700 and 6500 series were offered side by side), as well as in the 1890 catalogue. Nor did it prevent odd products at odd times. Perhaps they just had an old number that was not used and just wanted to plug the gap, so to speak.

Anyway, their relatively relaxed approach to numbers was not helped by various users quoting the wrong numbers. This may have included people employed by the company; after all, human error is almost inevitable when dealing with a vast range of stock. It all seems a bit undisciplined.

This system carried on until about 1930, to my knowledge, in spite of the death of their leader in the First World War and the shake up that would have caused.

What happened then is a bit of a guess, but we do know that there was a change in the management in 1934. We also know that a different numbering system was instituted about that time, because we have five pages of a catalogue or catalogues.

From these pages, it is very difficult, if not impossible, to discover how the numbering system operated, but it does seem that they used many of the same principles as before. It appears that they had series numbered 337, 338, 339, 346, 347, 514, 515, and 553. That is not to say that there were not others; there probably were. All these had an oblique followed by a single figure number, which implies a series, but it does seem a bit erratic. One wonders if they kept up the rate of production – somehow I doubt it.

MORITZ GOTTSCHALK: No.594 Stand-alone
c1874 to c1875

NO.	DESCRIPTION	DATE	DIMENSIONS	DISTINCTIVE FEATURES
594	**only one of this series** (listed in Gottschalk catalogue 1876) eg: no known example	c1875	14"x14"x4" 355x320x100?mm	• m. Charniere

The stand-alone number 594 is described in the factory record as "*m. Charniere,*" and was clearly not one of the square ones, but what it was is unclear. Assuming the "m." stands for "mit" (with) and "Charniere" is borrowed from the French meaning hinge, we can say that it was probably with some form of space-saving device.

MORITZ GOTTSCHALK: 590 Series
c1875 to c1876

NO.	DESCRIPTION	DATE	DIMENSIONS	DISTINCTIVE FEATURES
595	**smallest of this series** (listed in Gottschalk factory record 1876) eg: no known example	c1876	13¼"x10¼"x11¾" 340x260x300mm	
596	**second of this series** (listed in Gottschalk factory record 1876) eg: no known example	c1876	18"x13"x17¾" 460x330x450mm	
597 (2-006)	**third of this series** (listed in Gottschalk factory record 1876) eg: Bernd Zimmermann, D	c1876	21¾"x17"x20½" 580x430x520mm	• thru gate up double ramp to gateway • lower crtyd w/2 houses & tower • up to gateway & crtyd w/corner bldg • main bldg w/wing, & very lg circ tower
598	**fourth of this series** (listed in Gottschalk factory record 1876) eg: no known example	c1876	29"x20½"x23" 740x520x585mm	
599	**largest of this series** (listed in Gottschalk factory record 1876) eg: no known example	c1876	33½"x22"x23" 850x560x585mm	

Nos.595 to 599 were entered in handwriting, and were described as "*m/ Auf?????*" What this means is anyone's guess, but it may mean "with steps" or "with ramps." We do have one example, however, that may have been No.597.

2-006 Moritz Gottschalk No.597 *(probably) (Courtesy Bernd Zimmermann)*
This may or may not be a No.597, but it is by Moritz Gottschalk. The roofscape, the towers and the lithographed papers on the buildings tell us that. The only slight worry is that the perimeter walls are not quite the same, but that was quite probably a function of the passage of time, this fort having been made at a different stage in its development.

In this, we can see all the typical Gottschalk detailing of the time. For example, all the buildings at the lower level are the same as on No.590, with the exception of the perimeter walls. The upper level features a splendid six-storey corner house, a larger main building, and a fine circular tower.

IMORITZ GOTTSCHALK: 600 Series
c1874 to c1875

NO.	DESCRIPTION	DATE	DIMENSIONS	DISTINCTIVE FEATURES
600	**smallest of this series** (listed in Gottschalk catalogue 1875?) eg: no known example	c1875	13"x13"x4" 330x330x100mm	• octagonal
601	**second of this series** (listed in Gottschalk catalogue 1875?) eg: no known example	c1875	15¼"x15¼"x5" 390x390x125mm	• octagonal
602 (2-009)	**third of this series** (identified by an example in the ownership below) eg: Musée du Jouet, Bxl, B	c1875	19"x19"x18" 480x480x460mm	• octagonal – one extra level • separate single slope ramp • 2 sizes of tower & 2 of houses • central 3-piece circular tower
603 (2-007) (2-008)	**fourth of this series** (illustrated in Gottschalk catalogue 1875?) eg: no known example	c1875	20½"x20½"x6" 520x520x150mm	• octagonal – two extra levels • separate single slope ramp • 3 sizes of tower & 2 of houses • central 3-piece circular tower
604	**largest of this series** (listed in Gottschalk factory record 1876) eg: no known example	c1875	31½"x31½"x7" 660x660x180mm	• octagonal
605	**largest of this series** (listed in Gottschalk catalogue 1875?) eg: no known example	c1875	31½"x31½"x7" 800x800x180mm	• octagonal – three extra levels

The first indication we have of Gottschalk's 1875 production, apart from the factory record, is their appearance on a single page of his catalogue. This was the sort of catalogue used by salesmen and customers. It was for Nos.600 to 605, strangely omitting No.604. It included an illustration of No.603, which looks like a photograph. We also have a drawing of No.603.

There were six fortresses in the series. They ranged from the smallest at 13" x 13" (330 x 330mm), to the largest, 31½" x 31½" (800 x 800mm), which would have required some carefully considered handling. Again, they gave the height of the box only, which ranged from 4" (100mm) to 7" (180mm), a fact of interest only to shopkeepers, who may well have had storage problems, and shippers by way of packing requirements.

Another interesting fact one can glean from this document is that, where No.602 had only one extra level, No.603 had two and No.605 had three. As one goes up the levels, the buildings and towers get smaller. This occurs on No.602, where there is a significant difference in the size of things between the levels. I would say, judging No.603 by the photo in the catalogue, that there may have been a size between these. What we do not know is how they dealt with the situation on No.605 – did they make a very small top level, did they make some larger ones for the lowest level, or both.

These octagonal forts were quite spectacular, and must have displayed well in the shops. The effect is somewhat reminiscent of a wedding cake. The only drawback is that playing with them in the traditional way, using toy soldiers, would have been difficult. On the other hand, they may have been excellent as fairy castles for use by the girls of the household.

The Next Steps

I have been reliably informed that there was at least one series between the 600 series and the next one of which I have evidence. This would have been the 1800 series, which must have come out about 1885, but that is all I know. I can say it seems unlikely that this was the only one. Even if I assume that a series was entered into the factory record five hundred numbers apart, that means many forts must have been around. I am afraid we shall just have to wait until some enthusiast comes up with more evidence than I can muster.

The two 2300-related series, the 2360 and the 2370, which first saw the light of day about 1890, were the next. Actually, they were probably brought out in 1892/93, but the catalogue is undated. In it, the two series of fortresses, bearing consecutive numbers, offered fourteen models for sale. This seems a very large number to have in one's catalogue at any one time, even though the 1875 factory record provided more.

Anyway, the first series provided a range of sizes from No.2361 at 10" x 10" (255 x 255mm) – which is really quite small by any standards – to No.2367 at 22¼" x 20½" (550 x 510mm). Of these, we have one example: No.2366. We also have illustrations of this and four others taken from the catalogue.

The second series ran from No.2368 at 19¾" x 20" (500 x 510mm), to No.2374 at 34" x 36½" (865 x 930mm), which would have been more than a handful to move around. Of these, we have illustrations of three, taken from the catalogue.

That these are "fortresses" is dubious. They are really no more than houses, grand houses it is true, with guns in the courtyard and sentry boxes, but accommodation suited to the gentry rather than common or garden soldiers. This is evidenced in their description in the catalogue: *"Fortresses. Building and walls etc. made of wood, each window opens. Buildings have doors front and rear and can be opened. Rear box has removable metal plate for lights to illuminate. All parts can be disassembled, and are provided with anti-tip devices."*

2-007

2-008

2-009

2-007 **Moritz Gottschalk No.603**: *illustration. c1875*
2-008 **Moritz Gottschalk No.603**: *in 600 series catalogue, c1875*
2-009 **Moritz Gottschalk No.602** *(Courtesy Musée du Jouet, Brussels)*

The catalogue illustration is most likely based on a photograph (2-008). One wonders why No.605 was not in the catalogue.

On the actual example of No.602 (2-009), the flat base piece and the courtyard are clumsy replacements, but overall it is a fine example. One small perimeter wall piece and several roof embellishments are missing. The pieces on the lower level are the same as on No.590, and the difference in the size of the pieces between the levels is most apparent. One wonders how they managed the intermediate levels on the larger sizes. They clearly had some larger buildings, as can be seen in the catalogue.

This claim is so amazing that it deserves some investigation. Unfortunately, I have not been able to handle the one example we have. We see from the illustrations in the catalogue, however, that they had doors that opened. I find it difficult to imagine, though, how every window could be opened. In fact, I have doubts about any window opening on such a small building.

MORITZ GOTTSCHALK: 2360 Series
c1890 to c1898

NO.	DESCRIPTION	DATE	DIMENSIONS	DISTINCTIVE FEATURES
2361 (2-010)	**smallest of this series** (illustrated in Gottschalk catalogue 1890?) eg: no known example	c1890	10"x10"x4½" 255x255x110mm	• small gateway – 90º on • no sentry boxes
2362 (2-012)	**second of this series** (illustrated in Gottschalk catalogue 1890?) eg: no known example	c1890	12¼"x10½"x4½" 320x270x110mm	• small gateway – 90º on • no sentry boxes
2363 (2-011)	**third of this series** (illustrated in Gottschalk catalogue 1890?) eg: no known example	c1890	15"x15¼"x4½" 380x385x110mm	• small gateway – 90º on • two sentry boxes • ornate tower on main building
2364 (2-013)	**fourth of this series** (illustrated in Gottschalk catalogue 1890?) eg: no known example	c1890	17"x19"x6½" 430x480x165mm	• small gateway – 90º on • one sentry box • central tower proud of main building
2365	**fifth of this series** (listed in Gottschalk catalogue 1890?) eg: no known example	c1890	17¾"x17"x6½" 450x430x165mm	
2366 (2-014) (2-015)	**sixth of this series** (illustrated by an example in the collection below) eg: Berndt Zimmermann, D	c1890	19¼"x17"x6½" 490x430x165mm	• large gateway – 90º on • two sentry boxes • building 90º to main building • central tower proud of main building
2367	**largest of this series** (listed in Gottschalk catalogue 1890?) eg: no known example	c1890	22¾"x20½"x7¼" 580x510x185mm	

It is not known for certain how long before Gottschalk produced these fortresses that he made dollhouses. As there are some dollhouses with relatively low numbers, it seems reasonable to assume that they were in production before the fortresses.

2-010 Moritz Gottschalk No.2361: *catalogue*
This is the first of the fortresses in the 2300 series. The photo is taken from the catalogue. The fortress is really quite small, but not so small as to prevent the installation of opening doors. The No.2361 has two storeys and two bays at each side of the entrance. It is quite cramped. There are no sentry boxes, but there are a cannon and a couple of trees.

2-011

2-012

2-013

2-011 **Moritz Gottschalk No.2363**: catalogue
2-012 **Moritz Gottschalk No.2362**: catalogue
2-013 **Moritz Gottschalk No.2364**: catalogue
   These are the next three in the catalogue, and they demonstrate the progressive increase in size of the fortresses. No.2362 has two storeys and three bays at each side of the entrance, but no sentry boxes and but one cannon and two trees. No.2363 is similar to No.2362, with a larger courtyard and embellishments on the roof over the entrance. There are two sentry boxes and two cannon. No.2364 is more imposing with three storeys and two bays at each side of the entrance. The base is higher. There are a sentry box, two cannon, but, now, three trees.

1890

2-014

Nº 2366/6.

2-015

2-014 Moritz Gottschalk No.2366: *catalogue, c1890*
2-015 Moritz Gottschalk No.2366 *(Courtesy Bernd Zimmermann)*

No.2366 is the only one in the 2300 series of which we have an example. The images are of the catalogue and the real fortress.

It has two bays on each side of a four-storey, two-bay wide entrance tower. The secondary building is set at right angles to the main building coming forward. On the example, this secondary building has a red roof, which is impossible to distinguish in the black and white photographs, so it is impossible to tell if there were others in the series with similar roofs. There are two sentry boxes, but there is no trace of the cannon or trees.

Note the opening doors. Unfortunately, the door on the secondary building opens to a vertical drop down the side of the box. This could be a nasty shock for anyone prone to sleepwalking, but could be a useful feature if you were given the job of disposing of dead enemy bodies.

In this light, it is no surprise that the style of fortress owed much to their experience of dollhouses – despite having to be built to a much smaller scale in order to accommodate toy soldiers, which tended to be much smaller than dollhouse inhabitants.

This heritage is most obvious in the somewhat domestic character of their design. In addition, the buildings were hollow like dollhouses, with doors that opened to provide access to the inside, providing endless play opportunities. And so we come to the question of the windows. The catalogue claims that all the windows open. One might expect this in a dollhouse, but cut-out window openings at the reduced scale of fortresses would have been a serious challenge to efficient production.

One also wonders about the electric lighting. Presumably it operated on batteries, but I am not too sure how compact batteries were in those days. This also applies to the light bulbs. How did they make it work?

MORITZ GOTTSCHALK: 2370 Series
c1890 to c1898

NO.	DESCRIPTION	DATE	DIMENSIONS	DISTINCTIVE FEATURES
2368 (2-016)	**smallest of this series** (illustrated in Gottschalk catalogue 1890?) eg: no known example	c1890	19¾"x20"x7" 500x510x180mm	• large gateway – face on • one sentry box • chains on drawbridge • tower on corner in courtyard
2369	**second of this series** (listed in Gottschalk catalogue 1890?) eg: no known example	c1890	17¼"x22"x8¼" 440x560x210mm	
2370 (2-017)	**third of this series** (illustrated in Gottschalk catalogue 1890?) eg: no known example	c1890	19¾"x22"x8¼" 500x560x210mm	• large gateway – face on • two built-up levels • 3 sentry boxes • chains on drawbridge
2371	**fourth of this series** (listed in Gottschalk catalogue 1890?) eg: no known example	c1890	22½"x26¾"x11¾" 570x680x300mm	
2372	**fifth of this series** (listed in Gottschalk catalogue 1890?) eg: no known example	c1890	25½"x26¾"x11¾" 650x680x300mm	
2373	**sixth of this series** (listed in Gottschalk catalogue 1890?) eg: no known example	c1890	29"x29½"x11¾" 740x750x300mm	
2374 (2-018)	**largest of this series** (illustrated in Gottschalk catalogue 1890?) eg: no known example	c1890	34"x36½"x12¼" 860x930x310mm	• four large gateways – face on • two and a half built-up levels • two different self-standing towers • five houses –one very large

Anti-tip devices were claimed as a special feature in their catalogue. These may have been metal spikes or nails projecting down from the buildings into holes in the base, which became standard practice in the industry. In fact, this system does not lend itself to use on hollow buildings and they may have used a somewhat cruder technique of simple blocks of wood attached to the base, over which the buildings fitted snugly. They were certainly using this method on the 3200 series.

There were two differences between the series. First, and most obvious, was size. The second series was considerably bigger, which leads to the conclusion that, combined with the fact that they were consecutive numbers, the two have to be taken together. In effect, this would make for fourteen forts with many similarities, providing a continuous range of sizes and costs.

The second difference was in the gateways, which are now facing out from the fortress, and in their make up: they were generally bigger and included various towers.

Architectural detail was provided by a technique used extensively in dollhouse production of the time – lithographed paper glued to the bare wood forms. This allowed as much decoration as one could possibly wish and, combined with turned-wood pinnacles and minaret-type details at roof level, admirably intricate designs were possible.

In the catalogue, the fortresses are set off with various separate elements. These are sentry boxes, cannon, and trees in varying amounts. The sentry boxes we know were a part of the package, but I am not so sure about the cannon or the trees. Maybe they were put on there for effect.

In the same catalogue was another series (the 2500 series), using the same papers and incidental details as the 2300 series. It was comprised of eight models numbered from 2592 to 2599. This series also provided a range of sizes. It went from the smallest, measuring 15¼" x 9½" (385 x 240mm) – which is larger than at least two of the earlier series – to the largest, which was an imposing 32¼" x 27½" (820 x 700mm), and included five gates and three drawbridges. This is, at least, smaller than two of the earlier ones, but still a mighty handful to move around.

Did they misjudge the earlier range? The answer is probably, but not by that much, given the market they had to supply, which was mostly relatively rich people living in large houses.

There was one small change in their style of catalogue that may have been significant. They no longer listed the height as the height of the box base; now it was the overall height when erected. This implies a change in who was using the catalogue. It could no longer be the exporters, importers, distributors, or the transport contractors; it could only be the retailers and the customers – the actual end user. The Lines brothers went through a similar learning process about forty years later.

1890

2-016

№ 2368/1.

2-017

№ 2370/3.

2-018

№ 2374/7.

2-016 **Moritz Gottschalk No.2368**: *catalogue*
2-017 **Moritz Gottschalk No.2370**: *catalogue*
2-018 **Moritz Gottschalk No.2374**: *catalogue*

No.2368 (2-016) is the first with the gateway facing out from the courtyard. It is quite small, although the "hill" on which it stands is bigger than earlier fortresses, with a free-standing tower in the corner of the courtyard. Three storeys high, it has two bays each side of the one-bay, wide entrance tower.

No.2370 (2-017) has the same main building as No.2366 (2-014), with a free-standing tower in the corner of the courtyard. The base is considerably higher, which allows a secondary building to be located at the turn of the ramp. There are two sentry boxes.

No.2374 (2-018) is the largest from the 2300 series; the image is taken from the catalogue. It stands on a fine "hill," and has four gateways all facing out from the main building. Around the courtyard at the top is a fine main building, two secondary buildings, and two different self-standing towers. At the entry level, there are two more buildings. There are six sentry boxes, four cannon, and twelve trees.

The range was described in the catalogue as follows: *"Fortress with driveway, fancy drawbridges, etc. Buildings etc. with illumination."* There was nothing about opening doors and windows, nor was there mention of electric light, unless "with illumination" meant that. There was also no more on the much vaunted anti-tip devices. The opening doors and gates were shown in the catalogue however, and their omission from the description in the catalogue does not mean that the other specialties were discontinued.

MORITZ GOTTSCHALK: 2500 Series
c1892 to c1898

NO.	DESCRIPTION	DATE	DIMENSIONS	DISTINCTIVE FEATURES
2592	**smallest of this series** (listed in Gottschalk catalogue 1890?) eg: no known example	c1892	15¼"x9½"x12¾" 385x240x325mm	
2593	**second of this series** (listed in Gottschalk catalogue 1890?) eg: no known example	c1892	17¼"x11¾"x13" 440x300x330mm	
2594	**third of this series** (listed in Gottschalk catalogue 1890?) eg: no known example	c1892	18"x15¼"x19" 460x390x480mm	
2595	**fourth of this series** (listed in Gottschalk catalogue 1890?) eg: no known example	c1892	21"x20½"x21" 530x520x530mm	
2596	**fifth of this series** (listed in Gottschalk catalogue 1890?) eg: no known example	c1892	23"x21½"22" 585x550x560mm	
2597	**sixth of this series** (listed in Gottschalk catalogue 1890?) eg: no known example	c1892	24¾"x24"x23¼" 630x610x590mm	
2598	**seventh of this series** (listed in Gottschalk catalogue 1890?) eg: no known example	c1892	28¼"x24"x23¼" 720x610x590mm	
2599 (2-019)	**largest of this series** (illustrated in Gottschalk catalogue 1890?) eg: no known example	c1892	32¼"x27½"x23½" 820x700x600mm	• 4 gateways to ramp, 1 to undercroft • 3 drawbridges but no sentry boxes • two upper levels crenellated • craggy bark on boxes

Only one fort from the range was illustrated. It happens to be the largest on offer and was a spectacular affair promising great play opportunities. It is unfortunate that moving it around without the aid of a fork-lift would have been difficult, but that would not have mattered if one could afford a nursery where it could be dumped and never moved again. Of course, it was probably so expensive that the purchaser would have had the necessary nursery anyway.

It appears that both series used the same papers, although the black and white illustrations in the catalogue give no clue as to their colors. One noticeable change was the incorporation of crenellation in the 2500 series in place of flat-topped perimeter walls in the 2300 series. Here the guns have suitable openings to fire through, and a step towards fortresses was taken.

MORITZ GOTTSCHALK: 2700 Series
c1892 to c1898

NO.	DESCRIPTION	DATE	DIMENSIONS	DISTINCTIVE FEATURES
2784 (2-020)	**only one of this series-** (one example exists to my certain knowledge) eg: SOFIA Foundation, CY	c1894	22"x13"x15" 560x330x380mm	• quite small, two-floor main building • two large square decorative towers • long ramp to an imposing gateway • two sentry boxes

Finally, there is another series that comes into this category. We do not have the catalogue, but we do have an example. We can deduce nothing as far as the range of their forts was concerned, and, of course, where in that range the example fits, if, that is, it fits at all – it may have been a one-off. It comes in the 2700 series, which is different from the 2300 and 2500 series but is still quite residential in style. It was No.2784, and it came out about 1895.

It appears quite ponderous in scale, the size of the buildings being on the large size compared with the living accommodation. There is a lot of space at roof level and above, and the gateway looks to be eminently defensible. Maybe this was another step in the "fortress" saga; it definitely provided more to defend the property. They, at least, provided two sentry boxes, but still to the same design, which was to continue into the next series.

2-019 Moritz Gottschalk No.2599: *catalogue, c1892 & c1894*

This is the only example we have of the 2500 series. It is taken from the catalogue. It is the largest in the series and is covered with embellishments. There are four gateways, all to different designs, controlling a long and winding ramp. There was a splendid main building, but, interestingly, it is to an apparently smaller scale than the gateways.

2-020 Moritz Gottschalk No.2784

No.2784 is the only evidence we have of a 2700 series; there were no doubt others. It is still basically a house, but it is one characterized by the heavy modelling of the buildings, but strangely not the wall around the courtyard. The gatehouse is particularly large and defensible, the other buildings reasonably so. The ramp is very long, necessitating the toe to be a separate piece. There are two sentry boxes.

The Next Generation of Fortresses

Evidence of another "generation" of Moritz Gottschalk fortresses comes in the form of a single page taken from a catalogue, which is likely to have been published about 1899. The name Gottschalk does not appear anywhere, but the graphics are so similar to those in the earlier catalogue that it would be too much of a coincidence to be anything else.

The models illustrated in the catalogue are from the 3200 series – Nos. 3203 to 3211 – and provide a range of sizes similar to the earlier series. The smallest measured 12¼" x 8" (310 x 150mm), to the largest, which was 25" x 18½" (635 x 470mm). In fact, there must have been other pages in the catalogue because we have examples of other forts in the same series. These are No.3213 and No.3217.

In some ways, this series is similar to the previous ones. For example, the buildings are still of hollow construction and make use of the wooden block system of "anti-tip" devices. A similar tree bark is used to cover the box base, painted in the same way.

Both series use lithographed paper coverings to provide details of fenestration, wall texture, and color. Because we have examples, we can now comment on these aspects, even though the catalogue illustrations are, again, black and white. The red- and blue-roofed buildings have cream-colored walls with red and black details and are set around yellow courtyards, which are protected by low red-capped walls.

Perhaps the greatest difference lies in the simplification of design, which would have produced a number of economies. For example, there were now no opening doors or windows giving access to the interiors, and some of the buildings were made of cardboard instead of wood. The depth of the buildings changed also, so that those in this later series were no greater than the very meanest of the 2300 series. This, in itself, provided significant savings in production, but, of course, it meant that they had to give up on their much vaunted electric lighting.

The architectural style is very different. Whereas the earlier series were clearly splendid residences – very ornate with windows large enough to imply a late baroque or even 18th–19th century style – the 3200 series are much more austere. For example, there are no more pinnacles and minaret-type details at roof level. They are, however, distinctly more defensible, with windows narrow enough to be considered arrow slits and the crenellated parapets of the roofs – yet more steps toward the fortress image, which the name implies.

The style of the earlier series is clearly a natural extension of the dollhouse manufacturer's production. One is then led to wonder why a change might have been thought necessary. It may have been that market forces were at work again. Toy soldier manufacturers were becoming more and more prolific and their products would have required accommodation as well as places to attack. Alternatively, it may have been that a simple differentiation of products was thought to be desirable.

MORITZ GOTTSCHALK: 3200 Series
c1899 to c1905

NO.	DESCRIPTION	DATE	DIMENSIONS	DISTINCTIVE FEATURES
3203	smallest of this series (listed in Gottschalk catalogue 1899?) eg: no known example	c1899	12¼"x6"x3½" 310x150x90mm	
3204	second of this series (listed in Gottschalk catalogue 1899?) eg: no known example	c1899	12½"x9¼"x4" 320x235x100mm	
3205 (2-024)	third of this series (illustrated by an example in the collection below) eg: Antique Toy World, US	c1899	13¾"x10½"x4½" 355x270x115mm	• ramp to dbridge & small gateway • main bldg w/2 flanking circ towers • ornate roof on central section • turrets on the towers doubtful
3206 (2-023)	fourth of this series (illustrated by an example in the collection below) eg: Soltau Spielmuseum, D	c1899	16¼"x12¼"x5" 415x310x125mm	• ramp to dbridge & small gateway • main bldg w/2 flanking circ towers • ornate roof on central section • turrets on the towers doubtful
3207	fifth of this series (listed in Gottschalk catalogue 1899?) eg: no known example	c1899	18¼"x13¾"x5¼" 465x350x135mm	• small gateway missing roof & chains • gateway & perimeter walls missing • roof of one tower missing • high lower perimeter wall
3208	sixth of this series (listed in Gottschalk catalogue 1899?) eg: no known example	c1899	20"x14¾"x6" 510x375x150mm	
3209 (2-026) (2-027)	seventh of this series (illustrated by an example in the collection below) eg: Bernd Zimmerman, D	c1899	21½"x16¼"x9½" 550x410x245mm	• two levels • two small gateways • four towers all different • one sentry box – old design
3210	eighth of this series (listed in Gottschalk catalogue 1899?) eg: no known example	c1899	23¼"x17½"x10¼" 590x445x260mm	
3211 (2-025)	ninth of this series (illustrated in Gottschalk catalogue 1899?) eg: no known example	c1899	25"x18½"x10¾" 635x470x275mm	• two levels • two free-standing towers • two gateways – one large • one sentry box – old design
3213 (2-028)	eleventh of this series (catalogue unavailable, example used) eg: SOFIA Foundation, CY	c1899	19¾"x22"x8¼" 500x560x210mm	• 3-arch colonnade on lower level • two built-up levels • roofs of three towers missing • one sentry box – old design
3217 (2-029)	fifteenth of this series (example handled & photographed) eg: Gerry Greene, US	c1899	34"x36½"x12¼" 860x930x310mm	• 4-arch colonnade on lower level • two built-up levels • two large gateways • papers brown w/exposure to light

GOTTSCHALK'S USE OF CATALOGUES

The production of catalogues was, and probably still is, an essential part of most toy manufacturing companies' marketing strategies. The approach they take to this aspect of their business tells us much about the company culture. Moritz Gottschalk was no exception.

Unsurprisingly, the toy industry has always revolved around the Christmas trade. Consequently, manufacturers have had to conform to time scales established by the retailers. This has meant delivering their products in the late summer and early autumn so that they are received as late as possible before they have to be put on display for the Christmas rush. For the shopkeeper an early delivery means carrying stock for too long and, thus, reduced profit margins; and a late delivery could mean missing the rush and a seriously bad financial year.

The combination of this relatively fixed delivery date and the lead times needed in order to achieve efficient production has led manufacturers to require a clear idea of how full their order book is looking by Easter.

Consequently, the tradition of holding annual international (and national) toy fairs, such as Liepzig and Nuremberg, from late January to early March has become firmly established and, for many years, they have been the primary sales opportunity for manufacturers and importers. For obvious reasons, the production of manufacturers' catalogues conformed to this schedule, with mid-January publication deadlines being the norm for the following Christmas.

Moritz Gottschalk used more or less the same technique for the first thirty-five years of being in business, a technique that was copied by his son who followed him. They would illustrate two or three items of a series side by side, and list the relevant details of all in the series underneath or down the sides in beautiful, handwritten notes. The relevant details were the number of each item and its size – length x breadth x height.

There was some question about the height. They started out by listing the height of the box only, which was needed by the exporters, importers, distributors, and transport contractors simply because they had to store them. This did not, however, serve the purposes of the retailer or the customer. It took them about thirty-five years to work out how to manage this conundrum.

In the early years, they also hand-wrote a short description of the product. For example, beside the 2500 series they wrote: *"Fortress with driveway, fancy drawbridges, etc. Buildings, etc. with illumination."* By the time of the 3200 series this practice had stopped.

They used photography extensively, even as far back as about 1870, when its commercial use was in its infancy.

What happened after about 1907 we do not know, simply because we have no catalogues to look at – that is, until after 1934, when we know there was a change in the management.

At this time, the Third Reich was on the upswing and there was a strong feeling of nationalism in the country. In the catalogues that were then in use, the flags shown on the 300 numbers, which seem to reflect this, were of two sorts. There was a plain swastika and there was one with horizontal stripes. By the time of the 500 numbers, there was just one, which was a cross with a swastika in the middle.

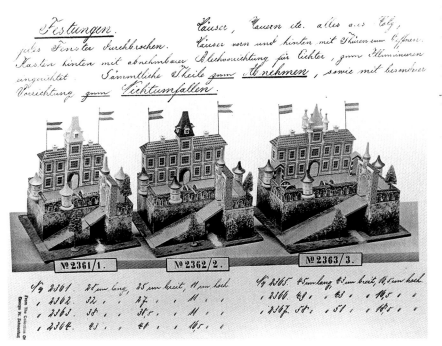

2-023

2-024

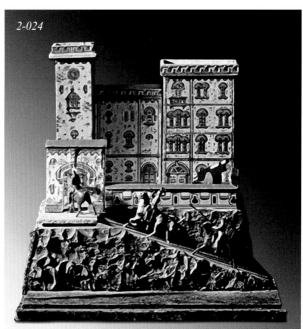

2-025

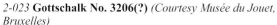

2-023 **Gottschalk No. 3206(?)** *(Courtesy Musée du Jouet, Bruxelles)*
2-024 **Gottschalk No. 3205(?)**
2-025 **Gottschalk No. 3211** *(catalogue)*

These are the three in the 3200 series. There is a complete change in the style of paper covering, and there is now no possibility of opening doors and windows.

The No.3205(?) (2-024), which is uncertain, is missing all its roofs and its drawbridge chains. It is quite small, so one wonders just how small the others were. The figures are Britain's 54mm scale cavalrymen.

The No.3206(?) (2-023) is also uncertain, but is probably the largest in the series with a single level. The turrets on top of the towers at the back are different, which seems a bit unlikely. There is no explanation, however, as to why. The drawbridge chains are present but not installed. The figures are approximately 45mm of contemporary German manufacture.

No.3211 (catalogue) (2-025), compared to No.2309, has a slightly larger main building, a much larger free-standing tower in the corner, a much more imposing gateway at the lower level, and an upper gateway that is now at right angles to the main building. There is one sentry box.

2-026

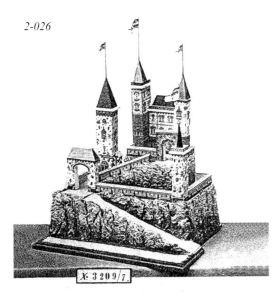

2-027

2-028

2-026 Moritz Gottschalk No. 3209 (catalogue), c1899
2-027 Moritz Gottschalk No. 3209 (Courtesy Bernd Zimmermann)
2-028 Moritz Gottschalk No. 3213
   These are two more examples in the 3200 series.
   No.3209 (2-026 & 2-027) is shown as a catalogue entry and "in the flesh." It can be seen as part of the progression in Gottschalk's development of these forts.

   No.3213 (2-028) is of a different style altogether. Perhaps the most significant change is in the base, where we have a colonnade. There are two slightly different levels in the courtyards. The three towers are missing their roofs and the upper gateway needs attention. There is one sentry box. The 40mm figures are of contemporary German origin.

2-029 Moritz Gottschalk No.3217, *c1899 & c1902*

To my knowledge, this is the last of the 3200 series. No.3217 (2-029) has the same sort of buildings as No.3213, but is much larger. It was made as a snow castle, but the loss of glitter has diminished its charm. It is complete with all its roofs. The darkening of the lithographed walls is probably caused by the accumulation of dust over a long period.

2-030 Gottschalk No.3566/1

This is one in the 3500 series, which came out about 1902. This No.3566/1 (2-030) seems to be part of a new series, but the continued use of the same papers make it feel like an extension. The main differences, compared with the 3200 series, are in the large circular tower, the small corner turrets on the courtyard wall, the treatment at the eaves, and the square penthouse on the top of the main building.

MORITZ GOTTSCHALK: 3500 Series
c1902 to c1908

NO.	DESCRIPTION	DATE	DIMENSIONS	DISTINCTIVE FEATURES
3566 (2-030)	**first of this series** (identified by an example in the collection below) eg: Berndt Zimmermann, D	c1902	unknown	• integral ramp to standard gateway • large four floor main & side bldg • very large tapering circular tower • square roof turret & 2 sm towers
356?	**second of this series** (identified by an example in the collection below) eg: Berndt Zimmermann, D	c1902	unknown	• integral ramp to db & 2 gateways • circ gateway tower & 4 small towers • large four floor main & side bldg • very large tapering circular tower

There are more in this style, but we have only two examples. One is No.3566; the other I cannot decipher, but it is clearly a part of the same series. As the numbers indicate, the series came out about two or three years after the main batch. Once again we can tell nothing of the range of which these forts were part. Nor can we tell why Gottschalk thought it necessary to produce more using the same papers. The only significantly different pieces were the giant circular tower and the turrets around the perimeter walls.

The End of an Era

This brings the story into the 20th century. Expansion and progress continued unabated, and we now come upon evidence of the next step in their development of military-related buildings.

This is the 3600 series, which were more in the nature of barracks than fortresses. In fact they resemble more their dollhouse heritage, the only concessions to the military being a sign which proclaimed it to be a "Kaserne" (German for barracks) and a sentry box or two. Actually without the sentry boxes, and with the correct sign, it could be any institution – a school, for example.

As far as I can make out, the range included four such buildings, graduated in size and complexity, from the relatively small to quite large.

MORITZ GOTTSCHALK: 3600 Series
1904 to c1907

NO.	DESCRIPTION	DATE	DIMENSIONS	DISTINCTIVE FEATURES
3620	**smallest of this series** (illustrated in Gottschalk catalogue 1904?) eg: no known example	1904	unknown	• two floors • look-out on the roof • two signs "Kaserne" • one sentry box
3621 (2-035)	**second of this series** (illustrated by an example in the collection below) eg: Noel Barrett Auctions, US	1904	unknown	• two floors • look-out on the roof • one sign "Kaserne" • one sentry box
3622	**third of this series** (illustrated in Gottschalk catalogue 1904?) eg: no known example	1904	unknown	• two floors • look-out on the roof • one sign "Kaserne" • one sentry box
3623	**largest of this series** (illustrated in Gottschalk catalogue 1904?) eg: no known example	1904	unknown	• three floors • wide entrance block • sign "National Guard" • two sentry boxes

In order to describe the range it is helpful to describe the two ends of it. No.3620 was the smallest, with two floors and a lookout at the top. At about 12" (30cm) in height overall, and about 9" (23cm) across the front, it was really quite simple. There was very little ornamentation on the outside, and there was just one sentry box.

At the other end of the range, No.3623 was the largest, with three floors, a basement, and a sizeable lookout well above roof level. At about 22" (56cm) in height it was a quite impressive structure. This, combined with a frontage of approximately 16" (40cm), all covered with ornamentation in the form of verandas, corner columns, steps up to the entrance, and the like; it was imposing indeed. It rated two sentry boxes, but no other indication that it had military connections.

There seems to have been at least two versions. One was signed "Kaserne" and flew the German flag, while the other was signed "National Guard" and flew the American flag. In our example (2-035) there was no sign but it flew the American Flag. This is a reasonably clear indication that some of them were being exported to America. One wonders how many of Gottschalk's products were exported in this fashion.

We know nothing of how the change from "fortresses" to barracks was accepted in the market place, because everything was overshadowed by the death of Moritz Gottschalk in 1905.

Although this was a sad event in itself, it nonetheless represented an opportunity for change. Practices, which had developed with the man himself over many years, could now be questioned and new ideas brought forward.

Initially, there was a short period of rest, while they girded their loins for the change which was imminent. In fact, they were sort of marking time when, in 1907, they brought out another series, the 4000 series, which was very similar in concept to the 3600 series, only much smaller and simpler.

The forts were in the nature of barracks, which we can only tell by the presence of sentry boxes and a flag flying from the roof. It was even truer than with the 3600 series that, without these, they could have been quite ordinary houses.

MORITZ GOTTSCHALK: 4000 Series
1907 to c1910

NO.	DESCRIPTION	DATE	DIMENSIONS	DISTINCTIVE FEATURES
4078	**smallest this series** (illustrated in Gottschalk catalogue 1907?) eg: no known example	1907	unknown	• one and a half storeys • look-out on the roof • two sentry boxes • small front area
4079	**second of this series** (illustrated in Gottschalk catalogue 1907?) eg: no known example	1907	unknown	• one and a half storeys • look-out on the roof • two sentry boxes • a front area same as 4078
4080	**third of this series** (illustrated in Gottschalk catalogue 1907?) eg: no known example	1907	unknown	• two and a half storeys • look-out on the roof • two sentry boxes • in a front yard with gates
4081	**largest of this series** (illustrated in Gottschalk catalogue 1907?) eg: no known example	1907	unknown	• two-and-a-half storeys • look-out on the roof • two sentry boxes • larger yard – double entry

This series, like the earlier one, went from quite small (about 10" (25cm) across) to quite large, with three floors and a double entrance (about 15" (38cm) across). There was little or no ornamentation on the building itself, such as verandas and columns applied to the façade, but, unlike the previous series, they all sported a fenced-off area in front. This no doubt served as a sort of parade ground.

Again, we have no knowledge of their acceptance by the buying public.

2-035 **Moritz Gottschalk No.3621** *(Courtesy Noel Barrett Auctions), c1904*
This is the second in the 3600 series. It shows how the series started relatively simply as far as ornamentation is concerned. Note the opening door and the suggestion of a basement.

The Start of a New Era

But here came the change. Dollhouse collectors have spoken of the change from blue-roof houses to red-roof houses for years, but to do so misses the point, at least as far as Gottschalk's toy forts were concerned. Yes, the roofs did change color, but more importantly, so did the whole method of their manufacture and decoration.

I have access to only two examples of the transition, which came out in about 1909 as the 4400 series. That these were part of a series is evidenced by an entry in an undated catalogue of Whyte, Ridsdale and Co. in England, who were offering a range of models, clearly by Gottschalk. These were numbered from G4423 to G4427, which may or may not be related to the Gottschalk numbering system, although they do bear an uncanny similarity to it.

The number that Gottschalk produced in the series is not known, but from the range of prices (4/6 to 36/-, which is very wide) in Whyte, Ridsdale & Co's catalogue, I am inclined to think it was rather more than rather less. This is not as important, however, as the changes it heralded. In this series, the towers still retained their blue roofs, but the main roofs were red. And so we see the beginning of the generally accepted transition – from blue to red roofs.

MORITZ GOTTSCHALK: 4400 Series
c1909

NO.	DESCRIPTION	DATE	DIMENSIONS	DISTINCTIVE FEATURES
4412 (2-042)	**smaller one of this series** (identified by an example in the ownership below) eg: Steve Sommers, US	c1909	11"x15"x13" 280x380x330mm	• main building w/red roof • two square towers (blue roofs) • standard gateway • base covered in lithographed paper
442? (2-040, 2-041)	**larger one of this series** (illustrated in Whyte & Risdale's catalogue) eg: Bernd Zimmermann, D	c1909	unknown	• two floor main building (red roof) • two square towers (blue roofs) • two standard gateways (one/level) • base covered in lithographed paper

But this was not the only change. Firstly, the buildings were no longer hollow. Initially, they were constructed from thin pieces of wood or thick cardboard, creating internal space in the manner of very small dollhouses. Now cut out of solid planks, they became quite two-dimensional, taking on some of the characteristics of theatrical scenery.

Secondly, the details, such as doors, windows, and stonework, were no longer lithographed on paper and stuck onto the wood. Now they were painted directly onto the wood, using stencils and spray paint to maintain a consistent quality.

Thirdly, the architectural style was changed. The nondescript "old" style of the 3200 series, and the 19th-century splendor of the 2300 and 2500 series were dropped, and a late medieval/baroque style of architecture was adopted in their place.

Ornamentation in the form of pinnacles on the main roof and on the gates, which is missing on one of the examples we have, must have been quite vulnerable to rough treatment. The fortress, fortunately, is perfectly usable without such decoration.

It was the 4700 series that first completely embodied this revolution and even, perhaps, took it one step further. The exact date at which it came onto the market is not known, although it seems likely to have been about 1910. It was certainly on sale in Britain by then, where it was featured in a Gamage's catalogue.

How long it was in production is also unclear, but there are examples in a Gottschalk poster from about 1920 and a Stukenbrock catalogue dated 1926. Of course, it must be remembered that others, usually wholesalers, used images of their forts, often with out-of-date graphics.

2-040 **Moritz Gottschalk No.4412** *(Courtesy Steve Sommers)*
On Moritz Gottschalk No.4412 note how all the detailing is now painted directly onto the wood. Note the doors and windows, their surrounds, and the various styles of cornice, all painted with shadow effect to give the whole a three-dimensional feel. This, together with the red roofs, marks the start of the new regime.
The source for the treatment of the base (lithographed paper on the front and bark elsewhere) and the wall around the courtyard, are a bit of a mystery – certainly they are like nothing done by Gottschalk before or since.
This is still very much a house, albeit a grand one, built to the domestic scale. Moritz Gottschalk No.4412 was typical of his production for years to come.

1909

2-041

Large Value Wood Forts, nicely painted in
attractive colours.

G 4423 —	G 4424 —	G 4425 —	G 4426 —
4/6 doz.	8/6 doz.	13/6 doz.	27/- doz.
	G 4427 — 36/- doz		

2-042

2-041 **Whyte, Ridsdale & Co., England** *(catalogue)*
2-042 **Moritz Gottschalk No.442?**

The extract from the catalogue of Whyte, Ridsdale & Co. is
undated, but it shows the fort to the right. It also shows clearly the
range on offer (though not necessarily the range of Gottschalk
which may have been greater).

Moritz Gottschalk No.442? is clearly in the same mould as
No.4412 (2-040) but it is now on two levels, and it sports two ramps
and two gateways. Note the pinnacle on the roof of the main
building, and the two on each of the gateways; they are missing from
No.4412. These were likely to have been vulnerable to rough
treatment, which might have been expected in the playroom.

GOTTSCHALK'S GROWTH AND THE EXPORT TRADE

Gottschalk must have timed his entry into the toy market to perfection. The rate at which the business grew was amazing. He started in about 1865 and soon had a "cottage industry" with a number of out-workers. It is not clear when he actually got into products made of wood. It was definitely by the time of his purchase of the new factory in 1873, when he had an in-house labour force of twenty, but it may have been a few years earlier.

The business experienced a number of setbacks. There were fires in 1872 and again in 1880, but Gottschalk seems to have recovered incredibly quickly and went on to even greater things each time. In other aspects, he was also extremely fortunate. For example, in 1875, just two years after they moved to the new factory, a train line opened up between Chemnitz and Marienberg. This immediately allowed expansion beyond their wildest dreams.

The plant grew with the business. Each year there was something new. There were new factories in 1873, 1880, and 1902. In addition, there was the erection of new buildings and extensions, sometimes quite major, whenever they were needed to fill the ever-increasing number of orders.

This can be demonstrated by their need for ever-increasing power. In 1873, when he bought a building to replace the one that had burned down the year before, they, at last, had access to a water mill. In 1885, this was found to be inadequate, so he installed steam power. In 1899, he even bought his own saw mill. In 1920, electricity was installed in the factory.

By the turn of the century, the company had a purpose-made factory built for their two hundred employees, and it remained until recently. Gottschalk had its own showrooms in Paris, London, and Amsterdam, as well as agencies in America and elsewhere.

By the early 1880s, all over the world the demand for children's toys was growing. Moritz Gottschalk was allied to Gamages in London and

F. A. O. Schwarz in New York, in an empire that included not only Western Europe and North America, but also Australia.

By way of example, we have the No.3213 (below left) which, according to a label on the underside, was retailed in the shop of Och Frères, in Geneva, Switzerland. No.3621 (below right), clearly made for the American market with the stars and stripes flying above, turned up there in 2010.

The modus operandi of the company was set by 1900 and it just kept on going. Despite the deaths of several leading lights, this approach continued until the depression and the rise of the Third Reich and a change of management in 1934. Then export became difficult and the company had to change – and change it did.

New lines, smaller fortresses, and a new numbering system are among the more easily identified changes. What happened to their export trade is not known, but one assumes that the European business kept them going until 1942, when toy production was halted. They then manufactured transport boxes for the armed forces.

After the war, the factory was taken over by the Soviet army and the grounds were used as soldiers' quarters. The factory returned to the production of toys by 1947. The whole toy industry, however, was controlled by the state, including exports. When the state began taking over middle-sized companies in East Germany in 1972, Moritz Gottschalk was nationalized.

MORITZ GOTTSCHALK: 4700 Series
c1910 to c1915

NO.	DESCRIPTION	DATE	DIMENSIONS	DISTINCTIVE FEATURES
4739 (2-047) (2-049)	**smallest of this series** (identified by an example in the ownership below) eg: Gerry Greene, US	c1910	unknown	• simple defensible ramp to dbridge • one regular gateway • one main building • one tower
4740 (2-048) (2-050)	**second of this series** (identified by an example in the ownership below) eg: Allen Hickling Toy Forts,	c1910	13"x9"x13¼" 330x230x335mm	• simple indefensible ramp to dbridge • one regular gateway • one main building • one tower
4741 (2-046)	**third of this series** (identified by an example in the ownership below) eg: Allen Hickling Toy Forts,	c1910	15"x10¾"x13" 380x275x330mm	• simple indefensible ramp to dbridge • one regular gateway • main building w/2-bay side building • one square flanking tower
4742 (2-051)	**fourth of this series** (identified by an example in the ownership below) eg: Bernd Zimmermann, D	c1910	16½"x11¾"x13½" 420x300x340mm	• simple indefensible ramp to dbridge • one regular gateway • main building w/2-bay side building • one square flanking tower
4744 (2-056)	**sixth of this series** (identified by an example in the ownership below) eg: Arnold Mueller, D	c1910	18½"x13½"x14" 470x340x355mm	• low level house & indefensible ramp • drawbridge & regular gateway • main building & 3-bay side building • corner & flanking sq towers
4747 (2-054)	**ninth of this series** (identified by an example in the ownership below) eg: Berndt Zimmermann, D	c1910	19"x15¼"x16" 485x385x410mm	• simple defensible ramp to dbridge • gateway & corner tower to ramp up • main blding w/3-bay side building • project porch & 2 flanking sq towers
4749 (2-055) (2-057)	**thirteenth of this series** (identified by an example in the ownership below) eg: Arnold Mueller, D	c1910	21½"x15¼"x20" 550x390x510mm	• double ramp & bridge to doorway • large square tower in the corner • two militaristic houses/buildings • squat circular tower

Unfortunately, I do not have access to any Gottschalk catalogues of the period, so it is impossible to be as definitive about the range on offer as it was for the earlier series. Examples, however, exist that are numbered from 4739 to 4751, as well as one or two without numbers but clearly in the range.

They were made of wood, die-cut cardboard, and bark from the same fir trees used to make the buildings. Assembly was simple – nails and glue – the demountable buildings being conventionally located by means of spikes set in their underside and slotted into holes in the base.

The early German baroque architectural style was portrayed very simply by the clever use of stencils, with sunny yellow courtyards, white battlements, cream buildings with ochre trim, and red roofs. The bark covering of the bases

was treated exactly as that on the 3200 series – crudely painted dark green and cream, with dry-brushed yellow and red highlights.

The one anomaly in this is the last in the series as we know it. This, if it was not a mistake, heralds a new series. How many others like this there were in this series is not known. In the example offered, just about everything is different from others in the series.

All the buildings are much more militaristic. There is a large, square tower, surrounded by quite large buildings, which would have to have been hollow. A heavy, squat circular tower and a different gateway overlooking a fixed bridge on the entry ramp complete the picture. In addition, the perimeter battlements vary in height, with the crenels quite widely spaced. Its architectural style is less classical and more down to earth.

2-046 Moritz Gottschalk No.4741
This is the third in the 4700 series. It is the smallest in the range to have almost all the buildings used in the series: the small square tower, a main building, a side building, a gateway, and the new type of courtyard wall. The side building was larger and there were some small buildings on the larger models, but they were relatively insignificant.

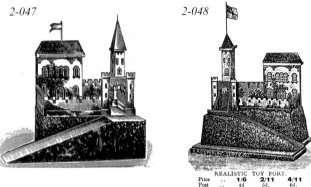

2-047

2-048

REALISTIC TOY FORT.

Price	..	**1/6**	**2/11**	**4/11**
Post	..	4d	5d.	6d.

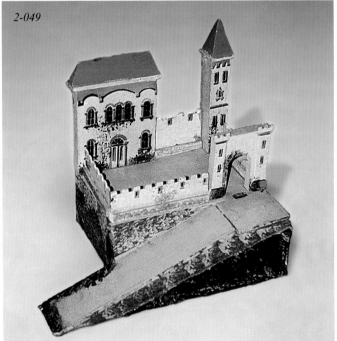

2-049

2-050

2-047 **Emil Schubert publicity c1916** (*Moritz Gottschalk No.4739*)
2-048 **Gamage's catalogue 1913** (*Moritz Gottschalk No.4740*)
2-049 **Moritz Gottschalk No.4739**
2-050 **Moritz Gottschalk No.4740**

The two examples of catalogues show how various companies used Gottschalk fortresses for advertising. Gamage's (2-048), the big London store, was selling the 4700 series specifically in 1910 and 1913. Emil Schubert of Grünhainichen used it on a handbill (2-047), c1916, to promote his activities in selling a wide variety of wood toys.

Gottschalk No.4739 is the smallest of the new series. It has a main building, a tower, and a gateway onto a small courtyard. Its style is definitely early German baroque. Also very much a house to domestic scale.

Gottschalk No.4740 is not much different from No.4739. The parts are all the same, but it is a little bigger and the ramp goes up the other way. There is a flat base making it more robust, and making it possible to close the underside.

2-051

2-054

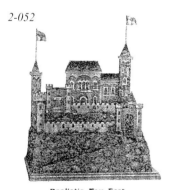

2-052

Realistic Toy Fort.

Enamelled grey with drawbridge.

1/6   2/11   4/6   6/6 (as illustration)   8/6
age 6d.   9d.   9d.   1/-   1/-
16/6 Carriage 1/- Do., size larger, 15/- Carriage 1/6
25/- with Moat to hold water.   Carriage 1/6

2-053 **Festungen**

aus Holz, mit feiner, wirkungsvoller Bemalung.

Nr.	1700	1701	1702	1703	1704
M.	1.80	2.50	3.—	3.60	5.—
Nr.	1705	1706	1707	1708	1709
M.	6.—	8.—	10.—	16.—	20.—

2-051 **Moritz Gottschalk No.4742** (*Courtesy Bernd Zimmermann*)
2-052 **Gamage's catalogue 1910** (*Gottschalk No.4746(?)*)
2-053 **Hermann Kurtz's catalogue 1912** (*Gottschalk No.4746(?)*)
2-054 **Moritz Gottschalk No.4744(?)** (*Courtesy Arnold Mueller*)
   Gottschalk No.4742 is very similar to No.4741, just little larger.
   Gottschalk No.4744 is quite different. Not only is it much larger again, but it has extra buildings. First the secondary building is larger than No.4742. There is an additional free-standing tower in the corner and another small building at the level of the base making for a bigger base plate. There is some uncertainty about this number.
   The two catalogues, Gamage's (2-052) and Hermann Kurtz's (2-053), both use the same image to represent the range. These being engravings rather than photographic images may mean there were few different ones. Both have prices arranged around them, displaying the range on offer.

2-055

No. **4751.**
55×39×51 cm

2-057

2-056

2-055 **Moritz Gottschalk No.4751** (catalogue)
2-056 **Moritz Gottschalk No. 4747** (Courtesy Bernd Zimmermann)
2-057 **Moritz Gottschalk No.4751** (Courtesy Arnold Mueller)

Moritz Gottschalk No.4747 has another level. It also has another tower, making three; the small building now elevated to the courtyard; a small corner tower; and some extra battlements. The ramp goes up the other way. This example is in bad shape in that two of the towers have lost their roofs, and the paint is a little worse for wear.

Moritz Gottschalk No.4751 is much higher than the others. We do not know how many there were like this. There is a re-entrant ramp as well as the entry bridge to get up. The buildings are militaristic in character and much more formidable than others in the series. It is possible to imagine this being well defended.

The catalogue is an enigma. It is almost certainly from a Gottschalk catalogue, but I cannot be sure.

Before leaving the 4700 series, there are a number of examples of Gottschalk fortresses being sold by different organizations. As we have already seen, Gottschalk himself had catalogues. There were also various others, exporters, distributors and big shops for example, who had an interest in the success or failure of the product. These had their own methods of selling, but nevertheless found images of the product line helpful. These were most likely supplied by Gottschalk. Unfortunately, I do not have any printed evidence of their activities in France, America, or Australia.

The next series up for examination is a real mess in the sense that I cannot make head or tail of it. The one thing they have in common is that they are all made up with parts that formed the last example in the 4700 series – the more militaristic aspects. We have examples that are No.48?8, No.4972, No.4974, No.4979 and No.4997.

MORITZ GOTTSCHALK: 4800/4900 Series
c1911 to c1915

NO.	DESCRIPTION	DATE	DIMENSIONS	DISTINCTIVE FEATURES
48?8 (2-061)	**the largest of this series** (identified by an example in the ownership below) eg: Ron Rosenburg, US	c1911	32"x24½"x25¼" 810x620x635mm	• levels on a hill of chunky cork • ramp to dbridge & gate, lg sq & circ towers • inter yd w/towers & ramp to dbridge & gate • mn bldg w/2 wings & lg sq tower
4972 (2-059) (2-060)	**smallest? of this series** (identified by an example in the ownership below) eg: Chris Atkinson, UK	c1911	unknown	• two levels on a hill of bark • ramp to dbridge & gate to yd w/sm bldgs • two circ corner towers & steps up • mn bldg w/1 corner & 1 free tower
4974 (2-058)	**third of this series** (identified by an example in the ownership below) eg: Allen Hickling Toy Forts,	c1911	35"x18"x22" 890x450x560mm	• two levels on a hill of chunky cork • ramp to dbridge & gate to yd w/sm bldgs • lg sq & two circ towers & ramp up • 4 main bldgs w/2 flanking sq towers
4979 (2-064)	**largest w/water in series** (identified by an example in the ownership below) eg: ??, US	c1911	30¼"x19"x20½" 770x480x520mm	• double ramp to dbridge over water tray • lg gateway to crtyd w/2 circ towers • large free-standing square tower • 2 x 2 main bldgs w/sq corner tower
4997 (2-062)	**smallest w/water in series** (identified by an example in the ownership below) eg: Bernd Zimmermann, D	c1911	unknown	• double ramp to dbridge over water tray • sm gateway to crtyd w/small bldgs • three circular corner towers • main bldg w/2 wings & lg sq tower

The first, Moritz Gottschalk No.48?8 (the third digit is indecipherable), is probably the largest. It is constructed on three levels – four if you count the ground. The only buildings that were not passed on from the 4700 series are a tall tower and some small, shed-like buildings. As the sizes increase, they just add more of the same buildings, which for such big castles tends to get a bit boring, but it is economically alluring for the manufacturer.

No.4972 is relatively small, but not so small that a second level was inappropriate. It has a more or less defensible upper level with a couple of large towers and a defensible house, but, surprisingly, no gate, so the enemy could march straight in. A much less defensible lower level had only a couple of squat towers and some shed-like buildings – somewhat like the old motte-and-bailey castles.

The bigger one, Moritz Gottschalk No.4974, has been converted by a junior French artist to contain toy soldiers, built in the same configuration only larger. Hence, we have buildings such as Commandant, Caserne Foch, Caserne Goumand, Ecurie, and Prison, not to mention many others. The whole fortress bears the name Fort de Valluax written over the gate. Needless to say these were not original, but make for a bit of fun.

2-058 **Moritz Gottschalk No.4974**
Moritz Gottschalk No.4974 is rather like a No.4972 in layout, but is much larger and utilizes a number of pieces from the earlier numbers in the 4700 series. In some ways this looks like a retrograde step, although, as far as I know, there was nothing of this size in the 4700 series.

2-059 **Moritz Gottschalk No.4972** *(khaki & black)*
2-060 **Moritz Gottschalk No.4972** *(yellow & dark brown)*
2-061 **Moritz Gottschalk No.48?8** *(Courtesy Ron Rosenberg)*
   Moritz Gottschalk No.4972 comes in at least two color schemes, but otherwise the two illustrated are identical. They are on two levels and have the same buildings as

others in the series. The yellow and dark brown example is missing a perimeter wall piece at the back and a small piece at the upper level.
   Moritz Gottschalk No.48?8 is a bit of a mystery. The third digit of the number is indecipherable. The fort is very large, on three levels, and its base is covered in cork. It has a main building with two towers surrounded by various smaller buildings and towers.

2-062

2-063

Festungen aus Holz in bester Ausführung.

Serie B.   Serie A.

Festungen in hervorragend schöner Ausführung, vollständig bemalt, massiv, aus tadellos getrocknetem Holz hergestellt.

Serie A. Aufgang, Zugbrücke, grosser Festungs-hof mit Gebäuden, Türmen usw. usw.

Nr.					Stück M.
2580.	Festung.	31 cm lang, 22 cm breit, 30 cm hoch	.	.	1.20
2581.	Festung.	32 cm lang, 23,5 cm breit, 32 cm hoch	.	.	1.60
2582.	Festung.	37 cm lang, 27 cm breit, 34,5 cm hoch	.	.	2.—
2583.	Festung.	42 cm lang, 30 cm breit, 36 cm hoch	.	.	3.25
2584.	Festung.	48,5 cm lang, 38 cm breit, 40 cm hoch	.	.	5.50
2585.	Festung.	62 cm lang, 49 cm breit, 58 cm hoch	.	.	10.50
2586.	Festung.	69 cm lang, 55 cm breit, 62 cm hoch	.	.	14.—

Serie B.   Festungen mit 1 Seitenaufgang, Zug-brücke, die über einen Wassergraben führt, 4 Türme, grosser Festungshof mit den nötigen Gebäuden, massive Ausführung.

Nr.					Stück M.
2587.	Festung.	60 cm lang, 41 cm breit, 46 cm hoch	.	.	8.50
2588.	Festung.	68 cm lang, 45 cm breit, 49 cm hoch	.	.	11.—
2589.	Festung.	77 cm lang, 48 cm breit, 52 cm hoch	.	.	13.50

2-064

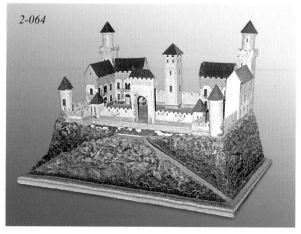

2-062 Moritz Gottschalk No.4997 *(Courtesy Bernd Zimmermann)*
2-063 Retailer's catalogue *(Gottschalk 4900 & 5200 series)*
2-064 Moritz Gottschalk No.4979

The numbering system seems to have gone seriously awry – see No.4751 (2-057) which appears to be in the same group.

Moritz Gottschalk No.4997 is the smaller of the two with water features, but it is not known where it fits in the range. It is in good shape, all the pieces appear good, but the metal container for the water is chipped and rusty. The gun, which is shown in the gateway, is not original.

Moritz Gottschalk No.4979 is the larger of the two with water features. It has an imposing gateway, even if the drawbridge is missing. The other pieces are well play-worn. The figures are 70mm.

The retailer's catalogue shows a serious error. The two series (A & B) relate to Gottschalk's 4900 and 5200 series – but there was a slip up somewhere, because the illustrations and the lists do not agree.

The two that follow from there are a bit of a problem, however. One is No.4979 and the other is No.4997, which is numerically further apart than one might expect. Were there really at least sixteen more fortresses? Or was there a mistake somewhere along the line? More to the point, No.4997 is the smaller of the two, which according to Gottschalk logic should come first. The one publicity handout I have has a picture of No.4979 and actually lists three sizes – rather unhelpfully numbered 2587 to 2589.

They both have water features out front, which are supposed to represent a moat. A metal-lined slot was let into the base to hold the water, which was crossed by means of the drawbridge. No doubt this presented some marvellous play opportunities, not to mention wet nursery floors. One wonders why Gottschalk did not repeat the feature. Maybe he got too much of an earful from the parents.

Consolidating the New Wave – The Next Two Series

The years from about 1909 to the outbreak of the First World War were times of intense activity in the Gottschalk factory. Up until then, they had been introducing new products at the rate of about 100 per year. Now, however, they produced at about twice that rate. From 1909 to 1914, they produced about 1100 new products.

Up to this point, with one or two minor exceptions, series were reasonably clearly differentiated, both in style and in time. However, the next two series, 5200 and 5500, shared the same components and overlapped in time. Known examples of the first are No.5259 to No.5265, and those in the second No.5517 to No.5525.

Both were launched well before the First World War and were available long after it was over. Both appeared in two versions – early and late. Although we do not know the timing of these versions, it seems likely that the war provided a natural break when they could have instituted the change.

The main difference lies in the covering of the base. The first was the same bark as the 3200, 4400, 4700, and 4900 series, and the second was a form of cardboard molded to give the impression of vegetation and drainage pipes high up. The first version also featured elaborate die-cut cardboard crenellation on the battlements. This was replaced by basic cut-out crenellation in the second version, which was followed in the later stages by a painted simulation of crenellation.

Variations in color scheme were relatively common. No.5259, for example, is known in at least the three color variations. There seems to have been no relationship between the two versions, early or late, and the color schemes.

No.5259 is also unique in the sense that it was the only "fortress" in the range to have flat buildings. Even more to the point, it was decidedly domestic

in character. It is true that flat buildings were used in the later 5500 series, but in this series the other examples all used more defensible elements.

MORITZ GOTTSCHALK: 5200 Series
c1912 to c1925

NO.	DESCRIPTION	DATE	DIMENSIONS	DISTINCTIVE FEATURES
5259 (2-065– 2-068)	**smallest of this series** (identified by an example in the ownership below) eg: Gerry Greene, US	c1912	unknown	• simple ramp to dbridge & gateway • courtyard w/one sq corner tower • open 3-bay first floor walkway • main building w/a high extension
5260 (2-069) (2-070)	**second of this series** (identified by an example in the ownership below) eg: SOFIA Foundation, CY	c1912	19"x13½"x14¼" 480x340x360mm	• roadway in front of ramp to dbridge • gateway gives on to courtyard • large 3-D house & 2-arch loggia • 1 large circ & 1 sq flanking towers
5261 (2-072)	**third of this series** (identified by an example in the ownership below) eg: Jim Osborne, UK	c1912	unknown	• roadway in front of ramp to dbridge • gate leads to crtyd w/sm sq tower • large 3-D house & 2-arch loggia • 1 large circ & 1 sq flanking towers
5263 (2-071)	**fourth of this series** (identified by an example in the ownership below) eg: Brightwells Auction, UK	c1912	unknown	• ramp to dbridge & shouldered gateway • 4-bay first floor walkway & sq tower • large 3-D house & 3-arch loggia • lg circ & lg sq flanking towers
5264 (2-073) 2-074)	**sixth of this series** (identified by an example in the ownership below) eg: Musée du Jouet, Bxl,, B	c1912	unknown	• 2 ramps to dbridges shouldered gateways • 2 corner turrets & a 6-arch walkway • 2 3-D hses w/2 & 3 arched loggias • lg circ & lg sq flanking towers
5265 (2-075) (2-076)	**largest of this series** (identified by an example in the ownership below) eg: SOFIA Foundation, CY	c1912	24"x19¼"x24¾" 610x490x630mm	• dble ramp to db & shouldered gtway • lg circular tower w/turret on top • side bldg w/2- & 3-arched loggias • 3-D house w/sm & lg sq towers

They had a square two-storey main building, with a three-storey wing alongside, and a small square tower, all with half-timbered upper floors. There was a piece with a rather nice open gallery at first floor level. In terms of materials and method of assembly, there was little change from the 4700 series.

The other style, on all the other fortresses in the 5200 series, was relatively three-dimensional with a large house, crenellated arched loggias, and large towers, both circular and square. These were somewhat like the later style in the 4700 and in the 4900 series. They were hollow, made of thin wood sheets framed up or of thick cardboard, in the case of the circular towers. The arches protecting the walkway under the loggias were also of cardboard.

c.1912

2-065

2-068

2-067

2-066

7/5259 (42×30×36 cm)
Festungen, gemalt und lackiert.
Fortresses, painted and varnished.
Fortalezas, pintadas y embarnizadas.

2-065 **Moritz Gottschalk No.5259** *(late version brown) (Courtesy Musée du Jouet, Bruxelles)*
2-066 **Universal Toy Catalogue** *1924-26*
2-067 **Moritz Gottschalk No.5259** *(late version cream)*
2-068 **Moritz Gottschalk No.5259** *(early version grey) (Courtesy Lynn Amari)*
   Moritz Gottschalk No.5259 (late version) is in two color schemes. One is cream with red roofs and a dirty yellow courtyard. The other is brown and white with red roofs. The courtyard, ramp, and road are also brown. It is difficult to tell if this is a repaint.

Universal Toy Catalogue 1924–1926 (Gottschalk No.5259) is a Gottschalk advertisement. The image, probably an engraving, is of the version that was not made after the First World War, so what it was doing here in 1924 was probably cost cutting.
   Moritz Gottschalk No.5259 (early version) has its buildings at the back, in an unusual order (see the other Nos.5259). If they were rearranged, this would be the exact fortress in the engraving used in the Universal Toy Catalogue 1924–1926.

2-069

2-070

2-069 Moritz Gottschalk No.5260 *(late version)*
2-070 Moritz Gottschalk No.5260 *(early version) (Courtesy Arnold Mueller)*

Moritz Gottschalk No.5260 (early version) is in excellent condition except for a few flakes of the bark box covering, and has a grey and white color scheme. The crenellation around the courtyard is created with cut-out cardboard.

Moritz Gottschalk No.5260 (late version) is almost the same as the early version. Note, however, the crenellation around the courtyard, and the pressed cardboard covering of the base. The figures are all 30mm scale by Britains and John Hill. The maker of the tents and the tin sentry box are unknown. The Dutch flags are not original, of course.

c.1912

2-071 **Moritz Gottschalk No.5263** *(early version) (Courtesy Brightwells Fine Art Auctions)*
2-072 **Moritz Gottschalk No.5261** *(late version)*

Moritz Gottschalk No.5263 (early version) is in poor condition. Two pieces of perimeter wall are missing (left front and back), the big house and several other pieces have severe

discoloration, the crenellation on the tower is badly damaged, and the drawbridge has seen better days. The green around the base and on the ramp appears to be a repaint.

Moritz Gottschalk No.5261 (late version) uses the same color scheme as the yellow and cream No.5264. It is complete and in good condition.

c.1912

2-073 **Moritz Gottschalk No.5264** (late version)
2-074 **Moritz Gottschalk No.5264** (early version) (Courtesy Musée du Jouet, Bruxelles)
   Moritz Gottschalk No.5264 (early version) is in a sombre grey and green color scheme with red roofs (2-074). It is missing two pieces of perimeter crenellation (just behind and below the upper gateway), but it is otherwise in good condition.

   Moritz Gottschalk No.5264 (late version) is in a yellow and cream color scheme with red roofs (2-073). The color of the river in front is a bit bright, compared to the older one. It is complete and in good condition

2-075

Model Fort.
As illustration.   Beautifully finished in colours.
Strongly made.   Size 24 × 19½ × 23 ius.   Price **32/6**
Post 9d.

2-076

2-075 **From Gamage's catalogue 1926**
2-076 **Moritz Gottschalk No.5265**

   Gamage's catalogue shows that nothing changed around this time in London, which was about fifteen years after the series was first brought out. The image is of the early version.

   Moritz Gottschalk No.5265 (late version) has been restored by me and, previously, by another. The three-arched walkway at the back was rebuilt and repainted as were the gateway and the small tower at the front. All the cardboard crenellation was replaced. The roofs were repaired and repainted. The courtyard, ramps, and the green around the base have been repainted.

The 5500 series used the flat form of buildings exclusively. These were almost the same as those on No.5259, but the main building was reduced in height, and it and the gateway were made more ornate by the addition of some applied cardboard. The other buildings all continued to have half-timbered upper floors.

MORITZ GOTTSCHALK: 5500 Series
c1913 to c1927

NO.	DESCRIPTION	DATE	DIMENSIONS	DISTINCTIVE FEATURES
5517 (2-077)	**smallest of this series** (identified by an example in the ownership below) eg: Bernd Zimmermann, D	c1913	11¼"x8"x12¼" 285x205x310mm	• side building & small square tower • simulated 4-bay first floor walkway • early crenellation on perimeter wall • ramp to an elaborate gateway
5518 (2-078) (2-081)	**second of this series** (identified by an example in the ownership below) eg: SOFIA Foundation, CY	c1913	12¼"x9½"x13" 310x235x330mm	• large flat house & side building • small square flanking tower • early crenellation to perimeter wall • ramp to an elaborate gateway
5519 (2-082)	**third of this series** (identified by an example in the ownership below) eg: Bernd Zimmermann, D	c1913	unknown	• side building & small square tower • one 3-bay open covered walkway • early crenellation around courtyard • ramp to a standard gateway
5520 (2-083)	**fourth of this series** (identified by an example in the ownership below) eg: Bernd Zimmermann, D	c1913	16"x10½"x13½" 410x270x340mm	• large flat house & side building • simulated 4-bay walkway • painted crenellation to yard wall • ramp to an elaborate gateway
5522 (2-084) (2-085)	**sixth of this series** (identified by an example in the ownership below) eg: Arnold Mueller, D	c1913	unknown	• large flat house & side building • 3-bay open walkway & 2 towers • 2-level courtyard & perimeter wall • ramp to an elaborate gateway
5524 (2-086) (2-087)	**eighth of this series** (identified by an example in the ownership below) eg: Steve Sommers, USA	c1913	21"x17"x16" 535x430x405mm	• main building & square tower • 4-bay walkway to circular tower • 2-level courtyd & verandah under • zig-zag ramp to elaborate gates
5525 (2-088)	**largest? of this series** (identified by an example in the ownership below) eg: SOFIA Foundation, CY	c1913	24"x19¼"x24¾" 610x490x630mm	• main building & 2 square towers • 3-bay walkway & circular tower • 2-level courtyd & verandah under • zig-zag ramp up cork-covered base

The buildings of both the 5200 and the 5500 series were now clearly medieval in character in two different architectural styles, which were sometimes mixed on the larger models. Both series adopted the same two styles, but there was one common element, which was used in later series also – a 1¼" (30mm) square

by 9" (230mm) tall, three-storey tower with a pyramidal roof – probably derived from a somewhat similar one in the 4700 series.

The pre-World War I versions of both series were less colorful than those that went before – especially the 4700 series. Although all the roofs were consistently bright red and the bark was painted with the same combination of dark green, cream, golden yellow and red, everything else was more sombre. The buildings tended to be a beige grey with the stones picked out in brown and cream; the courtyards were ochre or grey. Details were again represented by the clever use of stencils.

The largest of the 5500 series, No.5525, shows some of the characteristics of the 6000 series, which comes much later. The chunky cork covering was first used only on the largest of the 2300 and 2500 series, and later on No.48?8 in the 4900 series. It seems to be something that was reserved for these very big "fortresses" where the scale demands it.

2-077 **Moritz Gottschalk No.5517** *(late version) (Courtesy Bernd Zimmermann) Moritz Gottschalk No.5517 (late version) is a very late version. One indication of this is that it does not have the molded cardboard facing to the box; also, the painting on the box that is its replacement is quite crude. Also, there is simulated crenellation on the perimeter wall and a similar treatment for the walkway at first floor level on the middle piece at the back. There is no drawbridge and the ramp appears to be made of solid wood. These are all indications of savings being made in production. One wonders when it could have been made, and an explanation might be found in the raging inflation of 1922/23.*

2-078

2-079

HIGHLY FINISHED FORT
As illustration. Strongly made, in beautiful colourings. Size 15 x 10½ x 14 ins. Price 9/6 Post 9d.
Ditto larger. Price 18/6 Post 1/-.
Also as illustration but smaller. Price 7/6 Post 6d.

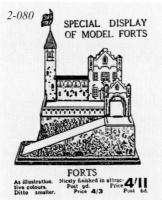

2-080

SPECIAL DISPLAY OF MODEL FORTS

FORTS
As illustration. Nicely finished in attractive colours. Post 9d. Price **4/3** Price **4/11** Post 6d.
Ditto smaller.

2-081

2-078 Moritz Gottschalk No.5518 *light grey (late version)*
2-079 Gamage's catalogue 1928
2-080 Gamage's catalogue 1929
2-081 Moritz Gotstschalk No.5518 *dark grey (late version) (Courtesy Bernd Zimmermann)*
  Gottschalk No.5518 (late version) is a light grey color scheme. It is in excellent condition. This would prove to be one of the most popular models in the marketplace.
  Gottschalk No.5518 (late version) is a dark grey color scheme. It is in bad shape – the

gateway, in particular, has severe discoloration. The paint work is generally in poor condition. The courtyard and horizontal surfaces are brown; this may be a repaint.
  Gamage's, the big toy super store in London, used Gottschalk's images of No.5518 (2-079) and another Gottschalk (the number unknown (2-080)) in 1928 and 1929. The image and the fort advertised did not always match up because the size specified is probably No.5520, although it is not clear. From the evidence of these advertisements, their pricing policy is difficult to fathom.

2-083

2-082

2-082 Moritz Gottschalk No.5519 *(Courtesy Bernd Zimmermann)*
2-083 Moritz Gottschalk No.5520 *(Courtesy Bernd Zimmermann)*
   *Moritz Gottschalk No.5519 (2-082) is almost certainly an early
version, and is very similar to No.5517 (2-077); for instance, it has
no door. The differences lie mostly in the quality of the pieces. The
walkway, now with three bays rather than four, is actually open,
the crenellation on the perimeter wall is cut, and the box is covered
in bark. The gateway is a much simpler design. Another difference
is that the ramp is more difficult to defend.*
   *Moritz Gottschalk No.5520 (2-083) is a later model in that the
first floor walkway and the perimeter wall crenellation are simulated
in paint. In some ways this is contradicted by the full treatment of the
elaborate main building, the drawbridge, and the covering of the
base. Nonetheless, it is an excellent example in splendid condition.
The 45mm semi-round mounted figures are of German manufacture.*

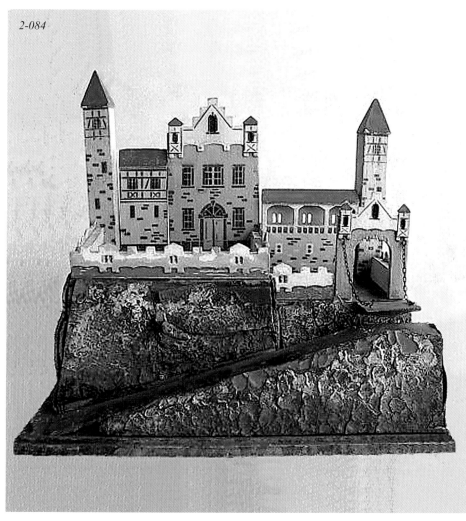

2-084

2-085

2-084 **Moritz Gottschalk No.5522** (*early version*)
2-085 **Moritz Gottschalk No.5522** (*late version*) (*Courtesy Arnold Mueller*)
    Moritz Gottschalk No.5522 (early version) is in more or less the same light grey color scheme as one of the Nos.5518. It is complete and in quite good condition, but it shows signs of wear on the crenellation, the roofs of the two towers, and the bark box covering at the front.
    Moritz Gottschalk No.5522 (late version) is exactly the same as the earlier one except for the crenellation on the walls surrounding the courtyard and the covering of the base. It is in excellent condition, sporting a yellow and cream color scheme. The 40mm figures are of German manufacture.

2-086

2-087

2-086 **Moritz Gottschalk No.5524** *(early version) (Courtesy Bernd Zimmermann)*
2-087 **Moritz Gottschalk No.5524** *(late version)*

   These fortresses show a remarkable increase in size and complexity, when compared to the No.5522 (2-084 & 2-085). The whole of the front, including the veranda and the complex ramp, and the change in levels of the courtyard, necessitating the second gateway, were all part of it. One can only surmise what No.5523 was like. What is most interesting is that the next one up is completely different.

   Moritz Gottschalk No.5524 (early version) (2-086) shows some considerable wear to the bark at the front of the ramp. Although it is complete, the open walkway at the back appears to be a different color. Maybe it is a replacement piece from a different fortress or a newer one. The 40mm knights are figures of German manufacture.

   Moritz Gottschalk No.5524 (late version) (2-087) is complete and in good shape. Note the late version covering of the box (molded cardboard) and the crenellation around the courtyard.

c.1913

2-088 Moritz Gottschalk No.5525

Moritz Gottschalk No.5525 could be a precursor to the large fortresses in the 6000 series. It is certainly one of the few to have a cork finish to the base. It has been lightly restored by me, in that the perimeter wall to the left-hand side has been replaced.

It is interesting to note that the perimeter walls around the courtyard are noticeably higher than others. This one feature alone begins to warrant calling it a fortress.

1914?

2-089

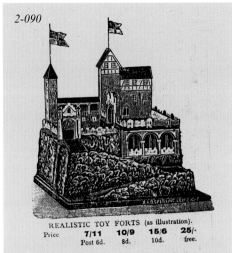

2-090

REALISTIC TOY FORTS (as illustration).
Price   **7/11   10/9   15/6   25/-**
Post 6d.   8d.   10d.   free.

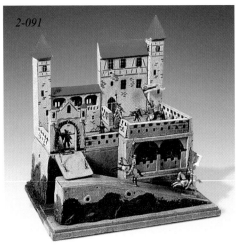

2-091

2-089 **Moritz Gottschalk No. unknown** *(earlier version) (Courtesy Bernd Zimmermann)*
2-090 **Gamage's catalogue 1913**
2-091 **Moritz Gottschalk No.6567** *(later version) (Courtesy Bernd Zimmermann)*

Moritz Gottschalk No.unknown (early version) is an anomaly. The number is not known but its similarity to No.6567 makes it probably No.6568 or No.6569. Maybe they were numbered in error – they would fit comfortably in the 5500 series or just a little later – say No.5568?. The 45mm mounted figures are of German origin.

Moritz Gottschalk No.6567 (late version) is another anomaly. The number is about 1150 entries in the catalogue after the others of similar design and construction (for example see Gottschalk No.5524 (2-086 & 2-087)). The 40mm figures are made by Merton in Germany.

Gamage's, the big London store, was selling them specifically in 1913. This is an engraving of an early version. It reveals that there were at least four fortresses in the series.

Now, mention must be made of an enigma, because it concerns two "fortresses" with a clear relationship to the 5500 series.

MORITZ GOTTSCHALK: 6500? Series
c1913 to c1925

NO.	DESCRIPTION	DATE	DIMENSIONS	DISTINCTIVE FEATURES
6567 (2-091)	**smallest of this series** (identified by an example in the ownership below) eg: Bernd Zimmermann, D	1914?	14½"x10½"x14½" 365x265x365mm	• ramp to dbridge & ornate gateway • 3 levels, including a 2-bay veranda • main building w/2 med sq towers • 3-bay, 1st floor open walkway
unknown (2-089)	**largest? of this series** (identified by an example in the ownership below) eg: Bernd Zimmermann, D	1914?	19¼"x14¼"x16½" 490x360x420mm	• ramp to dbridge & 2 ornate gateways • 3 levels including a 3-bay veranda • main & wing bldg & med sq tower • 4-bay first floor open walkway

These are two fortresses, one that bears the number 6567 and one that bears no number at all. Both are of the later version with molded cardboard on the base, although I know of others covered in bark, as in Gamage's catalogue, which are, therefore, earlier versions. They were obviously using pieces from the medieval "fortresses" just described.

The two are also clearly of the same basic design. The only question is how they could possibly come out when they did – one of them was illustrated in Gamage's catalogue of 1913 – with numbers that were not in use until fifteen years later. Of course, it was probably an error – others have been known – in which case the number could have been 5567 and not 6567. This seems much more likely.

The Great War and Its Aftermath

As the year 1914 drew to a close, the firm of Moritz Gottschalk faced its darkest hour. After nearly fifty years of continuous growth, development, and commercial success, the future looked bleak indeed.

The First World War had just broken out and Wilhelm, son of the great Moritz and owner of the firm, had been killed during the first few months of the conflict. If this were not challenge enough, the outbreak of hostilities also caused the firm's international markets in Britain, France, Australia, and, potentially, the USA to close. It threatened to draft all the younger workers into the army and to turn the factory production over to supporting the war effort. They faced great uncertainty, also, about the future leadership of the company.

With this grim prospect Wilhem's widow, Lina, took over the reins. In this, she was ably assisted by Kurt Wagner, who, following in his father's footsteps, had been a devoted employee of the firm and close associate of the family for more than thirty years. Exactly how the firm survived the war is not known, but survive it did, and when things began to settle down, in 1919, Kurt married Lina and became a partner in the business.

A Product Strategy for Recovery

Consciously or unconsciously, Gottschalk's business strategy, as it affected their toy fort production after the war, appears to have been one of retrenchment. This involved retaining the series already in production, but streamlining methods and materials – while trying out one or two new ideas to see if they would run. This would have had the effect of keeping their development costs to a minimum, production efficient, and their products cheap – thus re-establishing their trading network with as little delay as possible.

The existing 5200 and 5500 series formed the core of their production. The most obvious simplification took the form of a molded cardboard covering for the bases, replacing the tree bark used previously. This molding represented dressed stone walling with what can only be some form of circular drainage outlets at the upper level and, lower down, nondescript vegetation or moss-covered rock, invariably painted a dark green.

There were other changes of note. The elaborate crenellation made of die-cut cardboard was dispensed with. This was initially replaced with crenellation cut directly out of the wood, but this, too, was later replaced with an even simpler representation of crenellation stencilled onto straight-cut strips of wood.

These less ornate toy forts might have become a bit boring were it not for the firm commencing a new stylistic policy of producing a variety of color schemes. This extended only to the walls – ochre courtyards and red roofs with predominantly black and brown for the windows and doors remaining the norm. There are examples of three basic wall colors, each providing a significantly different effect: grey, brown, cream/white – all with white and brown highlighted stonework.

Of course, there was experimentation during this period and a number of developments were tried. First, there were experiments with finishes on the 5500 series. We have two fortresses with a plaster of Paris finish, molded to represent stone work. One is on a 5520 base (2-093) and the other on one from what is probably a 5521 (2-094). They used some of the pieces from the series but supplemented them with one or two new ones. The finish did not wear too well, so was dropped quite quickly.

2-092 **Moritz Gottschalk No.2/772**
2-093 **Moritz Gottschalk No.unknown 1**
2-094 **Moritz Gottschalk No.unknown 2**

Moritz Gottschalk No.2/772 is numbered strangely, almost as though it is not a Gottschalk item – but it is. The sand finish provides a refreshing change to the standard affair, but it is really difficult to paint on. The result is just woolly. This layout shows many of the characteristics of the 6200 series that was to come.

Moritz Gottschalk No.unknown 1 (2-093) is the first of two. It is complete, but shows the evidence of being knocked about a bit. This is inevitable with such a fragile finish. The plaster comes off if one so much as looks at it. It has a bark finish to the base.

Moritz Gottschalk No.unknown 2 (2-094) is the second one. It also shows evidence of being knocked about, damage that can happen even inside the box. Two things are worth noting: the gateway design comes to light again in the 6300 series and in Gottschalk No.6545 (2-127); and the base is covered with molded cardboard.

2-093

2-092

2-094

Then they tried a sandy finish. For this, they again used parts from the 5500 series, but they placed them on a much more complex box. It had a side entrance, a moat which ran all around the ramp, and a bridge allowing the ramp to pass over the moat. It was found that the spray paint used for the details did not take well on the sand, and the sharpness was lost, so this, too, had to be abandoned.

MORITZ GOTTSCHALK: Experiments
c1913 to c1925

NO.	DESCRIPTION	DATE	DIMENSIONS	DISTINCTIVE FEATURES
2/772 (2-092)	**sand-covered fort** (identified by an example in the ownership below) eg: Allen Hickling Toy Forts	unkwn	19¼"x14¼"x16½" 490x360x420mm	• moat all round the front of the fortress • bridge & ramp to dbridge & 2-turret gate • towers to walled crtyd w/lower balcony • rect tower, side bldg w/3-bay walkway
unknwn (2-093)	**plaster-covered fort 1** (identified by an example in the ownership below) eg: Allen Hickling Toy Forts	unkwn	16"x10½"x13½" 410x270x340mm	• ramp to dbridge & standard gateway • walled courtyard w/sm corner tower • rectangular tower & a main building • one open, 3-bay first floor walkway
unknwn (2-094)	**plaster-covered fort 2** (identified by an example in the ownership below) eg: Allen Hickling Toy Forts	unkwn	unknown	• ramp to dbridge & 2-tower gateway • medium sq tower & a sm wall tower • rectangular tower & main building • open, 4-bay, 1st floor walkway

These three fortresses all had bark on the bases, which probably dates them sometime before the introduction of the molded cardboard covering. The same cannot be said of the fourth one, No.55. It stands on a box that first had the number 5520 printed with a rubber stamp; this was erased and No.55 hand written in its place. Also rubber stamped on the bottom is *"Made in Germany."* The box itself was exactly the same size as that of a No.5520.

MORITZ GOTTSCHALK: 55? Series
c1920 to c1922

NO.	DESCRIPTION	DATE	DIMENSIONS	DISTINCTIVE FEATURES
55 (2-095)	**the only one of this type?** (identified by an example in the ownership below) eg: Allen Hickling Toy Forts	unkwn	16"x10½"x13½" 410x270x340mm	• ramp to dbridge & standard gateway • tower with cellophane windows • one open, 3-bay first floor walkway • missing a building & a wall piece

The buildings on top are incomplete in that a main building and some perimeter walling are missing. The buildings do include, however, an open three-bay walkway and an unusual tower. The open walkway was never on a No.5520 and neither was the unusual tower, which was slightly bigger than the normal tower. It was hollow and had windows which were cut out and backed with a sort of red cellophane – an effect recreated in the palace-like "fortress" using 6000 series parts, which will come later. It was almost as though the building was to be lighted but, as far as I can tell, it never was. It also has provision for a clock of some sort, which is missing.

There were other types of experiments. The first of these was a smaller-scale fort, as evidenced in No.5730. This was on two levels and had many of the elements of previous series with several newer pieces, only smaller. One particular innovation was the circular corner tower with an onion dome used at the corners of the perimeter wall, as well as two-turret gateways, a re-designed main building, and, all around, a higher wall with small turrets. This was the precursor of the 6300 series.

The next was No.5738. This had some easily recognizable pieces. There was the ubiquitous small square tower, which was to come back again and again, a gateway from the 4700 series, and a courtyard perimeter wall with simulated crenellation from the 5200 and 5500 series. Then there was the solid rectangular tower, which they had been toying with, but without the half timbering. Finally, there was a new main building. This had arrow slits for the most part, with just one window high up, and crenellation across the top – really defensible. Although painted a bright yellow, it was the precursor of the 5700 series (painted grey), which was to come on stream soon after.

2-095 **Moritz Gottschalk No.55**
Moritz Gottschalk No.55 is odd in that it was originally numbered 5520, which was then changed to 55. There are pieces missing: a main building and a piece of the perimeter wall. Of those that remain, the interesting one is the hollow tower. The windows were cut out and backed with red cellophane, almost as though it was to be lighted. The round "window" may have been for a watch serving as a clock.

2-096

2-098

A large Selec-
tion of Swords,
Guns, Popguns,
Water Pistols,
Pea Pistols, etc.

KT 234 MODEL FORTS. Medieval rather than modern, they gain immensely in pic-
turesqueness over the present-day version, for every bore revels in turrets, moats and drawbridges. Attractively finished and of strong construction. In every case the superstructure
can be dismantled and packed inside the base. Various designs. Prices 5/11, 9/9, 17/6,
37/6, 44/6, 72/-.

2-100

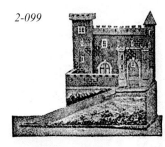

2-099

Forts.
As illustration, nicely finished, in attractive colours.
Size 13 × 9 × 11 in. Price 4/11   Post 9d.
Ditto smaller. Price 3/6   Post 6d.

2-097

2-096 **Moritz Gottschalk No.5738** *(Courtesy Bernd Zimmermann)*
2-097 **Moritz Gottschalk No.5730** *(Courtesy Bernd Zimmermann)*
2-098 **Hamley's catalogue 1929**
2-099 **Gamage's catalogue 1924**
2-100 **Moritz Gottschalk No.5753**

Moritz Gottschalk No.5738 is the forerunner of the 5700 series.
It is not known whether it was one of several; it probably was,
because Gamages had it in their catalogue in 1924 (2-099).
Except for its color, it was one of a more aggressively defensive
sort of "fortress" (2-101).

Moritz Gottschalk No.5730 is most unusual. It is to a much
smaller scale than anything Gottschalk produced up to this point. It
came into its own with the 6300 series (2-120 & 2-123). Two

features are worth noting – the circular towers with a form of onion
dome and high walls around the courtyard. It is not known whether
it was one of several, or not. It has molded cardboard on the base.

Moritz Gottschalk No.5753 is a fine example of a grand house,
which is complete. The three distinctive features are the access way
under the first floor walkway, placed at right angles to the other
buildings, its very fine double-fronted main building, and some very
special walling around the courtyard. Its grey color is significant in
the light of the fortresses that were to come. It has bark on the base.

According to their catalogue, Hamley's, another large store in
London, was selling these in 1929 (2-098). It appears to be derived
from a Gottschalk No.5753 on a large ground enclosure surrounded
by a moat – a very fancy version of the motte-and-bailey.

Then came Gottschalk No.5753, painted an attractive pale grey with light blue interior spaces on the walkways. There were two new pieces: the four-bay, open, first floor walkway with an arched gateway under it and a magnificent main building with two wings at the sides of a wide entrance.

MORITZ GOTTSCHALK: Miscellaneous
c1919 to c1924

NO.	DESCRIPTION	DATE	DIMENSIONS	DISTINCTIVE FEATURES
5730 (2-097)	**small scale castle** (identified by an example in the ownership below) eg: Cooper-Schiffer, USA	unkwn	unknown	• small scale on two levels • two ramps to two 2-turret gateways • a main & a side building • 3 square towers & 2 circular towers
5738 (2-096) (2-099)	**defensible castle type** (identified by an example in the ownership below) eg: Bernd Zimmermann, D	unkwn	unknown	• ramp to dbridge & fortified gateway • walled yard w/simulated crenellation • rectangular tower & medium sq tower • main bldg w/arrow slits & crenellation
5753 (2-100) (2-098)	**defensible grand house** (identified by an example in the ownership below) eg: Gerry Greene, USA	unkwn	unknown	• bark base w/ramp to db & 2-turret gate • entry level w/4-bay walkway & sq tower • 4-bay walkway w/arch & med sq tower • main bldg w/2 lg sq flanking towers

The base took a lot from the 4900 series, which also provided the big square towers, the small shed-like building, and the small wall turret. The buildings were completed by two medium, square towers and a two-turret gateway. Everything was surrounded with a really decorative perimeter wall. This had a life of its own on the top of an amazing castle structure in Hamley's catalogue of 1929, but I do not know of it being the precursor of anything else.

A Product Strategy for Development

Maybe Lina Gottschalk and her new husband Kurt were finding their feet at the head of the firm. Maybe they were trying to be different without extending themselves too much. Anyway, once recovery from the effects of the war was on the way and surviving the 1922–23 runaway inflation in Germany was assured, they could start to look to the future. Some real growth and development was essential if they were not to lose their market position.

They needed a business strategy for developing the product line. For this, they decided to go back to where they were before the war, producing "fortresses"

in batches of about ten types at a time, all using the same basic concept. This time, however, the concept they came up with was to make "fortresses" that really deserved the name – truly defensible structures, even to the inclusion of guns.

This brought on the production of a proper run and the launch of the 5700 series, of which known examples are No.5790 to No.5799. The same production style and methods were adopted, thus maintaining a relatively cautious approach to the market. They had already created No.5738, giving them a chance to test the market; it was to be the starting point for the series. Once again, a range of sizes was offered from No.5790 at 14¼" wide x 10" deep (356 x 250mm) to No.5799, which was 35½" across (900mm).

The buildings mostly were painted a sombre grey with white stonework, apart from the small conical and/or pyramidal red roofs on the towers. The result was a range of stark forts of an indefinite architectural pedigree, which, with the addition of enclosed and turret guns, became modern in the style they probably imagined would be built along the Maginot Line. There were only two known variations, one that was numbered Gottschalk No.5792, which was a bright yellow, and another, Gottschalk No.5794, which was a friendly brown.

The first five in the series were much alike. The pieces of No.5738 were used with very little change. Substituting a small circular tower for the small square one and the introduction of a new two-turret gateway were, in effect, the only changes.

2-101 Moritz Gottschalk No.5790

Gottschalk No.5790 is the first of the fortresses that are more like forts. It is most obviously derived from Gottschalk No.5738. Of course, the color is changed from yellow, the small tower is now circular instead of square, and there is a new gateway.

c.1923

2-102

2-102a

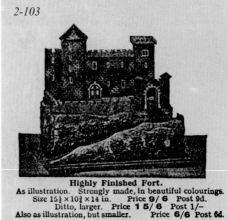

2-103

Highly Finished Fort.
As illustration. Strongly made, in beautiful colourings.
Size 15½ × 10¾ × 14 in.   Price **9/6** Post 9d.
Ditto, larger.   Price **15/6** Post 1/–
Also as illustration, but smaller.   Price **6/6** Post 6d.

2-102 Moritz Gottschalk No.5792 *(yellow)*
2-102a Moritz Gottschalk No.5792 *(grey) (Courtesy Bernd Zimmermann)*
2-103 Gamage's catalogue 1924

Moritz Gottschalk No.5792 is bigger than No.5790 (2-101), but not by much. The buildings at the back now have a large circular tower with a main block on one side and a side building on the other. The fact that one is colored yellow (2-102) is perhaps the most striking, since it was made at a time when they were attempting to be more fort-like. The grey version (2-102a), from which two side perimeter walls around the courtyard are missing, is more what we expect. The crenellation on the perimeter wall of both is real, not simulated.

Gamage's catalogue shows that these were on sale in England at the time.

2-104

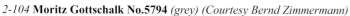

2-105

2-104 **Moritz Gottschalk No.5794** *(grey) (Courtesy Bernd Zimmermann)*
2-105 **Moritz Gottschalk No.5794** *(brown)*

Moritz Gottschalk No.5794 (grey) has a double ramp and two levels. The inside of both levels is used, accessed by a cunningly concealed door in the side of the base and various ways through the upper level to the top courtyard. The buildings at the back are the same as Gottschalk No.5790. The figures are German semi-flats.

Moritz Gottschalk No.5794 (brown) is exactly the same, but painted in brown. This is the only example we have of a series 5700 "fortress" painted brown. The gateway is a replacement.

However, even on the No.5794, an exciting new concept was introduced. Access was provided to the interior of the boxes, which became much more than the mound on which the fort was built. Access to both the lower and upper levels was provided. Now one could see how people got from one level to the next. Of course, this was much more work, but their years of experience making dollhouses probably gave them an edge.

This was further developed in their later "fortresses" where guns were introduced. Apart from the emplacements and turrets that were required to accommodate the artillery, a few new pieces were added. These were a substantial square tower, slightly shorter and much fatter than the one which had become their standard on almost every fort, an even more substantial circular tower, a rather grim extended crenellated main building, and a side building to match.

MORITZ GOTTSCHALK: 5700 Series
c1923 to c1930

NO.	DESCRIPTION	DATE	DIMENSIONS	DISTINCTIVE FEATURES
5790	**smallest of this series** (identified by an example in the ownership below) eg: SOFIA Foundation, CY	c1923	11¼"x8"x12¼" 285x205x310mm	• ramp to db & crenellated gateway • yard wall w/simulated crenellation • buildings at rear derived from 5738 • circular tower instead of square one
5792 (2-102) (2-102a)	**third of this series** (identified by an example in the ownership below) eg: Allen Hickling Toy Forts	c1923	15¾"x11"x13¾" 400x280x350mm	• ramp to db & crenellated gateway • yard wall w/simulated crenellation • buildings at rear derived from 5738 • large circular tower w/side building
5794 (2-104) (2-105)	**fifth of this series** (identified by an example in the ownership below) eg: Allen Hickling Toy Forts	c1923	18¼"x13½"x13¾" 465x345x350mm	• double ramp to crenellated gateway • secret door & doorways + stairwell • crenellated wall around courtyards • buildings at rear same as 5790
5795 (2-106)	**sixth of this series** (identified by an example in the ownership below) eg: Bernd Zimmermann, D	c1923	unknown	• gate & ramp w/3-gun embrasures • upper walled crtyd w/med sq tower • main building as enlarged 5738 • large circular & large square towers
5797 (2-107)	**eighth of this series** (identified by an example in the ownership below) eg: Bernd Zimmermann, D	c1923	unknown	• trench (or moat?) around 3 sides • gate at rear & ramp to db & gateway • upper courtyard w/main & side bldgs • circular & another flanking towers
579? (2-109)	**largest of this series** (identified by an example in the ownership below) eg: Auction House, D	c1923	35½"x??"x??" 900x??x??mm	• ground level gate, high wall & towers • db & gateway to inside space • upper level same as extended 5738 • two large gun turrets
unknwn (2-108)	**special in this series?** (identified by an example in the ownership below) eg: Bernd Zimmermann, D	c1923	21½"x16"x14¼" 550x410x360mm	• bark base & ramp to db & gateway • walled crtyd w/2 towers & ramp up • gate to upper crtyd w/2 lg sq towers • good representation of White Tower

There was also a version with the turrets on the top. Not only was this very large, but it was on two very definite levels, with the lower of these surrounded by a high perimeter wall and towers. The lower part of the "fortress" proper was a very severe building, and the upper level, which was at the first floor level on the building below, was dominated by two very large gun turrets.

The final example in the series may not belong in the series at all. It does not have a known number and is known mainly by its name – the Tower of London – and a quite good representation of the actual fort it is. I put it here because of its grey coloring and its general appearance.

2-106 Moritz Gottschalk No.5795 *(Courtesy Bernd Zimmermann)*
Moritz Gottschalk No.5795 is considerably larger and was the first to be provided with guns. The buildings at the back included an enlarged square tower, an elaborate main building with a balcony, and a large circular tower. There is no gateway in the usual sense, but just a door. The guns are accommodated in an all-new front piece, which forms the entrance.

c.1923

2-107

2-108

2-107 **Moritz Gottschalk No.5797** *(Courtesy Bernd Zimmermann)*
2-108 **Moritz Gottschalk No.unknown** *(Tower of London) (Courtesy Bernd Zimmermann)*

Compared to Moritz Gottschalk No.5795 on the previous page, No.5797 is notably different in that it has no provision for guns. There is one new piece – an extension to the main building. It is not certain whether the trench running around the front three sides is a moat. It is missing a tower. The figures are of German origin.

Moritz Gottschalk No.unknown (Tower of London) is some form of special. The main building at the back is a good representation of the White Tower. Otherwise it is like other two-level "fortresses," with perhaps a few more towers than normal. It has bark on the base. It is missing the front part of the upper courtyard perimeter wall. The 54mm figures are Britains cavalry.

2-109 **Moritz Gottschalk No.579(?)**

Gottschalk No.579(?) is by far the largest in the series that we know of. It is modelled on the old motte-and-bailey. On the mound is the main building with a balcony, flanked by two towers, and protected by two very large gun turrets. The lower wall is high, has two large square towers and eight small ones.

Gottschalk Reverts to the Medieval Period

In fact, it has many special pieces. Whether they were made just for this one "fortress" I really cannot say, but they do not appear on any other examples, before or since. First and foremost is the main building, which could not be anything but the White Tower of the Tower of London, especially the unique tops to the towers. Both the gateways and one of the towers on the lower level are also special pieces, which I do not think were used again.

Looking back on any strategy, the acid test is whether it achieved what it set out to achieve. In this case, both their recovery and development strategies did: the firm of Moritz Gottschalk was still in existence not only in the decade after the war, but throughout the 1930s as well.

In fact, a good strategy is rarely enough on its own. That they survived so well can probably be just as well attributed to their most valuable asset: a reputation for quality of product, reliability of service, and good commercial sense that had been built up over more than fifty years with their importers and distributors around the world. This was going to be needed as they moved into another period of high activity. From about 1923 through about 1930, they produced at least three more series as well as a few stand-alone examples.

MORITZ GOTTSCHALK: 6000 Series
c1925 to c1930

NO.	DESCRIPTION	DATE	DIMENSIONS	DISTINCTIVE FEATURES
6081 (2-110)	**smallest? of this series** (identified by an example in the ownership below) eg: SOFIA Foundation, CY	c1925	15½"x12"x14¼" 395x305x360mm	• layout atop high bark covered base • re-entrant ramp to large gatehouse • 3-D house, gallery, & circular tower • walled courtyard with corner tower
608? (2-111)	**sixth? of this series** (identified by an example in the ownership below) eg: Peter Clark, DC, US	c1925	32"x25"x26" 810x635x660mm	• cork base & O-gauge train tunnel • re-entrant ramp to 2 lg gatehouses • lower stable yard & upper courtyard • 3-D buildings & large towers
6086 (2-112) (2-113)	**seventh of this series** (identified by an example in the ownership below) eg: Gerry Greene, US	c1925	19"x21"x25" 480x535x635mm	• baseboard missing from cork base • re-entrant ramp to 2 lg gatehouses • lower stable yard & upper level • 3-D building & large circular tower
6087 (2-114)	**largest? of this series** (identified by an example in the ownership below) eg: SOFIA Foundation, CY	c1925	38½"x25¾"x30½" 980x655x775mm	• cork base & O-gauge train tunnel • treble ramp & bridge to upper level • 2 square & 2 circular towers • three 3-D houses w/moat

The first of these came out in 1925/1926 and was most spectacular. It involved building large "fortresses" – as large as the biggest of their earlier ones. The immediate impression one gets when presented with these is that they have gone back to the medieval period. We have four examples from the series: No.6081 and No.608(?) – probably 6085 or 6088 – to No.6087. The first is a quite small example, but the last three are enormous.

Starting with the smallest one, we have No.6081. There are only two recognizable pieces from earlier "fortresses," which is a measure of how original this series was. Virtually everything was new with the exception of the circular tower at the corner, the short tower at the corner of the perimeter wall, and the covering on the base, for which, for some reason, they went back to using bark. For the larger fortresses, they used cork on the base, principally because the scale would have been wrong otherwise.

The buildings have a more robust look to them. On this smaller one, there is a three-dimensional house and medium-sized circular tower, linked by a first floor walkway, which is surprisingly two-dimensional. The gatehouse is considerably larger than anything they had produced before, and the wall around the courtyard is a new section. This was also used for the second-floor gallery and various oriel windows on the larger examples.

2-110 Moritz Gottschalk No.6081
Moritz Gottschalk No.6081 is one of the small forts. Nearly all the pieces are newly designed. The house is one of the new, not quite three-dimensional ones. The upper gallery piece is strangely two-dimensional. The bark-covered base is mounted by a re-entrant ramp leading to a large gateway.

2-111 Moritz Gottschalk No.608(?)

Moritz Gottschalk No.608(?) is one of the very large fortresses that they produced to attract the very top end of the market. These were very spectacular. The digit after 608 is undecipherable.

It is a large establishment on two levels, all on a large hill with O-gauge toy railway running underneath. It is complete. It is entered up a re-entrant ramp, through a very large gatehouse, and into the entry courtyard surrounded by high-level walkways and a square tower. Up a small ramp, through a large gateway is the upper courtyard where the main accommodation is found. This comprises two three-dimensional houses, a four-bay upper level walkway, two large towers, and various ancillary buildings.

2-112

2-113

2-112 Moritz Gottschalk No.6086 (*with base board*)
2-113 Moritz Gottschalk No.6086

Moritz Gottschalk No.6086 (2-113) is missing its base board. As a consequence it has also lost its drawbridge and chains.

Entry is up a re-entrant ramp, through a very large gatehouse, and into the entry courtyard with its large circular tower. Then up a short ramp, bypassing a medium square tower, to the base of a long ramp to a large gateway.

Entering the upper courtyard through the gateway, one arrives at the main accommodation. This comprises one three-dimensional house linked to a large circular tower by a three-bay (two-arch) high-level walkway and several ancillary buildings. It is missing the turret off the large circular tower and a small piece of perimeter wall, both at the upper level.

The Moritz Gottschalk No.6086 on the left (2-112) shows the castle on a base board.

2-114 Moritz Gottschalk No.6087

Moritz Gottschalk No.6087 is substantially the largest of this series of large fortresses. The O-gauge railway tunnels under the back along its length.

One gains the lower reception plaza via the treble ramp, past some defensive towers, and through a gatehouse. One goes through this lower courtyard, surrounded by buildings and towers, up and over a sloping bridge to another large gatehouse. This gives onto the main courtyard, which serves the living quarters. Once there, one is faced by three three-dimensional houses, a large square tower, and an upper level walkway, all linked together.

The fortress is missing several pieces. The front perimeter wall piece is the most obvious, but there are others. For instance, the lower gatehouse is missing one of its side buildings and both of the tunnel entrances are replicas. There appears to be something missing on the first landing of the ramp – a door leading under the lower courtyard perhaps.

The three larger "fortresses" of which we have examples are clearly all from the same mold.

Starting with the bases, they are all very big and covered in chunky pieces of cork. The ramps are extensive. Two of them, No.608(?) and No.6087, contain tunnels designed to take O-gauge trains. In the case of the former, the train just ran around a circle, half under the "fortress" and half in the open; in the latter, it ran straight through from side to side down its length.

Of course, there was a serious mismatch in time between that which the buildings were supposed to represent and that of the steam railway – or, perhaps the railway was built under an existing establishment, in which case I have fears for its foundations.

Moving up, they are all in the form of hill-top settlements, somewhat in the nature of film sets. More to the point, they are rather like the products of O & M Hausser, who were Gottschalk's competitors about this time. They all have at least two levels and two courtyards.

Most of the buildings are three-dimensional; those that are not give a very real impression of three-dimensionality. All are defensible in the sense that they only have arrow slits on the ground floor. Only one, the No.6087, has a moat with a bridge over it, although how a moat was supposed to be filled on the top of a rock makes one wonder. Nevertheless, the question of how they could have called these "fortresses" still remains. They are residences that are defensible to a degree, but not against a determined foe.

These bigger examples owed more to their heritage than did the small one. The pieces that are recognizable earlier designs are the four towers, including the ubiquitous medium square tower that graces so many of Gottschalk's "fortresses," and the upper level walkway that even had a version with an arched support structure, which was new. The two gatehouses are very much more robust than anything that went before, and the taller of the two is quite a significant structure.

The three-dimensional buildings are supported by various subsidiary two-dimensional half-timbered buildings. There are at least six of them and they are used differently for each "fortress" – Gottschalk No.608(?) has two, Gottschalk No.6086 has one, and Gottschalk No.6087 has three.

Taking the three from the largest "fortress," two of them are about 2½" x 5" x 8½" (65 x 130 x 215mm), 6" (150mm) to the eaves. Another, slightly narrower,

is 1½" x 5¾" x 6½" (40 x 145 x 165mm), 5" (65mm) to the eaves. These make for a large physical presence. Two have dormer windows, one has a balcony and one, the narrower, has an outside staircase to the upper floor of the adjacent house. These applied embellishments are all three-dimensional and give a really good, realistic feel to the "fortress."

Gottschalk kept the color schemes all much the same; that is, various browns and yellows with white or cream trim and black windows, and, of course, the red roofs. The courtyards were either brown or a bright yellow. It all made for a bright and cheery scene.

Moving on to the 6200 series in which mostly the same parts were used. The one common feature in this series is the ramps, which they owe to an earlier prototype (2-092). There is a moat around three sides and the ramp gets over it by means of a fixed bridge. There is also a drawbridge higher up.

MORITZ GOTTSCHALK: 6200 Series
c1926 to c1930

NO.	DESCRIPTION	DATE	DIMENSIONS	DISTINCTIVE FEATURES
6204 (2-115)	smallest(?) in the series (identified by an example in the ownership below) eg: SOFIA Foundation, CY	c1926	15"x13¼"x17¼" 380x335x440mm	• cardboard base w/moat on 3 sides • re-entrant ramp w/bridge to gatehouse • normal layout with walled courtyard • bldg, open walkway & sm sq tower
620? (2-116)	largest? in the series (identified by an example in the ownership below) eg: Peter Clark, DC, US	c1926	unknown	• bark covered base w/moat • re-entrant ramp & gatehse to yard • med sq & lg circular towers • main building & 3-bay walkway
6374 (2-117) (2-118)	medium sized fortress (identified by an example in the ownership below) eg: SOFIA Foundation, CY	c1926	19¾"x11"x17¾" 500x280x450mm	• bark base w/ramp to db & gatehouse • entry crtyd w/main bldg & sq tower • db to upper gate & crtyd w/side bldg • main bldg, gallery & lg sq tower
unkwn (2-119)	large palace-like fortress (identified by an example in the ownership below) eg: SOFIA Foundation, CY	c1926	26"x19"x24" 660x480x610mm	• bark base & ramp to db & gatehouse • entry crtyd w/2 med sq towers & ramp • db & upper gatehouse to walled crtyd • 2- & 3-D houses & cent tower w/turret

2-117

2-118

2-115

2-116

2-115 **Moritz Gottschalk No.6204**
2-116 **Moritz Gottschalk No.620?** *(Courtesy the Peter B Clark collection)*
2-117 **Moritz Gottschalk No.6374** *detail*
2-118 **Moritz Gottschalk No.6374**

Moritz Gottschalk No.6204 is on a molded cardboard covered base, rising out of a moat on three sides. The re-entrant ramp crosses the moat by means of a bridge leading up to a drawbridge and a large gatehouse. There is a walled courtyard and a small house linked to a small square tower via a gallery. The buildings are predominantly grey. It is complete and in good condition.

Moritz Gottschalk No.620(?) is much the same as Gottschalk No.6204, especially up to the gatehouse, except that the base is covered in bark. The courtyard has walling from the 6000 series, including the short square tower at the corner. The buildings at the back comprise a small house and medium square tower, linked via a medium circular tower and an open three-bay upper walkway. The fortress is complete and in good condition, but the digit after the 620 is undecipherable.

Moritz Gottschalk No.6374 is basically two courtyards on a double base covered in bark, one slightly higher than the other. The buildings are all taken from the 6000 series. Interestingly, the large square tower is too large to fit into the base without a door being cut into the base to allow it to stick out (see the detail image (2-117)). The fortress is complete and in good condition.

Thereafter the "fortresses" take on a more traditional form, but using pieces from the 6000 series. On the smallest one, the perimeter wall around the courtyard is different in that it is made up of simple pieces of wood without crenellation. It is also much duller, being painted a mid-grey, and, adding to the dullness, with the old molded cardboard covering to the base. Whether this, taken with the lack of crenellation on the perimeter wall, is an indication of date is not known.

Before moving on to the 6300 series, there were two others that should be mentioned, because they, too, mostly used the 6000 series pieces. One was Gottschalk No.6374, which came on somewhat later. It was quite small, but nonetheless it used three-dimensional pieces and gave a fine display. The two courtyards are on two levels and they give exactly the same sort of environment as the 6000 series, but smaller.

2-119 **Moritz Gottschalk No.unknown**

Gottschalk No.unknown is seriously different from the others derived from the 6000 series, even though all the pieces are from it or are in the same style.

It is essentially a very large house atop a high bark-covered base. The defenses are organized on the double-wall system. The house is three-dimensional and has two almost identical wings attached to a central large square tower; all painted the same very pale grey with red roofs.

Restored by me, this fort had been knocked about a bit. The two battlement sections immediately adjacent to the lower gatehouse are replacements, and all the roofs, horizontal surfaces, and the ramp were repaired and repainted. Also, new paper was put into the windows.

The other one was a completely different story. It does not have a number but it was clearly in the 6000 series. It was on two levels, but the lower level was only for defense with crenellated walls and towers all around. This recalls the famous *double wall* defensive system for castles, which became common practice in the 13th/14th century, or even before that with the motte-and-bailey system.

Above that is a single very large building using three-dimensional pieces taken from the 6000 series arranged in a formal symmetrical pattern around a central tower to give the impression of a palace all built at the same time. There is one other notable difference, also taken from an earlier prototype (2-095): the windows are cut out and backed with a red sort of cellophane as though the buildings were going to be lighted, but they were not.

This fortress has also been lightly restored by me. Two walls in the lower ring were missing and some touching up of the buildings was necessary, in particular the roofs, as was the repainting of all the horizontal surfaces, the crenels included.

Gottschalk Tries to Control the Environment

In 1927, Gottschalk made a move to control the exterior environment of the "fortresses." To do this they had to put everything in a box. The box served to protect the "fortress" and provide a depiction of the area surrounding it. It also gave the possibility of creating a large forecourt by means of a flap-down front; in this forecourt they provided the surroundings in the form of small trees and houses.

MORITZ GOTTSCHALK: 6300 Series
c1927 to c.1934

NO.	DESCRIPTION	DATE	DIMENSIONS	DISTINCTIVE FEATURES
6319/1 (2-120)	**smallest in this series** (identified by an example in the ownership below) eg: Allen Hickling Toy Forts	c1927	16"x19½"x11" 405x495x280mm	• in box with flap-down front • castle buildings from 5730 • front buildings from 6086 • two modern houses
6319/2 (2-122) (2-123)	**second in this series** (identified by an example in the ownership below) eg: SOFIA Foundation, CY	c1927	19½"x23"x13" 495x585x330mm	• in box with flap-down front • castle from 5730 & separate ramp • 3 houses from 4800/4900 series • front wall, towers from 6000 series
6319/3 (2-126)	**largest in this series** (identified by an example in the ownership below) eg: Allen Hickling Toy Forts	c1927	22½"x26½"x14" 570x675x355mm	• in box with flap-down front & ramp • castle from 5730 and 5700 series • 4 modern houses, garage & trees • front wall, towers from 6000 series
6319/?	**largest in this series** (listed in Gottschalk catalogue 1929) eg: no known example	C1929	unknown	• in box with flap-down front & ramp • opening panoramic side panels • 4 modern houses, garage & trees • front wall, towers from 6000 series

One of the first things one notices is that the numbering system has changed. Previously, when "fortresses" were basically of the same type, had similar pieces, but were of different sizes, they were given sequential numbers, with the number after the oblique indicating their place in the series. Now they were given the same number, with the number after the oblique again indicating their place in the series. In some ways this seems more sensible, but how long it went on is anybody's guess – at least for now. There is no hard evidence available to us.

The first, No.6319/1, takes its castle buildings directly from No.5730 (2-097). This is a smaller scale than normal, so it fits more neatly into the box. The gateway leads onto a fairly conventional courtyard with buildings ranged along the back.

The buildings at the front, that is on the hinged flap, are larger scale, probably from the 6000 series. Apart from the two modern houses on the apron, the gateway, in particular, is really very large. This cleverly gives a false sense of perspective, so that the "fortress" looks much further away, and the whole looks much bigger than it actually is.

The second one, No.6319/2, is much the same as far as the castle buildings are concerned. The buildings at the front, however, are much larger. The walls are high, constructed of the walls from the 6000 series, applied to a back piece which raises them up. The towers at the corners are the ubiquitous, small, square towers cut down, making a sizeable structure. The gateway is from the 5700 series, and the houses are the small shed-like buildings from the 4800/4900 series.

The third of this series, No.6319/3, which is in my possession, leaves me in something of a quandary. If I compare it with what I have of Gottschalk's own catalogue, it has many of the characteristics of the 1929 production. The castle buildings are almost identical. Larger pieces were taken from the 6000 series, cut down to fit with some from Gottschalk No.5730, and a circular tower came from the 5700 series. It has a moat across the front. The gateway at the top of the ramp is taken from Gottschalk No.unknown 2 (2-094), and it is large enough to accentuate the perspective effect.

The apron courtyard has four modern houses in it, including one with a double garage, and two trees (or at least the bases of two trees). The walls are high, as before, with quite large corner towers, but the gateway is very much larger. The courtyard is still larger than the castle, but the difference is less than it was with the other "fortresses," so the perspective effect is reduced.

There others in this series that I have seen in Cieslik's *Moritz Gottsshalk 1892–1931*. These show the side wall divided in half vertically, with the front half swung open on each side to make a wider panorama, incidentally bringing the "fortress" out of its cramped box. Needless to say, my examples do not have that facility.

c.1927

2-120

2-123

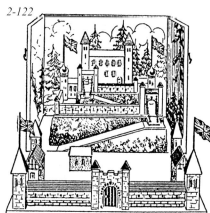

2-122

MODEL FORT
As illustration. Beautifully finished in colours.
Strongly made. Size 24 x 19½ x 23 ins.
Post 9d.   Price **27/6**

2-120 Moritz Gottschalk No.6319/1
2-122 Gamages catalogue 1928
Gottschalk No.6319/2
2-123 Moritz Gottschalk No.6319/2
(Courtesy Jim Osborne)

Moritz Gottschalk No.6319/1 is the smallest in the series. The pieces for the "fortress" come from Gottschalk No.5730. Those for the gateway and perimeter walling of the apron come from Gottschalk No.6087. The difference in scale, and thus size, provides an enhanced perspective making it appear larger than it was. The base of the "fortress" was covered with bark.

Moritz Gottschalk No.6319/2 is the middle size of the series. The pieces for the "fortress" were taken from Gottschalk No.5730, but those in front appear to have been specially made, and are considerably larger. The gateway is from the 5700 series. The small buildings are from the 4900 series. This example is painted light-grey with white stonework and red roofs.

Gamage's catalogue shows they were on sale in London at the time. Note how they used images with the British flag flying.

c.1927

2-126 Moritz Gottschalk No.6319/3

Moritz Gottschalk No.6319/3 is the largest in the series. While some of the pieces for the "fortress" can be traced to Gottschalk No.5730 (2-099) others cannot and are slightly larger. Particularly note the circular tower, the gallery and the gateways. There is a forecourt added to the "fortress" that contains a moat, thus necessitating a forward thrust ramp. The perimeter wall and buildings on the apron are more or less like the one before, but the four small houses are like those on Gottschalk No.6319/1 (2-120).

Now I would like to consider one or two items which do not fit in with anything else.

The first is Gottschalk No.6545, which may or may not have been part of a series. It is interesting because it has a presence, by which I mean so much packed into so small a space, while retaining its credibility. It uses many of the 6000 series pieces in a way that is consistent with that series, but it is really quite small.

It is on two levels and has an outer wall constructed in a circle – or rather a rough semi-circle. Because it is meant to go up against a wall, it has a flat back. The lower gateway is the one used on their experiments just after the First World War (2-094). Inside this circle stands the upper courtyard, which is rectangular except for one corner, which has been cut off. The buildings all fit together around a small courtyard on this upper level.

Next is a sort of series, in that there are at least three variations on a theme. This theme is West Point, the military academy in the United States, and the central tower is a quite good representation of the library tower at West Point. Of course, there the similarity ends, because there must be bits which make it more "fortress"-like. For example the system of ramps, a drawbridge, crenellated walls, and towers.

MORITZ GOTTSCHALK: Miscellaneous
c1926 to c1930+

NO.	DESCRIPTION	DATE	DIMENSIONS	DISTINCTIVE FEATURES
6545 (2-127)	**a stand-alone fortress** (identified by an example in the ownership below) eg: Allen Hickling Toy Forts	unkwn	26"x19"x24" 660x480x610mm	• bark-covered base on two levels • 3-D buildings from 6000 series • outer walls & towers crenellated • two ramps to two large gateways
6569 (2-130)	**smallest in the series** (identified by an example in the ownership below) eg: Bernd Zimmermann, D	unknwn	unknown	• labelled as West Point • 2 ramps, 2 courtyards, on 2 levels • 3-D modern buildings & one deck • crenellation all round
unknwn (2-129)	**largest in the series** (identified by an example in the ownership below) eg: Jeff Caulfield, USA	unknwn	unknown	• almost same as West Point • 2 ramps, 2 courtyards, on 2 levels • 3-D modern buildings & one deck • extra tower & crenellation all round

The first variation (2-130) was one with a small plaque, which describes it as "West Point." The second variation (2-129) was nearly the same, but not quite. It has an extra tower protecting the ramp and a real colonnade beside the entrance instead of one just painted on. Furthermore the side balcony is supported above a veranda.

They are actually quite large and are very impressive. But really none of these deserve the name "fortress." Let us face it, they are little more than an American hotel or block of flats of the era between the wars.

So we ring down the curtain on this stage of Moritz Gottschalk's development. The depression was just around the corner, and the management style was about to change. After the First World War and the rampant inflation of 1922/1923, this had been a golden era.

2-127 **Moritz Gottschalk No.6545**
Moritz Gottschalk No.6545 is altogether different. It is not known if it was part of a series or not. It is designed on the double-wall system of defense, in which an outer curtain wall surrounds an independent raised part. In this, the semi-circular outer wall is quite high, with towers every so often and a gatehouse that was taken from No.6319/3 for this "fortress." However the inner "keep" is rectangular. All the pieces for the "fortress" are derived from the 6000 series. There are a couple of pyramidal roofs and two small pieces of perimeter wall missing. The example has a flat back.

c.1926

2-129

2-130

2-129 Moritz Gottschalk No.6569 (West Point)
2-130 Moritz Gottschalk No.unknown *(Courtesy Jeff Caufield)*

Moritz Gottschalk No.6569 "West Point" is one of two versions shown here. There is also a tower at the top of the first leg of the ramp where the label was on the first one. There is simulated crenellation on the other two towers.

Moritz Gottschalk No.unknown is almost the same except the colonnade on the front has real depth behind it, and the deck to the right stands on a veranda. It gets its name from the buildings at the back, specifically the central tower, which is a reasonable model of the library tower at the real West Point. Across the front are ranged some formidable defenses in the form of towers and crenellated walls. The first leg of the ramp is defensible, and the second runs up between crenellated walls. There is a deck to the right. There is a label on the front of the ramp: "West Point."

GOTTSCHALK AND PRODUCT STRATEGY

Moritz Gottschalk was a book-binder with artistic skills. He could turn his hand to anything practical, such as woodworking, printing, etc. It was only a short step from this to using the same combination of technologies for diversification into different markets, such as toy grocery stores, stables, warehouses, and so-called "fortresses." The phrase "so-called" is used here because, although the translation has been checked – and double checked – "fortress" remains the best translation of the German word *"Festung"* used in his promotional literature.

In fact, "fortress" seems to be an inappropriate description of buildings, which were more in the nature of lightly fortified mansions with the occasional drawbridge, sentry box, and minor crenellation. We are definitely not talking of the military installations more usually described as forts, such as those built in the Celtic heartland by the kings of medieval England, at least not until after the First World War, when they managed to produce some reasonably defensible buildings – if not 100%.

Moritz and various members of his family were in business for about seventy years. During that time there was great need to adapt to a rapidly changing world. In terms of their design strategy, there were three major upheavals. One was when Moritz died and his son took over, another when his son was killed at the start of the First World War, and the third when his son's widow could not continue and she handed control of the business to her stepson in 1934.

The second happened right at the beginning of a four-year World War, which happened just as things were settling down in terms of development, and business was booming. The loss of their leader was clearly a disaster of major proportions at such a time. Much of the war took place quite near the German border, so all their export markets were closed. Luckily his wife was there and she proved more than capable. It was a question of just sitting tight until it was over.

The first of these more or less coincided with a revolution in the design of "fortresses," which happened at the end of the first decade of the 20th century. They went from reasonably 3-D constructions, covered with lithographed paper, to ones that were more in the nature of theatre scenery, with flatter buildings, details painted on with stencils, and red roofs for blue.

The second upheaval was at a time of major change in their business environment. This was the world recession of the 1930s, and the coming of the Third Reich. They could not continue as they had been doing. Not only had they lost a large proportion of their market, but they had to be politically adept to stay in business. This was achieved by changing the concept of "fortress" to be consistent with a more modern context.

Apart from these really important changes, there were many smaller ones. For example, somewhere about the time of the first shake up, there was a new way of locating the buildings. This was the installing of nails, or something similar, in the underside of the pieces matching holes drilled in the base. It is not known if Gottschalk initiated this, but it certainly suited the thinner solid buildings they produced.

Then there was the covering of the boxes. From the arrival of the 2300 series, at the latest, the use of bark on the smaller fortresses and cork on the larger ones was standard practice. Immediately after the First World War, he introduced the use of molded cardboard as an alternative for the smallest ones. In general, they maintained this regime to the end.

Of course, there were other innovations. Electric lighting was a feature of most of the early fortresses with hollow buildings on them. This was a lot more difficult with the coming of solid buildings and the number dropped dramatically. Nothing is known, at least to me, about how they were made to work or what batteries they used.

Then there was the great experiment with water. This occurred just before the First World War. They produced several fortresses with real water in the moats, though this production did not last long. Whether making them was too expensive or on the basis of feedback from parents about playrooms awash with water, they were quickly abandoned.

When they decided to base a fortress on reality, such as in the West Point case, they went to some trouble to get it right. The museum building at the real West Point provided an excellent model to work from, as can be seen from the image. This attempt at getting it right came after the second big important change, and can be evidenced in their modern day fortifications.

Unfortunately, the destruction of all the Gottschalk records during and after the Second World War makes tracking of these changes extremely difficult, if not impossible. From the fortresses which remain, however, we get a good idea of the Gottschalk philosophy, which was to produce articles to support play in as exciting a manner as possible.

The Company Faces the Depression and the Second World War

By 1930, the world depression was already underway. The supply of "fortresses" in England just dried up. This has limited my access to the company's products as well as my knowledge of the company's fortunes. I have been able, however, with the help of my German friends, a bit of reading, and fairly simple deduction, to piece together some understanding of those ten years leading up to the Second World War.

The first few years of the depression must have been difficult for Lina and Kurt – trying to keep the company going before the Third Reich came to power. The loss of their markets in England, France, Australia, America, and elsewhere, must have made survival very tricky for a year or two.

I imagine that, as they aged, their response to a rapidly changing world became that much more limited. So much so that, in 1934, they decided to call it a day and hand over the reins to Alfred, who was Kurt's son.

Adolf Hitler had just become chancellor, and it looked as though Germany would pull through, at least to a limited extent. Alfred, it seems, responded to this by launching two new strategies.

The first was the production of fortifications, building more or less on their experience of the First World War, modified as they thought they were to be used in the Second World War – bunkers, gun emplacements, trenches, and so forth. Included with these were more urban-type buildings serving as command centres, police stations, and the like.

MORITZ GOTTSCHALK: Panzer Forts
c1935 to c1941

NO.	DESCRIPTION	DATE	DIMENSIONS	DISTINCTIVE FEATURES
444 (2-135)	**large command bunker** (identified by an example in the ownership below) eg: Vectis Auctions, UK	c1935	23½"x11½"x6¼" 600x290x160mm	• artillery observation, first aid post • command, communications bunker • wood, cardboard, & material • painted green and brown
unknwn (2-133)	**airfield HQ** (identified by an example in the ownership below) eg: Vectis Auctions, UK	c1935	18½"x8¼"x4¾" 470x210x120mm	• large airfield type hanger/bunker • smaller bunker for personnel • wood, cardboard material • painted green and brown
unknwn (2-134)	**closed fort** (identified by an example in the ownership below) eg: Vectis Auctions, UK	c1935	17¼"x12¼"x6" 440x320x150mm	• fortified position, machine gun post • crew trench and defensive wire belt • wood, cardboard, & material • painted green and brown
unknwn (2-132)	**large bunker for infantry** (identified by an example in the ownership below) eg: Vectis Auctions, UK	c1935	31"x23½"x??" 790x590X??mm	• six bunkers (various), pill box • trench system w/wire obstacles • wood, cardboard, & material • painted green and brown

2-132 **Moritz Gottschalk Large Bunker for Infantry & Pioneers** *(Courtesy Vectis Auctions)*

Moritz Gottschalk Large Bunker for Infantry & Pioneers (modelled on examples from the Hindenberg Line of the First World War) is from about 1938. It has six bunkers (various functions), a forward trench system with pill box and wire obstacles. These were modelled on earthworks that were the most up-to-date defenses of the time. They were constructed of wood and cardboard and covered with composite material painted in green and brown. The 70mm figures are by Elastolin.

MORITZ GOTTSCHALK: Command Centres
c1935 to c1941

NO.	DESCRIPTION	DATE	DIMENSIONS	DISTINCTIVE FEATURES
unknwn (2-137)	**HQ building** (identified by an example in the ownership below) eg: Vectis Auctions, UK	c1935	23½"x11½"x6¼" 600x290x160mm	• three storey, semi-domestic bldg • paper-covered wood & cardboard • colored red & mottled brown
unknwn (2-136)	**SA 'home'** (identified by an example in the ownership below) eg: Vectis Auctions, UK	c1935	unknown	• 2-storey bldg & 3-storey tower • roughcast finish on wood • smooth roof • light grey walls & red roof

I am not going to go into the modern fortifications here, apart from one or two examples taken from the catalogues of Vectis Auctions. No doubt they served a purpose in the rise of the Third Reich and allowed the company to pursue their other lines without too much hindrance. But being almost entirely about earthworks and more conventional buildings, they are not germane to the story of the "fortresses" anyway.

2-133

2-135

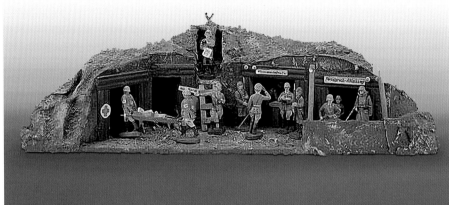

2-134

2-133 **Mortiz Gottschalk Airfield HQ** (*Courtesy Vectis Auctions*)
2-134 **Moritz Gottschalk Closed Fort** (*Courtesy Vectis Auctions*)
2-135 **Moritz Gottschalk No.444** *Command Bunker* (*Courtesy Vectis Auctions*)

The Moritz Gottschalk Airfield HQ (modelled on examples from the First World War) is from about 1935. It includes a large hanger-type bunker, and a small bunker for personnel. The 70mm figures are by Elastolin.

The Moritz Gottschalk Closed Fort (modelled on examples from the First World War and the Siegfried Line of the 1930s) is from about 1935. It is a large fortified position with rooftop machine gun post, crew trench, and defensive wire belt. The 70mm figures are by Elastolin.

The Moritz Gottschalk No.444 large Command Bunker (modelled on examples from the Hindenberg Line of the First World War) is from about 1935. It includes an artillery observation post, a command bunker, a first aid post, and a communications bunker. The 70mm figures are by Elastolin.

c.1935

2-136

2-137

2-136 **Moritz Gottschalk HQ Building** *(Courtesy Vectis Auctions)*
2-137 **Moritz Gottschalk SA Home** *(Courtesy Vectis Auctions)*
These are two examples of their more urban type of building.
The Moritz Gottschalk HQ Building shows its rich dollhouse heritage, although it is about half the size of most dolls houses. The figures are 70mm made by Elastolin and/

or Lineol, and are of such a size that the inside of the building would have been useless. The building itself was used only for background. 54mm scale figures would be better suited.
The Moritz Gottschalk SA Home is also small for the figures, and would be more suitable for 54mm scale. All the comments made for the HQ building also apply here. The figures are again by Elastolin and/or Lineol, although, as they are all sitting or lying down, the mismatch of scales is not so apparent.

The second strategy was the production of at least two new ranges. One was a range of what could honestly be called "fortresses." They were definitely defensible and were of a period in history that could be described as generically medieval.

The other range was a modern version somewhat along the lines of the 5200, 5500, and 6000 series, which are more in the nature of lightly fortified domestic buildings.

There are no known numbers on any of the real examples to hand, so we can only glean a little from those in the catalogue. All the known numbers have three digits before an oblique, and one digit after it. The three digits before the oblique seem to refer to the series. The digit after the oblique refers to the "fortress" itself – number 1 applying to the smallest, 2 to the next size up, and so on. In this first strand of Alfred's second strategy, three such series have been identified.

MORITZ GOTTSCHALK: 337 Series
c1935 to c1941

NO.	DESCRIPTION	DATE	DIMENSIONS	DISTINCTIVE FEATURES
337/2 (2-138)	**second in the series** (illustrated in Gottschalk catalogue) eg: no known example	c1935	12½"x8"x11" 320x200x280mm	• solid ramp to small gateway • rectangular court with crenellation • one central rectangular tower • small main buildings & small tower
337/3 (2-139)	**third in the series** (illustrated in Gottschalk catalogue) eg: no known example	c1935	16½"x9"x12½" 420x230x320mm	• solid ramp to small gateway • rectangular court with crenellation • two small square towers • one long crenellated main building
337/4 (2-140)	**fourth in the series** (illustrated in Gottschalk catalogue) eg: no known example	c1935	16½"x10½"x13½" 420x270x340mm	• solid ramp to medium gateway • rectangular court with crenellation • 2 medium (different) square towers • long crenellated main building
337/5 (2-141)	**fifth in the series** (illustrated in Gottschalk catalogue) eg: no known example	c1935	17¾"x11½"x14¼" 450x290x360mm	• solid ramp to crenellated gateway • rectangular court with crenellation • 1 small & one large square towers • main buildings, one with arch
337/6 (2-142)	**largest in the series** (illustrated in Gottschalk catalogue) eg: no known example	c1935	15¾"x11¾"x14¼" 400x300x360mm	• solid ramp to crenellated gateway • semi-circular court w/wall & bldg • 1 large & one medium square tower • one long crenellated main building

MORITZ GOTTSCHALK: 338 Series
c1935 to c1941

NO.	DESCRIPTION	DATE	DIMENSIONS	DISTINCTIVE FEATURES
338/2 (2-143)	**second in the series** (illustrated in Gottschalk catalogue) eg: no known example	c1935	16½"x10½"x13¾" 420x270x350mm	• solid ramp to medium gateway • rectangular court with small tower • 1 large & 1 small square towers • 1 main building & a side building
338/4 (2-144)	**fourth in the series** (illustrated in Gottschalk catalogue) eg: no known example	c1935	21"x16"x15¾" 530x410x400mm	• double solid ramp to medium gate • rect court + rounded corners • 1 large circular 1 small sq tower • 1 crenellated bldg with steps up
338/6 (2-145)	**largest in the series** (illustrated in Gottschalk catalogue) eg: no known example	c1935	33½"x20"x22¾" 850x510x580mm	• solid ramp to medium gateway • semi-circ court with small bldg • 1 large sq & 1 large circ tower • four main buildings 1 crenellated

MORITZ GOTTSCHALK: 339 Series
c1935 to c1941

NO.	DESCRIPTION	DATE	DIMENSIONS	DISTINCTIVE FEATURES
339/2 (2-146)	**second in the series** (illustrated in Gottschalk catalogue) eg: no known example	c1935	22½"x18½"x16½" 570x470x420mm	• double ramp to 2 med gateways • 2 courts w/crenellated walls • 1 med & one small square tower • two main & one side buildings

If these digits represent an order of production, the numbers are so close together it could only mean that they produced many different "fortresses" close together. Given that the numbers to our knowledge start at 337, one wonders where all the others are. Where did they start? How far did they go?

In these more defensible "fortresses," involving the more fort-like structures that they had on offer, the old system of covering the bases still held sway. Cork was used on only the largest bases, bark for the next size down, and a finer smaller-scale something – I do not know what – for the smaller bases.

The buildings on top of the bases are even more mixed. In the 338 series for example, the only consistent element is the gateway, although all the parts are consistent in their details – windows, doors, etc. On the other hand, in the 337 series, none of the gateways are the same, and, of the ten towers on the five models we know about, seven are different. Such variety makes identification very difficult, and can hardly have been good for any attempt at mass production.

Extracts from Gottschalk's catalogues

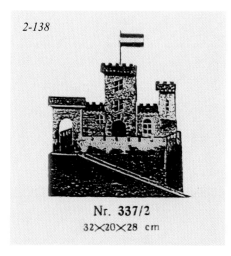

2-138

Nr. **337/2**
32×20×28 cm

2-139

Nr. **337/3**
42×23×32 cm

2-140

Nr. **337/4**
42×27×34 cm

2-141

Nr. **337/5**
45×29×36 cm

2-142

Nr. **337/6** 40×30×36 cm

2-138 **Moritz Gottschalk No.337/2** *(catalogue)*
2-139 **Moritz Gottschalk No.337/3** *(catalogue)*
2-140 **Moritz Gottschalk No.337/4** *(catalogue)*
2-141 **Moritz Gottschalk No.337/5** *(catalogue)*
2-142 **Moritz Gottschalk No.337/6** *(catalogue)*

These are five of the more defensible "fortresses." The 337 series is characterized by considerable crenellation throughout. They are all quite small.

Moritz Gottschalk No.337/2 (2-138). If one assumes there was a 337/1, then this is not the smallest in the series. It is, in any case, smaller than 337/3. It does not appear to have a base plate.

Moritz Gottschalk No.337/3 (2-139) is the next largest and the first to boast a base plate.

Moritz Gottschalk No.337/4 (2-140). Note the steps to the level above on the back building. Steps are a challenging feature because it is difficult to get the scale right. This is not featured elsewhere in the series.

Moritz Gottschalk No.337/5 (2-141). Note the arch through the back building, although one wonders where it leads. This is a rare example of a two-storey building in the series.

Moritz Gottschalk No.337/6 (2-142), being the largest in the series, is still barely as big as the smallest in the 338 series. Does this mean that the two series had to be seen together, at least in terms of size?

Extracts from Gottschalk's Catalogues

Nr. 338/2
42×27×35 cm

Nr. 338/4   53×41×40 cm

Nr. 338/6
85×51×58 cm

2-143 Moritz Gottschalk 338/2
(catalogue)
2-144 Moritz Gottschalk 338/4
(catalogue)
2-145 Moritz Gottschalk 338/6
(catalogue)

Notice the swastika on the flags on every building. All of these "fortresses" are of a size worth calling a "fortress."

Moritz Gottschalk No.338/2 (2-143) is the second smallest in the series and, as such, is quite large; in fact, it is larger than any in the 337 series. Note the gateway, which is common to all the "fortresses" in the series.

Moritz Gottschalk No.338/4 (2-144). This is a series of big "fortresses." The windows and the smaller square tower, as well as the gateway, were used by others in the series.

By some margin, Moritz Gottschalk No.338/6 (2-145e) is the largest we have of the 338 series. It certainly rates with the very large fortresses produced in the 6000 series, but this one appears to be to a larger scale. Its base is covered in cork. The gateway is the only piece that is shared with others in the series.

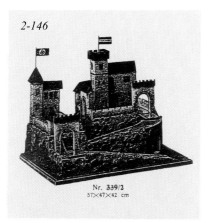

2-146

Nr. 339/2
57×47×42 cm

2-146 Moritz Gottschalk 339/2 *(catalogue)*
This is the second smallest in the series, although how many there were in the series is unknown.
This is the most like the old 6000 series and bears a passing resemblance to Gottschalk No.6374 (2-118). The base is covered with bark.

2-147

Nr. 346/2
65×56×44 cm

2-148

zum Beleuchten

Nr. 347/1
36×20×31 cm

2-149

Nr. 347/3
42×27×38 cm

2-147 **Moritz Gottschalk No.346/2** *(catalogue)*
2-148 **Moritz Gottschalk No.347/1** *(catalogue)*
2-149 **Moritz Gottschalk No.347/3** *(catalogue)*

Moritz Gottschalk No.346/2 (2-147) is the last of the truly defensible "fortresses," and even that is a bit doubtful. But it does have crenellation on the gateways and at roof level. This one has big, hollow side structures to the main building. They have opening doors rather like Gottschalk dollhouses. One has to go back to the 2300 and 2500 series for similar features.
Moritz Gottschalk No.347/1 (2-148 is the start of the less defensible "fortresses." It was claimed to have lighting. This is the smallest in the series.
Moritz Gottschalk No.347/3 (2-149) is the third up in the series, and the largest we have. It is not clear from the catalogue, but it was also lighted.

MORITZ GOTTSCHALK: 346 Series
c1935 to c1941

NO.	DESCRIPTION	DATE	DIMENSIONS	DISTINCTIVE FEATURES
346/2 (2-147)	**second in the series** (illustrated in Gottschalk catalogue) eg: no known example	c1935	26"x22"x17¼" 650x560x440mm	• double ramp to 2 med gateways • rectangular court with crenellation • one centralized main building • 2- & 3-D side bldgs w/crenellation

MORITZ GOTTSCHALK: 347 Series
c1935 to c1941

NO.	DESCRIPTION	DATE	DIMENSIONS	DISTINCTIVE FEATURES
347/1 (2-148)	**smallest in the series** (illustrated in Gottschalk catalogue) eg: no known example	c1935	14¼"x8"x12¼" 360x200x310mm	• simple ramp to small gateway • rectangular court w/small tower • 1 medium & 1 small square towers • 1 crenelated main bldg & lighting
347/2 (2-149)	**second in the series** (illustrated in Gottschalk catalogue) eg: no known example	c1935	16½"x10½"x15" 420x270x380mm	• simple ramp to medium gateway • rectangular court w/small tower • central rectangular main building • two side buildings

Then we come to three "fortresses" which are somewhat less defensible, but not quite as domestic as others.

Although we only have three catalogue illustrations to go by, it is clear that they were less warlike. Admittedly, they had some crenellation, but they were generally more palace-like. It is difficult to be adamant on the basis of so few examples, but it would appear that the 346 series were much larger than the 347.

Now we have come onto the even less defensible structures; there is no information in the catalogues about actual sizes. There are, however, images of the "fortresses."

Of this second strand of Alfred's second strategy we have six real examples and six from the catalogue. As far as the numbering system goes, the same issues apply here as for the more defensible "fortresses." I have no idea of the order in which they were produced unless the numbering system is a guide, which, because they introduced a new system unknown to me, may or may not be the case.

In spite of this, we can deduce some similarities according to the numbers, especially around the bases and ramps. For example the three "fortresses" bearing the number 515 before the oblique all had a semi-circular base and a ramp rising to a circular sort of lookout associated with the gateway. The buildings on the top, however, were all quite different on each example – even the gateways were all different. The only thing we can conclude for certain is that the "fortresses" in the series got bigger as the number after the oblique rises.

MORITZ GOTTSCHALK: 514 Series
c1935 to c1941

NO.	DESCRIPTION	DATE	DIMENSIONS	DISTINCTIVE FEATURES
514/1 (2-150)	**smallest in the series** (illustrated in Gottschalk catalogue) eg: no known example	c1935	unknown	• arched (3) ramp to small gateway • small courtyard w/curved end • one large circular tower • 2 main buildings w/1 to ground
514/3 (2-151)	**largest in the series** (illustrated in Gottschalk catalogue) eg: no known example	c1935	unknown	• arched (3) ramp to med gateway • medium courtyard w/curved end • 1 circular tower & 1 square tower • 2 main buildings w/1 to ground

MORITZ GOTTSCHALK: 515 Series
c1935 to c1941

NO.	DESCRIPTION	DATE	DIMENSIONS	DISTINCTIVE FEATURES
515/1 (2-152)	**smallest in the series** (illustrated in Gottschalk catalogue) eg: no known example	c1935	unknown	• semi-circ ramp to small gateway • semi-circ court w/small tower • one large circular tower • two main buildings
515/3 (2-153)	**third in the series** (illustrated in Gottschalk catalogue) eg: no known example	c1935	unknown	• semi-circ ramp to medium gate • semi-circ court w/small tower • 1 large circular & square tower • two main buildings
515/5 (2-154)	**fifth in the series** (illustrated in Gottschalk catalogue) eg: no known example	c1935	unknown	• semi-circ ramp to large gateway • semi-circ court w/small b'lding • 1 large & 1 medium square tower • two main buildings

Extracts from Gottschalk's catalogues

2-150

514/1

2-151

514/3

2-152

515/1

2-153

515/3

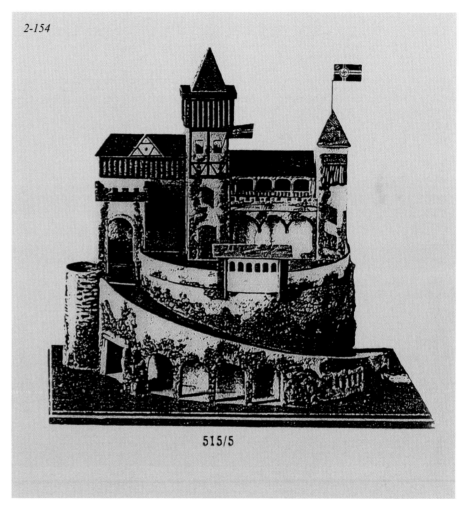

2-154

515/5

2-150 **Moritz Gottschalk No.514/1** *(catalogue)*
2-151 **Moritz Gottschalk No.514/3** *(catalogue)*
2-152 **Moritz Gottschalk No.515/1** *(catalogue)*
2-153 **Moritz Gottschalk No.515/3** *(catalogue)*
2-154 **Moritz Gottschalk No.515/5** *(catalogue)*

Moritz Gottschalk No.514/1 (2-150). The only parts which make this one of a series are the ramp, gateway, courtyard, and the lower part of the building on the right. Apart from their general style, the other buildings are completely different.

Moritz Gottschalk No.514/3 (2-151). All that was said about No.514/1 can be said here. Everything up to courtyard level is the same. Everything above that is completely different.

Moritz Gottschalk No.515/1 (2-152). Clearly smaller than No.515/3, there is little to make this one of a series except the swirling ramp and the semi-circular courtyard.

Moritz Gottschalk No.515/3 (2-153). The perforation of the ramp by openings of various shapes and sizes is a distinctive feature.

Moritz Gottschalk No.515/5 (2-154). This is by far the largest from the 515 series, at least as far as we know. The perforation of the ramp by openings of various shapes and sizes is an even greater distinctive feature.

2-155

Burg zum Beleuchten

553/3

2-156

2-155 **Moritz Gottschalk No.553/3** *(catalogue)*
2-156 **Moritz Gottschalk No.553/4 or 5** *(Courtesy Bernd Zimmermann)*

   Moritz Gottschalk No.553/3 has lower parts that bear a strong resemblance to those of the 514 series, as does the general mass of the other buildings. The gateways, the large circular crenellated tower, the large entrance to the basement, and the arches under the ramp are all more or less the same. The big difference is that this one has lighting while the 514 series does not.

   Moritz Gottschalk No.553/4 or 5 is clearly of the same series as the illustration in the catalogue. The only differences are the side building by the tower and the shape of the window under the courtyard. The battlements on the tower appear to have gone missing.

2-157 **Moritz Gottschalk No.unknown 1b** *(Courtesy Bernd Zimmermann)*
2-158 **Moritz Gottschalk No.unknown 1a** *(Courtesy Bernd Zimmermann)*
2-159 **Moritz Gottschalk No.unknown 2** *(Courtesy Bernd Zimmermann)*

The following are some of their later "fortresses." None of their numbers are known. It is not known where they come by date; nor is their sequence in the catalogue.

Moritz Gottschalk No.unknown 1a & 1b are clearly from the same series and appear to be the same size, but their numbers are unknown. The two gateways are different, as is the direction of the ramp. Otherwise the only significant difference is in the modelling of the small tower. Unusually, the single arch under the ramp is pointed. The chains from the drawbridge are missing on both.

Moritz Gottschalk No.unknown 2 has several of the same features as No.unknown 1a; note the gateway, courtyard, and both the square and circular crenellated towers. The main building is quite different, though, and the side building is an added feature. The arches under the ramp are also different in that they are rounded. Note that the water comes from under one arch only. The 40mm figures of knights are by Merton and Elastolin of Germany.

2-160 **Moritz Gottschalk No.unknown 3** *(Courtesy Bernd Zimmermann)*
2-161 **Moritz Gottschalk No.unknown 4** *(Courtesy Bernd Zimmermann)*

Moritz Gottschalk No.unknown 3 comes from a different series. It appears to have been well used. Some crenels are missing from the front tower, as are the chains from the drawbridge. The upper level walkway on the long building at the back seems to have is origins way back to the 5200 series. The ramp has three arches under it. Note that the water comes from under one arch only. The perimeter wall is not crenellated.

Moritz Gottschalk No.unknown 4 again comes from a different series, although the main building is the same as No.unknown2 (2-159) and the tower is the same as No.unknown3 (2-160). The ramp and courtyard with fancy arches under the bay are completely different. The drawbridge is missing its chains. The 40mm figures of knights are by various makers in Germany.

MORITZ GOTTSCHALK: 553 Series
c1935 to c1941

NO.	DESCRIPTION	DATE	DIMENSIONS	DISTINCTIVE FEATURES
553/3 (2-155)	**third in the series** (illustrated in Gottschalk catalogue) eg: no known example	c1935	unknown	• ramp w/3 arches to db & gateway • crtyd w/crenellated wall & curved end • main building w/rectangular tower • lg, circ, crenellated flanking tower
553/4 or 5 (2-156)	**only one in the series** (illustrated in Gottschalk catalogue) eg: no known example	c1935	23"x13¾"x19¾" 585x350x500mm	• ramp w/3 arches to db & gateway • crtyd w/crenellated wall & curved end • main building w/rect tower • lg, circ, flanking tower w/side bldg

Of the actual forts of which I have seen examples, only one bears any resemblance to those in the catalogue, which displays a remarkable similarity to No.553/3. In fact, it is only one side building wider, and the opening in the retaining wall under the courtyard is a horizontal oblong rather than two windows. Otherwise they are identical – maybe it was No.553/4 or No.553/5.

MORITZ GOTTSCHALK: "Fortresses"
c1935 to c1941

NO.	DESCRIPTION	DATE	DIMENSIONS	DISTINCTIVE FEATURES
unkwn(1a) (2-158)	**residential "fortress"** (identified by an example in the ownership below) eg: Bernd Zimmermann, D	c1935	unknown	• simple ramp up to db & gateway • crenellated crtyd w/sm sq tower • main building w/half-timbering • lg, circ, crenellated flanking tower
unkwn(1b) (2-157)	**residential "fortress"** (identified by an example in the ownership below) eg: Bernd Zimmermann, D	c1935	19"x11"x14½" 485x280x370mm	• simple ramp up to db & gateway • crenellated crtyd w/sm sq tower • half-timbered main building • lg, circ, crenellated flanking tower
unkwn(2) (2-159)	**residential "fortress"** (identified by an example in the ownership below) eg: Bernd Zimmermann, D	c1935	18"x11"x14½" 455x280x370mm	• ramp w/2 arches to db & gateway • crenellated crtyd w/long main bldg • sq tower & half- timbered side bldg • lg, circ, crenellated flanking tower
unkwn(3) (2-161)	**residential "fortress"** (identified by an example in the ownership below) eg: Bernd Zimmermann, D	c1935	unknown	• ramp w/3 arches to db & gateway • crtyd w/lg, circ corner tower to ground • mn bldg w/walkway & 3 side bldgs • large, circ, crenellated tower
unkwn(4) (2-160)	**residential "fortress"** (identified by an example in the ownership below) eg: Bernd Zimmermann, D	c1935	unknown	• ramp on 2 sides to db & gateway • crenellated crtyd w/lg semi-circ bay • long main bldg as No.2 & side bldg • lg, circ, crenellated flanking tower

All of the "fortresses" in the catalogue now fly the flag of the Third Reich or the Swastika. Sometimes they are seen to be flying both at the same time. Better safe than sorry, I guess.

In any case, this seems to have carried Gottschalk through to the war and even into its early years. But the story comes to an end in 1942, when toy manufacturing gave way to making transport boxes for the armed services.

After the Second World War

Immediately after the war, the factory was expropriated by the Soviet army and the grounds were used as soldiers' quarters. For the first two years, production consisted of wooden household articles. There was no production of toys. But in 1947, Gottschalk toys and dolls houses were seen again at the Leipzig fair.

MORITZ GOTTSCHALK: "Fortresses"
c1950 to c1960

2-162 **Moritz Gottschalk No.unknown 5**
Comparison with the pre-war forts makes it easy to identify this as a Gottschalk production. Of course, the colors are somewhat more garish, and the painting more formalized, but there is no doubt about its heritage. Note particularly the vegetation.
This style continued into the 1950s, but did not last long.

NO.	DESCRIPTION	DATE	DIMENSIONS	DISTINCTIVE FEATURES
unknwn (5) (2-162)	**residential "fortress"** (identified by an example in the ownership below) eg: Kind'museum, Baden, CH	c1950	unknown	• curving ramp up to db & gateway • crenelled crtyd w/2 lg circ towers • main building w/half-timbering • large, central, circ crenellated tower

Eventually, toy forts began to find a place again. Initially, they built on their experience of the years before the war, but the quality was not there to do a proper job. This, combined with the emergence of new materials and pressures of the marketplace, led to a gradual deterioration of the brand.

Their production was ever more controlled by the state throughout the 1950s. By 1960, the Gottschalk name had became absorbed in the explicitly state-run VEB Holzspielwaren Marienberg, and ceased to exist for all practical purposes.

This situation continued throughout the 1960s, until it was all nationalized in 1972. The remnants were absorbed into the large, state-owned company called VEB-VERO.

THREE

THE HAUSSER BROTHERS WERE ELASTOLIN:
Toy Forts of Quality

The Hausser brothers, Otto and Max, started their toy company in 1904 in Ludwigsberg, near Struttgart. They had earlier traded under the name of Müller and Freyer, wholesalers and manufacturers of toys and haberdashery with a special interest in dolls. It was this experience, especially that with dolls, which was to provide the basis for the development of composition to make small figures.

"Composition," which is a mixture of sawdust, casein, kaolin, and animal glue, amongst other things, had been used since about 1850 for the limbs of dolls. The first use of this method to make small figures was in 1898 by a company called Pfeiffer of Vienna, whose trademark was "Tipple Topple." The Haussers used Pfeiffer's experience as a starting point and called their particular composition Elastolin, which, over the years, has become the common name for the material.

They started with figures. A wire skeleton was set up for each figure and composition was molded onto it. A standing soldier was 10cm high; just before the First World War, they began to produce the 7cm models for which they became famous. Despite drawbacks, they manufactured throughout the war years, albeit at a reduced level. One such drawback was the death of Max Hausser, who was killed on the Western Front in 1915 and never saw the international success of the company.

After the war the company made a swift recovery, taking up where they had left off. They did not produce toy forts until some time after the war, in the early 1920s, just when they were beginning to establish an international reputation.

They began with wood, making large forts with only the bases made of sacking covered with a thin layer of composition, and some small plants for decoration. Soon, by 1925 at the latest, they had moved on to composition for the buildings also. For this, they applied a thin skin of composition over the wood to provide three-dimensional detail.

By 1928/1929, they were creating complete forts of composition. This material is inherently unstable when used in large quantities, leading to warping and cracking in the drying process. This is why the series was made to such a small scale.

About 1930, Kurt and Rolf Hausser, Otto's sons, joined the company.

By 1934, they were making wooden forts again, which were turned out at a sort of medium size. From the middle of the 1930s up to the Second World War they had a range of forts from the very small to the very large – in wood and composition. In 1936, with the company still growing and in need of room for expansion, they moved to Neustadt bei Coburg, four kilometers away. It was not until quite late in the war, in 1943, that they went over to a war footing, making mainly wooden items for military use.

After the Second World War, Hauser Brothers were slow to get going again, which was only to be expected due to the shortage of materials and a skilled workforce. It was not until the early fifties that they produced forts again.

At first, in 1953, they produced a few wooden castles, which were a development of those they produced just before the war. These were supplemented by two forts, also from just before the war, with toy railway tunnels running through the base. In 1956, the year that Otto Hausser died, they started production of their castle series using framed cardboard, somewhat in the manner of Tri-ang.

Plastic became available as an alternative material for their figures and castles, and, in 1961, they started two series at the same time, as well as figures, using the new wonder material. One series included middle to large forts made up of separate pieces, which then had to be assembled. The other was of monolithic vacuum-formed plastic, quite large, but small in scale. They added to these ranges continuously for the next twenty years – until they filed for bankruptcy in June 1983 and ceased production at the end of the year.

The First Toy Forts

There are no records available until 1925, so any historical presentation of the early years depends on pictures in the catalogue of 1925 or the actual forts themselves. Unfortunately, no examples are known, at least to me. We have to rely on documentary evidence in the form of photos in catalogues and price lists. There is no information available to me on when they started production of toy forts.

Five castles are mentioned in the 1925 catalogue. They were Nos.13514, 13516, 13518, 13520, and 13525. They ranged from the relatively small to the very large.

The first one had a large house with a very small courtyard protected by a small, square tower. The second, of which we have no illustration, had more or less the same accommodations as No.13518 – that is, a house, a tower, a gate, and castle walls. No.13520 was clearly larger, with the addition of a substantial covered cloister or stabling. No.13525 was larger again. Not only did it have the cloister or stabling of No.13520, but also a smaller cloister or walkway, two gates (one of which was in three parts), and a small, five-sided tower.

ELASTOLIN TOY FORTS: 13514-13525 Series (wood)
c1922 to c1926

NO.	DESCRIPTION	DATE	DIMENSIONS	DISTINCTIVE FEATURES
13514 (3-001)	smallest of this series (listed in Elastolin catalogue 1925) eg: no known example	c1920	13¾"x13"x17" 350x330x430mm	• integral ramp • painted wooden structure • round arched gateway • lg house and small sq tower
13516	second of this series (listed in Elastolin catalogue 1925) eg: no known example	c1920	16"x15¼"x16" 410x390x410mm	• integral ramp • painted wooden structure • large house and square tower
13518 (3-002)	third of this series (illustrated in Elastolin catalogue 1925) eg: no known example	c1920	19½"x18"x25½" 500x460x650mm	• integral ramp • painted wooden structure • large house and square tower
13520 (3-003)	fourth of this series (illustrated in Elastolin catalogue 1925) eg: no known example	c1920	32"x23"x31" 810x530x790mm	• integral ramp • painted wooden structure • lg house, sq tower & cloister
13525 (3-004)	largest of this series (illustrated in Elastolin catalogue 1925) eg: no known example	c1920	23½"x21"x33½" 700x530x850mm	• integral ramp + lg gateway • painted wooden structure • lg house, sq tower & cloister • lg gate, sm cloister & tower

The castle mounds were made of sackcloth coated with a thin layer of composition. This was scuffed up while still wet to give an illusion of a natural surface, and small shrubs were pushed into the soft material as a form of realistic decoration. The approach path was given a smooth finish to differentiate it from the natural areas.

The superstructure, in fact the whole castle structure, was made exclusively of wood, which gave a smooth, finished surface, and made for a toy-like appearance. Smudges of color were applied to this using a rag, and on top of this a representation of stonework was painted by hand. On the whole, this made for reasonable toy castles, but they did not really satisfy Otto Hausser, who was looking for something better – at least more realistic.

3-001 **Elastolin No.13514** *(catalogue)*
  This and the following three examples are the only evidence we have of the 13514 series. The actual source of this illustration of No.13514 is unknown, but it comes to me from Andreas Pietruschka. It appears to be of an earlier date than the others.

c.1920

3-002

3-003

3-004

3-002 **Elastolin No.13518** *(catalogue)*
3-003 **Elastolin No.13520** *(catalogue)*
3-004 **Elastolin No.13525** *(catalogue)*
   These are illustrations reproduced from *Figuren Magazin.* They are all photographs of the forts in prime condition, including the vegetation on the bases, just as they would have come from the factory. The bases are made of composition smeared onto sackcloth. The buildings above are clearly made of wood, giving them a toy-like feeling. Of course, this really only makes sense when they are compared with the next phase in their development.
No.13518 is the forerunner of No.13518½.
No.13520 is the forerunner of No.13520½.
No.13525 is the forerunner of No.13525½.

THE ELASTOLIN NUMBERING SYSTEM

This technical note is mostly based on two sources. First, we have the catalogues and price lists, even though they are seriously incomplete, especially in the early days of production. These were conveyed to me by Andreas Pietruschka, Peter Müller, and the staff of *Figuren Magazin*. Second, we have used common sense and logic, as far as they can be applied.

The Elastolin numbering system – or more properly "systems" – were a law unto themselves.

All the forts prior to the Second Word War had numbers in the 13500s. This includes the large wooden types that they started with, the small all-composition types, and their 1930s series of wooden forts. The large wooden forts were later sold covered in composition. For these they chose to use the same numbers as before, but with a "½" added. Later, they added "½" to any forts subsequently made with composition.

This system implies that they knew when they started how many of each sort they were going to produce. How else would one start with numbers in the late teens and early twenties, only then to go on to produce a series of small composition castles numbered 13509½ to 13513½? To compound the matter they went on to produce another series numbered 13501 to 13507, finally producing 13520, 13522 and 13526.

In an attempt to bring some semblance of order, here is a listing of their production up to the Second World War, in chronological order.

Dates issued	Numbers of castle	Types of castle
1920?	13514, 13516, 13518, 13520, 13525	The first large wooden castles
1925	13518½, 13520½, 13525½	The same covered with composition
1928 to 1930	13509½ to 13513½	Small all composition series
1930?	13517½	Large one covered with composition

	13500 to 13506	Medium-sized wooden castles
1933/1934	13500 to 13506	Medium-sized wooden castles
1934	13530, 13540	Unknown, not illustrated
1934/1935	13507	First one with tunnel
1938	13518N, unknown	Two types with tunnel
1938	13522N, 13524N, 13526N	Large wooden castles

After the war they did a little better. They still managed, however, to use two different numbering systems, the 800 series and the 9700 series, which is fine, but led to some of the forts with two numbers. They then mixed up their series, giving them all 9700 numbers, which led to the production of several pairs with the same number.

Here is a listing for their production after the Second World War.

Dates issued	Numbers of castle	Types of castle
1953	850, 856, 862	Medium wooden castles
1957?	866, 868	Developed from 13518N
1956 to 1963	870i, 870ii, 871, 872, 874, 878	Cardboard & wood castles
1961	9750, 9756, 9762, 9766, 9768	Previously 850, 856, 862, 866, & 868
1961 to 1979	9705, 9744 to 9749, 9780	Several pieces making large castles
1961 to 1976	9715, 9722, 9725, 9727, 9729 to 9745	One piece vacuum formed

How they survived such confusion remains a mystery!

The Transition to 65% Composition

Otto Hausser's "something better" came with the introduction of composition as a finishing material. They developed the technique of applying a thin coating of composition to the basic wooden forms, giving an excellent representation of building materials. Stonework looked like stonework and clay tiles looked like clay tiles.

So the castles did not change their form, but were given a complete makeover. While representing the forms and spaces adequately, when made of wood they had a sort of hard shiny appearance. Now they had a real effect that could be felt – literally.

ELASTOLIN TOY FORTS: 13518½-13525½ Series
c1926 to c1943

NO.	DESCRIPTION	DATE	DIMENSIONS	DISTINCTIVE FEATURES
13518½ (3-005)	**third of this series** (identified by a example in the ownership below) eg: Allen Hickling Toy Forts	c1925	19½"x18"x25½" 500x460x650mm	• integral ramp to db & gateway • wood structure + composition • large house and square tower • electric lighting from 1930
13520½ (3-006)	**fourth of this series** (identified by a example in the ownership below) eg: Allen Hickling Toy Forts	c1925	32"x23"x31" 810x530x790mm	• integral ramp to db & gateway • wood structure + composition • house, square tower & cloister • electric lighting from 1930
13525½ (3-007)	**largest of this series** (identified by a example in the ownership below) eg: Rob Wilson, UK	c1925	23½"x21"x33½" 700x530x850mm	• integral ramp + gateway ½-way • wood structure + composition • house, square tower & cloister • sm cloister, tower, 3-piece gate

There appears to be no record of what happened to Nos.13514 and 13516. No examples are known to exist. There were relatively minor changes to the other three, but nothing to alter the main mass of the buildings.

In contrast, the house, which retained its overall shape, underwent changes on three façades. The two gable ends had different window arrangements, but were otherwise identical. On the long sides, there were more windows placed in an irregular pattern and some windows were projecting, while others were ornamented. They were not identical.

The roof also was considerably different, now having seven small dormer windows and a chimney on the front, but none on the back.

The square tower had more ornate windows, and there was machicolation all around at the top. In addition, as with all the castle walls, the tops were properly protected with overhanging tiles.

The gateways on Nos.13518 and 13520 underwent a makeover and the steps in the courtyard disappeared (at least on later versions), as did the ventilator on top of the stable block. The base remained the same. On No.13525 the unique additional pieces actually remained relatively as they were, except for their finish.

I cannot believe that these improvements made much difference to the play value. The castles were all the same size and configuration. Attacking and defending them still presented the same challenges. So why change them? It can only have been the elusive goal of quality, and this they achieved mightily.

3-005 **Elastolin No.13518½**
This and the following examples are from the second series of large castles. They were produced and developed from 1925 to the Second World War.
No.13518½ is the smallest and is reasonably complete, though it is missing the plants that were used for decoration of the base.

c.1925

3-006 **Elastolin No.13520½**
3-007 **Elastolin No.13525½**

   The only basic differences between this No.13520½ (3-006) and its predecessor, No.13520 (3-003), was a change to the gateway and the omission of ventilator on the cloister (or stabling) roof. Of course, there was also the fact that it was now covered in composition.

   It is in relatively good condition, but it is missing the columns on the cloister, and the plants used to decorate the base. It is very common for these to get lost.

   No.13525½ (3-007) also lost its ventilator from the cloister (or stabling) roof, and was covered in composition. It also has its plants missing. Otherwise this is in very good condition. The figures are from Elastolin's own series of 40mm medieval knights.

If one is to have quality figures in lively poses and combinations, it seems only sensible that they should have equally splendid surroundings.

Not to be outshone by their competitors, from 1930, all of the larger series and most of the other castles were equipped with electric lighting. A battery was located in the mound, and fed a single bulb in the house.

The Move to Castles of 100% Composition

In 1928, Hausser tried their hand at producing forts entirely of composition. This proved more difficult than they had bargained for. Large amounts of composition proved extremely difficult to handle. Large cracks and warping during the drying process were the problem. The only solution was that the size had to be drastically reduced.

So they produced what, for them, was a series of mini-castles. These varied in scale but were all small; too small, some say, to permit any real play. They could only be used as background. They were Nos.13509½ to 13513½. There

ELASTOLIN TOY FORTS: 13509½-13515½ Series
c1928 to c1943

NO.	DESCRIPTION	DATE	DIMENSIONS	DISTINCTIVE FEATURES
13509½ (3-009)	**first of this series** (identified by a example in the ownership below) eg: Allen Hickling Toy Forts	1930	13¾"x11¾"x8¼" 350x300x210mm	• single defensible ramp • gateway to single courtyard • castle walls with tower & gun ports • buildings on back side with circ tower
13510½ (3-008) (3-010)	**smallest of this series** (identified by a example in the ownership below) eg: Allen Hickling Toy Forts	1928/ 1929	13"x11¾"x9¾" 330x300x260mm	• separate ramp & splendid entrance • 2-level crtyd with two drawbridges • bailey with towers on the wall • various buildings + large sq tower
13511½ (3-011)	**third of this series** (identified by a example in the ownership below) eg: Allen Hickling Toy Forts	1928/ 1929	17¼"x11"x14¼" 440x280x360mm	• single integral defensible ramp • gateway to single courtyard • buttressed castle with one gun port • buildings to rear + large sq tower
13512½ (3-012)	**fourth of this series** (identified by a example in the ownership below) eg: Allen Hickling Toy Forts	1928/ 1929	14¼"x15"x16½" 360x380x420mm	• double integral ramp • gateway to single courtyard • castle walls with corner turret • buildings to rear with lg circ tower
13513½ (3-014)	**largest of this series** (identified by a example in the ownership below) eg: Allen Hickling Toy Forts	1930	16"x13½"x8¾" 410x340x220mm	• single integral indefensible ramp • gateway to single courtyard • walls with corner tower & gun ports • sm building to rear with circ tower
13515½ (3-013)	**not in production** (identified by a *Figuren Magazin* photograph) eg: Figuren Magazin, D	1930	19¾"x15¾"x17" 500x400x435mm	• single integral ramp • two drawbridges to 2-part courtyard • fortified castle walls with tower • 3 buildings with large circular tower

was another larger one, No.13515½, the size of which may have been the reason why it only reached the stage of a wax model. It never went into production.

No.13510½ was the smallest in size and scale, but it was a really good castle. There were courtyards on several levels and two drawbridges. The entrance way was something to be marvelled at. The ramp with a gatehouse as the first part of the entrance was a separate piece. A second gatehouse, housing the drawbridge mechanism, was on the main base together with its drawbridge. It was like no other toy castle, with a sort of early barbican protecting the only way in.

The trouble was that the gateways themselves were only 20mm high – only big enough for a horseman which would be about 15mm high – all a bit on the small side. Why they did not try this at a larger scale remains a mystery. The uppermost level was a single courtyard surrounded on two sides by buildings, with a very large square tower.

Compared to No.13510½, No.13515½ would have been equally splendid had it gone into production, perhaps even more so, since it was almost twice the size. It also had two drawbridges, but not an entrance to compare with that on 13510½. On the other hand, it did have a number of buildings and it was truly defensible with a large circular tower.

All the others in this series had single courtyards and were somewhat larger in scale. The largest of these was No.13512½. The base was probably the most noticeable thing about it, because it was higher than any of the others; the very large, circular tower was also impressive. The fort was approached by a double ramp leading to a gateway into a single courtyard with quite substantial buildings to the rear.

No.13511½ was also quite impressive with its massive square tower by the gateway. These towers were a characteristic of the series, most notably on all but Nos.13509½ and 13513½. One wonders how effective they would have been as a keep, if keeps are what they were, especially where they were separate from the living accommodation. Perhaps, they were just an embellishment to appeal to the user. In any case they do appear slightly out of scale with the rest of the buildings.

Another characteristic was the height of the gateways. They were at least the height of the roof tops of the two-storey living accommodations. This is probably an example of the necessary enlargement when you reduce the scale of the rest of the castle. One still has to be able to drive one's horses through, otherwise one can only stand in front of a building without the embarrassment of entering it.

Nos.13509½ and No.3512½, the smallest and the largest in the series, were the most realistic, if slightly mundane castles in the range.

These small castles stayed in the catalogue up to the Second World War.

3-008

3-009

3-010

3-008 **Elastolin No.13510½** *with snow*
3-009 **Elastolin No.13509½**
3-010 **Elastolin No.13510½**
These are in the series of 100% composition castles, and show some of the problems, such as warping, inherent in that.

No.13509½ is one of the smaller ones (3-009), but is nonetheless a fine defensible Schloss.

No.13510½ (3-010) is the smallest of the range in size and scale. *It is designed on the*

motte-and-bailey principle. There is plenty of space for the riff raff and their cattle, inside the gate at the lower level, where they will not inconvenience the lord. The living accommodation is ample to justify the tower, which would have acted as a keep in times of trouble. The gateway complex is to be marvelled at.

The snow-covered version (3-008) may, or may not have been made in the factory, but it is certainly well done.

1928-1929

3-011

3-012

3-011 Elastolin No.13511½
3-012 Elastolin No.13512½

In this series, the castles were generally made on the small side because of the nature of the material. Having no "skeleton" to hold them together, they were subject to cracking and warping in the drying process if made any larger.

No.13511½ (3-011) is one of the classics in both the large tower and the large gateway types. The amount of living accommodation is really very small, which makes it more of a hunting lodge or summer castle. In this case, the size of the tower is a bit of an anomaly, if not impossible.

No.13512½ has a larger base than any in the range (3-012), and it is often found warped or cracked.

The living accommodation of this also is small, suggesting a hunting lodge or summer castle, but it is not so marked.

1930

3-013

3-014

3-013 Elastolin No.13515½ *wax model*

No.13515½ is a completely different kettle of fish. This is a wax model. Why it was never put into production we shall probably never know. Maybe it had to do with the fact that it was significantly larger than the others in the series.

Perhaps they thought that it would be too difficult to make. It served a purpose about thirty-five years later, when they produced "Burg Schaffhausen" (No.9734) in much the same format – only stretched a little.

3-014 Elastolin No.13513½

No.13513½ is one of the simpler castles. It is not full-blown, but is more of a small Schloss. Nevertheless, it is, without doubt, defensible. Look at the loopholes all round; there are about fifteen of them. That represents quite a lot of firepower.

CONSTRUCTION USING "ELASTOLIN" COMPOSITION

"Elastolin," which was a name thought up by the Hausser brothers, is now accepted as a generic term for almost any composition figure or castle. It is used to describe any product of O & M Hausser, as well as the basic material itself.

Since the mid-1850s this material had been extensively used by doll manufacturers. In fact, Neustadt bei Coburg, where Hausser had their factory from 1936, is also called "doll town" *("Puppenstadt")*. This particular method of manufacture was discovered in about 1898 by a company called Pfeiffer of Vienna, whose trademark was "Tipple-Topple;" Hausser acquired Pfeiffer in 1925.

It was not until Pfeiffer perfected their method of manufacturing that small figures came into being. The basic raw materials, sawdust and glue, were always to hand and very cheap. One fundamental ingredient, without which the operation would not have been viable, was also easily available – namely labor.

Basically, the manufacturing method was that an accurately machined brass mold of a particular product was made, but in two halves. A porridge-like mixture of sawdust, casein, glue, and kaolin was pressed by hand into the separate halves of the mold, and a wire strengthener was placed in one half. The two halves of the mold were joined and pre-dried in the air, and afterwards heated for a period at no more than 80ºC. The length of the cooking time depended on the thickness of the product.

After cooling, the product was removed from the mold, trimmed, and painted by hand. There were no base coats, fillers, or undercoats whatsoever; the molding was of a sufficiently high quality to take paint straight away.

The quality of the result depended on skilled mixing and the appropriate drying technique.

About 1925, Hausser developed the technique of applying a thin coat of the composition onto a wooden base. The pattern of windows, doors, arrow slits, machicolation, and other details was then pressed onto the basic form. This was then allowed to dry as above, but it took much less time because of the thinness of the composition.

The series which used 100% composition presented a completely different challenge in dealing with seriously large lumps of material. It required no little skill to avoid the cracking, splitting, and warping that could occur. Luckily, Hausser had the sort of skilled workforce, having the years of experience with the material, that was necessary to deal with it.

Hausser Goes to Wood for the Second Time

In 1933/1934, Hausser gave up on introducing new castles made of composition, for the time being anyway. That is not to say they did not continue to make the models they already had; they did. Anyway, they needed to fill out their range on offer with some medium-sized castles, and 100% composition could not cope with the size.

Why they went to wood without a thin coating of composition as a finish, which had become their trademark, is a bit of a mystery. Maybe they wanted a range of prices and found it cheaper. Certainly their reputation for top quality products was put at stake, because there is little to choose between this range and a similar set put out by Lineol at the time.

The wood models were Nos.13500 to 13506. Compared to the castles they had already introduced, they were quite naïve in design – much more toy-like. Unlike all of Hausser's designs up until then, they were not really castles, but neither were they forts. They were more in the nature of fortified houses, and none were more so than these.

One characteristic of these buildings was their circular towers of various sizes. These were instead of square towers, which had dominated before. It is certainly the towers that made any claim to defensibility justified, because apart from them there is very little. The argument about them being used as a keep still applies.

It seems that Hausser had abandoned the policy of making new castles with a house, a tower, a gateway, and other parts, which became the standard for all their castles. At least the six I know of in this series were all different. The houses and towers were different sizes and styles. Nothing was standard any more. This has to be related to the finish on the buildings. The molding required for giving each piece a composition finish was expensive, so, for economic reasons, one could not have many different designs.

As for architectural style, it is difficult to place the castles in history. They appear to be a sort of generic Middle Ages style. All one can say is that the houses with the higher numbers were less like town houses than others in the range, and they were made to a larger scale.

These castles do appear to provide quite a range, with the lower numbers being the smallest, and the largest being No.13506, which was nearly as big as No.13518½ – the smallest of the large castles. They certainly filled the middle range Hausser was looking for. They could now offer to the buying public a full range from the smallest to the largest.

Apart from the addition of a few specialty items, this took them comfortably up to the Second World War.

ELASTOLIN TOY FORTS: 13500-13506 Series
c1933 to c1943

NO.	DESCRIPTION	DATE	DIMENSIONS	DISTINCTIVE FEATURES
13500 (3-016)	**smallest of series** (illustrated in Elastolin catalogue) eg: no known example	1933/ 1934	10½"x12½"x13¾" 270x320x350mm	• composition base & no ramp • no gateway to single court • painted wooden structure • house, tower, out-building
13501 (3-017)	**second of the series** (illustrated in Elastolin catalogue) eg: no known example	1933/ 1934	12½"x13"x16½" 320x330x420mm	• composition base w/single ramp • sml gateway to single court • painted wooden structure • house, tower, out-buildings
13502 (3-018)	**third of the series** (identified by example in ownership below) eg: Bernd Zimmermann, D	1933/ 1934	15¾"x15"x18½" 400x380x470mm	• compo base w/single ramp • gateway to single courtyard • painted wooden structure • house, tower, out-buildings
13503 (3-019)	**fourth of the series** (illustrated in Elastolin catalogue) eg: no known example	1933/ 1934	17"x15¾"x23½" 430x400x600mm	• compo base w/single ramp • gateway to single courtyard • painted wooden structure • house, tower, out-buildings
13504 (3-020)	**fifth of the series** (illustrated in Elastolin catalogue) eg: no known example	1933/ 1934	19¾"x16½"x21¼" 500x420x540mm	• compo base w/single ramp • gateway to single courtyard • painted wooden structure • house, tower, out-buildings
13505	**sixth of the series** (mentioned in *Figuren Magazin*) eg: no known example	1933/ 1934	unknown	
13506 (3-021)	**largest of this series** (illustrated in Elastolin catalogue) eg: no known example	1933/ 1934	16½"x21"x22½" 420x530x570mm	• compo base w/single ramp • gateway to single courtyard • painted wooden structure • house, 2 towers, out-buildings

There were two other castles which were mentioned in a price list, also dated 1934. These were No.13530 and No.13540. I know nothing about these products, least of all how they fitted into the scheme of things. Maybe they never went into production. Maybe we will never know.

1933-1934

3-016 **Elastolin No.13500** *(catalogue)*
3-017 **Elastolin No.13501** *(catalogue)*
3-018 **Elastolin No. 13502** *(Courtesy Bernd Zimmermann)*
    These are all from the series of small to medium-sized castles, which is the follow-up series to the very large castles and the very small castles. They are all much simpler in concept, and extended the range of castles they had on offer. The idea was to keep all their series on the books, thereby appealing to a wider range of customers. Made of painted wood, they were quite naïve in design – much less realistic and more toy-like. The images from the catalogues are from Figuren Magazin.

3-016

3-017

3-018

3-019

3-020

3-021

3-019 **Elastolin No.13503** *(catalogue)*
3-020 **Elastolin No.13504** *(catalogue)*
3-021 **Elastolin No.13506** *(catalogue)*

All of these illustrations are taken from Figuren Magazin.
No.13503 is the last of the very small ones in this series. It has an interesting low, circular tower at the corner of the courtyard.

No.13504 is the first of the larger ones in this series (No.13505 is missing). In particular, it has the same house as No.13506, which is the one feature that distinguishes the larger scale of these castles.
No.13506 is the largest in the series. There may be a shallow conical roof missing from the towers.

The Period Leading to the Second World War

The range of large forts stayed as it was for about nine years. Then, in about 1934/35, they came up with the idea of an O-gauge toy railway tunnel running under the castle. This was No.13507. It was probably an attempt at broadening the market, an initiative that Hausser continued well into the 1960s. It necessitated a quite large castle because of the scale of the trains and the consequent scale of the tunnel. This model, which was a bit dubious architecturally, was not to be continued for long.

ELASTOLIN TOY FORT: 13507
c1935 to 1938

NO.	DESCRIPTION	DATE	DIMENSIONS	DISTINCTIVE FEATURES
13507 (3-022)	**only one of the series** (illustrated in Elastolin catalogue) eg: no known example	1934/ 1935	23½"x21½"x21" 600x550x530mm	• integral ramp & toy railway tunnel • wooden structure • house, large square tower & arch • large gateway

By 1938, they had come up with a much more sophisticated solution. They stopped production of No.13507 and returned to the style of about twelve years earlier, with their composition-covered wood forts, and they introduced two forts with provision for toy trains, which was clearly a good idea. They continued

3-022 **Elastolin No.13507** *(catalogue)*
This was the first castle to have a railway running through the base. It was successful in that it alerted the market to the possibility of this feature. However the design of the castle was not up to the standards that Hausser was used to and it was replaced three years later, in 1937.

with O-gauge trains because it was not only the most common scale at the time, but the trains were reasonably in scale with the castles they wanted to use.

It is not clear why they produced two when there was not much difference in size or style, but produce two they did and continued with them in different materials for the next forty years. Both of these castles were equipped with electric lighting.

ELASTOLIN TOY FORTS: 13518N Series
1938 to c1943

NO.	DESCRIPTION	DATE	DIMENSIONS	DISTINCTIVE FEATURES
13518N (3-023) (3-025) (3-026)	**smallest of this series** (identified by a example in the ownership below) eg: Rob Wilson, UK	c1938	24"x18"x24" 610x460x610mm	• integral ramp & gateway • wood structure w/compo finish • large house and square tower • circular tower & electric lighting
unknown (3-024)	**largest of this series** (illustrated in Elastolin catalogue) eg: no known example	c1938	23¾"x19¼"x25½" 605x490x650mm	• integral ramp & gateway • wood structure w/compo finish • lg house, sq tower, cloister • circular tower & electric lighting

This is where the numbering system broke down. Somehow one, or both, of these new castles – it is not at all clear – got a number which had been allocated about twelve years previously. It was 13518N. The earlier ones were 13518 and 13518½, which was understandable given that they were, in effect, the same castle, but these newer castles were not the same at all. They also introduced a circular tower for the first time, which added to the variety of pieces available and made for more believable castles. They produced castles with this number for about five years. There is no explanation of which I am aware.

ELASTOLIN TOY FORT: 13517
1938 to c1943

NO.	DESCRIPTION	DATE	DIMENSIONS	DISTINCTIVE FEATURES
13517 (3-027) (3-028)	**only one in series** (illustrated in Elastolin catalogue 1939/40) eg: Bernd Zimmermann, D	1938	18½"x14½"x20½" 470x370x520mm	• integral ramp on foam(?) base • wood structure w/compo finish • house and circular tower • gateway & electric lighting

Around this time they brought out No.13517N, which was a relatively small castle. It was like the others in the series of wood castles finished in composition, but had only a circular tower. It also featured electric lighting.

3-023

3-024

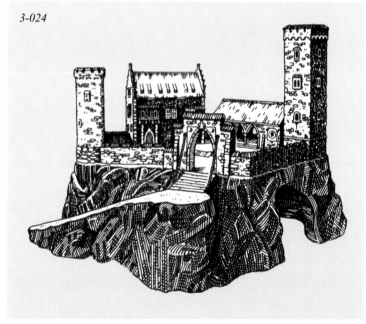

3-025

3-023 Elastolin No.13518N *(catalogue)*
3-024 Elastolin No.13518(?) *(catalogue)*
3-025 Elastolin No.13518N *front view*

    These are two castles which featured an O-gauge toy railway tunnel through the base. Both the No.13518 drawings are Elastolin catalogue illustrations. This is an example of how the Hausser numbering system became confused. It seems that the No.13518N was given to the smaller of the two forts, because there is an advert from 1939/1940 which names it. The number of the larger one remains a mystery.

    These are two of the longest running castles in Hausser's catalogue, being featured there, in various manifestations, for more than forty years. Over this time, they went from a 65% composition to a 95% plastic castle, but always kept the same buildings.

1938

3-026

3-027

3-028

3-027 Elastolin No.13517

This castle is further evidence of a snarl-up in the numbering system. No.13517 should have been No.13517½ if the logic of the system was to be followed. This is because it has composition on it. It may have come out after the Second World War, since it has a foam plastic base, which Hausser tried out for a very short period in the mid-1950s.

3-026 Elastolin No.13518N *rear view*
    This is the rear view, showing that Hausser managed to provide a castle truly in the round. This would have been a practical feature on any railway layout. In the real world, the tunnel exit under the dwelling cannot be considered a safe structural option, and the noise inside the house would have been frightful.

3-028 Elastolin No.13517 *(detail of label)*
    The underside of No.13517 shows its label with the number of the castle and its price.

ELASTOLIN'S USE OF CATALOGUES

Virtually all of Hausser's records from 1904 to 1946 were lost or destroyed during the Second World War, so it is difficult to accurately date their products except by using logic and a basic knowledge of social history.

I do not have much in the way of catalogues myself, and those I do have are often partial or abbreviated versions. Much of what is included in the text is reported by others, most often without any clear reference.

I do not have any of the early ones, that is those before 1939. What I do have are illustrations obviously taken from catalogues, but there is little by way of writing with them – mostly the original author's comments. Wherever I do not have an image of an actual fort, I have included catalogue versions.

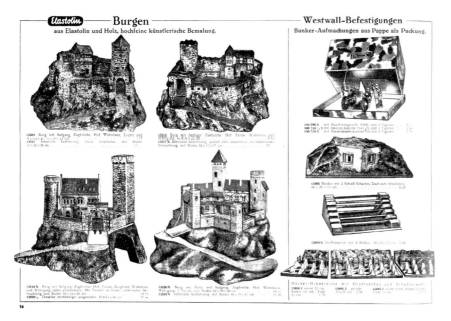

The 1939/40 catalogue contained eight castles. Here they went the route of four images (all apparently photographs), with written descriptions of them, and four similar forts, beneath. Of those illustrated there were two of the 100% composition type (13509½ and 13513½), one of those with a toy train tunnel under (13518N), and one of their last three before the war (13526N). Of the types that were merely described there was one of the 100% composition type (13511½), two of their larger forts (13517N and 13520½), and one of their last production before the war (13524N).

After this, I do not have anything until 1961. By that time, presumably with printing becoming cheaper, they had gone for many illustrations (now all hand drawn) and not so much writing – but still in black and white. Just the fort number and its dimensions were deemed to be enough.

The 1961/62 catalogue contained thirteen castles, all illustrated, but demonstrating what a mess they had got into with the numbers. They were: 9770, 9771, 9772, 9774, 9778, 850(9750), 856(9756), 862(9762), 9744, 9745, M925(9725), M927(9727), and M929(9729).

In 1966, Polks of New York (Hausser's agent in the USA at the time) produced a catalogue that showed that they had, at last, sorted out the numbering problem. It again used hand-drawn images and was printed in black and white. They made a big point of 9734 and 9747 being new, which they certainly were, having been produced that very year.

This Polks catalogue contained fifteen castles (only five illustrated). They were: 9727, 9729, 9730(illustrated), 9732 (illustrated), 9734, 9747 (illustrated), 9750, 9756 (illustrated), 9762, 9766, 9768, 9770, 9772 (illustrated), 9774, and 9780.

The 1973/74 catalogue, now with photographic images printed in color and in leaflet form, had six castles (all illustrated). There were five castles from the vacuum-molded series: 9715, 9729, 9731, 9732, and 9734. It also had one from the injection-molded series: 9747.

The catalogue of 1976/77 was in loose-leaf form. It contained thirteen castles (all illustrated), and claimed that they were lifelike and painted by hand (the castles not the images!). They were: 9715, 9725ii, 9729, 9731, 9732, 9733, 9734, 9735, 9740, 9705, 9747, 9749, and 9766.

Clearly, Hausser decided each year what they wanted to push and went for it. In any case, they would have found it difficult to put everything into their catalogues, which for the last twenty years had to share space with their other products (figures and the like).

In 1938, they also added to the range with three wooden forts. These were No.13522N, No.13524N, and No.13526N. Again these were offered according to size with No.13526N being the largest.

ELASTOLIN TOY FORTS: 13522N-13526N Series
1938 to c1943

NO.	DESCRIPTION	DATE	DIMENSIONS	DISTINCTIVE FEATURES
13522N (3-030)	**smallest of this series** (illustrated in Elastolin catalogue) eg: no known example	1938	15"x14½"x15¾" 380x370x400mm	• integral ramp & compo base • wooden structure • house w/circular tower & wing • large gateway
13524N (3-032)	**second of this series** (identified by an example in the ownership below) eg: Bernd Zimmermann, D	1938	13¾"x16"x16½" 350x410x420mm	• integral ramp & compo base • wooden structure • house, large & small sq tower • large gateway
13526N (3-031)	**largest of this series** (illustrated in Elastolin catalogue) eg: no known example	1938	20½"x19¾"x19" 520x500x480mm	• integral ramp & compo base • wooden structure • house + integral two sq towers • arched gateway & corner tower

These wooden forts were much more detailed than those of the previous five years. They were much less naïve and more pleasingly made in every way – equipped with small towers, alcoves, chimneys, and the like. Other details, such as half-timbering, windows, and doors, were sprayed on using stencils. They were also larger.

This completed the series of large forts up to the Second World War. Five of the six forts that were introduced in 1938 continued in some form or other after the war.

Starting Up Again after the War

When the Second World War was over, Hausser slowly returned to production. By 1947, production was getting going for figures only. The shortage of materials made the production of castles impossible. Figures were a different story. In the main, they used only materials that were waste from other processes – sawdust from the sawmills, animal glue from food production, etc. Toy castles, however, as they were made then, required quite large amounts of wood, which was required for the building industry.

Eventually, in 1953, the situation got a little better and they produced some castles again.

They began with two wooden castles, No.850 and No.862, which owed much to their predecessors from just before the war. With very minor changes, No.850 came from No.13522N, and, with some slightly more significant changes, No.862 came from No.13526N.

In 1955, they came out with another castle, No.856. It, too, was based on one of the castles from before the war – No.13524N, but there were major changes this time. It is true that the base, the gateway, and the mass of the main building were the same, but that is where it ended. The large square tower was moved to the middle, the smaller square tower was omitted, and a substantial circular tower was brought into the corner.

3-030 **Elastolin No.13522N** *(catalogue)*

No.13522N is a catalogue illustration reproduced from Figuren Magazin. These forts are from the pre-war offerings of Hausser's series of large forts. They were designed to fill some perceived gaps in the range with some that were slightly smaller than the very large ones.

They were simple, painted wood constructions, and provided a bit of color to the playroom. They were not very castle-like except for the drawbridge and the tower; they were more of a fortified mansion.

3-032

3-031

3-031 **Elastolin No.13526N** *(catalogue)*
3-032 **Elastolin No.13524N** *(Courtesy Bernd Zimmermann)*
   No.13524N (3-032) is slightly more defensible than the smaller one in the series (3-030), but it is still a bit residential. It is interesting to note how they went to extreme lengths to make them all different. One would have thought they could at least have made some of the towers the same.

No.13526N (3-031) is a catalogue illustration. This one in particular shows how much care was taken to provide a rich play experience. The towers are much more defensible than others in the series, and the gatehouse is especially so. The interesting shape of the courtyard is bordered by a corner tower, as well as complex buildings.

ELASTOLIN'S GROWTH AND PACKAGING

Growth

O & M Hausser's business grew at a slow but steady rate in the beginning, but it was not until some time after they introduced their 70mm figures that the business really took off. This was in about 1920.

The sculpture, generally, and the variety of poses were remarkable. Clearly people loved them. But these were the figures. The castles grew out of their figure production, but they presented a different challenge. What they needed was a range of castles equally remarkable.

So, in about 1920, they brought out their first wooden range, which evolved, by about 1925, into a range that was combined with composition. These were large and represented a more realistic world. Then, in about 1928, they went for 100% composition, again going for realism, even though the castles had to be small scale. In about 1933, they produced a middle-sized, mostly wood range. These three series combined, with one or two supplements, provided Hausser's pre-war offering.

After the war, the shortage of materials caused a slow recovery. But, in 1953, they began to re-build the range, starting with a revamp of a few of their pre-war castles. Then, three years later, they brought out a completely new style, using a concept well tried by Lines Bros. Ltd. in the UK. Only when this was established did they bring out two new series using plastic, so that, by 1961, they had four series on the market simultaneously.

In essence they believed in a step-by-step strategy – always making sure that the one step was secure before taking the next.

Packaging

Before the Second World War packaging was simple and effective. Castles were placed in large brown strawboard boxes with a small but classically colored Hausser label (3-033). After the war, it was a different story. Now, coming from behind, they faced serious competition and needed packaging that would stand out.

So, by about 1956, packaging for all of these castles consisted of a strongly patterned, bright, four-colored, corrugated cardboard box (3-035). This bore

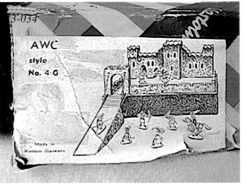

a black and white sticker bearing the picture of the castle and its number (3-034). From the 1970s, this label was replaced by a color photo sticker.

ELASTOLIN TOY FORTS : 850-862 (9750-9762) Series
1953 to c1965

NO.	DESCRIPTION	DATE	DIMENSIONS	DISTINCTIVE FEATURES
850 (3-036) (3-037)	**smallest in this series** (identified by a example in the ownership below) eg: Allen Hickling Toy Forts	1953	14½"x13"x17¾" 370x330x450mm	• integral ramp & various bases • wooden structure • house w/circular tower & wing • standard gateway
856 (3-038) (3-040)	**middle of this series** (illustrated in Elastolin catalogue) eg: *Figuren Magazin*, D	1955	15½"x13¾"x20" 390x350x510mm	• integral ramp & various bases • wooden structure • house, square & circ towers • large gateway
862 (3-039) (3-041)	**largest of this series** (illustrated in Elastolin sales catalogue 1953) eg: *Figuren Magazin*, D	1953	19"x17¾"x21" 480x440x530mm	• integral ramp & various bases • wooden structure • house + integral two sq towers • arched gateway & corner tower

There was one other change that applied to all three in the series. In 1955, they decided to simplify the making of the bases and to cast them out of Styrofoam, 30–40mm thick, with the same area and basic form.

This certainly achieved the aim of making the bases easier to manufacture, but it seems that the mound was too easily damaged as a result of being played with. The continuous poking with the metal locating pins of the parts and the general frailty of the material proved too much. It did not measure up to their goal of quality.

The castles, being made of wood and spray painted, were most colorful. Their smooth walls and roofs gave an impression more of toy forts from an earlier time. With their bright red roofs, blue windows, beige and reddish walls with half-timbered construction and gaudy green foliage, they were the bright spots in a child's room. They were really beautiful in children's eyes.

The series continued the policy of all the castles being different, as they were before the war. This design feature resulted in considerable costs for the manufacturing process, which meant that they were more expensive in the shops. No doubt Hausser thought that this variety, in combination with the colorful painting, justified the extra cost.

In 1957/58, they decided to change the material used for the base to a early sort of plastic. They used a form of the spray-molding technique. This was the first of Hausser's experiments with molding plastic and was to lead to the developments of vacuum- and injection-molding that took them forwards from 1961 for more than twenty years.

In 1961, these three wooden castles, still made of wood with plastic bases, were re-numbered 9750, 9756, and 9762.

3-036

3-036 **Elastolin No.862i** *(Courtesy Bernd Zimmermann)*
3-037 **Elastolin No.862ii** *(catalogue)*

This castle and the two that follow are those that led Hausser's recovery in the castle business after the Second World War, and got them back into making and selling toy castles.

This example shows its heritage from before the war, but there are inevitable simplifications. All the buildings would have been easier to make, except for the gatehouse. It is nonetheless slightly smaller, mostly in the courtyard.

3-037

3-038

3-039

3-040

3-041

3-038 **Elastolin No.856i** *(catalogue)*
3-039 **Elastolin No.850i**
3-040 **Elastolin No.856ii** *(Courtesy Bernd Zimmermann)*
3-041 **Elastolin No.850ii** *(Courtesy Musée du Jouet, Brussels)*

No.850i (3-039) *has a composition base. These were only made for about two years. One can easily see its heritage in No.13522N (3-030) from before the war. It is nearly the same; just the chimneys and an oriel window were missed off of this later version.*

No.850ii (3-041) *is the same castle but with a plastic base. From about 1958, their use of plastic for the series*

was their first foray into the market with that material. From here they used different technologies, but all their new castles were plastic-based. Also new was the drawbridge, which was changed for the new metal type. This was to be used on all forts from here on in.

No.856i (3-038) *is an example on a Styrofoam base. There is evidence of how badly these fared in play. Its roots in No.13524N (3-031) from before the war are not so clear. It is obviously constructed in the same style but the parts are completely different.*

No.856ii (3-040) *is the same castle with a plastic base from about 1958. The 40mm knights are by Elastolin.*

ELASTOLIN TOY FORTS: 866-868 Series
1957 to 1961

NO.	DESCRIPTION	DATE	DIMENSIONS	DISTINCTIVE FEATURES
866 (3-043)	**smallest of this series** (identified by a example in the ownership below) eg: SOFIA Foundation, CY	1957	21¼"x21¼"x18¼" 540x540x465mm	• integral ramp in a plastic base • wood structure/composition finish • large house and square tower • circular tower & gateway
868	**largest of this series** (illustrated in Elastolin catalogue) eg: no known example	1957	25½"x25½"x19¼" 650x650x490mm	• integral ramp in a plastic base • wood structure/composition finish • lg house, square tower & cloister • circular tower & gateway

Also in 1957, at the same time as the three castles were getting a new base, there was a reintroduction of the castles with toy trains running through the mound. These were given No.866 and No.868, which were a continuation of No.13518N. They also had bases that were made of plastic, but there was no change to the castles themselves.

Some researchers place the castles with trains running through them in the 9700 series. There is a strong case for doing so. The parts were used by others in the series, and the plastic molding was consistent with them.

ELASTOLIN TOY FORTS: 9766-9768 Series
1961 to c1981

NO.	DESCRIPTION	DATE	DIMENSIONS	DISTINCTIVE FEATURES
9766 (3-042)	**smallest of this series** (illustrated by an example in the ownership below) eg: Bernd Zimmermann,D	1961	21¼"x21¼"x18¼" 540x540x465mm	• ramp in a vacuum formed base • plastic structure ex castle walls • large house and square tower • circular tower & gateway
9768 (3-044)	**largest of this series** (identified by a example in the ownership below) eg: Allen Hickling Toy Forts	1961	25½"x25½"x19¼" 650x650x490mm	• ramp in a vacuum formed base • plastic structure ex castle walls • large house, cloister, square tower • circular tower & gateway

In 1961, only a few years after these castles had been resuscitated after the war, plastics became the name of the game. Hausser had perfected, as far as it was possible, the vacuum-forming technique, and they now went ahead at full speed. The bases benefited most from the new regime – noted by the stone arch around the railway tunnel entrance.

New numbers were called for and the two castles with the trains running under them were now constructed of plastic and given the Nos.9766 and 9768. Only the castle walls and the drawbridge proved impossible to make of plastic, so they continued to be made of wood and metal as before.

Castles Made of Cardboard

In 1955, a whole new series was designed, which was brought out in 1956. It was the first decade of the German economic miracle – the consumer demand was great and the range of goods grew year on year, but the customers' purses were light and they lived in small, narrow flats. This was the cautiously optimistic feeling of the time, which continued into the 1960s. There was a clear need for something new to fill the gap.

ELASTOLIN TOY FORTS: 870-878 Series
1956 to c1966

NO.	DESCRIPTION	DATE	DIMENSIONS	DISTINCTIVE FEATURES
870 version 1 (3-050)	**Rotbraune Kastell** (identified by a example in the ownership below) eg: SOFIA Foundation, CY	1956	18"x14½"x10¼" 460x370x260mm	• separate ramp • standard gate & metal dbridge • cardboard & framed structure • large house & large sq tower
870 version 2 (3-053)	**Rotbraune Kastell** (illustrated in Elastolin catalogue 1956) eg: Figuren Magazin, D	1963	18"x14½"x10¼" 460x370x260mm	• separate cut back ramp • standard gate & metal dbridge • cardboard & framed structure • large house & sm square tower
871 (3-051)	**Hellbraune Kastell** (identified by a example in the ownership below) eg: Allen Hickling Toy Forts	1960	13¾"x9¾"x8¾" 350x250x220mm	• separate cut back ramp • sm gateway & metal dbridge • cardboard & framed structure • lg house w/main & twin towers
872 (3-052)	**Schwarze Kastell** (identified by a example in the ownership below) eg: SOFIA Foundation, CY	1960	15¾"x25½"x12½" 400x650x320mm	• separate cut back ramp • gate base extension & metal dbridge • cardboard & framed structure • lg house, 2 lg sq towers
874 (3-049)	**Blaue Kastell** (illustrated in Elastolin catalogue 1956) eg: Figuren Magazin, D	1956	20"x17¾"x14¼" 510x450x360mm	• separate ramp • gateway & metal drawbridge • cardboard & framed structure • lg circ & corner bldg w/towers
878 (3-050)	**Camelot Burg** (illustrated in Elastolin catalogue 1956) eg: Figuren Magazin, D	1956	21"x11½"x22½" 530x290x570mm	• moat w/gate & metal dbridge • cardboard & framed structure • lg house w/main & twin towers • two large square corner towers

So, Hausser came up with a new design using cardboard shaped around wooden formers. It was very similar to those of the British company Lines Bros. Ltd., who, using their trade name Tri-ang, had been making forts in this style since 1939. Each castle came apart piece by piece to be stored in a box, which also served as the mound on which the castle sat. This was, above all, cheap, and did not take up too much room, both of which characteristics were in demand. These simple, individual castles, which were nonetheless appealing to the eye, were to prove very lucrative for the company.

"Kastelle" (castles) – is what the company called their new line. At the start, these were No.870, No.874, and No.878. Combined with their three large wooden forts and the two models with railways, this gave them a range of castles to respond to the demands. The 1956 catalogue, containing the three new models, provided a range of castles on the market priced at 9.75DM to 65DM.

1957

3-042

3-043

3-044

3-042 **Elastolin No.9766** *(Courtesy Bernd Zimmermann)*
3-043 **Elastolin No.866**
3-044 **Elastolin No.9768**
These are the two castle designs that featured an O-gauge toy railway tunnel through the base. They had been in the catalogue since 1938, and they featured in it, and in its various manifestations, for another twenty-five years.

When they first came out in 1957, they differed from the pre-war models only in the plastic base, which was at the cutting edge of technology, and the use of the new metal drawbridge. Everything else was exactly the same.
The main design difference between the early ones and the later ones was in the arch around the openings to the railway tunnel – the early ones (3-043) were larger and more cave-like, while the later ones (3-042 & 3-044) were slightly smaller and had a constructed stone arch.

CASTLE CONSTRUCTION USING WOOD-FRAMED CARDBOARD

This method of wood-framed construction was applied to the *"Kastelle"* range which came out in 1956. This was not new ground broken by Hausser, who must have known that Tri-ang in Britain had had a similar range since 1939. What they saw was a design that was economical of space, and a method of fabrication that was cheap. It fit miraculously into the pattern of demand they faced.

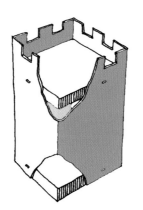

Starting with the towers, they took cardboard, stamped out individual pieces, folded them, and stapled them to small wood formers. The parts were then stable enough for battlements, which were cut out separately and stapled on. This also allowed just a suggestion of machicolation on the lower edge of the battlements.

The rest of the buildings, stamped out with the necessary doors, windows, and arrow slits, just followed on.

The castle walls surrounding the courtyard were made out of wood.

The box acted as storage for the parts and formed the mound on which the castle sat. They made a simple rectangular or square frame for the sides out of wood, and stapled a piece of thick cardboard on top for rigidity, and to make the courtyard.

All the pieces had a metal pin or pins on the underside, which fit exactly into holes in the box. This was so that they could be easily taken off to be laid in the box. It also ensured the correct placement of the pieces when the castle was being erected again. Sadly, it should be noted that this was begun before the Health and Safety Regulations made it impossible.

It was all worked out so that the pieces fit exactly into the box, very often so exactly that it was quite a puzzle how to fit them all in. This, of course, added to the pleasure of having the castle.

This series proved to be most lucrative for Hausser, just at a time when it was most needed. They were struggling to get the castles off the ground and needed a "banker." These castles provided just that, and gave them the boost they needed to ride the surge of demand when plastics came onto the scene in 1961 and beyond.

Hausser extended this range in 1960, when they added two more castles, No.871 and No.872. In 1963, they withdrew the original No.870, only to replace it with another, almost the same, but with the gateway moved to the other side, a small tower replacing the large one in the corner, and a ramp cut back at the top so that, to be effective, it had to project out at the front.

The castle, which they put into their "export" edition, No.870, was to prove the most popular. Whether this was because of its bright coloring or something else, we will never know, but each of these castles had its own basic color. No.870 was red-brown, known as the *"rotbraune Kastell,"* No.871 was beige, known as the *"hellbraune Kastell,"* No.872 was black, known as the *"schwarze Kastell,"* and No.874 was blue, known as the *"blaue Kastell."* No.878 was completely different in every respect and was known as the *"Camelot-Burg."*

The first four of these castles bore no direct indication of stonework on the walls. Rather, a combination of glue and sawdust was applied to the bare card, then the appropriate base color was applied, which was brought to life by the addition of cream, yellow, ochre, and green highlights, using a dry brush technique. This was all set off by the tops of the battlements being emphasized in a striking red color.

The fifth castle in the series, No.878, was still made with cardboard shaped around wooden formers, but it was totally different in design. First of all, it did not come apart to be stored in its box, partly because there was no box. The individual pieces were fixed to the base, which was quite shallow and also made of cardboard.

The towers were much bigger, with deep wells in which a 70mm figure could comfortably stand (and a 40mm figure could be completely protected), and the walls were much higher than others in the series. It was all surrounded by a moat crossed by a metal drawbridge to a gateway, which was the weakest part of the design. True it had a larger opening than others, but it was only the thickness of a piece of cardboard – quite out of character with the rest of it.

The color was meant to represent stonework. First, a spray was used to apply blue and cream in large areas letting the color of the cardboard show through. Then, small rectangles of a whitish color, apparently at random, were applied using a stencil. This was accentuated by thin black lines to represent some of the joints, also using a stencil. Finally the windows and arrow slits were highlighted in black.

A particular detail of this castle was the shield above the entrance. Originally this had the red stallion's head from the story of Prince Eisenherz von Thule by Hal Foster on it. However, Hausser had to refrain from marketing the castle for copyright reasons. This is why advertising material and catalogues from the later 1950s show the same castle with the unmistakable dragon of King Arthur. Maybe this is how it came to be named the *"Camelot Burg."*

This series did eventually came to be numbered 9770 to 9778, even though the pieces had no plastic in them.

ELASTOLIN TOY FORTS: 860 Series
c1955

NO.	DESCRIPTION	DATE	DIMENSIONS	DISTINCTIVE FEATURES
860	**smallest of these** (identified by mention in *Figuren Magazin*) eg: no known example	unknown	11¾"x9"x?" 300x230x?mm	• gateway • cardboard & framed structure • flat wooden buildings
unknown (3-054)	**first version** (identified by illustration in *Figuren Magazin*) eg:*Figuren Magazin*, D	1955	unknown	• large central gateway • cardboard & framed structure
unknown	**second version** (identified by mention in *Figuren Magazin*) eg: no known example	unknwn	unknown	• large gateway • cardboard & framed structure
unknown (3-055)	**largest of these?** (identified by illustration in *Figuren Magazin*) eg: no known example	1955	14½"x12¼"x?" 370x310x?mm	• very large gateway • cardboard & framed structure • conical structures & circular tower

Somehow, at the beginning, there were three other castles which never got into production in a big way. The first was a small, dark grey model with the number 860. The second was conceived as a fort for Knights of the Cross; it was blue, had no number, and was dated December 1955. It was in two versions based on different versions of the large gate. The third was violet with a lavish gate supported by conical structures and a circular tower, also dated December 1955. Very little is known about these.

3-048

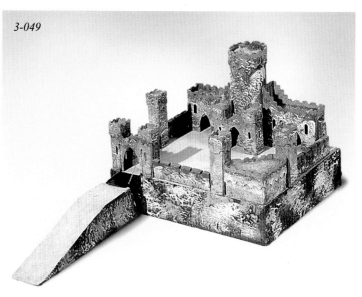

3-049

3-050

3-048 Elastolin No.870i *"Rotbraune Kastell" (first version)*
3-049 Elastolin No.874 *"Blauwe Kastell" (Courtesy Figuren Magazin)*
3-050 Elastolin No.878 *"Camelot Burg" (Courtesy Bernd Zimmermann)*

These three forts are from the "Kastellen" series. They were the first three produced in 1956.

No.870i was the very first in the series. It was the subject of Hausser's hugely successful "export" edition, which was actually to test the market. There was a second version, which was to come out in 1963.

No.874 was quite an elaborate castle with many pieces. The corner feature in front was unique. It was the so-called "Blauwe Kastell."

No.878 was the odd one in this series, being quite unlike any of the others, except in the method of construction. This one was actively promoted as a castle for use with 70mm figures. It was a very strong design except for the gateway, which was somewhat weak. Unlike the others in the series, it was sold pre-assembled in one piece.

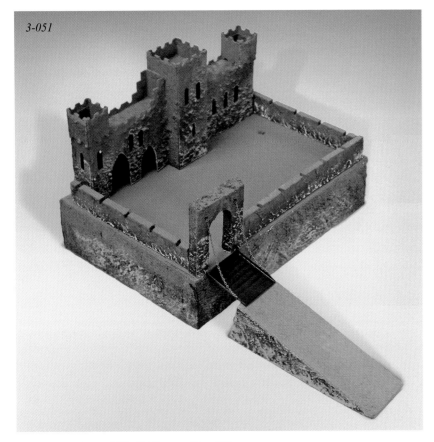

3-051

3-052

3-051 Elastolin No.871 *"Helbraune Kastell"*
3-052 Elastolin No.872 *"Schwarze Kastell"*

   These two castles comprised the second wave in this series in 1960.

   No.871 was the smallest of the "Kastellen" range, and was also the simplest in design. It was actively promoted as for 40mm figures. The courtyard and ramp may have been re-paints, at least on the horizontal surface.

   No.872 was also part of the second wave. The extension to the courtyard that carries the gateway was made separately. The towers are very tall.

3-053 **Elastolin 870ii** *"Rotbraune Kastell" second version*
3-054 **Elastolin unnumbered (1)** *(Courtesy Figuren Magazin)*
3-055 **Elastolin unnumbered (2)** *(catalogue)*

No.870ii was the second version of this castle. The only substantive changes were a reduction in size of the corner tower and a curtailment of the ramp, necessitating it to come straight out in front. One other change that cannot be explained was the reversal of the positions of the gate and the corner tower.

The two small images are of the forts, which were a sort of practice run before the "export edition" of No.870i (3-048).

Unnumbered (1) was conceived as a fort for Knights of the Cross, and is one of two versions based on the treatment of the gateway. Neither was ever put into production, though a few may have made it onto the market.

Unnumbered (2) was similar to unnumbered (1) in that it never was on the market in a meaningful way. Note its distinctive gateway and the round tower in front of the same back piece as several other versions (see 870i (3-048), 870ii (3-053) or 871 (3-051)). Perhaps they found these two pieces too difficult to make economically.

HAUSSER'S TREATMENT OF SCALE

This refers to both their buildings and their toy soldiers, which only matters when one wishes to benefit from combining them.

Until just before the Second World War, when Hausser produced a range of 40mm figures, they were working at a considerable disadvantage. At first, they produced figures at 100mm, only changing to 70mm just before the First World War; these did not "catch on" until later. To produce castles to a compatible scale was no easy task.

A castle of reasonable proportions, built to a compatible scale, would be truly enormous. Even their largest castle, No.13525, which is not a castle at all in terms of its accommodation, would have to be at least twice its actual size (about 72" x 72" or 183x183mm). This is clearly impractical in terms of handling during production, storage, and transport, not to mention the spatial demands placed on the potential buyer. So clearly a solution had to be found.

The problem was how to make the toy forts small enough to satisfy all these requirements, yet appear large enough to be realistic.

One way to make them smaller is to reduce the scale of the buildings, but the figures rapidly become giants with gateways through which they cannot pass, and battlements that provide no protection. Another way is to make the open spaces of the castle smaller, but the courtyards soon become too small to parade in and the ramps become unreasonably steep.

The answer lies in a combination of strategies, and Hausser made a fine effort. Their initial choice of size for the figures was a constant problem, which did not get any better until they produced their 40mm figures, but the small figures they made with composition before World War II were of the modern variety. It was not until 1960, when they launched their extensive range of 40mm medieval plastic figures, together with plastic versions of their 70mm range, that medieval characters became readily available.

They had not had anything like these before and could not use them in their repertoire. Now, however, they could and did identify castles according to the figures that were meant to go with them.

This problem was to raise its ugly head again almost as soon as it was solved. A new technology using plastic, seized on by Hausser, enabled the making of complete castles all in one piece. This was vacuum-forming, which, while providing a solution to many of the problems, cost and weight

3-056

3-057

in particular, did not allow very large forts to be made. This meant small scale again. Even the 40mm figures were really too large, although not by much, and they made a fine effort to integrate them in most cases.

Of course, they did not have to face these problems in their parallel set of forts, which were made with a different technology to a slightly larger scale. The 40mm figures were fine on these, although there were still questions about the 70mm figures. The demand for the one-piece forts was tremendous, however, so we can conclude that the problems were not experienced by many of their customers.

Plastic Castles with Removable Pieces

Hausser launched into the world of plastics in 1961. They used two main molding techniques – injection molding and vacuum forming – and these two formed the basis of the two series that they marketed. There were one or two techniques in addition to these, for example the so called "blow molding" technique (*"Blastechnik"*), but they were very few and far between.

Taking the injection-molded forts first, the most important thing to note is that they were not only injection-molded. The larger parts, such as the base, were also vacuum-formed, but, in the main, the buildings were all injection molded.

"Romantic castles and proud knights in magnificent armour are a wonderful toy for youngsters." So ran the copy on the title page of a small leaflet of the Hausser firm from the late 1950s. The highest quality of the Hausser products are those with individual gatehouses, towers, houses, and walls, all hand painted, standing on their rocky mound or on a base with a moat around. They were the top items in the catalogue.

Their castles, particularly those described in this series, with their pointed Gothic arches, Roman doors and windows, towers with bay windows, and battlements towering on their mound, were wonderful toys. They look realistic due to their wall structures, with windows and arrow slits in them. The battlements, the darker joints in the stones, the painted roofs, the grey or brown rock base, and the harmonious paint effects give them a solid feel.

All the parts (until the Norman castle No.9748) consist of individual, sprayed plastic pieces, or half-rounds to be glued together to make round towers or gateways. These separate wall and roof parts were then stuck together as necessary. The castle walls around the courtyard were in one piece. Most parts were used for different castles in the series, somewhat like a unit construction system. For the whole series there were:

- Two types of square tower: one large, used since the 1920s, and one very large;
- Two types of circular tower: one simple, used since the late 1930s, and one as on the "Water Fort;"
- Two types of gate: one a simple gateway from the 1920s, and one a gatehouse;
- One type of house: the one used since the 1920s;
- Two types of castle wall: one high, and one relatively short but thick, which was truly defensible and thoroughly justified use of the title "castle" when one was built using them.

This series was unlike any other in that there was no big launch. Previously, manufacturers would launch a series with at least four or five models, and even more if your name was Moritz Gottschalk, for example. Hausser probably thought that issuing one or two every so often was a good way to manage the uncertainty of the marketplace – and indeed it was. They only issued a new model when there was demand for it.

They started with just one castle, which was the largest they ever made. Said to be made for 40mm and 70mm figures, this was the famous "Water Fort" (*"Wasserburg"*) which came in two versions – No.9744 and No.9745i (so numbered to differentiate it from a similarly numbered one that came later). One had a moat and the other did not – the difference being just that. One had a large base, including the moat, while the other just sat on the floor.

The castle originally came in a box, which had a lovely lid with a label showing a tournament in progress in the Middle Ages. Behind the action is the castle, looking splendid on its substantial hill.

ELASTOLIN TOY FORTS: 9705 & 9744-9749 Series
1961 to 1983

NO.	DESCRIPTION	DATE	DIMENSIONS	DISTINCTIVE FEATURES
9705 (3-060) (3-061)	second of this series (identified by a example in the ownership below) eg: Allen Hickling Toy Forts	1966	24"x13¾"x11¾" 610x350x300mm	• no ramp • injection molded plastic structure • large house, sq & circular tower • gatehouse & castle walls
9725ii (3-063)	fourth of this series (illustrated in Elastolin catalogue 1976/77) eg: *Figuren Magazin*, D	1973	26¾"x19"x??" 680x485x??mm	• 1-piece castle & separate towers • vacuum formed base structure • three houses & gateway • "blow molded" sq & circ towers
9744	first of this series (illustrated in Elastolin catalogue 1961/62) eg: no known example	1961	17¾"x18½"x18" 450x470x460mm	• no ramp • injection molded plastic structure • large sq tower with turret & well • gatehouse, high walls, circ towers
9745i (3-053)	first of this series (identified by a example in the ownership below) eg: SOFIA Foundation, CY	1961	28¼"x30"x19¼" 720x760x490mm	• base + moat & integral ramp • injection molded plastic structure • large sq tower with turret & well • gatehouse, high walls, circ towers
9746 (3-064)	third of this series (identified by illustration in *Figuren Magazin*) eg: no known example	1971	22½"x22¾"x??" 570x580x??m	• vacuum formed mound & ramp • injection molded plastic structure • large three storey fort • gatehouse & castle walls
9747 (3-062)	second of this series (identified by a example in the ownership below) eg: Bernd Zimmermann, D	1966	29½"x30"x18" 750x750x475mm	• vacuum formed mound & ramp • injection molded plastic structure • lg house & sq + circular towers • gatehouse & castle walls
9748 (3-065)	fifth of this series (illustrated in Elastolin catalogue) eg: no known example	1979	30¾"x33¾"x??" 780x860x??mm	• vacuum formed mound & ramp • injection molded plastic structure • two small houses & square tower • built-in gateway
9749 (3-066)	fourth of this series (illustrated in Elastolin catalogue 1976/77) eg: no known example	1973	21"x21¼"x??" 530x540x??mm	• vacuum-formed mound & ramp • injection-molded plastic structure • large square tower • gatehouse & castle walls

1961

3-058 **Elastolin No.9745i** *"Die Wasserburg"*
   No.9744 and No.9745i were the first and the largest of the plastic revolution – they came out in 1961. They were basically the same castle – the "Water Fort" ("Die Wasserburg") – but No.9745 had a base of a moat and shallow ramp. It came in the injection-molded series, although parts, such as the base, were vacuum formed. It shows the move towards realism started with No.878 in the "Kastellen" series, particularly in the high walls and impressive gatehouse. It was also promoted as suitable for use with 70mm figures.

HAUSSER'S MARKETING STRATEGY

Virtually all of Hausser's records from 1904 to 1946 were lost or destroyed during the Second World War, so it is difficult to piece together anything much from before that time.

Very little is known about their export business. How and when they opened up in different countries is a bit of a mystery, at least to me.

The 1920 catalogue was in English, French, and Spanish, as well as German, which indicates a presence all over Europe and North and South America. It is also known that they had an arrangement with Blockhouse NY in New York, and had outlets and/or representatives in Sweden, Holland, Switzerland, Czechoslovakia, and France. The means by which they got there is unknown.

It is known that they came to England in 1925, as is evidenced in their advertising for agents. Unfortunately, this was not too long before the recession of 1929, when the trade really slowed up. After that came the Third Reich in 1933, and the consequent focus on the German army, which concentrated the market in Germany.

We can say something about Hausser's practice after the Second World War, however. The first post-war catalogue was not published until 1954, but after that they regularly produced catalogues, in color, of all types and sizes. These were aimed mostly at the end user but that helped the seller, too.

After the war, they took nothing for granted. They tested the market thoroughly whenever they were launching a new product line, to see if it would work. A good example is the testing they did when they launched the *"Kastellen"* range of cardboard castles in 1956.

In the last half of 1955, six months before the big launch, they put out a so-called "export" edition. How this was an "export" edition is a bit of a mystery, because it was also available in Germany. This test of the market used the No.870 and it nearly took over the Hausser workforce. According to factory records 6,500 were made and sold in those six months alone. So it was clear that they were onto a winner.

Also, when they came to production of the vacuum-formed plastic castles, which for them was something untried, they first produced three small, simple ones. Of course, this was partly to let the workforce learn the process, but it was also so that they could get out of it if necessary. Only about five years later did they start to expand their ideas until, by the mid-1970s, they were able to really "go to town."

Hausser always strove to have castles on the market that covered all price ranges. This necessitated seeing all their castles as one range.

For example, in the early 1960s, when plastics were just settling in, it was sensible to see all four types of castle together. The price in the shops for the series of vacuum-formed castles was 6.25DM to 9.75DM. The price of the series of cardboard castles (*"Kastellen,"* Nos. 870–878) ranged from 11.50DM to 34.50DM, the series made of wood (Nos. 850–862) ranged from 19.75DM to 39.50DM, and the price of the most exclusive series, the injection-molded series, varied from 54.50DM to 72.50DM.

One can see from this example that the two series of plastic castles extended the range on offer at both ends of the spectrum, providing them with a possible response at any level.

The moated base was delivered separately in a large grey, flat box. There were three versions of this base, all of which were the same as far as the moat was concerned. The variations were in the well(s) and the fixing for the circular towers:

• One well with no raised discs on which to fit the towers
• Two wells, one under the main tower, and no raised discs on which to fit the towers
• Two wells, one under the main tower, with raised discs on which to fit the towers

There is no record of when these were issued.

Hausser did not produce another in the series until five years later in 1966. Then they produced two, both for 40mm figures. These were No.9705 and No.9747. Interestingly, they were quite different from the first castle in the series and from each other, and they were completely different in their use.

One was a castle to play with on-the-floor or for the sand pit, as recommended in the Hausser advertisement of the time. It is No.9705 and called *"Nüremburg."* It contained all the usual parts, which were to become part of all their castles in the future: a house; a square tower; a circular tower with a small doorway to add on; a gatehouse; and six pieces of thick wall. Of these, the design of the house and the towers came from before the war; only the gatehouse and the walls were new.

The wall pieces, with places on which to stand a 40mm figure and galleried arches to put figures underneath, were especially realistic. For virtually the first time, defenders of the castle had some protection. All the pieces in the set were colored a light grey, with red roofs and details.

The illustration on the lid of the original box is a child playing, building a castle with additional parts. This combination with additional parts was encouraged by Hausser, and could lead to many different possibilities. Of course, they sold the parts separately if you wanted them.

The other was the so-called *"Braune Kastell"* (Brown Castle), which was a more conventional castle and the model for most of what followed. On its vacuum-formed base were the same parts as those on the smaller forts with a toy train tunnel from before the war (No.13518N), but with a bigger gatehouse, and in this case they were all brown. Given its dimensions, it was the biggest of all the forts built for 40mm figures, and perhaps also the most attractive. It looks good, from the two towers on opposite sides, with the square one artificially raised, to the house in an elevated position above the courtyard. With the thick walls and gatehouse fitting snugly on the rocky base leading one in, it became one of the favorite Hausser castles.

It was another five years, in 1971, before the next castle was introduced as a sample. It was No.9746, which was a Roman style of castle. It was also made for 40mm figures. It is the rarest of any in the series primarily because it was only available as a sample for a comparatively short time. Why it was introduced as a sample is not known, nor is it known why it never made it properly into the series.

This should really be classified more as a vacuum-formed castle than anything else, but it did have some injection-molded parts. The gatehouse and two pieces of wall fitted neatly into the vacuum-formed base at the front; the main building, also vacuum-formed but separately from the base, stood to the rear.

Hausser felt the need for a more substantial castle and, two years later, in 1973, they brought out No.9749. This rather individual structure, without a house or anything similar, is actually more of a fortification than a castle.

With a vacuum-formed, rather flat base, this model owes much of its conceptual design to both of the earlier castles. Its centrally located gatehouse, with two flanking wall pieces at the front, is an almost direct copy of them. One is led through to the centrally located tower at the back, with two further castle walls as part of the vacuum forming. The tower is the very large one from the "Water Fort." There is a well and steps giving access to the tower in the courtyard. It is advertised as being suitable for 40mm and 70mm figures.

Also in 1973, they introduced a real oddity. This was No.9725(ii), which, without putting too fine a point on it, was a blunder, because they already had one with that number in the vacuum-formed series. The reason that it was an oddity, though, was that it was a partial cross-over to the vacuum-molded series: it had three houses, a gateway, walls, and a well incorporated in the base. Also, it was the only other castle to have hard plastic removable parts made by the blow-molding technique (*"Blastechnik"*). The two towers, one square, the other circular, were those in question.

Then Hausser's customers had to wait another six years, until 1979, shortly before the company went out of business, for the final castle in the series – and what a castle it was. Designed and modeled by Josef Tonn, it was completely different from anything that went before. It was No.7948 known as *"Normannenburg."*

It was a perfect early Middle Ages fort – not castle – for 70mm figures. The drawbridge was built directly into the massive, imposing walls, and the two houses sat on top of them. The walls were part of the base, which was vacuum-formed and provided the foundation for the two wood-framed houses. These were made by the blow-molding technique (*"Blastechnik"*), so there were no glued joints in them.

CONSTRUCTION USING INJECTION MOLDING

Vacuum molding was an important development for Hausser, but it was not the only, nor the most important, form of molding plastic. There was also injection molding.

The first injection molding machine was patented by two American brothers, Isaiah and John Wesley Hyatt, in 1872. The industry progressed slowly over the years, producing collar stays, buttons, and hair combs. Then, in the 1940s, the Second World War created a huge demand for inexpensive, mass-produced products. In 1946, the first screw injection machine was built, allowing much more precise control over the quality of articles produced. This system is still in use today.

Injection molding is a process for producing parts from both thermoplastic and thermosetting plastic materials. Molds are made by a mold maker (or toolmaker) from metal, usually steel or aluminum, and precision-machined to form the features of the desired part.

Raw materials are chosen based on the strength and function of the final part; each material has different parameters for molding that must be taken into account. Most polymers may be used, including thermoplastics, such as nylon, polyethylene, and polystyrene.

With injection molding, granular plastic is fed from a hopper into a heated barrel. As they are moved forward by a screw-type plunger, the plastic is forced into a heated chamber, where it is melted. This is forced through a gate into the mold cavity. The mold remains cold so the plastic solidifies almost as soon as it is filled and hardens to the configuration of the mold cavity. Once the part is cool, the mold opens and the part is ejected.

This process is economically suited to the production of many of the same parts. Consequently, for the castle manufacturer, what was needed was a series of castles all requiring the same parts, but assembled in different configurations. Ideally, to reap the economic benefits of the method, it was a series that was to continue year after year.

Once the system was set up, the result was a large number of parts. Some of these were complete in themselves, while others needed to go through a further process of construction. For example, walls came out complete, but the halves of a circular tower needed to be glued together. All of these parts needed to be generic, in the sense that they applied to various castles, which, over time, Hausser developed.

But this did not solve the whole problem. The biggest part was still the mound, which did not lend itself to injection molding techniques. So the castle manufacturer had to find other methods to complete the job, and Hausser had just the one method – vacuum forming. This is why the two series, the one using primarily injection molding and the other vacuum forming, started together in 1961.

3-061

3-062

3-060

3-060 **Elastolin No.9705** *(with extra pieces)*
3-061 **Elastolin No.9705** *"Nüremburg"*
3-062 **Elastolin No.9747** *"Braune Kastell"*

Nos.9705 (3-061) came out in 1966. Any piece would go together with any other and the idea was that you could make your own layout. The set is as it was marketed as "Nüremburg," and designed *for play in the playroom or on the beach. They also sold separate pieces of No.9705 to allow more scope. No.9705 (with extra pieces) is an example of what could be done.

No.9747 (3-062) also came out in 1966 and became one of the favorite castles. Said to be for 40mm figures, it was a more realistic style of toy castle. The position of the parts being at different levels was very attractive.

3-066

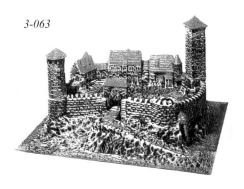

3-063

3-064

3-065

3-063 **Elastolin No.9725ii** *(catalogue)*
3-064 **Elastolin No.9746** *"Römerburg" (Courtesy Figuren Magazin)*
3-065 **Elastolin No.9748** *"Normannenburg" (Courtesy Figuren Magazin)*
3-066 **Elastolin No.9749** *(Courtesy Figuren Magazin)*

These are four in the injection-molded series of castles with removable pieces.

No.9746 (3-064) is the rarest of the castles in this series because it was only made for a very short time, and that was as a sample. Introduced in 1971, it is not known why it was made as a sample only.

No.9725ii (3-063) was introduced to the market in 1973. There was a bit of a cross-over between this series and that of the all-in-one single castles. The two towers could be removed.

No.9749 (3-066) also came out in 1973, but was not so much a castle as a fortification. Claiming to be suitable for 40mm and 70mm figures, it was made to defend something – if not itself.

No.9748 (3-065) is the late model "Norman Fort," which came out in 1979. It was made specifically for 70mm figures. It is one of two known to make use of the "blow molding" technique ("Blastechnik").

The Plastic, All-In-One, Single-Piece Series

In 1961, the same year that the injection molding series was launched, Hausser also introduced by far their largest series, which was to last more than twenty years. It was the vacuum-molded series of all-in-one single-piece plastic castles.

They looked amazingly realistic and were light and easy to handle for any child playing in the house or the garden. In the early 1960s, they were clearly the most reasonably priced in the Hausser catalogue, achieved through the relatively low outlay and simple manual work. They quickly became the most popular.

The two series should, in some ways, be seen together, in that the one complemented the other not only in price but in use. And that was not all: the two forms of manufacture were used together in practice, many castles having parts of both forms. For the sake of clarity, however, I think it best if they are kept separate.

Hausser started off with three castles, all of them very sensibly quite small. If you are going to start marketing castles made with a new technology, it is wise not to bite off more than you can chew. So these castles were No.9725(i) (so numbered because later, in 1973, they produced another one, completely different, also numbered 9725), No.9727, and No.9729. They were the only three to be made entirely with vacuum molding.

No.9725(i) was clearly the first to come off the drawing board. It was smaller in scale than the other two and owed much to the design of old-style wooden castles. There is no gateway on this or on the other two, which goes to show that they had yet to devise the trick of combining vacuum forming with parts made separately. The courtyard does look a little barren.

ELASTOLIN TOY FORTS: 9715-9745 Series
1961 to 1983

NO.	DESCRIPTION	DATE	DIMENSIONS	DISTINCTIVE FEATURES
9715 (3-077)	**fourth of this series** (illustrated by an example in the ownsership below) eg: Allen Hickling Toy Forts	1973	21"x16¾"x13" 535x425x330mm	• 1-piece castle • vacuum-formed structure • gate & semi-circular courtyard • L-shaped building & circ tower
9725i (3-068)	**first of this series** (illustrated in Elastolin catalogue 1961/62) eg: *Figuren Magazin*, D	1961	13½"x11½"x??" 345x290x?mm	• a small scale one piece castle • vacuum-formed structure • house, cloister & circular tower • lg court in front & no gateway
9727 (3-069)	**first of this series** (illustrated in Elastolin catalogue 1961/62) eg: *Figuren Magazin*, D	1961	11"x13½"x??" 280x345x?mm	• 1-piece castle ("Romerturm") • vacuum formed structure • large scale, two-room tower

9729 (3-070)	**first of this series** (identified by an example in the ownership below) eg: SOFIA Foundation, CY	1961	13¾"x11½"x9" 350x290x220mm	• 1-piece castle • vacuum-formed structure • house & circular tower at rear • sm sq corner bldg, no gateway
9730 (3-072)	**second of this series** (illustrated in Polks, NY catalogue 1966) eg: *Figuren Magazin*, D	1964	17¾"x15¾"x12¼" 450x400x310mm	• 2-piece castle extension • vacuum-formed structure • gateway & semi-circular yard • L-shaped bldg w/sq tower
9731 (3-074)	**fourth of this series** (illustrated in Elastolin catalogue 1973/74) eg: *Figuren Magazin*, D	1973	17¾"x15¾"x10¼" 450x400x260mm	• 1-piece castle replaced 9730 • vacuum-formed structure • gateway & semi-circular yard • L-shaped bldg w/sq tower
9732 (3-071)	**second of this series** (identified by an example in the ownership below) eg: Allen Hickling Toy Forts	1964	22"x22½"x13¾" 565x565x330mm	• 2-piece castle (tower extens'n) • vacuum-formed structure • house, chapel, & central circ tower • one main gateway & one other
9733 (3-075)	**fourth of this series** (identified by an example in the ownership below) eg: Allwyn Brice, UK	1973	22"x22½"x13¾" 565x565x280mm	• 1- piece castle replaced 9732 • vacuum-formed structure • house, chapel, & central circ tower • one main gateway & one other
9734 (3-073)	**third of this series** (illustrated in Elastolin catalogue) eg *Figuren Magazin*, D	1966	28½"x23½"x16¾" 745x620x425mm	• 2- piece castle (tower extension) • vacuum-formed structure • two gateways & three houses • with central circular tower
9735 (3-076)	**fourth of this series** (identified by an example in the ownership below) eg Allen Hickling Toy Forts	1973	28½"x23½"x16¾" 745x620x425mm	• 1-piece castle replaced 9734 • vacuum-formed structure • two gateways & three houses • with central circular tower
9740 (3-079)	**sixth of this series** (identified by a example in the ownership below) eg: Allen Hickling Toy Forts	1976	22¾"x22¾"x10" 580x580x255mm	• 1-piece castle & central gateway • vacuum-formed structure • L-shaped building & circ tower • large square tower & chapel
9741 (3-078)	**fifth of this series** (illustrated in Elastolin catalogue) eg: *Figuren Magazin*, D	1975	24¾"x25¼"x??" 630x640x?mm	• 2- piece castle (tower extens'n) • vacuum-formed structure • 9740 with large forecourt • lg gate & 2 forecourt houses
unknwn (3-080)	**seventh of this series** (identified by an example in the ownership below) eg: Allen Hickling Toy Forts	1982	22½"x15½"x8" 570x395x200mm	• 1-piece castle • vacuum-formed structure • 2 houses, chapel & central tower • gateway & 2 low circ towers

No 9727, the "Romerturm," became one of the most treasured of these vacuum-formed castles. It is not clear why exactly; maybe it is because it was so different. Just the one tower-like structure, albeit sub-divided in two, with two apse-like integral towers one each side of the gate. The door is larger than on the other two, so it could be used for 70mm figures in a pinch, although it was designed for 40mm figures.

Of the first three, No.9729 was the most like the ones which were to follow. It was to a much larger scale than No.9725(i), which made for a much smaller

3-068

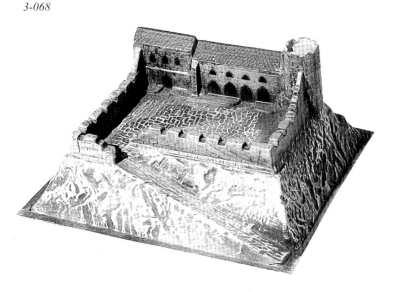

3-070

3-069

3-068 **Elastolin No.9725i** (catalogue)
3-069 **Elastolin No.9727** "Römerturm" (catalogue)
3-070 **Elastolin No.9729**

These are the castles that Hausser used to launch their series of plastic forts in 1961. The three small castles were obviously the way to begin a series.

No.9725i (3-068) was clearly the first to be designed. It was very small, even more like a farm than No.9715 (3-077). It is the first of two forts numbered 9725, hence the "i."

No.9727 (3-069) was a Roman tower fort. Note the simplicity of everything.

No.9729 (3-070) is the third of Hausser's launch of the series. This is the most advanced of the first three in the launch, so it becomes clear how they struggled with vacuum forming at the beginning.

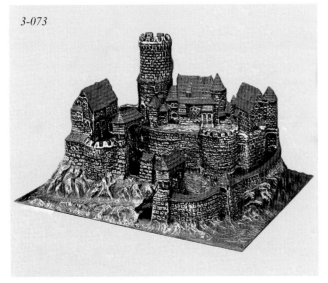

3-071 **Elastolin No.9730** (catalogue)
3-072 **Elastolin No.9732**
3-073 **Elastolin No.9734** *"Burg Schaffhausen"* (catalogue)

These forts are from the series of all-in-one, single-piece castles.

No.9730 was brought out in 1964. It is a clear indication of improvement in Hausser's design capability and shows that they were slowly getting the hang of vacuum forming.

No.9732 (3-072) was part of the big surge in production of plastic castles, also brought out in 1964. This is the first appearance of their new gateway design and their tower extension piece. The figures are some of Hausser's own 40mm range of Landsknechts.

No.9734 was brought out in 1966. It was by far the biggest so far and had two gateways and three houses. A most impressive castle, it showed how well they had taken on the technology. It owed a lot to the wax model of the very small composition fort which never made it onto the market (3-013).

courtyard. The towers were more thought out and the house showed considerably more design awareness.

These three have the pale-color plastic that was used early on, beige-ochre-light brown, also gray-beige, requiring a more expensive and individual paint style. From about 1968, all the vacuum-formed castles were cast in a dark color, mostly black but also dark grey and, more rarely, dark brown. From this time the castles were more simply painted, and the result was gloomier and more monotonal castles. However, they were still attractive play things.

Castle Construction Using Vacuum-Formed Plastic

Vacuum forming, commonly known as Vacuforming, is a simplified version of thermoforming. A sheet of plastic is heated to a forming temperature, stretched onto a single surface mold, and held against the mold by applying a vacuum between the mold surface and the sheet.

It is usually – but not always – restricted to forming plastic parts that are rather shallow in depth. Relatively deep parts can be formed if the form-able sheet is mechanically or pneumatically stretched, prior to bringing it into contact with the mold surface and before the vacuum is applied.

Normally, so-called draft angles must be incorporated in the mold design (a recommended minimum of 3°), otherwise release of the formed plastic and the mold is very difficult. This is why the castles made by this method appear to be tapered towards the top. All these molds have small holes all over, which act as air vents allowing the vacuum to work.

Suitable materials for use in vacuum forming are conventionally thermoplastics, the most common and easiest being High Impact Polystyrene Sheeting (HIPS). This is molded around a wood, synthetic resin, structural foam or aluminum mold, and can form to almost any shape.

A mold for the mound, house(s), tower(s) and walls was made – a whole castle at once. A "positive" shape of the developing castle could be seen from above. This construction, which brought all the individual pieces together, provided a sturdy metal shape – the so-called "shape box" of the vacuum forming machine. For each type of castle there was a unique individual mold.

Industrial plastic was heated by means of infra-red lamps in the metal frame. Then, thus warmed, the now somewhat floppy plastic sheet was pressed onto the mold by high pressure from above and, at the same time, air was sucked out via the air vents, thus creating the vacuum.

After rapid cooling by means of cold air, the castle could be taken off the mold. The extra bits on the edge were cut off using a big pair of scissors.

Some castles had additional height added to their towers by means of a sleeve, formed in two half-round parts using injection molding, which fitted over the already molded tower. This could be removed if one wanted, but when it was on it provided the castle with a more imposing appearance.

This process did not include the entire gateway. The upper part of it could not be molded with the rest. So this was injection molded in two halves, assembled together with the metal chain for the plastic drawbridge (also injection molded) and the winding mechanism, and glued together and added to the appropriate spot on the castle.

The raw material was then painted in the painting department. Painting was carried out by hand.

In the beginning, when they used a light plastic, a dark color was applied and then wiped off leaving the paint in the joints. Later, when the basic plastic tended to be dark or black, a light color could be applied using a short, wide, dry brush for all the walls. Then gray was applied for the courtyards and green for the scenery.

Finally, solid red or dark green was used for the roofs and blue for the water, if there was any, giving these castles a very lovely appearance.

There was a pause, then, in the introduction of new castles, which lasted until the middle of the 1960s, when, combined with new castles in the injection molding area, there was a surge in creativity.

First, in 1964, came No.9730 and No.9732. Of these two, No.9730 showed only minor developments. Most important was the introduction of a gateway with an overhead piece. Not that this was any great shakes, but it represented a breakthrough, because it was then possible to have a drawbridge, which was a great play feature for the children. Otherwise it was much the same as before, only a little larger.

No.9732 was a significant advance on anything that had gone before. Apart from the obvious point that it was even larger, with more buildings such as a chapel and two gateways, it also displayed two major developments.

One was the use of a simple extension piece, which fitted on the top of the basic tower to increase its height. It enabled a much more imposing effect and was to be used on at least three other castles.

The other innovation was a gateway, which owed much of its impressive appearance to the gatehouse on the "Water Fort." Now it was possible to have a wind-up mechanism for operation of the drawbridge. This development was to be seen on all the castles throughout the series and greatly enhanced their play value.

Next, in 1966, came No.9734. It was named *"Burg Schaffhausen"* and was, at 28½" x 23½" (725mm x 600mm), by far the largest vacuum-formed castle Hausser had made to date. It had three substantial houses, an imposing tower, and two gatehouses, both with drawbridges. It incorporated both of the developments that had been established in 1964: the tower extension and the gateway innovation. It represented the state of the art as far as toy castles were concerned.

Seven years later, 1973 was a big year, as they brought out five castles. They introduced "cleaned up" versions of the three they had brought out seven years earlier. In fact, they issued two of them without their tower extensions, and one with a cleaned up gateway. These were given numbers in sequence, directly next to the original numbers, which implies they knew all along that they were going to do this.

One of the new ones was No.9715. This was a large castle, something like No.9731, but the gateway was of the new model and it had a round tower at the apex of the buildings.

Then, in 1975 and 1976, they introduced two forts overlapping in style. The first was No.9741, called *"Burg Brauneck"* and had two courtyards. The yard at the front was entered via a massive gatehouse and had a reasonably large circular tower at the corner. The inner courtyard was reached via the first courtyard and another gatehouse, and had two large houses with an imposing circular tower, a chapel, and a reasonably large square tower.

The second was No.9740, which was a direct copy of the inner courtyard of *"Burg Brauneck,"* with an added approach ramp.

Finally, six years later in 1982, just before the company went under, they brought out for general release a middle-sized castle, which had no number. It had previously, in 1975, been on the market in a big department store, probably made exclusively for them. Behind the by-now-standard gateway, the way in wound its way up and around a circular tower into the courtyard, where there were two large houses and a chapel.

There were two others which must be placed in this series, but they have no date of issue. They were No.9722 and No.9745(ii). The latter represents another blunder, because No.9745 was also the number of the "Water Fort."

ELASTOLIN TOY FORTS : 9722 & 9745 Series
1975 to c1983

NO.	DESCRIPTION	DATE	DIMENSIONS	DISTINCTIVE FEATURES
9722 (3-081)	**unplaced in this series** (illustrated in Elastolin catalogue) eg: *Figuren Magazin*, D	unknown	30¾"x21¾"x?" 780x550x?mm	• 1-piece castle • vacuum-formed structure • two gateways & two courtyards • 4 houses & 3 towers (1 square)
9745ii (3-082)	**unplaced in this series** (illustrated in Elastolin catalogue) eg: *Figuren Magazin*, D	unknown	30"x24¾"x?" 760x630x?mm	• 1-piece castle • vacuum-formed structure • house, outbuildings & 3 towers • central gateway, lg court w/well

No.9722 was a large castle built up around two courtyards. With its two gatehouses, each with its drawbridge, and three towers, one with an extension, it could easily be defended. No.9745(ii) was a more open affair with a well in the middle of the only courtyard. It, too, could have been defended. It had four towers of varying heights, one at each corner, but no extension.

I think they must have come quite late on the scene, because they are the two largest of the vacuum-formed castles. Clearly, they were really beginning to get the hang of this style of production. One might say it was a bit late in the day.

Looking at these castles altogether, one can see how they were perfect for 40mm figures and their siege equipment. Whether the children playing with them were conscious of this or not is irrelevant. If they had only 70mm figures

3-074

3-075

3-076

3-077

3-074 **Elastolin No.9731** *(catalogue)*
3-075 **Elastolin No.9733**
3-076 **Elastolin No.9735**
3-077 **Elastolin No.9715**

No.9715 (3-077) is the only one of the four that came out in 1973 that was completely new. Compared to any of the previous castles in the series, it was hardly more than a lightly fortified farm. The gateway shows the innovative design in practice. It was made in two parts and stuck together afterwards.

No.9731 (3-074) came out in 1973 and is a revision of their 1963 version, replacing it (3-071). This one has a more effective gate.

No.9733 (3-075) also came out in 1973, and replaced No.9732 (3-072). The only difference was that there was no tower extension piece.

No.9735 (3-076) also came out in 1973, and replaced No.9734 (3-073). The only difference is that this one did not have a tower extension piece either.

3-080

3-078

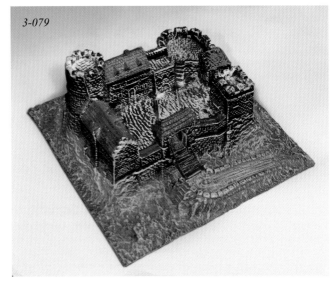

3-079

3-078 **Elastolin No.9741**: *"Burg Brauneck" (catalogue)*
3-079 **Elastolin No.9740**
3-080 **Elastolin unnumbered**

No.9741 (3-078) was issued in 1975, strangely, before No.9740 (3-079), which is in effect part of it. It was named "Burg Brauneck." It has a formidable gateway and a forecourt, which would have been accommodation for the castle's forces and a serious challenge to anyone coming in that way. Over another moat and through the second gateway was the more residential part of the castle, all protected by a tall tower (with an extension).

No.9740 (3-079) is a duplicate of half of "Burg Brauneck" (or was half of "Burg Brauneck" a duplicate of this one?). Since this was brought out a year later, in 1976, it would appear to be the "spin-off"; maybe we will never know. This one had no tower extension.

The unnumbered one (3-080) was brought out in 1982, just before the company folded, though it may have been sitting on a shelf earlier. It is said to have been on sale in a department store earlier, in 1975. Who knows what sort of arrangements they had with individual stores?

3-081

Unknown & 1964

3-081 **Elastolin No.9722** *(Catalogue)*
3-082 **Elastolin No.9745ii** *(Catalogue)*
3-083 **Elastolin No.9780** *four set up together (Courtesy Figuren Magazin)*
3-084 **Elastolin No.9780**: *"Sternschanze (Catalogue)*

Two of these forts are from the series of all-in-one, single-piece castles. The other is a fortification from later in history.

Nos.9780 was brought out in 1964. It was something completely different, representing a fortification from a different period. Hauser tried it out to see if there was a market for it. As it turned out, although it was a nice idea, the market was just not there and they withdrew it from the catalogue in 1967.

No.9780 x 4 is an example of how four No.9780 units might look together.

The date of release of No.9722 is not known. The design of the castle, with its two gateways and two courtyards, is really defensible, and shows many of the features that Hausser developed, so probably came quite late onto the scene. For example, it has a large square tower which does not feature in the series until the release of "Burg Brauneck" in 1975.

Nos.9745ii(3-082) is the other undated castle. It is a bit more peaceful than one or two others, particularly when compared with No.9722.

3-082

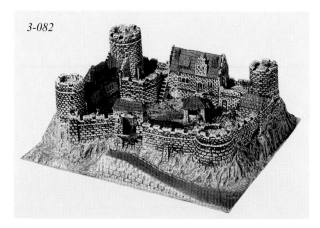

3-083

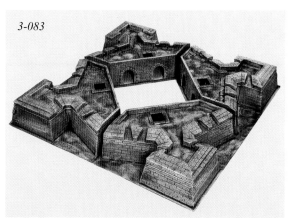

3-084

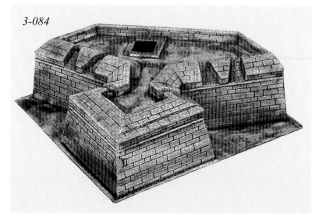

and a smaller-scale castle, this did not prevent them from playing. They just carried on regardless.

Castles of a Later Period in History

Hausser, for a short period 1964–1967, produced a different sort of fortification. It was a completely new thing for collectors. Not a fort with towers, gates, and battlements, as in the conventional style, but a simple, angular fortification. It went perfectly with the 40mm Landsknechts, the artillery that went with them, and the 40mm mercenaries in knights' armour from the period.

Huge walls, deep and wide ditches – these were the new bastions that the landed gentry had built at strategic locations. With the increasing use of gunpowder, and with field artillery becoming ever more powerful in the 15th century, the old fortifications had to be reinforced. These were built in front of existing old fortifications such as gates and city walls.

ELASTOLIN TOY FORT: 9780
1964 to 1967

NO.	DESCRIPTION	DATE	DIMENSIONS	DISTINCTIVE FEATURES
9780 (3-083) (3-084)	**the only one of this series** (mentioned in Polks, NY, catalogue 1966) eg: *Figuren Magazin*, D	1964	25¼"x25¼"x?" 640x640x?mm	• vacuum-formed structure • star-shaped battlements • lg crenels & access below • arched way in from yard

Added to the walls, these large, additional projections allowed the defenders to put more men and artillery on top. They gained dominance over the field of fire from these positions. Big, funnel-shaped crenels were a feature of three defenses and, seen from above, they were star-shaped.

Hausser took as a model the Rosenberg fortification, which rises over the town of Kronach. They produced a substantial model of one wing designed by Josef Tonn, gave it No.9780, and named it *"Sternschanze."* To build a complete star, creating an enclosed courtyard, one needed four such pieces. This made for a fortification 1280mm square, which was quite realistic, but a bit big for a child's room.

The painting of these pieces was relatively easy. The light-colored raw material was covered in a darker, usually grey/green, varnish, which, while still wet, was gently wiped off again, leaving the joints expressed. The whole was finished with some green grass.

The relatively short period during which these fortifications were available from Hausser indicates that they did not prove very attractive to the customer. They withdrew them from the range in 1967.

So we come to the end of the Hausser story, the end of a sixty-year stint of wonderfully realistic toy forts. We know it ended in bankruptcy – they all do – but we do not know why. Maybe we will find out more as time goes on. We miss them.

FOUR

THE REST OF GERMANY:
Makers of Toy Forts to the World

From about 1800 until the First World War, there were very many firms in Germany producing toy forts and castles. I do not profess to be an expert on all of them, but I do have a number of the forts and know of a considerable number more. So this is going to be a review of the field, in a somewhat haphazard fashion, though I have tried to give it some structure by presenting them in a roughly chronological order.

Until the 1914–1918 war, with very few exceptions, Germany was the undisputed world market leader in the production of toys. Of course, this included the production of toy forts and castles. For the fifteen years after the war, things got somewhat more difficult for them. There was growing competition, raging inflation in the country, the world depression, and the rise of the Third Reich.

Then came the 1939–1945 war, and after it the occupation of many of the toy making regions by Russia. Although they made a slow recovery, this spelled the end of their domination.

This chapter does not include the products of Gottschalk or the Hausser brothers, which are the subjects of separate, dedicated chapters.

The first forts, identifiable as such, were part of villages made up of small blocks of wood. These blocks formed the houses of the settlement and one or two major buildings, such as churches and the town hall. Occasionally, there was a large fortified house or the ruins of one.

Then came the forts made up of many pieces that could be assembled into specific forts. These were by manufacturers unknown to me, although I do have some examples.

Christian Hacker started to make forts about 1850. Moritz Gottschalk came onto the scene about 1870, closely followed by Emil Schubert. They led the way for wooden forts. About the same time, manufacturers in metal came on the scene. Rock and Graner and, to a slightly lesser extent, the firms of Lutz and Marklin started production.

By this time, several firms started producing wooden forts, with Carl Moritz Reichel, Emil Weise, Richter and Wittich, and Emil Rudolph leading the opposition to Moritz Gottschalk. Weise was taken over by Carl Krause, and he and Weber came in about 1900.

Then began a mad rush led by the distributors Oscar Beier, Carl Nötzel, Moko, and others. I do not know the names of the manufacturers they represented, but their work is well known. They were swiftly followed by the rise of the firms of Albin Schönherr and Emil Hinkelmann, who were manufacturers. Together with Moritz Gottschalk, these were the backbone of the German toy industry as far as toy forts and castles were concerned.

The First World War came and things slowed up a bit, at least for the duration. After the war, however, Moritz Gottschalk's heirs were still going strong and, accompanied by Richter and Wittich, Emil Hinkelmann, and Emil Schubert, continued to produce. Emil Neubert was a newcomer, as was the firm of Hausser Brothers.

They continued, through the disastrous national inflation, until the World Recession of 1929–1930, which had the effect of making exports difficult. With the rise of the Third Reich, the focus on modern defenses became paramount until once again World War loomed. By 1942, this had a cataclysmic effect on the production of toy forts and the market collapsed completely.

The industry recovered slowly after the war. This was a time when Germany was split into eastern and western zones. In the west, it was not until the early 1950s that Elastolin came back, supported by the firms of Eco and Big Plastik. In the east VEB Holzspielwaren and the various nationalized industries struggled to get going again.

By the middle of the 1980s, the coming of television and computers had put an end to it all. Now older children could create their own environments, and the gaming aspects of it had a dynamic fascination.

Static three-dimensional toy forts and castles became objects for the very young.

In the Beginning

Early in the nineteenth century, the first manufactured toy forts and castles appeared. They were elements in the sets of small wood blocks cut into the shape of buildings (4-002, 4-003 & 4-006), which were to be laid out as miniature towns and villages.

Each set contained a number of houses, usually in two sizes, and one or two special buildings. Most common among these buildings – sometimes made out of more than one piece – were churches, civic buildings, and gatehouses, but forts and castles (or the ruins of them) were also sometimes included (4-005).

Small castles were also made and sold separately. Later, some of these had tiny toy soldiers to man them. They may have been sold as cake decorations – they were small enough.

About the same time, the same basic technology was being applied to the production of building blocks – usually wood cubes that were to be stacked together to form quite large buildings (4-007). The idea was to provide blocks of a generic nature intended to be used in the creation of many different buildings.

The more sophisticated sets had blocks cut as roofs, arches, and columns, and it was only a small step from here – usually by the provision of a few crenulated blocks – to sets specifically made for constructing forts and castles. These had the added advantage of falling down with splendid realism when bombarded by toy cannon.

Some of these are still being sold today.

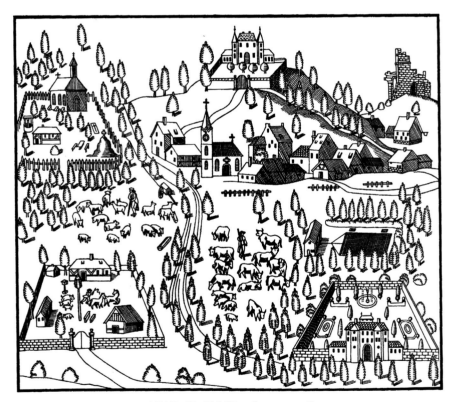

4-001 **Bestelmeier catalogue (1803):** *No.916 "Very large scene"*
This is a very large village set by Georg Hieronymus Bestelmeier of Nuremberg from about 1800. This is so large it is difficult to imagine it for sale as such. It may have been made up of various smaller sets – a village set, a couple of large house sets, a church set, and two or three farm sets, for example. Note the ruinous fortress on the hill (rear right), and the large houses (rear center and right front), either of which could have been fortified.

4-002

4-003

4-002 **From a sample book:** *large town*
4-003 **Unidentified manufacturer:** *town blocks*
(Courtesy Noel Barrett Auctions)
These are typical of the sort of blocks available about 1840. They do not include a fortress or castle, but those may have been sold separately.
The blocks could be arranged in any order, according to the whim of the player. Whether you could make a town, village, or farm, and whether it could be fortified or not depended on how many blocks you had.
Blocks like these, or developed from them, are still available today.

1800 to the Present

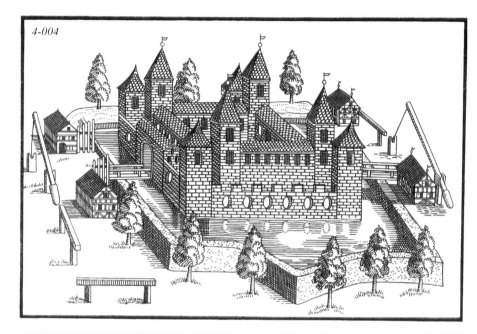

4-004

4-007

4-005

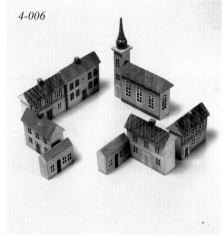

4-006

4-004 Bestelmeier catalogue (1803): *No.830 "Fortress"*
4-005 Example from a sample book: *ruined castle*
4-006 Unidentified manufacturer: *more modern town*
4-007 Unidentified manufacturer: *castle blocks*

The fortress (4-004) and the ruined castle (4-005) are examples of major buildings in the village or town sets. These come from catalogues of about 1800 and 1840.

The small photograph of the more modern town buildings (4-006) shows how the tradition continues.

The castle blocks (4-007), which are incomplete, are typical of the time. They have doors, windows, loopholes, roofs, and other details on their various faces so that a realistic castle could be created. These blocks also have the effect of falling down most realistically when attacked with guns.

The First Real Pioneers

About 1850, most of the surviving early examples of small towns had evolved away from this generic concept and were designed to represent specific, mostly real buildings. This meant that the blocks had to be assembled in one particular configuration, coincidently making them something more in the nature of a puzzle with a unique solution.

One such was *"The Siege of Sebastopol"* (4-010), also named *"Die Belagerung von Sebastopol,"* and *"La Siège de Sebastopol."* This fort celebrated the famous, if somewhat indecorous, victory in the Crimean War of 1854–55. It was also produced, again in three languages, as *"The Attack on the Lion Tower"* (4-011), *"Der Sturm auf die Löwenburg,"* and *"L'escalade du Fort-des-Lions."* Which came first is a bit of a mystery, but the fort was identical in each.

UNIDENTIFIED
c1860

NO.	DESCRIPTION	DATE	DIMENSIONS	DISTINCTIVE FEATURES
unknown (4-008, 4-009, 4-010 & 4-012)	**one in this series** (identified by an example in the ownership below) eg: SOFIA Foundation, CY	c1860	15¾"x15¾"x15½" 400x400x395mm	• The Siege of Sebastopol • 72 blocks & 5 flags • one building, five square towers • three floors
unknown (4-011)	**one in this series** (identified by an example in the ownership below) eg: Gisbert Freber, D	c1860	15¾"x15¾"x15½" 400x400x395mm	• The Attack on the Lion Tower • 72 blocks & 5 flags • one building, five square towers • three floors

The toy is made of seventy-two wooden components (4-009), covered with lithographed paper, and five flag poles with flags flying. When assembled, it measures 15½" (395mm) high (not counting the flagpoles) and 15¾" x 15¾" (400 x 400mm) square (at the bottom of the base).

It is erected on its base, which is formed of four sloping pieces of wood, joined in two pairs by brass hinges. The two unhinged ends are joined together by threading a stiff wire through four cloth loops at each corner – two fixed to each end. The whole is then firmed up by a square platform piece, which sits on small ledges just inside and at the top of the side pieces.

The superstructure is built of vertical slabs mitred at the corners (4-008). This style of construction, which is designed to be destroyed or, at least, severely damaged by toy guns, collapses very realistically bit by bit.

It is somewhat monochromal dressed brownstone, with strongly expressed quoins and window surrounds of a lighter stone. Apart from the very bright red, orange, and gold flags, the only colors are in the windows on the upper floor, where muted red window bars and light green curtains can be seen with doors that are green with ornate gold handles. The doors on the ground floor are brown, sporting a magnificent gold lion.

4-008 **Unidentified manufacturer**: *The Siege of Sebastopol*
This was an interesting toy that combined traditional features of a toy fort with those of two other traditional toys – wooden building blocks and puzzles. The former, which required a certain amount of constructional understanding and manual dexterity, could be built in any form that the user wished. This became especially true in this case, when the toy fort blocks were combined with some plain wooden blocks – otherwise it could be sensibly put together with only minor variations. In this respect it was more in the nature of the second traditional toy – a puzzle, which by definition has only one solution. However, unlike a conventional jig-saw, this one is fully three-dimensional and definitely not interlocking.

4-009 **Unidentified manufacturer**: *"The Siege of Sebastopol" – the pieces*
4-010 **Unidentified manufacturer**: *"The Siege of Sebastopol" – the box top*
4-011 **Unidentified manufacturer**: *"The Attack on the Lion" –Tower*
4-012 **Unidentified manufacturer**: *"The Siege of Sebastopol" – the box & pieces*

   The pieces laid out like this (4-009) give a clear impression of how many there were and their relative sizes.

   The box tops (4-010 & 4-011) show the different graphics that the two types had. One appears to have been aimed at the British market, thus the portrayal of ships. The other appears to be aimed at the French, for which French uniforms take pride of place. The Attack on the Lion-Tower box was badly damaged and has been restored.

   The box, with the pieces in it, shows how there was just enough room for all of them.

Another fort made along the same lines and about this time was "Fort Ali Musjid." This was named after the first battle in the Second Afghan War (1878–1880), more commonly referred to as the Battle of Ali Masjid.

Its being in Afghanistan accounts for the small turrets at roof level attached to the main building, which in their profusion of pointed roofs could only have come from thereabouts, though I have no idea how this relates to the actual fort. All the photographs I can find of the actual fort show only a hill top or the fort after it was taken. To say it got a bit knocked about during the battle would be an understatement.

The manufacturer is unknown to me, but it is clearly made by competent craftsmen. The box is typically German, and the skill with which the contents are made is also German. This is particularly true of the figures, who, even though they are wearing Eastern type uniforms, were almost certainly made in the Erzgebirge region of Germany.

The forts are built up of many pieces, all of natural wood, which makes them ideal targets for the guns supplied with both sets. These guns, although made of wood, were both capable of being fired. Some of the blocks have windows made of colored paper, which were stuck in slight depressions in the wood.

UNIDENTIFIED
c1880

NO.	DESCRIPTION	DATE	DIMENSIONS	DISTINCTIVE FEATURES
unknown (4-013)	**the smallest of this series** (identified by an example in the ownership below) eg: SOFIA Foundation, CY	c1880	12½"x8¼"x2¾" 320x210x70mm	• Fort Ali Musjid (1) – 42 pieces • unfinished wood with windows • buildings arranged in a line • two circular towers
unknown (4-014)	**the largest of this series** (identified by an example in the ownership below) eg: SOFIA Foundation, CY	c1880	11¼"x11¼"x9" 285x285x230mm	• Fort Ali Musjid (2) – 127 pieces • unfinished wood with windows • buildings surrounding a courtyard • four circular towers

At least two versions were made, though there may have been more. They both sit upon a structure built-up of separate blocks. The larger is a square layout (4-014), while the smaller one is a line of buildings (4-013), as one might find along a street. The only reason for more than one version must have been price – having a range of forts available on the market.

Another example of this type of fort is the delightful small castle produced by the firm of Carl Brandt (4-015). The company started in Gossmitz in 1856 and continued well into the 20th century. They made all types of toys, but became

known over time for their production of building blocks. They made town blocks, country houses, and castles – all nicely boxed with a label that showed how they should be used; four versions of castles are known to have existed.

CARL BRANDT
c1900

NO.	DESCRIPTION	DATE	DIMENSIONS	DISTINCTIVE FEATURES
280, IV (4-015, 4-016 & 4-017)	**only one in this series** (identified by an example in the ownership below) eg: Musée du Jouet, Bxl. B	c1880	unknown	• sm castle puzzle/target by Carl Brandt • long ramp and drawbridge • buildings surrounding a courtyard • 60 painted blocks one circular tower

Their small fort – it only measures about 6" x 6" x 6" (150 x 150 x 150mm) with a ramp extension of about another 6" (150mm) – is a really quite realistic model. The buildings are made of about fifty-five pieces of painted wood with the base covered in bark. The windows and doorways are cut out.

4-013 **Unidentified manufacturer**: *"Fort Ali Musjid" small size*
The "Fort Ali Musjid" above is the small-size version of the larger one on the next page. It is quite unrealistic in its layout, being a line of buildings, no doubt excellent for target practice, but not much else. It is a little fort-like, however, in that there are more battlements and fewer turrets.

4-014

4-015

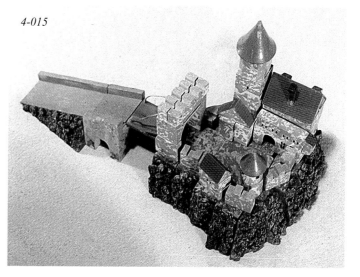

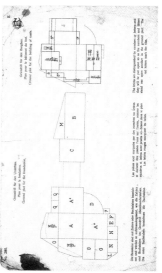

4-014 Unidentified manufacturer: "Fort Ali Musjid" large size

4-015 Carl Brandt: Small fort (above) and its instructions for assembly (below)

The "Fort Ali Musjid" large version is much more plausible than the smaller version. What the fort actually looked like is in question, but I doubt it was like this. Can you imagine a building like this in the wilds of the Kyber Pass in the latter part of the 19th century? More likely, it was something much more militaristic and basic.

The small castle by Brandt (4-015) has all the charm of something small and well made. It is difficult to imagine shooting at it with guns, but, if the box is to be believed, they did. It is a multiple toy just like "The Siege of Sebastopol."

Forts Made of Metal

Sometime around 1875, the manufacturers in metal became a force to be reckoned with. They tended to manufacture very large pieces, often with a water feature, such as a lake or a fountain. They tended towards the spectacular – more to be looked at and admired than played with (4-018).

Probably the first on the scene was Rock and Graner of Biberach in Baden-Wuerttemberg, established in 1813. They produced dolls, piggy banks, carriages, ships, and a few castles. Their castle production developed enormously after Henry Graner died in 1877. Their output was substantial for about thirty years, until toy trains really took off.

They specialized in large, rocky mountain scenes with buildings, including castles. Often they had lakes and fountains, and occasionally small trains. It seems unlikely that the trains were operational, but the fountains most certainly were.

ROCK & GRANER: Metal Forts
c1872 to 1910

NO.	DESCRIPTION	DATE	DIMENSIONS	DISTINCTIVE FEATURES
unknown (4-020)	"Mountain Castle" (photographs supplied by Peter Kirk [dec'd]) eg: Prague Museum, CSK	unknown	unknown	• castle & six houses on mountain • train and village below • small harbour & park also below • central important house
809 (4-023)	"Burg" (illustrated in Rock& Graner catalogue) eg: no known example	unknown	unknown	• major castle with lake below • gatehouse on island in lake • two towers + connecting bridge • farm on meadow below
2068 (4-022)	"Water Castle" (illustrated in Rock & Graner catalogue) eg: no known example	unknown	25½"x18"x18½" 650x460x470mm	• very large castle 3 towers on hill • dbridge to gatehouse on 2nd hill • water mill below at harborside • lakeside buildings and fountain
1863	"Hill, lake and fountain" (illustrated in Rock& Graner catalogue) eg: no known example	unknown	unknown	• large castle on hill & gatehouse • drawbridge to adjacent hill • tunnel through hill with castle • lakeside building and fountain
2219 (4-018)	"Bergpartine No.6½" (illustrated in Rock& Graner catalogue) eg: no known example	unknown	unknown	• large church & house on hilltop • settlement of houses below • watermill and industrial buildings • lake w/fountain, boat, fish, & swan

In 1846, Ludwig Lutz of Ellwangen started his company producing metal wreaths and some toys. By about 1870, they started making toy castles. At first, they made castles with the craggy scenery of Rock and Graner and with the water features. Later forts were designed to stand on the floor and, without fountains and hills, to have scenery, if there was to be some, added to them.

2219. Halbe Größe. Bergparthie 6½.

4-018 Rock and Graner catalogue: *2216 Bergparthie No.6½*

Rock and Graner specialized in water effects. This is clearly demonstrated in this "fort." It has a fountain and a water wheel, not to mention a substantial lake with fish and a swan along with two men in a boat. The fact that they are all to a different scale does not seem to be important.

At the bottom of the hill there is a working settlement, while at the top there is sizeable church and a house of some measure. Then there are buildings for look-out and defense that come into the category of forts and castles with which we are concerned.

4-020

c.1850-c.1910

4-021

4-022

2068 Festung Nº 7
2069 ditto   " 8 lang 65 breit 46 hoch 47
            Centimètres.

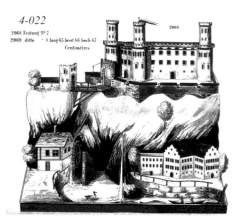

4-023

4-020 **Rock & Graner**: *Mountain castle (Courtesy Peter Kirk)*
4-021 **Unidentified maker**: *Remnant from a scene*
4-022 **Rock & Graner catalogue**: *2068 Festung No.8*
4-023 **Rock & Graner catalogue**: *No.809 Burg*

The mountain scene (4-020) is typical of the production of Rock and Graner about 1880. Apart from the seven houses of different sizes and functions, there is a railway, roads, a small park, and a harbour.

The remnant from a scene (4-021) is one such house, although the scene cannot be identified. The windows are glazed, and the chimney is operational, so that it may be lighted with a candle.

The two extracts from the catalogue (4-022 & 4-023) show castles on hilltops with lakes plus their fountains, boats, ducks, and fish below.

These were suitable for use with the toy soldiers, which were becoming much more available. They were made to a scale which was more appropriate, and provided a suitable object for a siege – or somewhere to defend. What is more, a flat surface, such as a floor on which they stood, provided the perfect base for the soldiers because of their flat bases.

LUDWIG LUTZ: Metal Forts
c1870 to 1891

NO.	DESCRIPTION	DATE	DIMENSIONS	DISTINCTIVE FEATURES
unknown (4-024)	**grand house** (illustrated in Ludwig Lutz catalogue) eg: no known example	c1880	unknown	• formal hill w/garden on top • metal construction • fountain in garden •3-storey house & 2 wings
unknown (4-025)	**house with rock garden** (illustrated in Ludwig Lutz catalogue) eg: no known example	c1880	unknown	• lake w/fountain & ducks • big rocky garden • steps up via summer house • modest 2-storey house on top
unknown (4-026)	**hill w/house & railway** (illustrated in Ludwig Lutz catalogue) eg: no known example	c1880	unknown	• rocky hill with path • imposing 5-bay mansion • circular railway under • farmyard & animals below
unknown	**working quay** (illustrated in Ludwig Lutz catalogue) eg: no known example	unknown	unknown	• waterfall from lake with bridge • three buildings in background • various industrial types on quay • fountain in the harbour
unknown	**mountain scene** (illustrated in Ludwig Lutz catalogue) eg: no known example	unknown	unknown	• mountain and lake below • large palace on mountain top • bandstand, park, & house below • train running through mountain
1242	**castle** (illustrated in Ludwig Lutz catalogue) eg: no known example	c1885	17¼"x17"x19" 440x430x480mm	• central approach & gateway • courtyard w/4 corner towers • large central circular tower • circular tower on central tower
1244 (4-028) (4-029)	**soldier carousel castle** (illustrated in Ludwig Lutz catalogue) eg: no known example	c1885	19¾"x18½"x13¾" 500x470x350mm	• large castle with soldier carousel • three levels with terraces • three circular towers • tunnel through the castle
1245 (4-027) (4-034) (4-038)	**castle** (listed in Ludwig Lutz catalogue) eg: Christies Auction, UK	c1880	24½"x21"x27½" 620x530x700mm	• central approach & gate • courtyard w/4 corner towers • cent bldg w/2 flanking rect twrs • sq penthouse w/circ tower on top

They were known for the high quality of their toys, which included trains, boats, and other toys as well as castles, until they were bought out by Gebruder Märklin in 1891.

The firm of Friedrich Wilhelm Märklin was started in 1859 at Göppingen in Baden-Wuerttemberg, close to Rock and Graner. Initially they produced dollhouse furniture, gradually branching out into larger toys. In the 1890s, they began with toy trains and have become known world wide as manufacturers in that field.

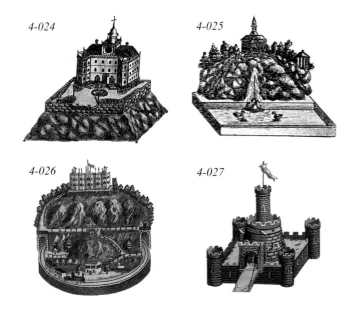

4-024   *4-025*   *4-026*   *4-027*

4-024 **Lutz catalogue:** *Grand house with formal garden*
4-025 **Lutz catalogue**: *House on hill with fountain and lake*
4-026 **Lutz catalogue**: *Mountain with railway in tunnel below*
4-027 **Lutz catalogue**: *Fort No.1242*

The two black and white illustrations (4-024 & 4-025) are from an earlier catalogue than the colored illustrations. Silber & Fleming of Wood Street in London had the Grand House with the Formal Garden in their catalogue in 1884. It is probably safe to say that they were both available in 1884 if not earlier.

The two illustrated underneath were from a later catalogue. The mountain (4-026) shows that Lutz was producing in the same style as Rock and Graner, as well as more military forts.

The Fort No.1242 (4-027) demonstrates a very different style, almost certainly prompted by the rise in the toy soldier industry. It would be difficult to imagine playing with forts like this to be anything but based on military operations. These where what Gebruder Märklin wanted when they took over the Lutz affairs in 1891.

There was a period, however, about 1880 to 1910, when they produced toy castles as well as trains. This was a relatively small part of their production until they bought out Ludwig Lutz in 1891. Then, with some of Lutz's skilled workers, many of Lutz's forts were taken over without change, given a new number, and put directly in the Märklin catalogue. From about 1895, for fifteen years, the firm of Gebruder Märklin produced a fine range of metal toy forts.

4-029

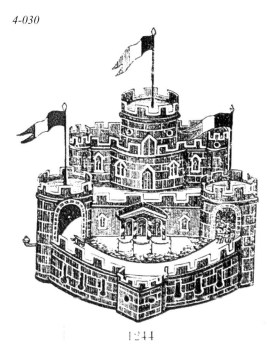

4-030

1244

4-031

4-028

4-028 **Ludwig Lutz:** *Fort No.1244 (catalogue)*
4-029 **Ludwig Lutz**: *Fort No.1244*
4-030 **Gebruder Märklin**: *Fort No.1244 (catalogue)*
4-031 **Gebruder Märklin** *(Courtesy Noel Barrett Auctions)*

Here we have the full story of the takeover of Ludwig Lutz by Gebruder Märklin. This was a remarkable toy (4-029) in that it combined a music box and a ring around which troops of the player's choosing could parade. It was designed by Lutz more to be looked at than played with. The ring was actually a disc which rotated under a fixed, somewhat smaller disc. This left a ring about 2" (50mm) wide around the outside on which the troops were set up. The idea was to put your parade of toy soldiers on it so they could "march"

round through the opening on the one side, through the castle, and out again via the opening on the other side. None of this was changed by Märklin.

Actually Märklin changed as little as possible (4-031), and all of it in the paint work. Note the following: i) the scale of the stonework was changed; ii) the windows are completely different although their distribution remains, except in the top tower; iii) the gun ports are differently spaced, and replace the port holes in the extension, although this does not apply in their catalogue illustration; iv) the stonework around the openings is no longer red; v) the painting of the portico is more in keeping with their guardhouses. The overall effect is one of greater realism. The Märklin catalogue (4-030) illustration is taken from 1895, just three years after the takeover.

GEBRUDER MÄRKLIN: Metal Forts
c1870 to 1910

NO.	DESCRIPTION	DATE	DIMENSIONS	DISTINCTIVE FEATURES
1244 (4-030) (4-031)	soldier carousel castle (listed in Noel Barrett's auction catalogue) eg Noel Barrett Auctions, US	c1891	19¾"x18½"x13¾" 500x470x350mm	• large castle with soldier carousel • three levels with terraces • three circular towers • tunnel through the castle
3820	very large castle complex (listed in Gebruder Märklin catalogue L9-1909 p.123) eg: no known example	c1907	53¾"x41¼"x26½" 1360x1050x670mm	• large castle with 2 soldier carousels • 2 main buildings 1 castle, 1 barracks • three level castle with central tower • lower barracks building & 3 levels
8104	explodable fort (listed in Gebruder Märklin catalogue 1909) eg: no known example	c1909	21"x6¼"x15" 530x160x380mm	• castle on a mountain top • central tower and two wing towers • all collapses under fire
8131	castle (listed in Gebruder Märklin catalogue M9-1909 p.524) eg: no known example	c1907	15¾"x11¾"x19¼" 400x300x490mm	• fort designed to stand on floor • operating drawbridge from gateway • two storey main building • two towers on the roof
8132 (4-032)	castle (listed in Gebruder Märklin catalogue M9-1909 p.524) eg: C Kohler Auctions, CH	c1904	15¾"x11¾"x16½" 400x300x420mm	• fort designed to stand on floor • operating drawbridge & two towers • main building with two wings • circular central tower on the roof
8133	castle (listed in Gebruder Märklin catalogue M9-1909 p.525) eg: no known example	c1907	20"x19"x15¾" 510x480x400mm	• fort designed to stand on floor • operating drawbridge & two towers • large courtyard with corner towers • square central tower on the roof
8134	castle (listed in Gebruder Märklin catalogue M9-1909 p.525) eg: no known example	c1904	20"x18½"x16½" 510x470x420mm	• large barbican & internal gateway • large courtyard with corner towers • two storey main building w/stairs • circular central tower on the roof
8135	castle (listed in Gebruder Märklin catalogue M9-1909 p.525) eg: no known example	c1895	17¼"x17"x19" 440x430x480mm	• fort designed to stand on floor • 1st floor courtyard with four towers • circular main bldg & sloping sides • tall circular central tower on the roof
8136 (4-033) (4-034)	castle (listed in Gebruder Märklin catalogue M9-1909 p.525) eg: Allen Hickling Toy Forts	1895	24½"x21"x27½" 620x530x700mm	• fort designed to stand on floor • 1st floor courtyard with two towers • square main bldg & flanking towers • square upper level circ central tower
8141	castle/fortress (listed in Gebruder Märklin catalogue L9-1909 p.525) eg: no known example	c1905	30¼"x18½"x19¾" 770x470x500mm	• removable barracks & wood towers • only one drawbridge
8142	castle/fortress (listed in Gebruder Märklin catalogue L9-1909 p.525) eg: no known example	c1905	35½"x25½"x21½" 900x650x550mm	• removable barracks & wood towers • brook and one drawbridge
8143	castle/fortress (listed in Gebruder Märklin catalogue L9-1909 p.525) eg: no known example	c1905	39¾"x30¼"x23" 1010x770x580mm	• three-level hill • removable barracks & wood towers • three buildings & four towers • brook and two drawbridges
8144/1	castle/fortress (listed in Gebruder Märklin catalogue L9-1909 p.525) eg: no known example	c1906	29½"x23¾"x17" 750x550x480mm	• medium hill with landscaping
8144/2	castle/fortress (listed in Gebruder Märklin catalogue L9-1909 p.525) eg: no known example	c1906	39¼"x30"x23¼" 1000x760x590mm	• large hill with landscaping • two buildings and two towers
8146/1	fort (listed in Gebruder Märklin catalogue L10-1910 p.664) eg: no known example	unkwn	21½"x15¾"x15" 550x400x380mm	• wood and tin with drawbridge • main building and entrance • two square flanking/corner towers • provision for electric light
8146/2	fort (listed in Gebruder Märklin catalogue L10-1910 p.664) eg: no known example	unkwn	27½"x19¼"x17¾" 700x490x450mm	• wood and tin with drawbridge • main building and entrance • two square flanking/corner towers • provision for electric light
8146/3	fort (listed in Gebruder Märklin catalogue L10-1910 p.664) eg: no known example	unkwn	33½"x22¾"x17¾" 850x580x450mm	• wood and tin with drawbridge • main building and entrance • two square flanking/corner towers • provision for electric light
8147	castle/palace (listed in Gebruder Märklin catalogue L10-1910 p.664) eg: no known example	unkwn	38½"x28¾"x23½" 980x730x600mm	• entrance with drawbridge • castle with two tin wings • two circular wing towers • four square corner towers of wood

There were others of course, but they were relatively small-time when it came to forts. Georges Carrette and Gebruder Bing were two of the better known names to be involved, but their interests lay predominantly elsewhere; they were mainly concerned with toy trains.

4-032 Gebruder Märklin: *Fort No.1832*
This is a typical example of Gebruder Märklin's product. It is missing its small central turret on the roof, but is complete otherwise.
It was modeled on the Ludwig Lutz No.1247, and was probably on the market earlier than 1904, but I have no evidence for that. Although the bright red door surround is a typical Lutz feature, I still think this was by Märklin – maybe an early example.

4-033

4-034

4-036

4-035

4-033 **Gebruder Märklin**: *Fort no.1836 (catalogue)*
4-034 **Lutz No.1245** or **Märklin No.1836**: *Upper section of the fort only*
4-035 **Unidentified manufacturer**: *Fort (Courtesy Rob Wilson)*
4-036 **Ludwig Lutz**: *Fort no.1245 (catalogue)*

These are typical examples of the work of Lutz, Märklin, and others. The three Lutz or Märklin examples (4-033, 4-034 &4-036) are of the same fort, which was one of the more popular they produced. It was certainly large enough for play with small toy soldiers and would not have looked amiss with the somewhat larger ones that Britains started making about 1894.

The castle by the unknown manufacturer (4-035) is much more realistic. It is also a smaller scale, so is not in the same league. However, it does have a certain charm about it, and it would have been possible to play with 10mm soldiers.

The First Conventional Toy Forts of Wood

When I name these toy forts "conventional," I mean that they came as parts in a box, which when turned over became the hill on which the fort was erected. Among these, we have to remember Moritz Gottschalk, who has a chapter of his own. He was indeed one of the first. This chapter is about some others.

One of the first, if not the first, was Christian Hacker. He was Moritz Gottschalk's main competition in the early years. He set up his factory in Nuremberg in 1835, and started producing first-class dollhouses, rooms, shops, and stables, but the first known fortress was listed in the account books of the company in 1848.

In 1865, he went into partnership with his son George. When George died in 1882, the firm went rapidly downhill until it was sold to Chistoph Kalb in 1885. Through various owners, in various combinations, the company continued strongly from then until it finally folded in 1927.

Christian Hacker sold toys all over Europe and the rest of the world. He supplied directly to shops in Paris, London, and New York, and to many others through specialist distributors. Although these comprised mostly dollhouses and related rooms, shops, and stables at a large scale, there were, nonetheless, a number of forts from the very large to the relatively small. All of these were at the highest level of the market, which was reflected in the relative complexity of finish.

The earliest image we have is one from a wholesalers catalogue dated 1885 (4-037). Only one fort, the largest, is illustrated, though there were eleven different sizes offered, ranging from 11" x 9¾" (280 x 250mm) to 29" x 29½" (740 x 750mm), and in price from 2.80 marks to 27.00 marks.

CHRISTIAN HACKER
1865 to c1915

NO.	DESCRIPTION	DATE	DIMENSIONS	DISTINCTIVE FEATURES
unknown	**castle** (identified by an example in the ownership below) eg: Allen Hickling Toy Forts	unknown	14¾"x11"x18½" 375x280x420mm	• heavy base w/cork simulated rock • drawbridge to gate & central ramp • courtyard with two circ corner towers • two-storey main bldg with two wings
unknown (4-039)	**castle** (identified by an example in the ownership below) eg: Allen Hickling Toy Forts	unknown	25"x12"x25" 640x310x630mm	• heavy base w/cork simulated rock • drawbridge to gate & central ramp • courtyard with two circ corner towers • two-storey main bldg with two wings
288/1– 288/11 (4-037)	**fortress** (illustrated in a wholesalers (A Wahnschaffer) catalogue) eg: no known example	1885		• double ramp to dbridge & 2 towers • single ramp to gateway & courtyard • one 4-storey & one 2-storey building • large square tower
281/1– 281/2	**very small fort** (listed in Christian Hacker price list) eg: no known example	c1900		• simple four-sided design • ramp & tower with flags
288/1– 288/3	**fortress** (illustrated in Christian Hacker price list) eg: no known example	c1900	varies	• double ramp to drwbridge & 2 towers • single ramp to gateway & courtyard • one 4-storey & one 2-storey building • large square tower
289/1– 289/3 (4-038)	**real fortress** (illustrated in Christian Hacker price list) eg: no known example	c1900	varies	• single ramp to gateway & drawbridge • 2nd ramp up to main courtyard • two-storey main building • two large & two small square towers
309/0– 309/4 (4-040)	**castle** (identified by an example in the ownership below) eg: Baden Toy Museum, CH	c1900	varies	• large fort with simulated rock base • ramp to gateway with drawbridge • 2 main buildings 1 linked to sq tower • massive circ tower on raised base
310/0– 310/3	**smaller castle** (listed in Christian Hacker price list) eg: no known example	c1900	varies	• smaller simpler fort • similar ramp and smaller base • courtyard with simpler buildings • smaller circular tower
431	**castle** (listed in Christian Hacker price list) eg: no known example	c1900	26¾"x28¾"x29½" 680x730x800mm	• ramp up to first level • gateway and drawbridges • large sq & sm round & sq towers • one four-storey building and balcony
484/0– 484/3	**castle** (illustrated in Christian Hacker photo catalogue) eg: no known example	c1915	varies	• simulated rock base of cloth • ramp on 2 sides & drawbrge midway • a massive gate & one small tower • large four-storey half timbered house
502	**castle with clockwork** (illustrated in Christian Hacker photo catalogue) eg: no known example	1915	25½"x23½"x23½" 650x600x600mm	• very large simulated rock hill • clockwork in courtyard for soldiers • one large building in courtyard • half-timbered house on top of hill
505/1– 505/ (4-041)	**castle/fortress** (illustrated in Christian Hacker photo catalogue) eg: no known example	c1915	varies	• simulated rock base of cloth • ramp to gate to entrance yard • drawbridge to main yard & 2 towers • 3-storey house linked to sq tower
515	**very large castle/ fortress** (illustrated in Christian Hacker photo catalogue) eg: no known example	c1915	unknown	• two simulated rock hills using cloth • long ramp & 2 span bridge link • many buildings on both sides • four medium towers & one large one

Hacker kept track of his production by giving each model a number, usually handwritten on the underside of the item. This number had three digits and then an oblique with a single digit to indicate the size. It seems that this three-figure number did not change over the years. This is unlike Moritz Gottschalk, who had a separate number for each size and number, leading to very high numbers.

1885-c.1915

4-037

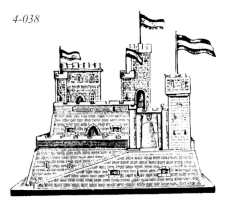

4-038

4-037 **Wholesaler** (catalogue 1885): No.288
4-038 **Christian Hacker** (price list c1900): No.289
4-039 **Christian Hacker**: early model
4-040 **Christian Hacker**: No.309
4-041 **Christian Hacker** (photo catalogue c1915): No.505

These illustrations give an idea of how Hacker's forts developed over the forty years leading up to the First World War. It is known that he was producing forts for thirty years prior to this, and for ten years after the war, but there are no records available. It seems unlikely, however, that he initially produced such a wide range, although it is only reasonable to assume that the quality would have been just as fine.

Of note is the treatment of the bases, moving from solid masonry in 1895 to the use of cloth to simulate natural rock in 1915. Also worthy of note is the introduction of exposed wood framing in the buildings, which takes away some of their stark military character.

That these were made to a much larger scale than much of his competition is clear, and, indeed, they were much larger in size, but what set these apart were their finishes. This, combined with the complexity of design, put them in a class of their own.

4-039

4-040

4-041

SORTING OUT WHO DID WHAT

It is really difficult to sort out the German manufacturers. Not only were they extremely prolific in their output, but it seems that they combined manufacturing with wholesaling and exporting – selling work other than their own. This is, of course, with the exception of Moritz Gottschalk and the Hausser Brothers, who, it appears, handled their own product.

Much of their documentation, such as advertising, catalogues and factory records, was destroyed in the turbulent environment in which they worked. This environment included two world wars – both of which they lost, sustaining severe damage – several other wars, a catastrophic national economy, the coming of the Third Reich, and occupation by the Russians. All in all, this was one hundred years of upheaval and change, all of which makes following their progress extremely difficult.

Besides this, there were so many of them. In many cases it is possible to identify a manufacturer, but not to know his or her name. This was an ideal situation for the emergence of wholesalers. They could save the prospective purchasers a lot of time and trouble by assembling a large range from different sources. Of course, they did not acknowledge their suppliers. This is complicated by the fact that the manufacturers often copied others' designs, leading to forts that were very similar (if not exactly the same). Those few who have written anything about them have virtually given up in despair. I sympathize.

For example, I have two complete catalogues – at least as far as forts are concerned – probably dating from before the First World War. One is from E. Emil Schubert published just before the war, and the other from D. H. Wagner & Sohn probably about 1900. Schubert's contains 21 models in 101 sizes, while D. H. Wagner's contains 38 models in 141 sizes. Wagner's catalogue has forts from Richter & Wittich, Hacker, Gottschalk, and Weber, or remarkably similar copies of them; Schubert's catalogue contains forts of Gottschalk, or copies of them. The problem of identifying manufacturers even extended to their advertising, where there are several examples of manufacturers using images of others' forts, without acknowledgment. This leads to confusion – not least in my mind.

4-042   4-043

4-044   4-045

These are a selection of castles in Wagner's and Schubert's catalogues that are the same as, or copies of, forts by other manufacturers. Clockwise from the top left they are: Gottschalk in Schubert's; Richter & Wittich, Gottschalk, and Hacker, all in Wagner's. There were many others by lesser manufacturers. Below is an example of their advertising – in this case Schubert using a Gottschalk image.

E. Emil Schubert Started Quite Early

E. Emil Schubert started his firm in 1874 in Grunhainichen, just about the same time that Moritz Gottschalk started to produce castles. Of course, like so many others, he did not manufacture only toy castles, but they were an important part of his operation.

From the start it was claimed that he was involved in the *"production of fortresses, stables and shops,"* but we have no evidence of forts from that time. The earliest examples are from about 1880 or perhaps a little earlier.

To my knowledge there is a small fort with glass in the windows (4-048), which was to be lighted by a candle. It is slightly burnt where this means of providing light got out of hand, broke a window, and destroyed the door, but is otherwise in quite good condition. It dates almost certainly to the 1880s, maybe a little earlier, and is almost certainly by Schubert. Two medium-sized castles (4-047 & 4-049), built in a similar way, were produced about this time or perhaps a little later. They have all the same detailing, even down to the approach pathways. The only difference is in the circular corner tower, variations of which were used by many manufacturers.

Two much bigger castles (4-050 & 4-051) were produced at a somewhat later date, probably about 1895, when the fragility of the glazing gave way to windows and doors painted on. These had fancy ramps, two drawbridges, and everything a grand palace should have.

EMIL SCHUBERT: The Early Days
c1880 to c1900

NO.	DESCRIPTION	DATE	DIMENSIONS	DISTINCTIVE FEATURES
unknown (4-048)	**the smallest of the series** (identified by an example in the ownership below) eg: Allen Hickling Toy Forts	c1880	14½"x10¼"x10½" 365x260x270mm	• simple ramp up one low level • gateway and drawbridge • walled courtyard with sq & circ towers • glazed main bldg lighted by candle
unknown (4-049)	**medium of this series** (identified by an example in the ownership below) eg: Bernd Zimmermann, D	c1885	unknown	• re-entrant ramp up one low level • sq tower, gateway, & dbridge on the turn • walled courtyard with sq & circ towers • 7-bay, 3-D glazed main bldg & 2 candles
unknown (4-047)	**medium of this series** (identified by an example in the ownership below) eg: Christies Auctions, UK	c1885	28½"x20½"x23¾" 725x520x605mm	• re-entrant ramp up one low level • sq tower, gateway & dbridge on the turn • walled courtyard with sq & circ towers • 9-bay, 3-D glazed main bldg & 2 candles
unknown (4-050)	**very large castle 1** (identified by an example in the ownership below) eg: Bernd Zimmermann, D	c1895	unknown	• twin re-entrant ramps up one high level • 2 main gateways & 2 with drawbridges • bright painted bldgs with 2 corner towers • long main bldg with 2 sq & 2 circ towers
unknown (4-051)	**very large castle 2** (identified by an example in the ownership below) eg: Bernd Zimmermann, D	c1895	unknown	• twin re-entrant ramps up one high level • 2 main gateways & 2 w/drawbridges • bright painted bldgs w/2 corner towers • long main bldg w/2 sq & 2 circ towers

4-047 Emil Schubert: *medium palace*
This is the largest of the early palaces with glazed windows. The smallest we have is illustrated on the next page. They are clearly from the same manufacturer, although the smaller one is older, which is evident in the finishes. They would have been part of a series, probably five or six, which would have ranged from the small to the quite large.

The window openings were cut out and a piece of glass, with drapes and glazing bars already painted on it, was stuck on the backside of the wall. The door was treated in the same way, but was not transparent. The source of lighting was then provided by two candles of the Christmas tree variety, a hole in the roof allowing the smoke to escape.

The figures are 30mm semi-flat horsemen of German origin.

4-050

4-048

4-049

4-051

4-048 **Emil Schubert***: small palace*
4-049 **Emil Schubert***: medium palace (Courtesy Bernd Zimmermann)*
4-050 **Emil Schubert***: very large palace 1 (Courtesy Bernd Zimmermann)*
4-051 **Emil Schubert***: very large palace 2 (Courtesy Bernd Zimmermann)*

These four examples represent the range of the series in both size and time.

The earliest is the small one on the left (4-048). The palace had a near call when fire broke out as a result of the candle burning out, which took a window and the door. Also something unfortunate happened to the crenellation on the front tower. The rest is in remarkably good condition.

The next (4-049) dates from slightly later, but still has glazed windows and the dreaded candle lighting. Again, the glass is substantially missing, though it seems that fire was not to blame on this occasion.

The dates of the two to the right are difficult to establish, but it is safe to say they are both later than the glazed ones. It would appear that the upper one (4-050) is very slightly larger and, of course, carries larger stencilled windows. The lower one (4-051) has lost its pediment, decorated with a black eagle, which was over the central section of the rear building. The low wall that lined the upper sections of the ramps is also missing.

The figures on the upper one are 40mm plastic knights by Merton, while those on the lower one are 48mm knights from the Spenkuch factory.

According to a catalogue from just before the First World War, Schubert had started to produce castles with more or less the same characteristics.

Three series dominated their production. They seem to have been brought out at separate times, although they were available in the same catalogue. They were the 100, the 700, and the 900 series, which are clearly related because of stylistic similarities. That is not to say they were the same, but they came from the same stable.

They were all on three levels, with the main buildings on the top level. The main differences lie in the form of the access ramps and the layout and form of the buildings at the entry level. At first, they had a simple built-in ramp, with no buildings on the entrance level. Next was a separate ramp with access, via a drawbridge, to the entrance level with buildings on it. The final development was a large curving ramp which doubled back on itself, with a building at the turn.

EMIL SCHUBERT: 100 Series
c1895 to c1915

NO.	DESCRIPTION	DATE	DIMENSIONS	DISTINCTIVE FEATURES
100/2 /0	**the smallest in this series** (listed in Emil Schubert catalogue) eg: no known example	c1895	15"x10"x11¾" 380x250x300mm	
100/0	**the second in this series** (listed in Emil Schubert catalogue) eg: no known example, D	c1895	16½"x10¼"x12½" 420x260x320mm	
100/1	**the third in this series** (listed in Emil Schubert catalogue) eg: no known example	c1895	19"x11"x13¾" 480x280x350mm	
100/1½ (4-052)	**the fourth in this series** (illustrated in Emil Schubert catalogue) eg: no known example	c1895	20"x12½"x15¾" 510x320x400mm	• integral ramp up to entrance yard • gateway, two sq towers & dbridge up • gateway to walled yard with circ tower • L-shaped main building & corner tower
100/2	**the fifth in this series** (listed in Emil Schubert catalogue) eg: no known example	c1895	22"x13"x19" 560x330x480mm	
100/3	**the sixth in this series** (listed in Emil Schubert catalogue) eg: no known example	c1895	25½"x15¾"x19¾" 650x400x500mm	
100/4	**the largest in this series** (listed in Emil Schubert catalogue) eg: no known example	c1895	25½"x25½"x20½" 650x650x520mm	

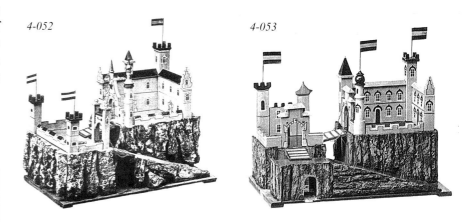

4-052

4-053

4-054

4-052 **Emil Schubert**: *100/1½ (catalogue)*
4-053 **Emil Schubert**: *700/3 (catalogue)*
4-054 **Emil Schubert**: *900/1 (catalogue)*

Catalogue examples of the new wave of castles produced by Emil Schubert about 1895–1910. They came out at intervals during the period. Major differences lie in the ramp and the lower courtyard.

EMIL SCHUBERT: 700 Series
c1905 to c1915

NO.	DESCRIPTION	DATE	DIMENSIONS	DISTINCTIVE FEATURES
700/0	**the smallest in this series** (listed in Emil Schubert catalogue) eg: no known example	c1905	15"x9½"x9¾" 380x240x250mm	
700/1	**the second in this series** (listed in Emil Schubert catalogue) eg: no known example, D	c1905	17"x11¾"x11¾" 430x300x300mm	
700/2	**the third in this series** (listed in Emil Schubert catalogue) eg: no known example	c1905	19¾"x12½"x13¾" 500x320x350mm	
700/3 (4-053)	**the fourth in this series** (illustrated in Emil Schubert catalogue) eg: no known example	c1905	22"x13¾"x15¾" 560x350x400mm	• partly integral ramp up to dbridge & gate • entry yard, bldg w/2 towers & dbridge up • gateway to walled yard with circ tower • L-shaped main building with tower
700/4	**the largest in this series** (listed in Emil Schubert catalogue) eg: no known example	c1905	25½"x14¼"x15¾" 650x360x400mm	

EMIL SCHUBERT: 900 Series
c1910 to c1915

NO.	DESCRIPTION	DATE	DIMENSIONS	DISTINCTIVE FEATURES
900/0	**the smallest of this series** (listed in Emil Schubert catalogue) eg: no known example	c1910	15¾"x15"x11¾" 400x380x300mm	
900/1 (4-054)	**the second in this series** (illustrated in Emil Schubert catalogue) eg: no known example, D	c1910	17¾"x16½"x13½" 450x420x340mm	• lg curving, 2-stage ramp w/bldg & towers • drawbridge & gate to entry yard w/bldg • drwbrdge & gate - main yard w/circ tower • L-shaped main building & corner tower
900/2	**the third in this series** (listed in Emil Schubert catalogue) eg: no known example	c1910	20½"x18"x15" 520x460x380mm	
900/3	**the fourth in this series** (listed in Emil Schubert catalogue) eg: no known example	c1910	21¼"x20"x17" 540x510x430mm	
900/4	**the largest of this series** (listed in Emil Schubert catalogue) eg: no known example	c1910	23¼"x21½"x19¾" 590x550x500mm	

4-055 **Emil Schubert***: 700 series castle (Courtesy Musée du Jouet, Bruxelles)*

This is typical of the 700 series castles. The castles were developed slightly over time and, even within a series, there was variation. Thus this castle may not conform exactly to the catalogue we have. It is clearly one of the smaller ones.

The castle is populated by 45mm Merton figures.

4-056

4-057

4-056 **Emil Schubert**: *900 series castle*
4-057 **Emil Schubert**: *900 series castle*

These are examples of the 900 series. The earlier one has smooth painted walls and stuck on windows and doors. The roughcast effect on the walls came later – as did the stencilled doors and windows. These differences are typical of the variations one might expect over time, even within a series.

They are both missing parts. For instance, the later example (4-057) is missing the low flanking walls in front of the building halfway up the ramp, as well as the safety rail on the upper part and the wall on the lower part of the ramp. The other (4-056) is missing a large portion of the "brick built" ramp. There are slight differences: the proportion of the arch in the gateway, the building at the rear of entry level, the construction of the crenellation, and, of course, the finish.

Throughout the period 1895 to 1915, Schubert produced a number of series. These included very small ones, as in the 300 and 500 series, enormous ones, such as in the 400 and 600 series, as well as those in between. In this way, he could supply the needs of practically any customer.

EMIL SCHUBERT: 300 Series
c1900 to c1915

NO.	DESCRIPTION	DATE	DIMENSIONS	DISTINCTIVE FEATURES
300/2/0	**the smallest in this series** (listed in Emil Schubert catalogue) eg: no known example	c1900	10½"x7½"x9" 270x190x230mm	
300/0	**the second in this series** (listed in Emil Schubert catalogue) eg: no known example, D	c1900	11½"x8¼"x9" 290x210x230mm	
300/1	**the third in this series** (listed in Emil Schubert catalogue) eg: no known example	c1900	11¾"x8¾"x10¼" 300x220x260mm	
300/2	**the fourth in this series** (listed in Emil Schubert catalogue) eg: no known example	c1900	11¾"x9½"x11" 300x240x280mm	
300/3 (4-058)	**the fifth in this series** (illustrated in Emil Schubert catalogue) eg: no known example	c1900	15"x9½"x11¾" 380x240x300mm	• part integral ramp up to entrance yard • square tower with 2-D building at rear • drawbridge to gateway to walled yard • L-shaped 2-D building & corner tower
300/4	**the largest in this series** (listed in Emil Schubert catalogue) eg: no known example	c1900	16½"x10½"x13" 420x270x330mm	

4-058   *4-059*

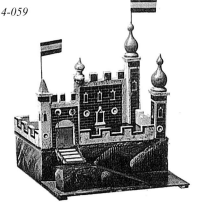

EMIL SCHUBERT: 500 Series
c1905 to c1915

NO.	DESCRIPTION	DATE	DIMENSIONS	DISTINCTIVE FEATURES
500/0	**the smallest in this series** (listed in Emil Schubert catalogue) eg: no known example	c1900	7½"x7½"x7" 190x190x180mm	
500/1	**the second in this series** (listed in Emil Schubert catalogue) eg: no known example, D	c1900	8"x9"x8¾" 200x230x220mm	
500/1½	**the third in this series** (listed in Emil Schubert catalogue) eg: no known example	c1900	9½"x9¾"x9¼" 240x250x240mm	
500/2	**the fourth in this series** (listed in Emil Schubert catalogue) eg: no known example	c1900	9¾"x11"x10½" 250x280x270mm	
500/2½	**the fifth in this series** (listed in Emil Schubert catalogue) eg: no known example	c1900	10½"x11"x10½" 270x280x270mm	
500/3 (4-059)	**the sixth in this series** (illustrated in Emil Schubert catalogue) eg: no known example	c1900	11¼"x11¼"x11¼" 300x300x300mm	• separate ramp up to drawbridge & gate • walled main courtyard w/sq corner tower • main side building & tower at rear
500/4	**the largest in this series** (listed in Emil Schubert catalogue) eg: no known example	c1900	14¼"x13¾"x15" 360x350x380mm	

4-058 Emil Schubert: *300/3 (catalogue)*
4-059 Emil Schubert: *500/3 (catalogue)*
  Even the largest in these series were really small, but this suited Emil Schubert in his search for a wide range of castles to offer his clientele. His other series completed the range.
  The buildings in the 300 series (4-058) were very two-dimensional; those in the 500 series less so, but still not very realistic. They were so small they could have been nothing more.
  The one unique feature is that the buildings of the 500 series (4-059) were covered in paper, providing stone detailing, windows, and doors. This is most unusual for Schubert.

Of the two series of very large castles, I only have an image of one of the 600 series. The "footprint" of the 400 series was basically rectangular, whereas the 600 series was square. In terms of size, the smallest of the 600 series started more or less where the average ones left off and went up from there. This, of course, would make sense in the provision of a range for sale – there would be no need for unnecessary duplication. The biggest were at least twice the size of the largest medium-sized castle.

EMIL SCHUBERT: 400 Series
c1900 to c1915

NO.	DESCRIPTION	DATE	DIMENSIONS	DISTINCTIVE FEATURES
400/2/0	**the smallest in this series** (listed in Emil Schubert catalogue) eg: no known example	c1900	22½"x15"x14½" 570x380x370mm	
400/0	**the second in this series** (listed in Emil Schubert catalogue) eg: no known example, D	c1900	26½"x15¾"x15¾" 670x400x400mm	
400/1	**the third in this series** (listed in Emil Schubert catalogue) eg: no known example	c1900	28¾"x19¾"x21¼" 730x500x540mm	
400/2	**the largest in this series** (listed in Emil Schubert catalogue) eg: no known example	c1900	32¼"x22½"x22½" 820x570x570mm	

EMIL SCHUBERT: 600 Series
c1905 to c1915

NO.	DESCRIPTION	DATE	DIMENSIONS	DISTINCTIVE FEATURES
600/1	**the smallest in this series** (listed in Emil Schubert catalogue) eg: no known example	c1905	22¼"x23½"x19¾" 580x600x500mm	
600/2 (4-060)	**the second in this series** (illustrated in Emil Schubert catalogue) eg: no known example, D	c1905	28"x28¾"x23½" 710x730x600mm	• long integral ramp up to gate & walkway • 3 bldgs on walkway round central moat • dbridge & gate to yard w/circ tower • L-shaped main building & corner tower
600/3	**the largest in this series** (listed in Emil Schubert catalogue) eg: no known example	c1905	32"x32"x30¼" 810x810x770mm	

I can say that both series boasted "water features," which means water-filled moats. Judging by the prices charged for them, they were definitely much more complicated. The method of holding the water, presumably some form of metal lining, would alone have accounted for a substantial part of the increase in cost.

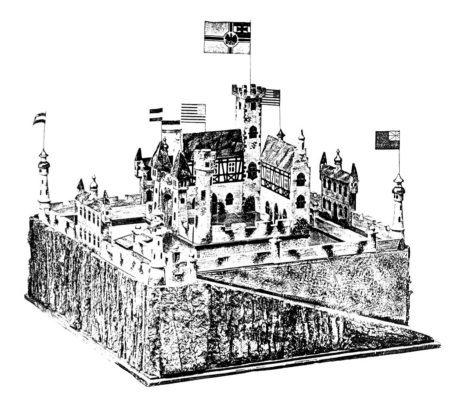

4-060 Emil Schubert: *600/2 (catalogue)*
This is a catalogue illustration of one of the largest castles that Schubert produced. The actual castle, which bears a striking similarity to the 1000 series on the next page, stands in the middle of a man-made lake. Around the outside stand three two-storey houses and four circular towers. Unfortunately, these houses, and the towers, appear to be to a smaller scale than the castle itself, which contributes to a loss of the feeling of grandeur. The flags are unrealistic.

The production of the in-between sizes was relatively simple. They comprise the 200, 800, and 1000 series. There are no examples of the 200 series, so we have no idea what they looked like. It is a different story with the 800 and 1000 series.

EMIL SCHUBERT: 200 Series
c1895 to c1915

NO.	DESCRIPTION	DATE	DIMENSIONS	DISTINCTIVE FEATURES
200/1	**the smallest in this series** (listed in Emil Schubert catalogue) eg: no known example	c1895	17"x13"x15¾" 430x330x400mm	
200/2	**the second in this series** (listed in Emil Schubert catalogue) eg: no known example	c1895	19¾"x14½"x17" 500x370x430mm	
200/3	**the largest in this series** (listed in Emil Schubert catalogue) eg: no known example	c1895	22½"x16"x20½" 570x410x520mm	

The 800 series was a well-used configuration of base and buildings. It was, in principle, the same as the 100 and 700 series, but a mirrored image of them, with the entry courtyard on the right as you look at it. Basically the same building distribution was used, but with much more complex forms. More elaborate shapes were evident and the whole was much more broken up.

EMIL SCHUBERT: 800 Series
c1910 to c1915

NO.	DESCRIPTION	DATE	DIMENSIONS	DISTINCTIVE FEATURES
800/0	**the smallest of this series** (listed in Emil Schubert catalogue) eg: no known example	c1910	15¾"x15"x11¾" 400x380x300mm	
800/1	**the second in this series** (listed in Emil Schubert catalogue) eg: no known example, D	c1910	17¾"x16½"x13½" 450x420x340mm	
800/2	**the third in this series–** (listed in Emil Schubert catalogue) eg: no known example	c1910	20½"x18"x15" 520x460x380mm	
800/3 (4-061)	**the fourth in this series** (illustrated in Emil Schubert catalogue) eg: no known example	c1910	21¼"x20"x17" 540x510x430mm	• part-integrated ramp to dbridge & gate • entry yard w/building w/2 towers to rear • dbridge & gate to main yard w/2 circ tower • 2 separate main bldgs w/3 flankingr towers
800/4	**the largest of this series–** (listed in Emil Schubert catalogue) eg: no known example	c1910	23¼"x21½"x19¾" 590x550x500mm	

The 1000 series was in some ways more complicated. In fact, it was two series in one; in the numbers, one given the suffix "a" and the other "b." There was little difference in form, although the "a" castles had two drawbridges and the "b" only one.

The main difference is in the painting. Both used stencils to provide detail. The "a" series, however, used older equipment and was quite crude by comparison. The "b" series used much more sophisticated stencils, which provided pointed arches over the windows and doors, not to mention the stonework in the walls.

EMIL SCHUBERT: 1000 Series
c1910 to c1915

NO.	DESCRIPTION	DATE	DIMENSIONS	DISTINCTIVE FEATURES
1000/0 a & b	**the smallest of this series** (listed in Emil Schubert catalogue) eg: no known example	c1910	15¾"x15"x11¾" 400x380x300mm	
1000/1 a & b (4-063) (4-064)	**the largest in this series** (identified by an example in the ownership below) eg: Allen Hickling Toy Forts	c1910	17¾"x16½"x13½" 450x420x340mm	• part-integrated ramp to gateway • walled entry yard with building to rear • drawbridge & gate to yard w/circ tower • main buildings on two sides & corner tower
1000/1½ a & b	**the third in this series** (illustrated in Emil Schubert catalogue) eg: no known example	c1910	20½"x18"x15" 520x460x380mm	
1000/2 a & b (4-062)	**the fourth in this series** (listed in Emil Schubert catalogue) eg: no known example	c1910	21¼"x20"x17" 540x510x430mm	• part-integrated ramp to dbridge & gateway • walled entry yard with building to rear • dbridge & gate to main yard w/circ tower • main bldgs on two sides & corner tower
1000/2½ a & b	**the largest of this series** (listed in Emil Schubert catalogue) eg: no known example	c1910	23¼"x21½"x19¾" 590x550x500mm	

In 1914, E. Emil Schubert was joined in the business by one of his sons, Emil Arthur Schubert, who became an active partner in 1916.

About this time, there was a major change in direction for the company. They no longer made the old castles, but branched out into three-dimensional, beautifully painted models. It seems likely that this was copied by others or was copied from others, or, at least, this is one school of thought. Another has it that Schubert had nothing to do with it. He did, however, sell them, because they are in the catalogue.

4-061

4-064

4-062   4-063

4-061 **Emil Schubert**: *800/3 (catalogue)*
4-062 **Emil Schubert**: *1000/2a (catalogue)*
4-063 **Emil Schubert**: *1000/1b (catalogue)*
4-064 **Emil Schubert**: *1000/1b castle (Courtesy Musée du Jouet, Brussels)*

The catalogue illustration of the 800 series (4-061) shows one of the larger ones. One can see how the buildings were broken up to look much more realistic.

The catalogue illustrations (4-062 & 4-063) show the different paint treatments of the "a" and "b" series. Also clearly visible are the two drawbridges on the "a" castle.

Above is an example of a castle in the 1000 series (4-064). It is a mixture of the two castle types, having the form of the "b" series, but the paint style of the "a" series. In any case it shows its heritage in the buildings of the 800 series. It is missing two walls at the entry level, and part of the main building at the upper level.

The first of these was one called "Wartburg." Probably this was meant to be the residence of the "kings" of Thuringia, but whether this was meant to be the real Wartburg Castle, or not, I am not entirely sure. It is true that they both have two towers and a lot of the detailing is similar, but there the similarity ends. If nothing else, the size alone would have been prohibitive in a toy.

Nevertheless, it was a truly magnificent toy castle (4-065 & 4-065a). It is somewhat more on the residential, peaceful side than most of the others in the range – hardly warranting the name fort or castle. The two wings of the main building were clearly different, one being essentially a residential area while the other contained the chapel. A small outbuilding stands on the other side of the courtyard, next to the bridge. The stable yard is at the entry level, with its servant quarters carefully sited next to the gate to receive visitors.

In the painting, the attention to detail is quite amazing when compared with other toy buildings. The stonework of the walls and the tiling on the roofs is all depicted. From the doors with their hinges and latches to the detailed sundial-type clock on the stable block tower, everything is as good as it gets with painting.

At least three or four manufacturers made almost identical forts, so I can only be certain the one in his catalogue was made by Schubert. One thing is certain: it was the only one in my catalogue which was given a name. All the others were described as merely a castle, a fort, or a fortress.

EMIL SCHUBERT: 107 Series Wartburg Castle
c1915 to c1925

NO.	DESCRIPTION	DATE	DIMENSIONS	DISTINCTIVE FEATURES
107/0	**the smallest of this series** (listed in Emil Schubert catalogue) eg: no known example	c1915	15¾"x15"x11¾" 400x380x300mm	
107/1 (4-069)	**the second in this series** (illustrated in Emil Schubert catalogue) eg: SOFIA Foundation, CY	c1915	17¾"x16½"x13½" 450x420x340mm	• part-integrated ramp to dbridge & gate • walled entry yard with buildings + tower • bridge to main crtyd with sm outhouse • main buildings on two sides & corner tower
107/2	**the third in this series** (listed in Emil Schubert catalogue) eg: no known example	c1915	20½"x18"x15" 520x460x380mm	
107/3	**the fourth in this series** (listed in Emil Schubert catalogue) eg: no known example	c1915	21¼"x20"x17" 540x510x430mm	
107/4	**the largest of this series** (listed in Emil Schubert catalogue) eg: no known example	c1915	23¼"x21½"x19¾" 590x550x500mm	

The same can be said about another fort. It was a fairly standard fort, basically grey in color, with a couple of extra pieces and levels. There were several variations, involving particularly the position of the gatehouse at the top of the lower ramp and the various pinnacles at roof level. There was even one version (4-070) that had another quite large pentagonal tower and platform to the side, accessed through a part of the main building.

Equally exquisitely painted, the stonework and tiling are the same as with the Wartburg. On this castle, it is worth mentioning the vegetation, which is quite realistic about the battlements, and the delicate flowers all up the ramp. It must be said, however, that not all manufacturers could match this quality. Some produced a somewhat cheaper line.

EMIL SCHUBERT: 133 Series
c1915 to c1925

NO.	DESCRIPTION	DATE	DIMENSIONS	DISTINCTIVE FEATURES
133/1	**the smallest in this series** (listed in Emil Schubert catalogue) eg: no known example	c1915	22½"x15"x14½" 570x380x370mm	
133/2 (4-074)	**the second in this series** (illustrated in Emil Schubert catalogue) eg: Musée du Jouet, Bxl, B	c1915	26½"x15¾"x15¾" 670x400x400mm	• integrated ramp to dbridge & gatehouse • walled intermediate yard w/2 circ towers • drawbridge & gate to main courtyard • main buildings on two sides & corner tower
133/3	**the third in this series** (listed in Emil Schubert catalogue) eg: no known example	c1915	28¾"x19¾"x21¼" 730x500x540mm	
133/4	**the largest in this series** (listed in Emil Schubert catalogue) eg: no known example	c1915	32¼"x22½"x22½" 820x570x570mm	

Another in the range of which we have no examples was the 121 series. This was quite like the 133 series overall and had a few pieces of the 107 series (4-075). It was extremely like the 133 series in its layout and its buildings at the intermediate level, having anything significantly unique only at the upper level. It was also generally larger.

Yet another in the range that took Schubert through the war was the 137 series. This one had a moat with water (4-076). It was generally large, as were the others, but there the similarities stopped. These were quite unlike the Wartburg and the other two.

4-069

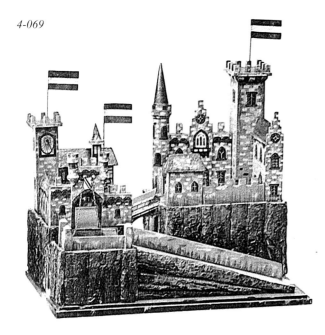

4-065a

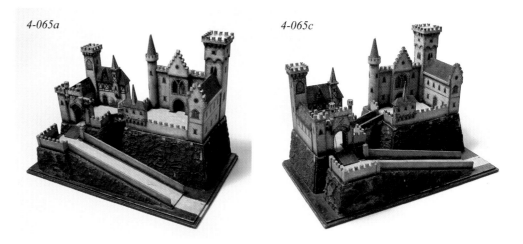

4-065c

4-065b

4-065a **Emil Schubert(?):** *Wartburg Castle front 1*
4-065b **Emil Schubert(?):** *Wartburg Castle back*
4-065c **Emil Schubert(?):** *Wartburg Castle front 2*
4-069 **Emil Schubert** *107/1 (catalogue)*

This castle represents the famous Wartburg Castle in Thuringia, Saxony. The exact period in history that it is supposed to represent is unclear, but it could be about 1200AD. It is a magnificent toy fort.

There is much uncertainty about the manufacturer, because it might have been made by one of several. At the time, it was common practice for manufacturers in the toy industry in Germany to copy the work of others. These images are thought to be of a fort by Emil Schubert. The one of the back shows how much care went into the making of these forts – the common practice was to leave the back blank, assuming it to be backed up to a wall.

The catalogue illustration (4-069) is taken from Schubert's catalogue from just before the First World War.

4-065

4-066

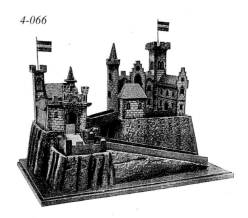

4-067

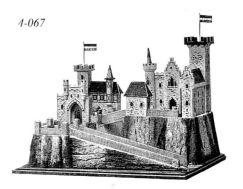

4-068

4-065 Unidentified manufacturer: *Wartburg Castle.*
This is another representation of Wartburg Castle from another manufacturer. There are several pieces missing from the fort in this example. Crenels from both towers and the battlements around both courtyards, and the long wall from the ramp having somehow got lost.

Catalogues from other manufacturers
The remaining three illustrations are taken from various catalogues. The one above (4-066) was from the distributor Meisterarbeit, while the other two (4-067 & 4-068) are from the catalogue of D. H. Wagner. It is surprising how they managed to produce such similar models.

4-070 **Emil Schubert or another**: *similar to the 133 series castle (Courtesy The Puzzle Museum, James Dalgety)*

These forts are remarkably fortress-like, from the ramp, which goes up so that attackers are disadvantaged by having to defend themselves left-handed, to the swathes of crenellation and the masses of towers.

Rarely can one be certain about the manufacturer of a particular item. This is a classic example. It shows evidence of two or three manufacturers – it may have been made by any of them.

4-074 **Emil Schubert**: *133 series castle (Courtesy Musée du Jouet, Bruxelles)*

This one is most likely to have been manufactured by Emil Schubert, although nothing can be certain.

There are several pieces missing. The roof off the main tower seems particularly vulnerable, as do the pinnacles. Of course, the battlements are a constant source of damage and loss, but on the whole they have survived well.

MANUFACTURERS AND PLAGIARISM

Throughout the history of toy fort manufacture, especially in Germany, there was no feeling of being any the less for taking on the ideas of others – there was no stigma attached to it. The basic idea was that there was always room for improvement – that one could always do better. After all, there are only so many variations one can think of in terms of toy forts.

I have taken one fort for an example, but I could have taken many others.

The forts in question have no "model" in the real world, but they have many features that were quite common. They could have been manufactured by anyone, but the most likely candidates are Emil Schubert, Richter and Wittech, ??Heymann, and D. H. Wagner amongst others, but notably not Moritz Gottschalk. They were distributed by Meisterarbiet (4-070a) and D. H. Wagner (4-070b), though probably by others as well; I only have catalogues from the two.

differences in the painting, which go from the main overall base color to the detailing of the vegetation.

Why they should have all produced a similar fort remains something of a mystery. Was it that this type of toy fort was particularly attractive? It certainly was not easier to make. Or was it something to do with competition in the marketplace? Maybe we shall never know.

There is another, completely different explanation, that has to do with the way the manufacturers were organized. If, in addition to their normal operations, they had a sort of cottage industry in which they gave instructions to outworkers to make a given fort, then some of the variations would be bound to occur. I feel this is a bit unlikely, however. It might explain the small painting differences, but I doubt that it accounts for the major ones.

4-070c

180/2/29

4-070b

No. 356/2

4-070a

4-071

4-072

4-073

There are three main differences among the various productions. One is in the position of the gate, with one facing down the ramp (4-071 & 4-072) and the other facing out over the general approach (4-070a & 4-073). The second is that on one model (4-070c) there is a large pentagonal tower located on a spur out of the rock base behind the gate, approached through one of the main buildings at the upper level. Thirdly, in some cases, there is a substantial building across the end of the courtyard at the entry level (4-071 & 4-072).

There are, of course, many minor differences, mainly concerning the shape of the roofs and detailing of the main tower. There are also considerable

EMIL SCHUBERT: 121 Series
c1915 to c1925

NO.	DESCRIPTION	DATE	DIMENSIONS	DISTINCTIVE FEATURES
121/1 (4-075)	**the smallest of this series** (illustrated in Emil Schubert catalogue) eg: no known example	c1915	17¼"x13½"x15¾" 440x340x400mm	• integral ramp to dbridge & gatehouse • walled intermediate yard w/two circ towers • drawbridge & gate to main courtyard • main buildings to rear w/sq & circ towers
121/2	**the second in this series** (listed in Emil Schubert catalogue) eg: no known example	c1915	20"x14½"x20½" 510x370x520mm	
121/3	**the third in this series** (listed in Emil Schubert catalogue) eg: no known example	c1915	22¾"x16½"x22½" 580x420x570mm	
121/4	**the fourth in this series** (listed in Emil Schubert catalogue) eg: no known example	c1915	26¾"x19"x24¾" 680x480x630mm	
121/5	**the largest of this series** (listed in Emil Schubert catalogue) eg: no known example	c1915	31½"x22¾"x27½" 800x560x700mm	

EMIL SCHUBERT: 137 Series
c1915 to c1925

NO.	DESCRIPTION	DATE	DIMENSIONS	DISTINCTIVE FEATURES
137/1	**the smallest in this series** (listed in Emil Schubert catalogue) eg: no known example	c1915	19¼"x15"x18" 490x380x460mm	
137/2 (4-076)	**the second in this series** (illustrated in Emil Schubert catalogue) eg: no known example	c1915	22¾"x16¼"x19¾" 580x420x500mm	• ramp to drawbridge & gatehouse over moat • walled courtyard with bldgs on four sides • main buildings with three square towers
137/3	**the third in this series** (listed in Emil Schubert catalogue) eg: no known example	c1915	26"x18½"x22½" 660x470x570mm	
137/4	**the largest in this series** (listed in Emil Schubert catalogue) eg: no known example	c1915	29½"x19¾"x24½" 750x500x620mm	

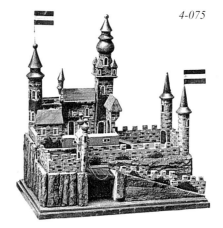 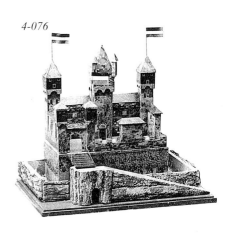

4-075   *4-076*

4-075 **Emil Schubert***: 121/1 (catalogue)*
4-076 **Emil Schubert***: 137/2 (catalogue)*
The similarity between the 121/1 castle and the several variants of the 133 series by several manufacturers is evident. The striking difference is in the dome-like affair on the top of the tower.
The 137 series is clearly a different model all together. From the moat – with water – to the buildings above, it came from a different source. The only thing that makes us consider it here is the fact that it comes from Schubert's catalogue.

After the war the more realistic fort continued to be manufactured. It is still not absolutely clear who did what, but we have three castles that come into this category. Two, which are very similar, are both built on a large hill (4-077 & 4-078). They both have a delightful chapel at a lower level, and rest of the buildings are almost the same. The one significant difference is that on one of them the ramp goes up through a tunnel, under a turret, although it arrives at the same place.

These are thought by some to be the work of two manufacturers, and that may be so. Alternatively, it could be the same model, by the same manufacturer, a couple of years apart. It is hard to tell, as we have no catalogue.

The third one (4-079) is almost certainly by Schubert. The painting of the gate and the door to the main building are typical of their work. The bark on the base would also point that way. The 70mm figures, which are out of scale with the castle, are of German origin.

In 1919, a big shake up came. E. Emil Schubert sold the firm to his two sons, Emil Arthur and Emil Kurt. It seems that, from then on, the products became more toy-like and less realistic. This had the consequence of making the production process much simpler and the products much cheaper.

EMIL SCHUBERT(?): Post-1918 Hill Series
c1918 to c1925

NO.	DESCRIPTION	DATE	DIMENSIONS	DISTINCTIVE FEATURES
unknown (4-077)	**one in this series** (identified by an example in the ownership below) eg: Allen Hickling Toy Forts	c1918	23"x14½"x20¾" 585x365x530mm	• integral ramp to db, gateway, & chapel • 2nd dbridge & gatehouse to main courtyard • basically cream bldgs & circular tower • main bldgs w/central hex tower at rear
unknown (4-078)	**one in this series** (identified by an example in the ownership below) eg: Allen Hickling Toy Forts	c1918	21¼"x14½"x23¼" 540x365x590mm	• integral ramp to chapel, gateway & tunnel • 2nd dbridge & gatehouse to main yard • grey bldgs & circular tower with terrace • main bldgs w/central hex tower at rear

EMIL SCHUBERT: Post-1918 Series
c1918 to c1925

NO.	DESCRIPTION	DATE	DIMENSIONS	DISTINCTIVE FEATURES
unknown (4-079)	**the only one in this series** (identified by an example in the ownership below) eg: Bernd Zimmermann, D	c1918	23¼"x15½"x15½" 550x390x390mm	• separate single ramp to dbridge & gateway • walled entry courtyard w/circ corner tower • up to walled main courtyard • main bldg on two sides w/square tower

4-079

4-077

4-078

4-077 Unidentified manufacturer: *post-1918 hill castle*
4-078 Emil Schubert (?): *post-1918 hill castle with access tunnel*

The manufacturer(s) of these two are unknown, but the one with the tunnel (4-078) is probably by Schubert. These show how two manufacturers could produce almost the same castle. Maybe this was symptomatic of a paucity of designs. The figures on the one on the left are 40mm Elastolin Landsknechts.

4-079 Emil Schubert: *post-1918 castle (Courtesy Bernd Zimmermann)*
This castle was produced to supplement the series that was brought out just before the 1914–1918 war. These were the last of the truly three-dimensional castles. From then on, they became more and more like scenery.
This is quite a small castle; if it were one of a series, which was Schubert's style, it would probably have been one of the small ones. The bark finishes to the base and the paint style (in particular the door to the house and the gateway) make one think of Schubert.
The 70mm figures, which are out of scale with the castle, are of German origin.

This did not happen overnight; it was a slow process of evolution. In this, there is a recognition that the buying public was becoming more middle class and that people had smaller houses. Nevertheless, the castles were, in the main, very colorful and provided excellent play opportunities.

I know only of small- and medium-sized castles, but this does not mean that there were no larger ones. They all show some imagination in the buildings, which is especially true of the later, two-dimensional ones. There appears to be an effort to make up for the lack of depth by implying it in the painting.

EMIL SCHUBERT: Post-First World War
c1920 to c1940

NO.	DESCRIPTION	DATE	DIMENSIONS	DISTINCTIVE FEATURES
unknown (4-080)	**quite large grey fort** (identified by an example in the ownership below) eg: Bernd Zimmermann, D	c1920	20"x19"x13" 510x480x330mm	• 2-sided integral ramp to dbridge & gate • entry courtyard with circular corner tower • dbridge & gate to walled main courtyard • main building w/sq & circ end towers at rear
unknown (4-082)	**small cream fort** (identified by an example in the ownership below) eg: Bernd Zimmermann, D	c1920	unknown	• separate single ramp to drawbridge & gate • main courtyard w/2 sq towers & bow front • main building w/blue roof & sq corner tower
115/1 (4-081)	**medium grey Schloss** (identified by an example in the ownership below) eg: Bernd Zimmermann, D	1913	21¾"x15¾"x17¼" 505x350x450mm	• separate single ramp to drawbridge & gate • main courtyard w/large sq tower • circular corner tower (not original?) • main bldg w/red roof & sq corner tower
unknown (4-083)	**small grey Schloss** (identified by an example in the ownership below) eg: Bernd Zimmermann, D	c1920	unknown	• separate single ramp to drawbridge & gate • main courtyard w/circ corner tower • main building w/red roof & sq corner tower
unknown (4-086)	**medium white Schloss** (identified by an example in the ownership below) eg: Bernd Zimmermann, D	c1930	unknown	• 2-sided integral ramp to dbridge & gate • entry courtyard with buildings to rear • dbridge & gate to main ctyard w/sq tower • 2-D bldgs w/cent sq tower at rear
unknown (4-084)	**small grey Schloss** (identified by an example in the ownership below) eg: Bernd Zimmermann, D	c1930	19"x10½"x17¾" 480x270x450mm	• integral single ramp to drawbridge & gate • main courtyard w/small sq corner tower • large range of 2-D bldgs at rear
unknown (4-085)	**small cream Schloss** (identified by an example in the ownership below) eg: Bernd Zimmermann, D	c1935	unknown	• integral single ramp to drawbridge & gate • main courtyard w/small sq corner tower • small range of 2-D bldgs at rear

Emil Kurt died in 1936 and his father, the great E. Emil Schubert, in 1938. The Second World War did not seem to affect the company too badly. When starting up again after the war, the new owner was Gotthart Schubert, who led them to 1970, when they were nationalized and absorbed in the VEB VERO.

4-080

4-080 **Emil Schubert**: *quite large grey fort (Courtesy Bernd Zimmermann)*
4-081 **Emil Schubert**: *medium grey Schloss (Courtesy Bernd Zimmermann)*

These are two of the Schubert's forts that led the way in the slimming down of their production. It was a process that took time, so it was not so noticeable in the beginning.

Both are complete in that there are no pieces missing.

There is some doubt about the circular tower at the back of the fort on the right (4-081) – it may be from another fort. Otherwise it is more of a house than a military establishment, which accounts for it being called a Schloss.

The 54mm figures, in First World War soldier uniforms, on the one to the right are German-made.

4-081

4-082

4-083

4-086

4-084

4-085

4-082 **Emil Schubert**: *an earlier small cream fort (Courtesy Bernd Zimmermann)*
4-083 **Emil Schubert**: *an earlier small grey Schloss (Courtesy Bernd Zimmermann)*
4-084 **Emil Schubert**: *a later Schloss (Courtesy Bernd Zimmermann)*
4-085 **Emil Schubert**: *a later Schloss (Courtesy Bernd Zimmermann)*
4-086 **Emil Schubert**: *medium white Schloss (Courtesy Bernd Zimmermann)*

These forts demonstrate Schubert's range through the years leading up to the Second World War. The move to simplification is clear. First, there came castles that were only slightly thinner; then, they were slimmed down progressively until the buildings were almost completely two-dimensional. This led inevitably to economies in production and, thus, a cheaper product. The way they compensated for this in design terms was to put more variety into the buildings. Then came the Second World War. The 45mm figures on the fort top left are by Elastolin, while those on the remainder are by Merton.

Carl Moritz Reichel Was an Early Bird

Carl Moritz Reichel started his company in February, 1833, in Niederlauterstein. The firm passed from fathers to sons, from then until 1972, when it was nationalized. There were manufacturers before them, D. H. Wagner and C. H. Oehme in particular, although these were more wholesalers than manufacturers. In terms of continuity, Reichel must rate as one of the longest running manufacturers in the field.

Reichel was never a major producer of toy forts. Although by 1895 he had a major operation with seventy-five workers, he concentrated more on dollhouses, rooms, and furniture. This does not mean that he can be discounted as a fort manufacturer – far from it. He was always there, keeping the big manufacturers on their toes.

As far as I can tell, he really started making toy forts in about 1880, but I cannot be sure about this, just as I am uncertain about the dates of his forts. The majority of his production had rectangular bases with two-dimensional buildings. There were a couple of exceptions involving exploding forts, and there is some confusion about his later efforts, which may have been made by several manufacturers.

CARL MORITZ REICHEL: Sea Fort
c1880 to c1890

NO.	DESCRIPTION	DATE	DIMENSIONS	DISTINCTIVE FEATURES
unknown (4-087) (4-088)	**small sea fort** (Identified by an example in the ownership below) eg: SOFIA Foundation, CY	c1880	11"x9"x8½" 280x230x215mm	• integral double ramp to gateway • walled entry courtyard • 2-D back piece w/paper covering

The first fort I have come across (4-087) may or may not be by Reichel, but it is in his style. The back piece is a picture looking out to sea from a fort. At sea is a wonderful depiction of a sea battle between two fleets of square-rigged ships, just at the time that they were turning to steam.

Now we come to forts that are definitely by Reichel, including two exploding ones. Like the small sea fort, they are paper-covered with a printed image of the castle mounted on it. The two ordinary forts (4-089 & 4-090) are simple boxes with an up-stand at the back and a gateway with battlements around. One is clearly about twenty years later than the other.

The two exploding forts (4-092 & 4-094) are triggered to explode by a missile hitting a target. This target is a piece of the castle in one case and the figure of a man in the other. Once so triggered, the castles blow up by their floor, and everything on it, being thrown upwards by a spring action, simulating a direct hit to the fort's arsenal.

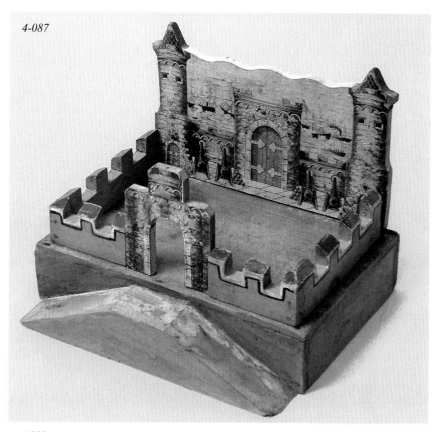

4-087

4-088

4-087 C. Moritz Reichel: *small sea fort*
4-088 C. Moritz Reichel: *backdrop to the sea fort*

The small sea fort (4-087) is delightfully simple. The interest lies in its setting, with the fort being blockaded by ships. These ships are square-rigged with steam assistance in some cases. In fact, the ships are themselves coming under attack, which can be deduced by the gunfire portrayed, although it is impossible to tell which is on which side.

The detail of the lithograph (4-088) shows the battle described above. It even shows some smaller boats with one under sail, bringing men ashore. The cannon on the fort are not being manned, so one assumes the ships are out of range.

CARL MORITZ REICHEL: Exploding & Other Forts
c1890 to c1910

NO.	DESCRIPTION	DATE	DIMENSIONS	DISTINCTIVE FEATURES
unknown (4-090)	**small fort** (identified by an example in the ownership below) eg: Allen Hickling Toy Forts	c1890	10¾"x7"x7" 275x175x180mm	• integral single ramp to gateway • walled entry courtyard • 2-D back w/paper covering
unknown (4-089)	**small bridge fort** (identified by an example in the ownership below) eg: Musée du Jouet, Bxl, B	c1905	unknown	• integral single ramp to gateway • walled entry yard (to the bridge) • 2-D back w/paper covering
unknown (4-091) (4-092)	**2-D exploding fort** (identified by an example in the ownership below) eg: Bernd Zimmermann, D	c1890	unknown	• no ramp • elevated gun platform • 2-D back w/paper covering
unknown (4-093) (4-094)	**3-D exploding fort** (identified by an example in the ownership below) eg: Bernd Zimmermann, D	c1910	unknown	• no ramp – elevated gun platform • 3-D fort above • 3 towers on front w/battlements • 3 towers on main bldg at rear

4-090

4-089

4-089 **C. Moritz Reichel**: *small fort*
4-090 **C. Moritz Reichel**: *small bridge fort (Courtesy Musée du Jouet, Brussels)*

   Both of these forts are small by any standard. The predominantly red one (4-089) is earlier and was probably made about 1890. There is no drawbridge and the whole is delightfully simple. The pieces were kept in the upturned base as in other forts, and were kept in place by a flap made of cardboard.

   The later fort (4-090) retains the simplicity. The main differences, apart from the picture on the back piece, were the battlements and the covering of the base. The gateway was also much more severe. It did not seem to worry Reichel that the scale of the shrubbery on the base was completely wrong. The idea of this being a forecourt to the bridge was ingenious.

4-091

4-092

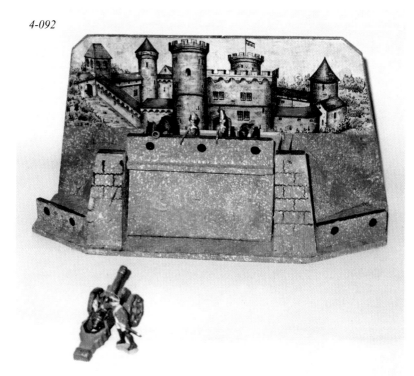

4-091 **C. Moritz Reichel**: *2-dimensional exploding fort (after) (Courtesy Bernd Zimmermann)*
4-092 **C. Moritz Reichel**: *2-dimensional exploding fort (before) (Courtesy Bernd Zimmermann)*
4-093 **C. Moritz Reichel**: *3-dimensional exploding fort (after) (Courtesy Bernd Zimmermann)*
4-094 **C. Moritz Reichel**: *3-dimensional exploding fort (before) (Courtesy Bernd Zimmermann)*

The two-dimensional fort (4-091 & 4-092), which we assume to be about the same age as the simple fort on the previous page, is also really simple. It is only a box in front of the fort proper. The lid forms a gun platform on which a few figures can be stood. When "exploded" the platform springs up, throwing the guns and men into disarray. There being no ramp up, its play value was really limited to only target practice – that is unless a ramp could be constructed somehow out of other materials to be found in the playroom.

The three-dimensional fort (4-093 & 4-094) is dated by the soldier "target person." He is clearly of First World War vintage, so 1910 is the earliest it could be. It has most of the drawbacks of the earlier one – in particular no ramp. The gun platform, however, stays in position in this case, the courtyard of the fort behind bursting open to simulate the "explosion." In this model, all the buildings were thrown into disarray, together with the guns and men – a much more satisfactory outcome.

After the First World War, the Reichel company produced mainly brown-colored forts, but not exclusively. These, in line with their heritage, were made mostly in two dimensions, covered with printed paper.

CARL MORITZ REICHEL: Various Forts
c1920 to c1935

NO.	DESCRIPTION	DATE	DIMENSIONS	DISTINCTIVE FEATURES
unknown (4-097)	**half-timbered Schloss**— (identified by an example in the ownership below) eg: Musée du Jouet, Bxl, B	c1920	14¾"x9"x14¾" 375x230x375mm	• integral single ramp to dbridge & gate • courtyard with corner front building • bldg, cent tower & gable at rear
unknown (4-100)	**half-timbered Schloss** (identified by an example in the ownership below) eg: Bernd Zimmermann, D	c1920	unknown	• integral single ramp to drawbridge & gate • main court w/small bldg in corner • main bldg w/large sq cent tower • gable & sq tower w/half timbering
unknown (4-099)	**half-timbered Schloss** (identified by an example in the ownership below) eg: Musée du Jouet, Bxl, B	c1935	unknown	• integral single ramp to drawbridge & gate • main court w/sm wall in corner • main bldg w/large sq cent tower • building & gable w/half timbering
unknown (4-095)	**sm ripple brown Schloss** (identified by an example in the ownership below) eg: Musée du Jouet, Bxl, B	c1935	unknown	• integral single ramp to gate • courtyard with corner building • range of two-D buildings at rear • central feature & 2 circ end towers
unknown (4-096)	**lge ripple brown Schloss** (identified by an example in the ownership below) eg: Allen Hickling Toy Forts	c1935	21½"x12¼"x16¼" 555x310x410mm	• integral single ramp to dbridge & gate • court w/2-storey corner building • range of 2-D buildings at rear • 1cent rect & two hex end towers
unknown (4-098)	**large rough beige Schloss** (identified by an example in the ownership below) eg: Bernd Zimmermann, D	c1935	unknown	• integral single ramp to drawbridge & gate • main courtyard w/small corner wall • main building w/large cent feature • circ + sq end towers w/sm windows

Some forts have bark on the base (4-096) and some do not (4-095). Some have black stone surrounds to the main gate (4-098), while some have white (4-099). Some have bright colors (4-100) and some do not (4-096). There are some with doors with a wavy surround (4-104), some without (4-097); some with hinges (4-103), some with just a line (4-101); and some with steps leading up to the door (4-102). This wide variety does not even consider the windows, sundial clocks, and half timbering.

4-097

4-097 C. Moritz Reichel: *colorful small half-timbered Schloss (Courtesy Musée du Jouet, Brussels)*

4-100

4-098 **C. Moritz Reichel**: *rough beige Schloss (Courtesy Bernd Zimmermann)*
4-099 **C. Moritz Reichel**: *small snow Schloss (Courtesy Musée du Jouet, Brussels)*
4-100 **C. Moritz Reichel**: *colorful large half-timbered Schloss (Courtesy Bernd Zimmermann)*
    The colorful, small, half-timbered Schloss (4-097) looks more calmly peaceful than some of the others. Its form and much of its detailing appear again in the large version (4-100). The main difference lies in the very big square tower right in the middle of the larger one. The small image (4-099) shows a smaller version in the range, this time in winter format. In all of these, one can recognize many of the parts in the heavily modified Schloss – although the color of the building and the blanket of snow may make it difficult to spot.
    The fourth Schloss (4-098) is probably the latest to be brought out. It is less like the others, as one could imagine, but the overall form, which is reminiscent of the big ripple brown Schloss, and the doors give it away – that is unless another manufacturer was copying the design.

CARL MORITZ REICHEL: Light Brown Schlossen
c1930

NO.	DESCRIPTION	DATE	DIMENSIONS	DISTINCTIVE FEATURES
unknown (4-102)	**light brown Schloss** (identified by an example in the ownership below) eg: Musée du Jouet, Bxl, B	c1930	unknown	• integral separate ramp to drawbridge & gate • main courtyard with corner building • bldg & cent tower w/oblique windows • doorways w/steps up & wall sundial
unknown (4-103)	**light brown Schloss** (identified by an example in the ownership below) eg: Allen Hickling Toy Forts	c1930	13"x8¼"x11" 330x210x280mm	• integral separate ramp to drawbridge & gate • main courtyard with corner building • main bldg & cent tower w/slit windows • normal doorways & wall sundial
unknown (4-101)	**lt brown bigger Schloss** (identified by an example in the ownership below) eg: Bernd Zimmermann, D	c1930	unknown	• integral reentrant ramp to dbridge & gate • access to entry court & gate w/tower • main court w/med hex corner tower • main building w/2 large sq end towers
unknown (4-104)	**lt brown bigger Schloss** (identified by an example in the ownership below) eg: Bernd Zimmermann, D	c1930	unknown	• integral reentrant ramp to dbridge & gate • access to entry court & gate w/tower • main courtyard w/lg circ corner tower • main building w/2 large sq end towers

4-098

4-099

    But there is one set of forts with some consistent features. They were the forts with a light brown smooth finish. It is true that other features demonstrated a wide variety, indicating the possibility that another manufacturer was involved, but it seems sensible to keep them together.

4-095

4-096

4-095 **C. Moritz Reichel**: *large ripple brown Schloss*
4-096 **C. Moritz Reichel**: *small ripple brown Schloss*

These two are obviously from the same stable. They were probably produced sometime during the build-up to the Second World War. Their rather dull coloring is a bit like camouflage, even though the detailing is vaguely reminiscent of the middle ages. The ripple effect is obtained photographically, using an oblique lighting source on a rough surface.

Apart from size, the main differences are small. The large one (4-096) has hexagonal towers, a higher middle section, a two-storey front building, tree bark on the base, a drawbridge, and battlements on the gateway. The smaller one (4-095) has only painted bushes around the base of the buildings.

4-102

4-103

4-101

4-104

4-101 **C. Moritz Reichel**: *larger light brown Schloss (Courtesy Bernd Zimmermann)*
4-102 **C. Moritz Reichel**: *small light brown Schloss (Courtesy Musée du Jouet, Brussels)*
4-103 **C. Moritz Reichel**: *small light brown Schloss*
4-104 **C. Moritz Reichel**: *larger light brown Schloss (Courtesy Bernd Zimmermann)*

These light brown models herald the coming war. It is an attempt at camouflage without it being too noticeable.

The two smaller ones (4-102 & 4-103) are slightly different, although the absence of much of the crenellation on one of them is misleading. There are clear differences, the color of the courtyard battlements for example. However, the small differences in the fenestration and the doors are more interesting, when you consider that these were printed and not easy to change.

The two larger models are also very nearly the same. The differences are in the form of the central feature and the corner tower, which are the most significant. The courtyard walls are replacements on the one with the circular corner tower (4-101). The use of figures demonstrates once again the effect of their size on the apparent size of the castle. The red-coated foot soldiers, which are 75mm, really make the castle look small when compared with the other (4-104), on which are 40mm green uniformed mounted lancers.

Finally there are two forts that are quite different. One (4-106) is a heavily modified fort with a Gottschalk wing added and the front building substituted, all under a blanket of snow. The other (4-105) is a highly colored one, with wood instead of cardboard battlements, so it might have been earlier.

The difficulty lies in the absence of an appreciable pattern. One cannot fathom a series or anything like that. So I have treated them all as one series. After about 1935, little is known of the Reichel family as far as the construction of toy forts is concerned. They continued through to nationalization mostly with dollhouse-related products.

CARL MORITZ REICHEL: Small Forts
c1920 to c1935

NO.	DESCRIPTION	DATE	DIMENSIONS	DISTINCTIVE FEATURES
unknown (4-105)	**red-roofed Schloss** (identified by an example in the ownership below) eg: Musée du Jouet, Bxl, B	c1920	unknown	• integral ramp to drawbridge & gate • courtyard with corner building • at rear main bldg w/wing & 2 towers • half-timbering & red roofs
unknown (4-106)	**winter Schloss** (identified by an example in the ownership below) eg: SOFIA Foundation, CY	c1935	14¾"x9"x14¾" 375x230x375mm	• integral ramp to drawbridge & gate • main courtyard w/small wall in corner • Gottschalk wing on main building • at rear main bldng, cent tower & gable

4-105

4-106

4-105 **C. Moritz Reichel**: *colorful wooden Schloss (Courtesy Musée du Jouet, Brussels)*
4-106 **C. Moritz Reichel**: *heavily modified Schloss*

The brightly colored wooden Schloss (4-105) is a bit of an enigma. The absence of cardboard for the battlements and the different surface treatment of the base may be an indication of another manufacturer. Alternatively, there may be some simple explanation to do with availability of materials, but, of course, this would not explain the different roofing details.

The heavy modification of the snowy model (4-106) has been carried out by at least two restorers. The first of these was of considerable ability; the addition of a piece of Gottschalk, and the moving of the front wall piece, was cleverly done. Exactly why he thought it necessary we will probably never know, but it makes for a very pleasant effect.

The second restorer was myself, and all I did was to make the snow seem real and generally tidy up a bit. Whether it was originally a snow scene or not seems unimportant now.

Emil Weise and Carl Krause

By about 1890, there were several companies quite well established and others just starting up. I treat Emil Weise and Carl Krause together not because they formed one firm, but because, in 1901, Emil Weise was taken over by Carl Krause, who carried on where Weise left off.

Emil Weise founded his company in Finsterwalde about 1880. He manufactured all types of wood products, specializing in toys such as fortresses, shops, warehouses, stables, and kitchens. Strangely, although he made dollhouse furniture, he does not seem to have gone into dollhouses like many of his competitors.

One feature that Weise used consistently on nearly all his forts was a circular tower with a conical roof. It was colored a reddish brown with windows stencilled in black. These were seen together with the battlements, which were another consistent feature, all painted to the same pattern, mostly a yellow ochre body color with red and white tops – a combination that was used by many others.

Weise also made practical furniture, such as desks, carts, ladders, and boxes. It may have been the breadth of his offering, amongst other things, that led to his downfall, because in 1901 he was declared bankrupt. It was then that Carl Krause, also of Finsterwalde, came to the rescue. He took over the complete operation, including the premises and showrooms.

EMIL WEISE
c1890 to 1901

NO.	DESCRIPTION	DATE	DIMENSIONS	DISTINCTIVE FEATURES
unknown (4-110)	**very small fortress** (identified by an example in the ownership below) eg: Allen Hickling Toy Forts	c1890	9¾"x12"x11¾" 250x305x300mm	• double-back ramp with drawbridge • flat arch with litho to main courtyard • one circular corner tower • large flat back piece with litho(2)
unknown (4-109)	**medium fortress** (identified by an example in the ownership below) eg: unknown	c1890	unknown	• ramp to flat gate with litho to ctyard • ramp w/drawbridge to gate with litho • two circular corner towers • large flat back piece with litho(2)
unknown (4-107) (4-108)	**small medium fortress** (identified by an example in the ownership below) eg: Allen Hickling Toy Forts	c1890	16¼"x17¼"x10½" 410x440x270mm	• two-sided ramp to drawbridge • flat gateway with litho to courtyard • two circular corner towers • large flat back piece with litho(1)
unknown (4-110a)	**medium fortress** (identified by an example in the ownership below) eg: SOFIA Foundation, CY	c1895	19¼"x19¾"x10½" 490x495x270mm	• two-sided ramp to flat gate with litho • drawbridge to gate with litho • two circular corner towers • large flat back piece with litho(3)
unknown (4-113a)	**large fortress** (identified by an example in the ownership below) eg: C Kohler auctions, CH	c1890	18½"x15"x13" 470x380x330mm	• fort w/simulated rock base (cork) • two reverse ramps to entry courtyard • drawbridge thru gateway to courtyard • large, flat back piece with litho(3)
unknown (4-110b)	**medium fortress (transition)** (identified by an example in the ownership below) eg: Allen Hickling Toy Forts	c1895	23"x15"x14" 590x380x355mm	• single ramp up fort with base (cork) • flat gate(litho) to yard w/flat bldgs(1) • drawbridge thru gateway to courtyard • main bldg w/tower & windows
unknown (4-113)	**large castle/fortress** (illustrated in Emil Weise catalogue) eg: no known example	c1898	unknown	• simulated rock base (cork) w/ramp • drawbridge thru gatehouse to yard • two large square towers on periphery • main bdgs w/large square tower

4-109

4-108

4-107 Emil Weise (catalogue 1895): *Castle/fortress/Schloss*
This is an illustration of probably the oldest example we have of Emil Weise's range of toy forts.
His trademark circular towers are clearly to the fore, although they are slightly fatter and the roofs slightly taller than the ubiquitous orange-brown ones he used afterwards.
The lithograph on the back piece is unrealistic compared to those on the later ones, which are quite photographic.

4-108 Emil Weise: *early medium fort*
4-109 Emil Weise: *medium fort*
4-110 Emil Weise: *small fort*
These are from the earliest series we have. The earliest of these is the medium fort (4-108) with its flat gateway with paper covering, and the somewhat unrealistic lithograph on the back piece. Note also the circular towers at the corners, which were the forerunners of Weise's trademark orange-brown towers.
The next in age is the small one (4-110). One first notices the change in style of the gateways. Gone are the flat, lithographed gateways and in come constructed, painted ones. Also, we have the first appearance of the orange-brown circular tower. The back piece was also changed. The lithography was more realistic, almost photographic. The lower drawbridge is a replacement.
The large one (4-109) is about of the same vintage. The most significant of the differences is the addition of an entrance court with a gateway using the lithograph of the back piece of the smaller one. The inner gateway is two-dimensional with another lithograph, as is the back piece. The top of the tower on the left at the back has been broken off, and there may be something missing from the tower on the right. Most noticeable, compared to the earlier fort (4-108), is the architectural detail in the lithography.

CARL KRAUSE
1901 to c1915

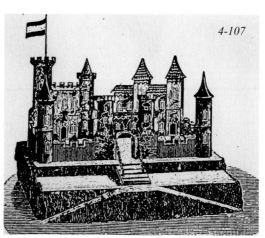

4-107

4-110

NO.	DESCRIPTION	DATE	DIMENSIONS	DISTINCTIVE FEATURES
10 (4-112)	**small med fortress (transition)** (identified by an example in the ownership below) eg: Allen Hickling Toy Forts	c1902	19"x12"x12" 480x305x305mm	• single rmp to ctyd w/2-D litho bldg • dbridge thru gate to main ctyard • 3 brown circular columns • main bldg w/windows & sq tower
unknown (4-112a)	**medium fortress (transition)** (identified by an example in the ownership below) eg: unknown	c1902	23"x15"x14" 585x380x355mm	• single rmp to ctyd w/2-D litho bldg • dbridge thru gate to main ctyard • 2 brown circular columns • L-form bldg w/windows & sq tower
unknown (4-111)	**very large fortress (+ water)** (illustrated in Carl Krause catalogue) eg: no known example	c1906	unknown	• reverse ramp up to moat w/water • dbridge & gateway to single ramp up • arrive at ctyard w/2-D litho bldg • L-form bldg w/windows & sq tower
unknown (4-114)	**large castle/fortress** (identified by an example in the ownership below) eg: Allen Hickling Toy Forts	c1905	25"x19¼"x20½" 635x490x520mm	• double rmp to gtway w/3 circ towers • 2ⁿᵈ ramp thru gatehse to main yard • one wing building & five towers • 3 main bldgs & large square tower

4-110a

c.1895-c.1900

4-110b

4-112a

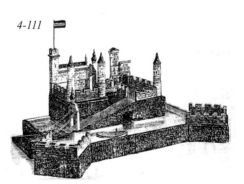

4-111

4-112b

4-110a **Emil Weise**: *medium fort*
4-110b **Emil Weise**: *early transition fort*
4-111 **Carl Krause catalogue (1906)**: *fort/moat*
4-112a **Emil Weise / Carl Krause**: *transition fort*
4-112b **Emil Weise / Carl Krause**: *smaller transition fort*

The medium-size fort top left (4-110a) is somewhat different from the others on this page. It is derived from the early one on the previous page.

The remaining four have been named "transition" forts because they have both flat and 3-D pieces, and they were produced by both Weise and Krause. The top middle fort (4-110b) gives us some cause for uncertainty; it has the early form of lithograph, together with a grey tower

with a gold "onion" dome top. The other two (4-112a & 4-112b) have the later form of lithography, with the ubiquitous orange-brown towers.

Focusing on the similarities is interesting. They all have a single ramp rising up from the left to the lower of two uneven mounds, with a drawbridge between them. Architecturally they all use the later form of gateway on the upper level, and the 3-D buildings all have the same fenestration, doorways, and a tower at one end. The older building has suffered over the years, and is now missing most of its fenestration.

The catalogue illustration (4-111) is dated 1906, but it may have been used earlier. It shows a "transition" fort located in the middle of a grand lake. While this provided endless play opportunities, the resulting mess must have been considerable – presumably cleared up by the hired help.

c.1900-c.1905

4-113

4-114

4-113a

4-113 Emil Weise catalogue (1898): *castle*

4-113a Emil Weise / Carl Krause: *large "transition" castle*

4-114 Carl Krause: *large maroon castle/fortress*

The Weise catalogue entry (4-113) shows an early move towards bigger, more rounded forts. This is probably Weise's first attempt at putting it into practice. We will probably never know how far he got on with the idea, but Krause certainly took it up with enthusiasm.

The fort at the left (4-113a) is called "transition" because it marked the beginning of a move away from flat buildings with lithographed paper covering. Everything is much more bulky than previously, and the gateway, at the head of a complex double ramp, is even more elaborate than earlier. The problem with this is that it is typical of much of both Emil Weise's and Carl Krause's productions, having parts from different times. This one is probably a Krause version because of the light colored battlements, which were typical of his production.

The maroon castle/fortress (4-114) is indeed large. All the buildings, of which there were relatively many, are truly 3-D and, for them, in a new style. All the windows and doors were stuck on and it could be viewed completely in the round. This example has many windows and doors missing.

It was almost as though there had been no interruption at all. The advertising continued to use many of Weise's images and it was not until about 1904 that new models began to appear. These included the use of water for the moat, something being tried by others at the time. I am not sure how long they continued, but it is reasonable to assume they continued until the First World War.

Richter and Wittich

Richter and Wittich set up their business in Eppendorf in 1891. They continued in business under those names for more than forty years, before being taken over by Richter's daughter Hilde in the run up to the Second World War. They continued after the war in Eppendorf, until nationalization in about 1971.

They claimed to be the largest wood and metal manufacturer, producing a wide range of toys and musical instruments. They never, however, used metal in the production of toy forts.

I know little of the history of the company, but I think I can trace a lot of their production up to the First World War, after it until the Second World War, and then, in a more sketchy manner, beyond that to nationalization.

There were two possible starting points. The interesting thing is that they were so different there may have been two companies involved. One is a rather gloomy set of castles (4-115, 4-116 & 4-117) using three-color lithography on a buff paper, which tended to go brown with age, with black on red trim. The other (4-118) was more of a palace which used bright four-color printing to bring a fresh feeling to the building.

RICHTER & WITTICH
1891 to c1915

NO.	DESCRIPTION	DATE	DIMENSIONS	DISTINCTIVE FEATURES
75/60 (4-115)	**large fortress** (identified by an example in the ownership below) eg: SOFIA Foundation, CY	c1891	27"x13½"x14" 685x340x355mm	• two base mounds with river between • 1 residential yard & 1 defensible • 2 db + gateways + five towers • one 4-storey bldg & 5-storey tower
unknown (4-116)	**medium fortress** (identified by an example in the ownership below) eg: Allen Hickling Toy Forts	c1891	19¼"x13¾"x15" 490x350x380mm	• single mound w/ ramp to drawbridge • gateway to main courtyard • one 2-storey bldg and square tower • one 4-storey bldg & 5-storey tower
/6 2 (4-117)	**medium fortress** (identified by an example in the ownership below) eg: Allen Hickling Toy Forts	c1895	18¾"x12¼"x13¾" 475x310x350mm	• ramp up ½-bark base to gateway • 2 circ towers & gateway at 1st level • 1 sq & 1 circ tower at 2nd level • 2 large sq towers & 3-storey bldg

unknown (4-121)	**palace/castle w/vegetation** (identified by an example in the ownership below) eg: SOFIA Foundation, CY	c1900	15"x10"x12" 380x255x305mm	• ramp up ½-bark base to gateway • 2 circ towers & gateway at 1st level • 1 sq & 1 circ tower at 2nd level • 2 large sq towers & 2-storey bldg
974/1	**small castle** (identified by an example in the ownership below) eg: SOFIA Foundation, CY	c1900	7"x10¾"x8" 180x275x200mm	• small fort or entrance way • steps to courtyard & 2 circ towers • entrance/gateway across back
unknown (4-118)	**palace/castle** (identified by an example in the ownership below) eg: Allen Hickling Toy Forts	c1900	18½"x11"x12½" 470x280x320mm	• ramp over moat to colorful palace • past 2 towers to 4- tower entrance • thru gateway to large courtyard • 2 square towers & 3-storey palace
unknown	**small medium palace/castle** (identified by an example in the ownership below) eg: Allen Hickling Toy Forts	c1905	15"x9¾"x12" 380x250x305mm	• 2 level fort but no ramp or gateway • 2 circ towers at 1st level & steps up • 1 sq & 1 circ tower at 2nd level • 2 large sq towers & 2-storey bldg
unknown (4-117)	**medium palace/castle** (identified by an example in the ownership below) eg: Allen Hickling Toy Forts	c1905	19"x12¼"x13¾" 485x310x350mm	• 2 level fort on ½-bark base w/ ramp • gateway to 1st level w/2 circ towers • dbridge to 2 sq towers at 2nd level • 2 large sq towers & 2-storey palace
unknown (4-125)	**large palace/castle** (illustrated in unattributable catalogue) eg: no known example	c1905	unknown	• large fort with bark base and ramp • gateway to 1st level w/2 circ towers • steps up to 2 lg sq towers & palace • 2 further sq towers at 2nd level
unknown (4-123)	**large palace/castle** (identified by an example in the ownership below) eg: Bernd Zimmermann, D	c1910	18½"x11"x12½" 470x280x320mm	• large fort with bark base and ramp • gateway to 1st level w/2 circ towers • steps up to 2 lg sq towers & palace • 2 further sq towers at 2nd level
unknown (4-124)	**large palace/castle** (identified by an example in the ownership below) eg: Mick Murphy, US	c1910	unknown	• integral rmp to db & gate at 1st level • four circular towers & steps up • one 2-storey building w/sq towers • 1 elevated large circular tower
unknown (4-122)	**large palace/castle** (identified by an example in the ownership below) eg: Ann Timpson, US	c1915	unknown	• very large fort w/bark base & ramp • gateway to 1st level w/2 circ towers • steps up to 4 lg sq towers & palace • 1 elevated large circular tower

It was really this use of four-color printing that saw them on their way. Whether they got new presses or bought the papers in, the result was the same – the forts were more saleable because of their attractiveness. They made a range of sizes including a version with vegetation at the windows and doors (4-121).

These two lines of development came to a head just before the start of the First World War. Because they changed direction quite radically in the design of their forts, it seems reasonable to surmise that something happened then. Maybe it had something to do with the war. They seemed to go backwards for a while, producing flat buildings in a cheap format.

4-115 **Richter & Wittich**: *large fortress*

This large fortress was made about 1891, right at the start of the firm. Its defensible nature is demonstrated by the number of towers in relation to the living accommodation and by the upper courtyard with the second drawbridge. The two bits of courtyard wall at the rear are replacements, as are the drawbridge chains. Everything else is original. The flags are, of course, totally inappropriate additions.

I have examples of small forts of this type (4-126), as well as evidence of several larger ones (4-127 & 4-128), such as the one they chose to lead their advertising. They also made other larger ones, but the quality was definitely down-market.

Whether or not they had been producing these earlier as a cheap alternative, I do not know, but I do know they launched the line quite aggressively, advertising it to the exclusion of their earlier forts. They did not last, however, even though they were still advertising them in 1925, and before long they went over to production without paper.

4-116

4-117

4-116 Richter & Wittich: *medium fortress*
4-117 Richter & Wittich: *medium-sized palace/castle*

The medium fortress to the left (4-116) is a smaller version of the one on the previous page. Most of the courtyard walls have been replaced, as have the drawbridge and its chains. The flags are not original and roofs have been repainted.

The medium-sized palace/castle above (4-117) shows the first move towards the future. Most parts are the same as on the older forts, but the differences lie in the bark on the sides and the simpler gatehouse. Note the towers with a turret on top, which are very similar to those on the brightly colored palace on the next page. The horizontal surfaces have been repainted (except the ramp) and the roofs also. The flags have been changed, but are equally inappropriate.

4-118

4-119

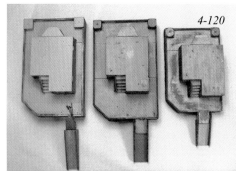

4-120

4-121

4-118 **Richter & Wittich**: *palace/castle with moat*
4-119 **Richter & Wittich**: *medium palace/castle*
4-120 **Richter & Wittich**: *the bases compared*
4-121 **Richter & Wittich**: *medium palace/castle with vegetation*

The colorful palace above (4-118) was made about 1900 and is covered in paper, but the printing shows a later technology. The result is brighter colors and better detail. The moat is not lined and could not therefore be filled with water. The flat main building is not quite as convincing as the three-dimensional type.

The medium palace/castle above right (4-119) has an almost identical layout as the earlier version on the previous page. The only differences lie in the overall finishes (i.e., the printed

paper), the gateway, and there being one more tower with a pointed roof. The drawbridge has been replaced.

The castle on the right (4-121) was probably the first with the new style of printing, made about 1900. Its layout is almost the same as the one above, but in this case the windows and doors all have decorative vegetation around them. The courtyard at the first level has a smaller area just inside the gateway.

The photograph in the centre (4-120) shows the bases of the three palaces/castles. They are clearly from the same source, though the buildings are different.

c.1910-c.1915

4-122

4-123

4-124

4-125

4-122 **Richter & Wittich**: *palace/castle (Courtesy Bernd Zimmermann)*
4-123 **Richter & Wittich**: *palace/castle*
4-124 **Richter & Wittich**: *the ultimate palace/castle (Courtesy Evelyn Ackermann)*
4-125 **Hermann Klassen (Lyra)**: **(***distributor's advert)*

These palaces/castles represent the final phase following this line of development. They show how, starting with the first colorful palace, then combining elements of both streams, one arrives at this point. Of the examples available to me, they were much bigger than the lead-up to them would imply.

Some of the ultimate forts are shown here. One (4-122), has the two circular towers in reversed position (i.e., the larger tower should be elevated), and one of the two towers at the first level is missing its turret top. The fort on the bottom left (4-124) has seen considerable service and is missing a gateway and several small elements. Apart from these relatively minor imperfections, these are the most realistic of all the Richter & Wittich forts up until the First World War.

RICHTER & WITTICH
c1910 to c1925

NO.	DESCRIPTION	DATE	DIMENSIONS	DISTINCTIVE FEATURES
unknown	**small fort no main building** (identified by an example in the ownership below) eg: Allen Hickling Toy Forts	unkwn	12½"x8"x8½" 315x205x220mm	• short ramp up to gateway • courtyard with four square towers
unknown (4-126)	**small palace/fort** (identified by an example in the ownership below) eg: Allen Hickling Toy Forts	unkwn	12½"x8"x8½" 315x205x215mm	• short ramp up to gateway • courtyard with two square towers • main building between two sq towers
unknown (4-128)	**large palace/fort** (identified by an example in the ownership below) eg: Bernd Zimmermann,D	unkwn	unknown	• double ramp up to gateway • courtyard with two square towers • three-sided palace with 4 sq towers
unknown	**palace w/roofs** (identified by an example in the ownership below) eg: eBay	unkwn	unknown	• double ramp up to 1st level • double ramp to gateway at 2nd level • two sq corner towers at 2nd level • two small bldgs & one large bld
unknown (4-127)	**eastern palace w/roofs** (identified by an example in the ownership below) eg: Allen Hickling Toy Forts	unkwn	13½"x10"x10¾" 340x255x275mm	• double ramp to 1st level bldg • 4 sq towers • double ramp to gateway at 2nd level • two small bldgs & one large bldg
unknown (4-129)	**larger palace/castle** (illustration used by Richter & Wittich in advertising) eg: no known example	c1915	unknown	• ramp up to drawbridge & gateway • main building between 2 sq towers
unknown (4-130)	**larger palace/castle** (identified by an example in the ownership below) eg: Bernd Zimmermann, D	c1915	unknown	• medium fort with built-in moat • ramp (missing) up to gateway • courtyard w/one square corner tower • one wing and tower of main building

RICHTER & WITTICH:
c1925 to c1972

NO.	DESCRIPTION	DATE	DIMENSIONS	DISTINCTIVE FEATURES
unknown	**small snow castle (grey)** (identified by an example in the ownership below) eg: Bernd Zimmermann, D	c1925	unknown	• double ramp up to db & gateway • courtyard with one small sq tower • main bldg w/central tower & kitchen • one wing w/half-timbered 4th floor
unknown (4-131)	**large snow castle (brown)** (identified by an example in the ownership below) eg: Arnold Mueller, D	c1925	unknown	• very lg fort w/massive tower (snow) • ramp up past chapel to db & gateway • upper crtyd w/walls & bldgs around • three free-standing bldgs incl tower
unknown (4-133)	**medium fortress (yellow)** (identified by an example in the ownership below) eg: Bernd Zimmermann,D	c1930	unknown	• ramp up to db & gatehouse • courtyard surrounded by walls • one 3-storey residential building • one-storey linking bldg to lg sq tower
68? (4-134)	**castle/fort (yellow)** (identified by an example in the ownership below) eg: Allen Hickling Toy Forts	c1935	19"x15¼"x16" 480x390x405mm	• double ramp up to db & gateway • courtyard w/three sq corner towers • main bldg in left corner w/lg sq tower
unknown (4-132)	**castle (grey)** (identified by an example in the ownership below) eg: Bernd Zimmermann,D	c1935	unknown	• ramp up to db & gatehouse • courtyard w/walls & gateway • one 3-storey residential building • 1-storey linking bldg to lg sq tower
unknown	**larger castle (grey)** (illustration used by Richter & Wittich in advertising) eg: Allen Hickling Toy Forts	c1935	21½"x17¼"x24" 545x440x610mm	• walled double ramp up to db & gateway • courtyard w/three sq corner pieces • 2½-storey main bldg w/2-storey wing • very large square tower w/roof

They started out with quite complex and ornate designs, some of them very large indeed. The two examples available to me, which I am certain were made by Richter and Wittich because they appear in their advertising literature, are both snow castles.

They both show a finish that consists of a coating of plaster incised to represent stone, and then spray painted at an angle to accentuate the modeling. The windows and doors were then sprayed on using stencils.

It is not clear when the next development occurred, but it appears to have been some time later. They started producing similarly robust designs, but now in a summertime decoration. Four examples are known to me, although there are many more which may, or may not, have been by Richter and Wittich.

They appear to have been made using the same techniques as their snow castles, albeit more sober and defensible. Maybe this could be attributed to the political climate in Germany in the 1930s; certainly this had a sobering effect. According to the advertisements, they continued with the same models until nationalization in 1972.

4-126 Richter & Wittich: *small palace/fort*
This small fort is one of a series produced at the same time as, or soon after, Richter & Wittich's mainstream forts – those more realistic, and certainly more expensive ones, which were described earlier.
It is not known if these were intended as a cheap line to set against the others. They were produced quite crudely, with flat buildings – if there were any – covered with four-color printed paper.

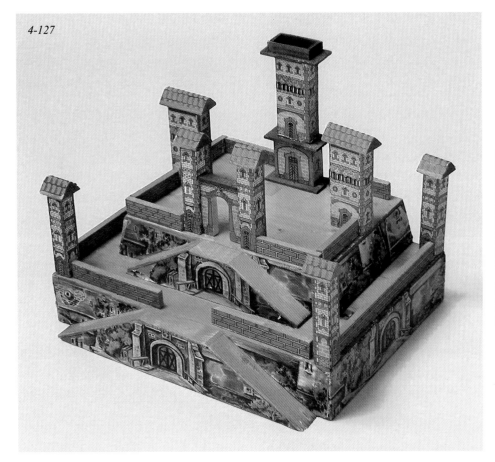

4-127

c.1910-c.1925

4-128

4-129

4-130

4-127 **Richter & Wittich**: *medium eastern fort*
4-128 **Richter & Wittich**: *large palace (Courtesy Bernd Zimmermann)*
4-129 **Richter & Wittich**: *(advertisement for palace/forts)*
4-130 **Richter & Wittich**: *small-sized palace/fort (Courtesy Bernd Zimmermann)*

The image of the largest palace/fort (4-128) illustrates the development of the cheaper line of forts, which ran until about 1925. The eastern fort (4-127), which is attributed to Richter & Wittich because of the similarity of technique, shows the development of a parallel line. It is missing a piece of courtyard battlement.

The lower two (4-129 & 4-130) are linked because they use the same papers on the base and the buildings. Those on the base should be seen with 4-128, and the dry moat (the drawbridge and ramp are missing on this one) is reminiscent of the one surrounding the earlier palace/fort (4-118). They were unlined and could not have held water.

c.1925–c.1972

4-131

4-133

4-134

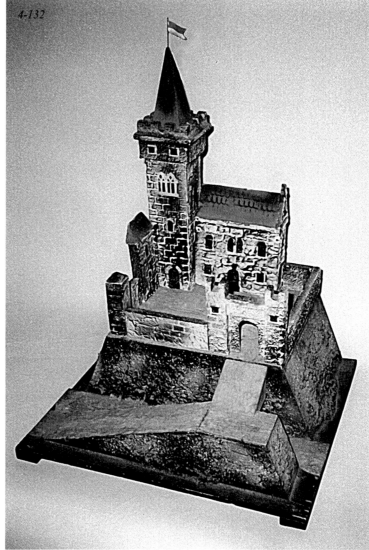

4-132

4-131 **Richter & Wittich**: *very large snow castle (Courtesy Bernd Zimmermann)*

4-132 **Richter & Wittich**: *medium castle (Courtesy Bernd Zimmermann)*

4-133 **Richter & Wittich**: *medium fortress (Courtesy Bernd Zimmermann)*

4-134 **Richter & Wittich**: *castle fort*

These forts are representative of those that Richter & Wittich produced to the end, although it must be pointed out that this represents about twenty-five years. I know the castle to the right (4-132) was still going strong when the Second World War broke out, because there are advertisements of the era showing it. In this period, the snow castles came first, probably about 1920.

They are robust in structure, well-painted, and display a wide range in size and color. The technique of incising the composition coating seems labor intensive but effective, although they used some form of grid as an aid.

The stenciling of the windows and doors was done over the rough texture of the walls and seems to work very well. The outlining of the openings with white helped in this. The color at the windows on the snow castle seems to work there, but was probably too much work to do on all of the castles.

Carl Weber Made Mostly Small Castles

Carl Weber founded his firm in 1844, although he may have been active as early as 1830. As with most of his competitors, his first forty or so years were spent mostly in the making of dollhouses and furniture. Probably, it was not until the 1880s that they turned their attention to toy forts in earnest.

Little is known about his early output. This lack of knowledge, combined with the fact that they went out of business in 1915, means that there is little information available to me. In fact, I have only remnants of a catalogue from about 1900 to identify some of his forts. From this there is one about which we are certain. This is a small fort numbered 4355 (4-136). There was an oblique, followed by a single digit, after this number indicating its place in the range, but I am afraid it proved indecipherable.

The larger forts are less frequently come across (4-135, 4-137 & 4-140). This is partly because, in all probability, fewer were made in the first place. Their size may, in fact, have played a role in their demise – the bigger the fort, the more space it takes up, and therefore the greater the gain when it was cleared out. At least I have access to two of them.

Now there is the question of their development – how did they move on. The small one (4-136) is a prime example. There is a range of candidates, all, or none of which, may have been produced by Weber. This is the trouble created by different manufacturers making more or less the same fort.

I have two that I think are by Weber (4-142 & 4-146), although I cannot be 100% certain, and I have one of which I am reasonably sure was not by him (4-147). Then there are a number of wholesalers who provided illustrations of very similar castles, Carl Nötzel (4-143), D. H. Wagner (4-144), and Meisterarbeit (4-145) among them. Of course, Weber's may not have been the original, it is just the way I came across them.

CARL WEBER:
c1890 to c1910

NO.	DESCRIPTION	DATE	DIMENSIONS	DISTINCTIVE FEATURES
3868/3 (4-135)	**large Schloss** (illustrated in Carkl Weber catalogue) eg: no known example	c1893	unknown	• 2-sided ramp to forecourt w/2 towers • dbridge & gateway to main courtyard • buildings surrounding ample space • 2-storey main building w/2 towers
3868 (4-137)	**large Schloss** (identified by an example in the ownership below) eg: Musée du Jouet, Bxl, B	c1893	18½"x20¾"x16" 470x525x405mm	• 2-sided ramp to forecourt w/2 towers • dbridge & gateway to main courtyard • buildings surrounding ample space • 2-storey main building w/two towers
4166 (4-140)	**large Schloss** (illustrated in Carkl Weber catalogue) eg: no known example	c1895	unknown	• separate double ramp to square area • dbridge & gateway to walled walkway • gateway to yard with bldgs around • sq central tower w/hex tower on top
4355/2	**small Schloss** (illustrated in Carkl Weber catalogue) eg: no known example	c1900	unknown	• integral ramp to double gateway • entrance yard w/misc bldgs & towers • entry to top level from underneath • 2-wing main bldg w/sq tower
4355 (4-136)	**small Schloss** (identified by an example in the ownership below) eg: Allen Hickling Toy Forts	c1900	13½"x9¼"x11½" 355x235x295mm	• integral ramp to double gateway • entrance yard w/misc bldgs & towers • entry to top level from underneath • 2-wing main bldg w/sq tower
4540/2 (4-139)	**very large Schloss** (illustrated in Carkl Weber catalogue) eg: no known example	c1900	unknown	• garden to extended ramp system • dbridge & gate to forecourt w/bldgs • entry to upper level underneath • main bldg w/three towers

4540 (4-138)	**very large Schloss** (illustrated in Carkl Weber catalogue) eg: Bernd Zimmermann, D	c1900	unknown	• garden to extended ramp system • dbridge & gate to forecourt w/bldgs • entry to upper level underneath • main bldg w/three towers
4548/1 (4-141)	**large Schloss** (illustrated in Carkl Weber catalogue) eg: no known example	c1900	unknown	• separate single ramp to db & gate • main courtyard with buildings around • 3-storey main building with wings • two corner towers

CARL WEBER (?): or Maybe Others
c1910 to c1925

NO.	DESCRIPTION	DATE	DIMENSIONS	DISTINCTIVE FEATURES
unknown (4-142)	**summer Schloss** (identified by an example in the ownership below) eg: Allen Hickling Toy Forts	c1910	16½"x11"x13" 420x280x330mm	• integral ramp to dbridge & gateway • entrance yard w/rear bldgs & towers • ramp to upper courtyard w/circ tower • main bldg w/two wings & sq tower
unknown (4-146)	**winter Schloss** (identified by an example in the ownership below) eg: Allen Hickling Toy Forts	c1910	16½"x11"x13" 420x280x330mm	• integral ramp to dbridge & gateway • entrance yard w/rear bldg & towers • ramp to upper courtyard w/circ tower • main bldg w/two wings & sq tower
358/1 (4-143)	**small Schloss** (illustrated in D. H. Wagner catalogue) eg: no known example	c1915	13½"x9¼"x11½" 355x235x295mm	• integral ramp to dbridge & gateway • entrance yard w/rear bldg & towers • ramp to upper courtyard w/circ tower • main bldg w/two wings & sq tower
180/5/3 (4-144)	**small Schloss** (illustrated in Meisterarbeit catalogue) eg: no known example	c1925	unknown	• integral ramp to dbridge & gateway • entrance yard w/rear bldg & towers • ramp to upper courtyard w/circ tower • main bldg w/two wings & sq tower
521/3 (4-145)	**small Schloss** (illustrated in Carl Nötzel catalogue) eg: no known example	c1910	unknown	• integral ramp to dbridge & gateway • entrance yard w/rear bldg & towers • ramp to upper courtyard w/circ tower • main bldg w/two wings & sq tower
unknown (4-147)	**multi-colored Schloss** (identified by an example in the ownership below) eg: Allen Hickling Toy Forts	c1925	19¾"x12¾"x15¼" 500x325x390mm	• integral ramp to dbridge & gateway • entrance yard w/rear bldg & towers • ramp to upper courtyard w/circ tower • main bldg w/two wings & sq tower

4-136

4-137

4-135

4-135 Carl Weber No.3868/3 *(catalogue)*
4-136 Carl Weber No.4355/? *(Courtesy Musée du Jouet, Brussels)*
4-137 Carl Weber No.3868/? *(Courtesy Musée du Jouet, Brussels)*

   Weber No.4355 (4-136) is the small Schloss that was the one on which several others were based. It is not known whether Weber was involved in all of these developments or not. It can be said that later models had several improvements – access to the upper level was achieved via a ramp and the buildings at the entrance level were reduced and simplified.

   Weber No.3868 (4-137) is a larger fort that was produced earlier than No.4355. Its actual size is not known, but it was clearly impressively larger. Not only were the ramps much grander, but so too were the buildings above, providing much more accommodation.

4-138 **Carl Weber No.4540/?** *(Courtesy Bernd Zimmermann)*
4-139 **Carl Weber No.4540/2** *(catalogue)*
4-140 **Carl Weber No.4166** *(catalogue)*
4-141 **Carl Weber No.4548/1** *(catalogue)*

These are some more of Weber's output of larger forts. The earliest on this page is No.4166 (4-140) which dates from about 1895. The latest is No.4548/1 (4-141) which came out about 1900.

Weber No.4540/? (4-138) is missing its drawbridge, the pediment over the central gateway, and one or two crenels, but is in good condition for its age. It shows some differences to the catalogue, the most significant being the form of the towers and the two additional wings on the main building. This may be just a matter of size, but more likely there were improvements being made all the time and these were just some of them.

4-142

4-143

4-144

4-146

4-145

4-147

4-142 **Summer version probably by Weber**
4-143 to 4-145 **Three catalogue entries of similar designs**
4-146 **Winter version probably by Weber**
4-147 **Multi-colored version probably not by Weber**

These are various developments of Weber No.4533/? (4-136). All seven models are different, but they are the same in the general disposition of parts and in that their upper level is accessed via a ramp. This was not the case with the "original."

The two on the far left (4-142 & 4-146), both of which show signs of a hard life (missing pieces of courtyard wall, oriel windows, crenels, etc.), were the most likely to have been by Weber. They are the most alike, but could still have been by different manufacturers.

The three in the center are from catalogues of (from top to bottom) Carl Nötzel, D. H. Wagner, and Meisterarbeit. Of these, the one by Carl Nötzel is most likely to be associated with Weber, and the others probably not – Meisterarbeit did not start operation until eight years after Weber gave up.

The one on the right (4-147) is quite different. It, also, is missing a piece of courtyard wall and some crenels, but, more importantly, the paint style is unlike any of the others.

Albin Schönherr Leaves Gottschalk

In 1895, Albin Schönherr left the employ of Moritz Gottschalk and set up his own workshop in Niederlauterstein. Despite the culture which prevailed of copying each others designs, it seems that he took very little from Gottschalk's forts. Most of his output was related to dollhouses, kitchens, and furniture, however, and in this there was said to be a strong similarity with Gottschalk's production.

Little is known of Schönherr's history, at least to me. We do have some illustrations from catalogues and the like, and some of his later production. The exact dates are not available, though, and those included here are all a bit of sensible guesswork. Similarly, the sizes are missing on many of them.

The forts of the first series were all made of wood with bark-covered bases. They were quite complex and would have been quite time-consuming to make. The second series forts, also made of wood with bark bases, were considerably easier. The larger forts retained many of the characteristics of the former series but made much of the complexity as add-ons.

ALBIN SCHÖNHERR: Early Castles
c1895 to c1915

NO.	DESCRIPTION	DATE	DIMENSIONS	DISTINCTIVE FEATURES
494/2 (4-148)	fairly complex fort (illustrated in Albin Schönherr catalogue) eg: no known example	c1895	22"x15¼"x18½" 560x390x470mm	• free-standing tower linked by bridge • ramp up 2 sides of bark base to gateway • main courtyard w/sq & circ corner towers • building with small & large sq towers
386/4 (4-152)	complex fort (illustrated in c1910 Albin Schönherr advertisement) eg: no known example	c1910	22¾"x15¾"x18½" 580x400x470mm	• integral ramp to gate and entrance court • walled yard with bldgs + 2 corner towers • ramp to second gate and main courtyard • main bldgs w/two large square towers
411/32/1 (4-150)	small complex fort (illustrated in Meisterarbeit catalogue) eg: no known example	c1910	unknown	• integral ramp to gate & foyer court • large 2-D entrance tower • main courtyard w/sq & circ corner towers • buildings w/2-D square tower
386/5 (4-151)	large complex fort (illustrated in Meisterarbeit catalogue) eg: no known example	c1910	27½"x17¼"x19¾" 700x440x500mm	• integral ramp to gate and entrance court • walled yard with bldgs + 2 corner towers • ramp to second gate and main courtyard • main buildings w/two large square towers
422/3 (4-149)	odd medium castle (illustrated in c1910 Albin Schönherr advertisement) eg: no known example	c1915	13"x8¼"x9" 330x210x230mm	• fort w/2-D bldgs w/litho facing • integral ramp to gate • walled main yard with corner building • large building to rear with three towers

That leaves just one odd one from before the First World War (4-149). Completely different from all the others before or since, it is predominantly a flat fort with all its detail supplied by the application of lithographic prints. This way of doing things was used earlier by several manufacturers, notably Moritz Gottschalk, Carl Moritz Reichel, Emil Weise, and Richter and Wittech, although it was still the early days for the technique. The fact that there are few examples of its use by Albin Schönherr may be attributed to the level of investment that they had in their existing methods.

4-148 Albin Schönherr No.494/2 *(catalogue)*
This is one of the earliest forts produced by Schönherr. The form of the free-standing tower has been taken from Gottschalk, who had just such a one in their contemporary series.
If the numbering system is the same as used by others in the business, this would have been the second largest in the series, making them definitely on the large side (depending, of course, on how many there were in the series).

c.1905–c.1915

4-152

4-149

4-150

4-151

4-149 Albin Schönherr No.422/3 *(advertisement)*
4-150 Albin Schönherr 411/32/1 *(Meisterarbeit catalogue)*
4-151 Albin Schönherr 386/5 *(Meisterarbeit catalogue)*
4-152 Albin Schönherr No.386/4 *(advertisement)*

Here are three forts from one long-running series, and one experimental one. The series was still being sold about 1924, as is witnessed by its inclusion in the Meisterarbeit catalogue (Meisterarbeit did not come into being as a company until 1923). The images of the two larger forts in the series (4-151 & 4-152) are almost identical, the one being a mirror image of the other – the Meisterabeit one is slightly larger. The smaller one (4-150) may be the smallest in the range; it nevertheless demonstrates the use of parts from others in the series in an effort to promote long runs.

The "experimental" fort No.422/3 (4-149) represents an attempt at a different style of production. Presumably it was an effort at learning from others, which included Moritz Gottschalk, Schönherr's previous employer. It was obviously a cheaper form of construction. It did not stay in the range for very long, although it acted as the forerunner for their next series.

It was probably after the First World War that the next series was introduced. It was again wood covered with lithographed paper, but it was to give the effect of stonework rather than architectural detail. The detail was the three-dimensional part of the structure.

There are but two certain examples of this, and one which might have been by another maker. Both of the examples that are certainly by Schönherr (4-153 & 4-155) are quite large and display a lot of imagination. The other one (4-154) is surprisingly flat, and displays more conventional fort details.

ALBIN SCHÖNHERR: Transitional Schlosser
c1920

NO.	DESCRIPTION	DATE	DIMENSIONS	DISTINCTIVE FEATURES
unknown (4-153)	**medium Schloss** (identified by an cxamplc in the ownership below) eg: Bernd Zimmermann, D	c1920	26"x18½"x20¾" 660x470x530mm	• ramp up two sides of ½ bark base thru tower • over river to dbridge & gate to courtyard • three parts of main bldg & short circ tower • main building divided w/small sq towers
unknown (4-155)	**large complex Schloss** (identified by an example in the ownership below) eg: Bernd Zimmermann, D	c1920	32¼"x22½"x26" 820x570x660mm	• rmp up two sides of ½-bark base w/3 arches • two free-standing towers protect db & gate • crtyd w/circ tower, bldg on wall & side wing • main buildings divided w/large square tower
unknown (4-154)	**small castle** (identified by an example in the ownership below) eg: Bernd Zimmermann, D	c1920	17¼"x11½"x15" 440x290x380mm	• integral simple rmp up to dbridge & gate • courtyard with corner building. • main bldg w/central feature & corner towers

4-153

4-154

4-155

4-153 **Albin Schönherr**: *medium Schloss (Courtesy Bernd Zimmermann)*
4-154 **Albin Schönherr?**: *small castle (Courtesy Bernd Zimmermann)*
4-155 **Albin Schönherr**: *large Schloss (Courtesy Bernd Zimmermann)*

The largest of these three (4-155) displays, by far, the most imagination. It is reasonably defensible with its two free-standing towers and other defenses, but is nevertheless as much a house as it is a fort, albeit a large one. The figures are 40mm knights by Merton.

The medium-sized fort (4-153) still has sufficient battlements for defense, but it is much simpler. The ramp still wraps around two sides, but the tower half-way up is a nice touch, as is the short round tower by the drawbridge. The windows are stuck on the surface.

The smallest of these three (4-154) is probably the most contentious. Here we have a castle using the same paper on the walls and, more importantly, the same doorways. Yet, it is so unlike the other two that doubts have to emerge. It could have been by another company, but more likely it was by Schönherr though with another designer, possibly separated in time. The figures on this one are also 40mm knights by Merton.

It must have been about 1925 when Schönherr got into a very productive phase of development. This was a series of fortified houses, all of which were built with some half-timbered parts and with one or two substantial towers. They all had a ramp, a drawbridge, a gateway, and a courtyard, along the back of which ranged a wide variety of buildings.

There were two types, principally distinguished by their ramp. One type had the notable feature of a ramp that was not straight – it wiggled its way up to the gateway. This meant that it had to be separate from the base proper. The other type had a straight ramp integral with the base.

Which came first is a matter of speculation. I think the straight ramp would have been easier and cheaper to make, so it is more than likely that it came later in an effort to make the forts more competitive.

ALBIN SCHÖNHERR: Schlösser with Non-straight Ramps
c1925 to c1942

NO.	DESCRIPTION	DATE	DIMENSIONS	DISTINCTIVE FEATURES
unknown (4-157)	**small snow Schloss** (identified by an example in the ownership below) eg: Bernd Zimmermann, D	c1925	15"x11½"x15¼" 380x290x390mm	• snow-covered wiggly ramp to db & gate • over river to courtyard with blue buildings • main building at rear in three parts • half-timbered bldgs w/gable & sq tower
unknown (4-160)	**med large snow Schloss** (identified by an example in the ownership below) eg: Rob Wilson, UK	c1925	unknown	• snow-covered wiggly ramp to db & gate • over river to courtyard with blue buildings • main building at rear in five parts • half-timbered bldgs w/circ tower
unknown (4-156)	**Schloss w/railway tunnel** (identified by an example in the ownership below) eg: Rob Wilson, UK	c1925	24"x18"x15" 610x455x380mm	• bark-covered base housing railway tunnel • wiggly ramp to drawbridge & gateway • courtyard with main building in four parts • half-timbered bldgs w/square & circ towers
unknown (4-159)	**Schloss w/railway tunnel** (identified by an example in the ownership below) eg: Noel Barrett Auctions	c1925	24"x18"x15" 610x455x380mm	• painted covering to base w/railway tunnel • wiggly ramp to drawbridge & gateway • courtyard with main building in four parts • half-timbered bldgs w/square & circ towers
unknown (4-161)	**medium large Schloss** (identified by an example in the ownership below) eg: Marc Azzini, B	c1925	22"x14¼"x21½" 550x365x545mm	• painted covering to base & wiggly ramp • drawbridge over river & gate to courtyard • corner buildings (two) & lg circ tower • half-timbered main buildings with gable
unknown (4-158)	**large Schloss** (identified by an example in the ownership below) eg: Noel Barrett Auctions	c1925	unknown	• painted covering to base & wiggly ramp • drawbridge & gate to courtyard • main buildings to rear in six parts • half-timbered main bldgs w/sq & circ towers

Other differences concerned the finish to the base. The non-straight type had bark or similar, while the straight-ramped type had a rough painted finish. The

bark type provided an up-stand at the edge of the courtyard, but the painted type necessitated some lengths of wall along the edge of the courtyard.

The buildings at the back were all different and can only be identified as by Schönherr by their characteristic windows and pointed doorways. They all had the same wall treatment, the same half-timbering details, and more or less the same type of roof finish.

4-156 **Albin Schönherr***: Schloss with railway tunnel*
The main feature of this Schloss is the railway tunnel, which would have made it very difficult to store the parts of the buildings. These were usually put in the upturned base, but here the tunnel openings would allow pieces to fall out. The walls of the base are made rough with the application of tree bark.

This is clearly a fortified house. There is provision for men to defend the place in the towers and other battlements. There is also the winding ramp thoroughly overlooked, even though it rises the wrong way for defense purposes!

4-157 **Albin Schönherr**: *small snow Schloss (Courtesy Bernd Zimmermann)*
4-158 **Albin Schönherr**: *similar large Schloss (Courtesy Noel Barrett Auctions)*
4-159 **Albin Schönherr**: *Schloss with similar characteristics (Courtesy Noel Barrett Auctions)*
4-160 **Albin Schönherr**: *Schloss under snow (Courtesy Rob Wilson)*
4-161 **Albin Schönherr**: *later Schloss with similar characteristics (Courtesy Marc Azzini)*
   These are Schlösser that were made by the same hand. The two snow castles (4-157 &
4-160), which seem to come from the same series, are strikingly similar. Note the finish
on the base and the river flowing beneath.

The small snow Schloss above left (4-157) is a classic example of the genre. In
particular, one cannot help noticing the size of the doors, typical of Schönherr – they
are too small in relation to the other parts. Also note the size of the window in the gable
in relation to the other windows. It appears too big – heaven knows what went on
behind it; perhaps there was an artist's studio there. The 40mm figures on this Schloss
are by Merton.
   Note the covering of the base on all the examples, which is extended up to eliminate
the need for battlement walls around the courtyard, an effect which is not very realistic.

ALBIN SCHÖNHERR: Schlösser with Straight Ramps
c1930 to c1942

NO.	DESCRIPTION	DATE	DIMENSIONS	DISTINCTIVE FEATURES
unknown	**small white Schloss** (identified by an example in the ownership below) eg: Bernd Zimmermann, D	c1930	17"x11"x15¼" 430x280x390mm	• integral ramp to drawbridge over moat • gate to walled court w/sm circ corner tower • main building at rear in three parts • half-timbered buildings with circular tower
unknown (4-162)	**small fawn Schloss** (identified by an example in the ownership below) eg: Bernd Zimmermann, D	c1930	16½"x14½"x15¼" 420x370x390mm	• integral ramp to drawbridge over moat • gate to walled court w/sm rect corner tower • main building at rear in three parts • half-timbered bldgs with central sq tower
unknown (4-164)	**large gray Schloss** (identified by an example in the ownership below) eg: Rob Wilson, UK	c1930	unknown	• integral ramp to drawbridge over moat • gate to walled court w/circ corner tower • main building at rear in five parts • half-timbered bldgs with large rect tower
unknown (4-163)	**large green Schloss** (identified by an example in the ownership below) eg: Bernd Zimmermann, D	c1930	18¼"x11½"x18" 465x290x460mm	• integral ramp to drawbridge over moat • gate to walled court w/sm sq corner tower • main building at rear in four parts • half-timbered bldgs with sq & circ towers
unknown	**large cream Schloss** (identified by an example in the ownership below) eg: Bernd Zimmermann, D	c1930	unknown	• integral ramp to db over moat (2 arches) • gate to walled court w/sm circ corner tower • main building at rear in four parts • half-timbered bldgs w/large square tower

There is no doubt Schönherr made other forts, but I have no evidence of them.

In 1938, Albin's son Paul took over the company. When he died in 1948, his widow and daughter took over. After some arguments with the authorities, they carried on until nationalization in 1972, during which period they were manufacturing mostly dollhouse furniture and the like.

4-164

4-162

4-163

*4-162 **Albin Schönherr**: small white Schloss (Courtesy Bernd Zimmermann)*
*4-163 **Albin Schönherr**: large green Schloss (Courtesy Bernd Zimmermann)*
*4-164 **Albin Schönherr**: large gray Schloss*

The gray Schloss above (4-164) has many of the typical features of these toys. The integral ramp, the wall finishes, the roof finishes (both of them), the small doorways, and the small square windows are to be found on all in the series. Least typical is the tower at the corner of the courtyard, which is larger than usual.

The two images to the left (4-162 & 4-163) are others from the series. Both are also typical, but the large green Schloss is slightly more unusual. There are two aspects of the design that stand out: the crenellated wall around the courtyard and the high level projecting piece in the middle of one of the back pieces. The men on both of them are 40mm figures by Merton.

The Hinkelmann Family Was in the Mix

Emil (it is interesting how frequently that name appears in connection with forts) Hinkelmann started his company in Grünhainichen in 1844. The business was kept in the family throughout its active life of about a hundred years. Like the vast majority of companies, they initially produced dollhouse-related goods, but they were known also for their boxes.

It is not known exactly when they started to produce toy forts, but it is known that they were in full swing by 1911, as evidenced in an advertisement of the time. On a visit, in 2004, to the grandson of Emil Ferdinand Hinkelmann, who led the firm just after the First World War, I saw about fifteen toy forts, all made in the period between the wars. All of them have the distinguishing feature of a base covering of small blocks of wood, covered with a paper of some kind, which was then stretched and heavily painted. This gives the impression of a craggy rocky hill supporting the fort.

From these, it may be deduced that they were involved in the making of copies of other manufacturers' products... or were they victims of such plagiarism by others? There are two forts bearing a striking resemblance to the works of Reichel, and another to that of Schubert. There may well be others unidentified by me.

EMIL HINKELMANN: Early Castles
c1910

NO.	DESCRIPTION	DATE	DIMENSIONS	DISTINCTIVE FEATURES
unknown (4-166)	medium castle (identified by an example in the ownership below) eg: Rob Wilson, UK	c1910	19¾"x22½"x16¾" 500x570x680mm	• angled ramp up to dbridge and gateway • crtyd w/one sq tower & lg circ tower • 2-storey bldg & arch to terrace • L-shaped bldg w/sq tower (missing)
unknown (4-167)	medium castle (identified by an example in the ownership below) eg: Bernd Zimmermann, D	c1910	19¾"x22½"x16¾" 500x570x680mm	• angled ramp up to dbridge and gateway • crtyd w/one sq tower & lg circ tower • 2-storey bldg & arch to terrace • L-shaped bldg w/sq linking tower

EMIL HINKELMANN: Various Castles
c1920 to c1942

NO.	DESCRIPTION	DATE	DIMENSIONS	DISTINCTIVE FEATURES
132/1	medium grey fort (identified by an example in the ownership below) eg: Rudolph Hinkelmann	c1920	unknown	• integral ramp up two sides of fort • dbridge & gateway to crtyd • various castle bldgs
150/1	medium grey fort (identified by an example in the ownership below) eg: Rudolph Hinkelmann	c1920	unknown	• integral ramp to gatehouse to entry crtyd • 3-D bldg w/sq rear tower to bridgehead • suspension bridge to high crtyd w/bldg • main bldg w/lg circ tower at rear
346/2	small/medium grey fort (identified by an example in the ownership below) eg: Rudolph Hinkelmann	c1920	unknown	• integral ramp up long side of fort • gateway to crtyd w/3-D bldgs & tower • 3-D bldgs & lg sq tower at rear • as medieval fort dist by Oehme (4-208)
347/0	small white fort (identified by an example in the ownership below) eg: Rudolph Hinkelmann	c1920	unknown	• similar to Emil Hinkelmann (4-169) • integral ramp to dbridge & lg gateway • same size as original overall • colors now white w/red roofs
347/1	large brown fort (identified by an example in the ownership below) eg: Rudolph Hinkelmann	c1920	unknown	• similar to Emil Hinkelmann (4-169) • integral ramp to dbridge & lg gateway • larger size as original overall • colors now brown w/red roofs
348	large cream fort (identified by an example in the ownership below) eg: Rudolph Hinkelmann	c1920	unknown	• separate ramp to db & 3-D gatehouse • ctyd w/3-D bldg & lg circ tower • 3-D ½-timbered main bldg at rear • bridge to lg circ tower
352/1 (4-169)	medium brown fort (identified by an example in the ownership below) eg: Rudolph Hinkelmann	c1920	unknown	• integral ramp to dbridge & gateway • ctyd & corner bldg & main bldg behind • 4-part bldg 2/sm & lg sq towers • similar to Mortiz Reichel (4-102)
354/1	small grey fort (identified by an example in the ownership below) eg: Rudolph Hinkelmann	c1920	unknown	• integral ramp to dbridge & gateway • ctyd & corner bldg & main bldg behind • 3 parts: gable, center tower, house • like Mortiz Reichel (4-097 w/snow)
unknown (4-170)	large dark grey fort (identified by an example in the ownership below) eg: Bernd Zimmermann, D	c1920	26¾"x14½"x17¾" 680x370x450mm	• separate ramp to dbridge & gateway • ctyd w/bldg, sq tower & bridgehead • small suspension bridge w/sm tower • L-shaped main bldg w/lg cir tower
unknown	small white fort (identified by an example in the ownership below) eg: Rudolph Hinkelmann	c1920	unknown	
unknown (4-168)	medium light grey fort (identified by an example in the ownership below) eg: Rudolph Hinkelmann	c1920	unknown	• circular ramp to db & gateway to ctyd • 2nd dbridge & gateway to crtyd w/tower • L-shaped main bldg w/sq link tower • copy of Emil Schubert (4-056)
unknown	small white fort (identified by an example in the ownership below) eg: Rudolph Hinkelmann	c1920	unknown	
unknown	very small cream fort (identified by an example in the ownership below) eg: Rudolph Hinkelmann	c1920	unknown	

4-165

4-166

4-167

4-165 **Hinkelmann (***advert 1911)*
4-166 **Emil Hinkelmann***: a
multi-colored version of the fort*
4-167 **Hinkelmann***, the more sober
fort (Courtesy Bernd Zimmermann)*

*The Hinkelmann advertisement
is from 1911 (4-165). The
interesting thing is that it seems as
though they used a mirror image of
the fort for some reason. This can
be seen by comparing the image
with those of the actual fort to the
right.*

*Of the two versions, the more
sober one (4-167) seems to be the
most realistic. Judging by the
stencilling of the windows and
doors, the brightly colored version
(4-166) was the later of the two,
though why there should have been
a difference escapes me. The 40mm
Elastolin figures on the more sober
fort are Landsknechts by Hausser.*

c.1920

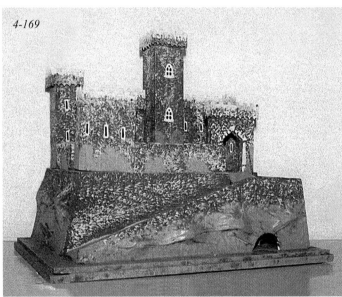

4-168 **Emil Hinkelmann**: *large fort (Courtesy Musée du Jouet, Brussels)*
4-169 **Emil Hinkelmann**: *large medium fort (Courtesy Musée du Jouet, Brussels)*
4-170 **Emil Hinkelmann**: *very large fort (Courtesy Musée du Jouet, Brussels)*
    These are three forts from the Hinkelmann's own collection. They all bear the hallmarks of Hinkelmann construction, though they also bear a strong resemblance to forts

attributed to others. Clockwise from the left, these others are D. H. Wagner, E. Emil Schubert, and Carl Moritz Reichel. It is difficult to be definitive about who copied whom — it could have gone either way, or indeed it could have been coincidence. There is no denying these are great forts, and it may be we should not get too hung up on the question of who owned the design rights.

So were the Hinkelmanns plagiarists or plagiarized? Maybe we will never know. They were certainly productive at quite a reasonable level of the market throughout the difficult times, and we assume they were successful.

They went out of business in 1938.

Emil Neubert Joins the Fray

Emil Neubert was a relatively late starter, when compared to the likes of Hacker and Gottschalk, but this did not deter him from being a prolific manufacturer of toy forts. It would seem that he was in the business for only about twenty-five years, but he played a major role in the production of toy forts, albeit at the cheaper end of the market.

He set up his company in 1924 in Marienberg-Hüttengrund, but that is the extent of my knowledge of him. I have no catalogues or advertisements, so it is difficult to say anything definitive about him or his product. I have no numbers or dates; all I have is the evidence of his forts, of which there were many. This means I am going to have to list these in groups of similar forts and make a best guess at a sequence of production.

It seems that he started with a series that was consistent with those manufactured by others in the field at the time. There were not any very large examples; they ranged from really quite small forts to what would have been middle of the range, had there been a full range.

They were reasonably complex designs, without any major changes of level, so they all ended up with a rectangular courtyard and buildings aligned along the back. They appear well painted with the details, such as their extensive use of half-timbering, windows, and doorways, applied with the use of stencils.

EMIL NEUBERT: The First Series
1924 to c1935

NO.	DESCRIPTION	DATE	DIMENSIONS	DISTINCTIVE FEATURES
unknown (4-172)	small brown fort (identified by an example in the ownership below) eg: Bernd Zimmermann, D	c1924	13¼"x9½"x12¾" 335x240x325mm	• integral single ramp to drawbridge • gateway to central walled courtyard • 2-D main building at rear w/square tower
unknown (4-175)	small grey fort (identified by an example in the ownership below) eg: Bernd Zimmermann, D	c1924	16¼"x10½"x14½" 410x270x370mm	• integral single ramp to drawbridge • gateway to central walled courtyard • 2-D main building at rear w/square tower
unknown (4-171)	small snow fort (identified by an example in the ownership below) Musée du Jouet, Bxl, B	c1924	unknown	• integral single ramp to drawbridge • gateway to central walled courtyard • 2-D main building at rear w/square tower • w/square & circular towers

unknown (4-174)	small medium fort (identified by an example in the ownership below) eg: Bernd Zimmermann, D	c1924	16"x10½"x15" 400x270x380mm	• integral single ramp to drawbridge • gateway to central walled courtyard • 2-D main bldg at rear w/sq & circ tower
unknown (4-173)	small medium fort (identified by an example in the ownership below) eg: Bernd Zimmermann, D	c1924	unknown	• integral single ramp to dbridge • gateway to central walled courtyard • 2-D main building at rear • sq & circ towers w/half-timbering
unknown	medium fort (identified by an example in the ownership below) eg: Bernd Zimmermann, D	c1924	18½"x13"x18½" 470x330x470mm	• integral single ramp to dbridge & gateway • central walled courtyard w/corner tower • 2-D main bldgs at rear w/two circ towers • feature w/2 sm towers & half-timbering
unknown (4-176)	medium fort (identified by an example in the ownership below) Musée du Jouet, Bxl, B	1924	unknown	• integral single ramp to dbridge & gateway • central walled crtyd w/2-D main bldg • w/1 lg sq & 1 lg circ towers • feature w/1 sm tower & half-timbering
unknown (4-177)	medium fort (identified by an example in the ownership below) Musée du Jouet, Bxl, B	1924	18"x13"x18½" 460x330x470mm	• integral single ramp to dbridge & gateway • central walled crtyd w/2-D main bldg • w/1 lg sq & 1 lg circ towers • feature w/1 sm tower & half-timbering
unknown	medium snow fort (identified by an example in the ownership below) eg: Bernd Zimmermann, D	1924	18"x13"x18½" 460x330x470mm	• (snow) integral ramp to dbridge & gateway • central walled crtyd w/2-D main bldg • w/1 lg sq & 1 lg circ towers • feature w/1 sm tower & half-timbering
unknown	large medium fort (identified by an example in the ownership below) Musée du Jouet, Bxl, B	1924	unknown	• integral single ramp to dbridge & gateway • central walled court w/wing building • 2-D main bldgs w/two circ towers • feature w/1 sm tower & onion roofs
unknown (4-178)	large medium fort (identified by an example in the ownership below) eg: Bernd Zimmermann, D	c1924	21¾"x14½"x18½" 550x370x470mm	• integral single ramp to dbridge & gateway • central walled court w/wing building • 2-D main bldgs w/two circ towers • feature w/1 sm tower & onion roofs
unknown (4-179)	large medium fort (identified by an example in the ownership below) eg: Bernd Zimmermann, D	1924	19¼"x13"x14½" 490x330x370mm	• integral single ramp to dbridge & gateway • central walled court w/wing building • 2-D main bldgs w/two circ towers • feature w/1 sm tower & half-timbering

4-171 Emil Neubert: *small snow fort (Courtesy Musée du Jouet, Brussels)*

This was one of the earliest of Neubert's forts, produced right at the beginning of his business.

Coming relatively late on the scene, he found it difficult to come up with anything new – to be original. So all of his forts seem to be somewhat like those of others. As time passed, this became less noticeable and he began to develop a style particularly his own.

This one is, of course, a snow castle, but is clearly from the series; note the half-timbering on the two sides of the central feature, door, and windows. The ramp also is a giveaway with its sloping end matching the slope of the sides of the fort.

1924–c.1935

4-172

4-173

4-175

4-174

4-172 **Emil Neubert**: *small brown fort (Courtesy Bernd Zimmermann)*
4-173 **Emil Neubert**: *small medium fort (Courtesy Bernd Zimmermann)*
4-174 **Emil Neubert**: *small medium fort (Courtesy Bernd Zimmermann)*
4-175 **Emil Neubert**: *small gray fort (Courtesy Bernd Zimmermann)*

These are some of the smaller forts in the first series.

The small brown fort (4-172) has most of the features of the series, but no large round towers and no half-timbering. The 40mm figures are by Merton.

The two small medium forts in the centre (4-173 & 4-174) are more easily recognizable as by Neubert. The big circular towers are a clue, even though they have different types of roofs.

The gateways too are clearly the same in spite of their different roofs. The fancy gable on the top one was a feature rarely used, but there is no doubt about its attribution. The drawbridge on the lower example would appear to be a replacement.

The small grey fort (4-175) is unusual simply because it is a rare example of this coloring in the first series. Again, there is no large circular tower for identification, principally because there would be no space for it, but the gateway and other features make up for it.

4-176 **Emil Neubert**: *medium fort (Courtesy Musée du Jouet, Brussels)*
4-177 **Emil Neubert**: *medium fort (Courtesy Musée du Jouet, Brussels)*
4-178 **Emil Neubert**: *large medium fort (Courtesy Bernd Zimmermann)*
4-179 **Emil Neubert**: *large medium fort (Courtesy Bernd Zimmermann)*

This is a selection from the larger forts in the first series. These all display a basic rough brown finish with large towers (usually round), different degrees of half-timbering, and other trademarks of a Neubert product.

The two medium forts (4-176 & 4-177) are classic examples of the genre. The one in the center is in near perfect condition, while the one on the left is missing its drawbridge and chains, and a dragon or similar has been nibbling at the battlements on the square tower, not to mention the point atop the roof on the circular tower.

The large medium fort to the right (4-178) has some fancy domes on anything slightly vertical. It also has a gate at the bottom of the ramp, borrowed, I think, from another fort. The wing side building coming out from one of the towers is an interesting innovation. The fancy gable treatment is also interesting.

The large medium fort below (4-179) shares many of the same features, but noticeably the two big towers are rectangular. The 45mm figures are by a unknown German manufacturer.

When things settled down after the rush of getting started, Neubert began to think about developing another series. The one he came up with showed many small differences to the first series, and, although none of them were particularly significant, the cumulative effect was amazing. Again it has proved impossible to put precise dates on the series, or on changes within the series.

One or two changes are worth a mention, however. These are the ones that showed up consistently throughout the series. The first was at the roofline, where the big, pointed roofs of the first series are noticeable by their absence; only a few small ones appear. There was also a change in the way they indicated doorways, which now showed a door, up some steps, slightly ajar – all done with stencils. This had to be seen in conjunction with the heavy stone surrounds which adorned the openings in the gateways.

Finally, there was the introduction of balustraded and covered walkways at a high level. This was achieved using a piece of cut-out cardboard, set proud of the wall to provide, very simply, the columns and balustrade. This feature was used even when all else had been discontinued as the Second World War loomed.

EMIL NEUBERT: The Second Series
c1935 to c1940

NO.	DESCRIPTION	DATE	DIMENSIONS	DISTINCTIVE FEATURES
unknown (4-182)	small beige fort (identified by an example in the ownership below) Musée du Jouet, Bxl, B	c1935	unknown	• integral single ramp to drawbridge • gateway to central walled courtyard • 2-D main bldg at rear w/2 sq towers
unknown (4-183)	small white fort (identified by an example in the ownership below) Musée du Jouet, Bxl, B	c1935	13½"x10¼"x13½" 340x260x340mm	• integral single ramp to drawbridge • gateway to central walled courtyard • 2-D main bldg at rear w/lg central sq tower • two flanking square towers
unknown (4-181)	medium beige fort (identified by an example in the ownership below) eg: Bernd Zimmermann, D	c1935	19"x12½"x17¼" 485x315x435mm	• integral single ramp to drawbridge • gateway to central walled courtyard • 2-D main building at rear w/central tower • 2 flanking towers – 1 sq & 1 lg circular
unknown	medium brown fort (identified by an example in the ownership below) eg: Bernd Zimmermann, D	c1935	19"x12½"x19" 480x315x480mm	• integral single ramp to drawbridge • gateway to central walled courtyard • 2-D main building at rear w/central tower • two flanking rectangular towers
unknown (4-184)	medium grey fort (identified by an example in the ownership below) eg: Bernd Zimmermann, D	c1935	19"x16¼"x20¼" 485x410x515mm	• integral single ramp to dbridge & gateway • central walled crtyd w/sm sq corner tower • 2-D bldgs at rear w/lg circ tower • walkways & med sq flanking tower
unknown (4-180)	medium large fort (identified by an example in the ownership below) eg: Bernd Zimmermann, D	c1935	21"x15"x19¾" 530x380x500mm	• integral single ramp to dbridge & gateway • central walled crtyd w/sm sq tower • 2-D bldgs at rear w/lg circ tower • one large square flanking tower
unknown	large grey fort (identified by an example in the ownership below) eg: Bernd Zimmermann, D	c1935	24½"x21"x21½" 620x530x550mm	• integral single ramp to dbridge & gateway • central walled crtyd w/sm oct corner tower • 2-D bldgs at rear w/very lg circ tower • walkways & med sq flanking tower
unknown	large brown fort (identified by an example in the ownership below) eg: Bernd Zimmermann, D	c1935	24½"x19¾"x23" 625x500x580mm	• single ramp on 2-arch bridge to dbridge • gateway to central crtyd w/oct tower • 2-D bldgs at rear w/very lg circ tower • one large square flanking tower
unknown	large brown fort (identified by an example in the ownership below) eg: Bernd Zimmermann, D	c1935	24½"x17¾"x22" 620x450x560mm	• integral single ramp to dbridge & gateway • central walled crtyd w/sm oct corner tower • bridge from corner tower to main bldg • 2-D bldgs at rear w/very lg circ tower
unknown (4-186)	large cream fort (identified by an example in the ownership below) Musée du Jouet, Bxl, B	c1935	unknown	• integral single ramp to dbridge & gateway • central walled crtyd w/sm oct corner tower • bridge from corner tower to main bldg • 2-D bldgs at rear w/very lg circ tower
unknown	large irregular fort (identified by an example in the ownership below) eg: Bernd Zimmermann, D	c1935	26½"x20½"x22½" 670x520x570mm	• integral single ramp to dbridge & gateway • central irregular walled courtyard • large square central tower w/main entrance • main buildings in sections at rear
unknown (4-185)	very large fort (identified by an example in the ownership below) eg: Bernd Zimmermann, D	c1935	29¼"x22½"x21½" 740x570x550mm	• single ramp on 2-arch bridge to dbridge • gateway to central crtyd with sq corner tower • 2-D bldgs at rear w/very lg circ tower • one large, circular flanking tower

Of course there were many other changes, but these were not consistently used – they would appear on only one or two forts. Thus we have bridges, various styles of gateway, slanted windows winding their way up towers, and even wells in some courtyards.

4-180 **Emil Neubert**: *medium large fort (Courtesy Bernd Zimmermann)*

This is one of the larger forts in the new series, which is clearly identifiable as by Neubert.

On the whole, this new series was larger than the previous one. Of course, there were small ones also, but they were generally fewer.

It was now that Neubert introduced his unique contribution – the high level covered walkway. Simply made and of very little depth, these appeared on almost all of his forts until the end of production.

There were other innovations, but many features stayed the same. His reliance on stencils with spray paint is a case in point, as well as the retention of the sturdy, tall circular towers in most cases, and the approach via a fairly simple ramp.

4-181

4-184

4-182

4-183

4-181 **Emil Neubert**: *medium fort (Courtesy Bernd Zimmermann)*
4-182 **Emil Neubert**: *small beige fort (Courtesy Bernd Zimmermann)*
4-183 **Emil Neubert**: *small white fort (Courtesy Musée du Jouet, Brussels)*
4-184 **Emil Neubert**: *medium fort*

These smaller forts were very much simpler than the larger ones. Gone are the fancy roofs, the large areas of half-timbering, and the sloping ends to the ramps. In come a new stencil design for entrances, with balustraded steps leading up to a partially open door, and a high level walkway in front of the upper level windows. Both these features became Neubert specialities.

Despite these changes, there really is not much to differentiate them from the small ones of the previous series. This is not true when one looks at the larger ones, where they are significantly more advanced. The small fort to the far left (4-182) is almost certainly more recent than the others – probably made in the lead-up to the Second World War.

4-185

4-186

4-185 **Emil Neubert**: *very large fort (Courtesy Bernd Zimmermann)*
4-186 **Emil Neubert**: *large fort (Courtesy Bernd Zimmermann)*
   These are the larger forts in the series, considerably larger than Neubert had made before. First we must consider the bases. They are noticeably higher than the earlier ones, with projections out at courtyard level to take the corner towers and other buildings on the walls. There are at least two openings to allow the moat to flow through – in the case of the very large one through a bridge for the ramp to go over.

The very large fort (4-185), which was probably one of the first in the series, has little apart from size to make it stand out from the smaller ones. That is unless you consider the two-arch bridge which formed part of the ramp – a fine feature by any standard. The other example is totally different (4-186); two particular features stand out: the bridge spanning from back to front and the well in the courtyard. That it has a wonderful gateway and the upper floors make this a four-storey building combine to make this an exceptional fort. The 40mm knights are of German origin.

As the Second World War came closer, standards were, of necessity, dropped. Catalogues, if there were any, are unavailable, at least to me, so, judging by their product, the quality of the design and finishes declined considerably. This was almost certainly due to the difficulty in getting supplies. Any semblance of a series disappeared, and it seems forts were produced in any way possible. Thin, two-dimensional wood buildings were the norm, though they still retained their high-level walkway.

And so ended Neubert's entry into the toy forts market. It was "short but sweet" as the saying goes – not even twenty years – but his impact was indeed significant. At least, he kept the others on their toes by his presence.

EMIL NEUBERT: The Last Forts
c1940 to c1943

NO.	DESCRIPTION	DATE	DIMENSIONS	DISTINCTIVE FEATURES
unknown (4-189)	**small brown fort** (identified by an example in the ownership below) eg: Allen Hickling Toy Forts	c1940	11¾"x9¾"x9½" 300x245x240mm	• single integral ramp to gateway • central walled courtyard • 2-D main building at rear • two flanking "square" towers
unknown	**small cream fort** (identified by an example in the ownership below) eg: Bernd Zimmermann, D	c1940	16¼"x10½"x14½" 410x270x370mm	• single integral ramp to drawbridge • gateway to central walled courtyard • 2-D main building at rear • central feature & two rectangular towers
unknown (4-188)	**medium beige fort** (identified by an example in the ownership below) Musée du Jouet, Bxl, B	c1940	19"x8¾"x16¼" 480x225x415mm	• single integral ramp to drawbridge • gateway to central walled courtyard • 2-D main building at rear • central feature & large circular tower
unknown	**medium large fort** (identified by an example in the ownership below) eg: Bernd Zimmermann, D	c1940	15¼"x10½"x17¼" 390x265x440mm	• single integral ramp to drawbridge & gate • central walled court w/corner circ tower • main building at rear with square tower • circular free standing tower
unknown	**large brown fort** (identified by an example in the ownership below) eg: Bernd Zimmermann, D	c1940	23¼"x15¼"x20½" 590x390x520mm	• integral ramp to entry yard w/circ tower • second ramp to drawbridge & gateway • central walled courtyard w/side building • main building at rear w/one lg circ tower
unknown (4-187)	**large brown fort** (identified by an example in the ownership below) eg: Allen Hickling Toy Forts	1940	26¼"x15¼"x24½" 665x390x625mm	• integral ramp to entry yard w/circ tower • second ramp to drawbridge & gateway • central walled courtyard w/side building • main building at rear w/1 tall circ tower

4-187

4-188

4-189

4-187 **Emil Neubert**: *large fort*
4-188 **Emil Neubert**: *small medium fort (Courtesy Musée du Jouet, Brussels)*
4-189 **Emil Neubert**: *small fort*

The large fort (4-187) may have been produced slightly before 1940, and the quality is beginning to show signs of the coming austerity. The buildings are quite two-dimensional and, although there is differentiation of levels and in the buildings, the painting is of a lesser quality. The figures are 54mm Swoppets by Britains.

Of the two below, the small one (4-189) was made noticeably nearer the end of production. It is very decidedly more two-dimensional without a drawbridge, and little effort was spent on the painting.

After the Second World War

After the Second World War, Germany was in a mess. This meant more than the physical fabric; it meant society in general. It was divided into zones – Eastern and Western – with different forms of government. Most of the industries concerned with the making of toy forts were in the Eastern Zone, which meant they were controlled by the Russians. Thus, they were state-controlled, and later, about 1972, they were nationalized.

In the Eastern Zone, it is difficult to be precise about who did what and when, because none of the records are available to me. I do, however, have one or two forts that are definitely from there.

One of their industries was VEB Holzspielwaren Marienberg. Marienberg was the town out of which Gottschalk worked before the war, but whether any of his workers were involved is not known. They produced a range of forts, which, given the circumstances, were quite good. It seems that they were all on the large side and were provided with electric lighting to the main buildings.

VEB HOLZSPIELWAREN MARIENBERG
1950 to c1972

NO.	DESCRIPTION	DATE	DIMENSIONS	DISTINCTIVE FEATURES
unknown	**medium fort** (identified by an example in the ownership below) eg: Bernd Zimmermann, D	c1950	15¼"x10½"x17¼" 390x265x440mm	• integral single ramp to dbridge & gateway • central walled crtyd with circ corner tower • very large circular tower to rear • main building w/sq tower & electric lights
unknown	**medium large fort** (identified by an example in the ownership below) eg: Bernd Zimmermann, D	c1955	23½"x16½"x19¾" 600x470x500mm	• integral reentrant ramp to dbridge • gateway to walled crtyd w/sm tower • main building w/2 flanking towers at rear • electric lighting to main building
unknown (4-191a)	**medium large fort** (identified by an example in the ownership below) eg: Musée du Jouet, Bxl, B	c1960	unknown	• separate single ramp to dbridge & gateway • walled courtyard with main buildings at rear • main building with central circular tower • electric lighting to one main building
unknown (4-190a)	**very large fort** (identified by an example in the ownership below) eg: Bernd Zimmermann, D	c1955	23½"x19¾"x18¾" 600x495x460mm	• integral reentrant ramp to dbridge & gate • walled court w/sm & lg circ towers to rear • ramp to 2nd level courtyard & main building • electric lighting to main building
721/6L (4-190b) (4-191)	**very large fort** (identified by an example in the ownership below) eg Allen Hickling Toy Forts	c1960	25¾"x17¼"x24¾" 655x440x630mm	• integral reentrant ramp to dbridge & gate • walled crtyd w/main bldg & circ tower to rear • 2nd level crtyd w/main bldg & lg circ tower • electric lighting to both main buildings
unknown (4-190)	**very large fort** (identified by an example in the ownership below) eg: Marc Assini, B	c1955	25¾"x20¾"x21¾" 655x525x550mm	• integral reentrant ramp to dbridge & gate • walled court w/sm & lg circ towers to rear • ramp to 2nd level courtyard & main building • electric lighting to main building

Apart from these, there were a number of others, but I cannot put a name to them, nor can I be certain they were made in the Eastern Zone. It would appear that they all stayed with wood and wood-related materials – they almost never ventured into the world of plastics for forts.

The examples I can get my hands on tend to be smaller and the finishes are not so good. They did, however, serve a public that seemed to have valued them, maybe because there was no alternative.

OTHER MANUFACTURERS FROM EASTERN GERMANY
1945 to c1972

NO.	DESCRIPTION	DATE	DIMENSIONS	DISTINCTIVE FEATURES
B25	**small fort** (identified by an example in the ownership below) eg: Bernd Zimmermann, D	c1955	unknown	• integral single ramp to dbridge & gateway • central walled crtyd w/sq corner tower • L-shaped main bldg to side & rear • squarc flanking towers
B26 (4-194)	**small fort** (identified by an example in the ownership below) eg: Bernd Zimmermann, D	c1955	unknown	• integral wrap-around ramp to dbridge • central walled crtyd w/sq corner tower • L-shaped main bldg to side & rear • sq & circ flanking towers (plastic roofs)
B?? (4-194a)	**small fort** (identified by an example in the ownership below) eg:: Allen Hickling Toy Forts	c1955	12"x12½"x12½" 305x315x315mm	• integral single ramp to dbridge & gateway • central walled crtyd w/sq corner tower • main building at rear • sq & circ flanking towers (plastic roofs)
B??	**small fort** (identified by an example in the ownership below) eg: Bernd Zimmermann, D	c1955	unknown	• integral single ramp to dbridge & gateway • central walled crtyd w/main building • sq & circ flanking towers (plastic roofs)
B?? (4-194b)	**medium fort** (identified by an example in the ownership below) eg: eBay	c1955	unknown	• integral single ramp to dbridge & gateway • central walled crtyd w/lg circ tower • 3-part main bldg w/electric lighting • bldgs w/lg sq linking tower
B29	**large medium fort** (identified by an example in the ownership below) eg: unknown	c1955	unknown	• gate to ramp to db over moat (2 arches) • gate to entry crtyd w/bldg & sq corner twr • bridge to gate & main courtyd w/circ twer • 4-part main building at rear w/sq link tower
unknown (4-193)	**small medium fort** (identified by an example in the ownership below) eg: Bernd Zimmermann, D	c1955	unknown	• integral single ramp to gateway • central walled crtyd w/sm sq tower • main bldg w/circ tpwer (plastic top) • crude stencil windows & door
unknown (4-192)	**small medium fort** (identified by an example in the ownership below) eg: Bernd Zimmermann, D	c1955	unknown	• integral single rmp to dbridge & gateway • walled court w/main building to rear • cent feature w/rect & sq flanking towers • crude stencil windows & door
unknown (4-193a)	**medium fort** (identified by an example in the ownership below) eg: Bernd Zimmermann, D	c1955	unknown	• integral single ramp to gateway • walled court w/small square corner tower • main bldg w/sm & lg flanking circ towers • turret (plastic top) & stencil windows

4-190 **VEB Holzspielwaren Marienberg** *(Courtesy Marc Azzini)*
4-190a **VEB Holzspielwaren Marienberg** *(Courtesy Bernd Zimmermann)*
4-190b **Packaging label for 721/6L**
4-191 **VEB Holzspielwaren Marienberg 721/6L**
4-191a **VEB Holzspielwaren Marienberg** *(Courtesy Musée du Jouet, Brussels)*

These are all typical large forts made by VEB Holzspielwaren Marienberg. They offer excellent play value with their multiple levels, re-entrant ramps, and interior spaces.

Constructed of wood, hardboard, and cardboard, they were as robust as any on the market at the time, which does not mean that they were in any way indestructible. The electric lighting, in particular, left much to be desired. The figures on the upper right example (4-191) are 54mm knights from Britains Swoppet range. Those on the lower right (4-190a) are a mixture of German manufacture including Elastolin.

The packaging label (above centre (4-190b)) is from VEB Holzspielwaren Marienberg, and has an image of the fort at lower left.

4-192 **Unknown manufacturer**: *small fort (Courtesy Bernd Zimmermann)*

4-193 **Unknown manufacturer**: *small fort (Courtesy Bernd Zimmermann)*

4-193a **Unknown manufacturer**: *medium fort (Courtesy Bernd Zimmermann)*

4-194 **Unknown manufacturer**: *B26 small fort (Courtesy Bernd Zimmermann)*

4-194a **Unknown manufacturer**: *B25 small fort with box*

4-194b **Unknown manufacturer**: *medium fort (Courtesy Bernd Zimmermann)*

These forts are all thought to be from the Eastern Zone of Germany during the 1950s and 1960s. They are all relatively small and are all by manufacturers unknown to me. The three in the upper right hand corner (4-194, 4-194a & 4-194b) are by the same manufacturer, who cared more for realism. The doors and windows are particularly well depicted.

The one above left (4-192) bears some of the characteristics of Neubert and of Schubert, but I do not think we can assume too much from that. The sloppy use of stencils for the doors and windows is particularly noticeable.

The small medium sized example below left (4-193) is from a different manufacture, but is typical of those produced in the Eastern Zone at the time. The medium-sized example top center (4-193a) is clearly different again, but is also typical of those produced in the Eastern Zone of Germany. It owes much to the work of La Hotte aux Jouets.

In the Western Zone things were very different. O. and M. Hausser were there, and though it took a while to get going, they did recover. They started with figures, and then, about ten years after the war ended, they were in full toy fort production.

When plastic came along in about 1957, two companies climbed on the band wagon and flourished alongside Hausser. They were Eco, based in Neumarkt, who seemed to copy Hausser's style, including vacuum-forming, and Big Plastik, based in Fürth, who used injection-molding. Later they were joined by Simba, who produced forts more in the traditional style, as much as the use of plastic would allow.

Eco's most popular fort was one they called "Camelot" (4-196). It is more of a settlement than a fort, and it is apparently smaller scale than the others, although this may be attributed to the fact that it is more of a settlement. Nonetheless, it still has the same gateway as the others making the buildings appear smaller.

Big Plastik started up about 1965, also in the Western Zone, thus avoiding all the hassle in the Eastern Zone. Their most popular product was one they called "King Arthur Castle" (4-200). It was a fine fort with a basement dungeon and a well – great play value. Simba likewise set up in the Western Zone and made several models.

ECO: Vacuum-formed Plastic
c1960 to c1990

NO.	DESCRIPTION	DATE	DIMENSIONS	DISTINCTIVE FEATURES
434000 (4-196)	**white fort ("Camelot")** (identified by an example in the ownership below) eg: Allen Hickling Toy Forts	c1965	24"x16¾"x8½" 610x425x215mm	• drawbridge over moat to gatehouse • entry court w/circ tower & building to rear • chapel crtyd w/chapel & 2 bldgs to rear • down to well & large circular tower front
unknown (4-195)	**white fort** (identified by an example in the ownership below) eg: Allen Hickling Toy Forts	c1965	22¼"x15¾"x12" 515x400x305mm	• dbridge over moat to gateh'se to rmp up • 2 sm circ towers & bldg to protect entry • up to crtyd w/main bldgs & sm circ tower • steps to upper level w/lg circ tower
5 (4-198)	**large white fort with lake** (identified by an example in the ownership below) eg: Allen Hickling Toy Forts	c1965	32½"x22½"x14¼" 820x570x360mm	• dbridge over moat to gateh'se to lake • entry court w/lg circ tower & bldg w/ruins • gateh'se to main crtyd w/circ twr & chapel • 2 bldgs with very lg central circ tower
11	**large brown fort** (identified by an example in the ownership below) eg: Allen Hickling Toy Forts	c1965	23½"x15½"x8" 595x395x200mm	• dbridge over moat to gatehouse • lg crtyd w/circ tower & battlements to sides • L-shape 5-part main bldng at rear & side
unknown	**very large white fort** (identified by an example in the ownership below) eg: Bernd Zimmermann, D	c1965	unknown	• db over moat to gateh'se & entry crtyd • lg sq & tall circ tower & bldgs to rear • gateh'se to main crtyd & chapel w/circ tower • main bldgs and corner redoubt
unknown	**very large white fort** (identified by an example in the ownership below) eg: Geoff Green, AU	c1965	unknown	• double dbridges & gateways over moat • walled court with small circular wall tower • main building at rear in six parts to rear • 3-storey buildings and a tower extension

BIG PLASTIK & SIMBA: Plastic Forts
c1970 to c2000

NO.	DESCRIPTION	DATE	DIMENSIONS	DISTINCTIVE FEATURES
unknown (4-200)	**Big Plastik fort** (identified by an example in the ownership below) eg: Allen Hickling Toy Forts	c1965	20"x20"x18¾" 510x510x475mm	• separate simple ramp to dbridge & gateway • court with basement dungeon & well • 3 square towers & building to rear
unknown (4-199)	**Big Plastik fort** (identified by an example in the ownership below) eg: Marc Azzini, B	c1965	unknown	• gateway with flanking semi-circ towers • walled courtyard with well • steps up to higher section to rear • maybe missing some parts
unknown (4-197)	**Simba fort** (identified by an example in the ownership below) eg: Musée du Jouet, Bxl, B	c1965	unknown	• small ramp up to dbridge & gatehouse • high walled court w/4 circ corner towers • main building at rear

4-195 Eco No.unknown

This relatively small fort would prove to be one of the most popular. It is a typical Eco product made with a vacuum-forming process. The feeling of a densely packed fortified settlement on a hilltop is very well done.

c.1965-c.2000

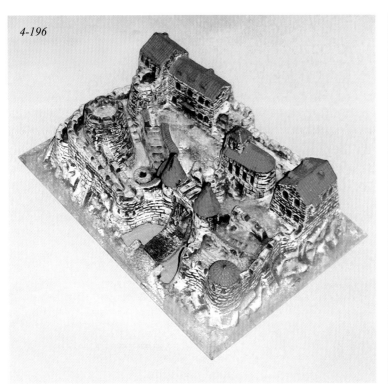

4-196

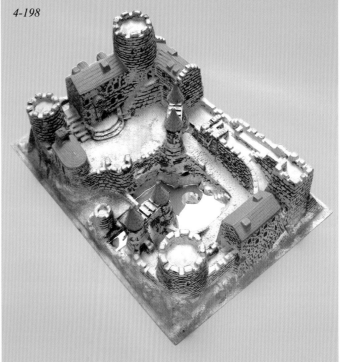

4-198

4-197

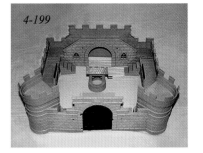

4-199

4-200

4-196 **Eco No.434000**: *Camelot*
4-197 **Simba**: *most common fort (Courtesy Musée du Jouet, Brussels)*
4-198 **Eco No.5**: *fort with interior lake*
4-199 **Big Plastik**: *fort (Courtesy Marc Azzini)*
4-200 **Big Plastik**: *King Arthur Castle*

These forts are all from the Western Zone of Germany during the 1960s. Above left and right are two typical forts made by Eco. Constructed of vacuum-formed plastic, they were not very robust, but this was offset by the savings on transport. The one on the left (4-196) is their most popular model, which they named Camelot, though it bears little resemblance to the popular image of Camelot of King Arthur's day. It represents a settlement with the remains of earlier fortification. The one on the right (4-198) is much bigger, and has the possibility of water in the interior lake. Everything considered, this is a magnificent design, again with evidence of earlier fortification. The keep is clearly defined at one end.

The example at the centre above (4-197) is by Simba, and is a fine example of the more traditional fort.

The two examples below are by Big Plastik. The one on the right (4-200) is King Arthur Castle, which, judging by the sales, was the most popular. It certainly had a lot going for it – different levels, interior and exterior spaces, etc. The one on the left (4-199) may have some pieces missing. It is a much simpler fort in spite of it having a well.

1890-1910

4-201

4-202

4-203

Unidentified German Manufacturers' Forts

None of these manufacturers got into this chapter, but they all deserve a mention here. The reason for their omission is simply that I do not know enough about them. Maybe the next author will provide the necessary information.

The first one on this page (4-201) shows many of the characteristics of Erzgebirge work, while the second one (4-202) shows how that work was developed during the next ten years or so. The last on this page (4-206), from perhaps a little later, shows how they chose an Eastern theme, thus allowing them to continue their bright colors.

The image above right (4-203) is somewhat different in that it may have been manufactured by several companies – Schumann, Schubert, and D. H. Wagner come to mind, but it may have been someone else. This fort has been seriously restored, but retains its character. The one below center (2-205) has much the same scenario. The 30mm huntsman figures are mainly by Heyde of Germany.

The last to get a mention (4-204), shows that lithography could provide a level of detail that would have been impossible by any other means. This technique was being used by others about this time – Richter and Wittich for example.

4-204

4-205

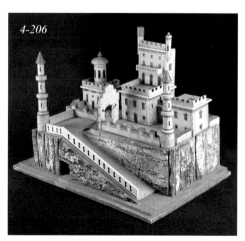

4-206

4-208

4-210

4-211

4-212

4-209

4-207

Unidentified German Manufacturers' Forts

These are all taken from the decade that was disrupted by the First World War.

Probably the first was the fort in illustration 4-208. This was distributed by J. D. Oehme and most likely others, but we do not know the manufacturer. The details were painted on by hand with the aid of stencils, which is true of all the forts on this page with the exception of the cardboard one. The figures are 30mm German flats.

Then came the two forts in illustrations 4-211 & 4-207, which may or may not have been by the same manufacturer, in spite of the similarity of the architecture – Schumann, Schubert, and D. H. Wagner come to mind as candidates. The obvious difference is that the one above is a winter scene and the one below is summer, which confuses the situation. The figures on the one above are 45mm marching soldiers of German make, whereas those on the lower one are 45mm Landsknechts produced by Elastolin. The small fort in illustration 4-212 is not dissimilar, but is clearly a different manufacturer.

The fort based on the Middle East or India (4-210) is quite unusual. It has many Eastern details, but stands on a base intended to represent a hill like the medieval forts of Europe, which makes me think of India as the more likely basis.

Finally, there is the cardboard fort in illustration 4-209. This bears many of the characteristics of the Erzgebirge. It is quite small in scale, as well as in size, but it is beautifully made if a little fragile – not very good for a toy. Noticeable in the design is the three-dimensionality of the palace; not only are the wings completely capable of housing a number of people, but there are four of them.

4-213

4-214

4-215

4-217

4-218

4-216

Unidentified German Manufacturers' Forts

These forts were part of Germany's recovery after the First World War. This was made in spite of major setbacks, including the runaway inflation of the German Mark in 1922-23. It was a fine effort.

The fort in illustration 4-217 came out in the early 1920s and was distributed by Oskar Beier. Notice the difference in treatment of the windows on the front towers and the rest of the painting – it is as though they came from another fort. It has been substantially restored but is still an excellent example.

The center left and bottom right forts (4-214 & 4-218) are of about the same vintage and are also fine specimens. Nothing is known of them except that the less domestic one (4-214) was distributed by Meisterarbeit.

The one at the top left (4-213) was by Lineol – No. F13. Using techniques similar to O & M Hausser, they produced this very large fort, which, although similar in many respects, was quite crude by comparison.

Of the other two on this page, brought out in the early 1930s, the brick built one (4-215) is quite simple in concept – just a generic fort with masses of crenellation.

The more palace-like one (4-216) is quite a different proposition. It is one of the few based on an actual palace, the English Queen's summer residence at Balmoral in Scotland. It is, of course, partial in its complexity, but the rest is a faithful representation. It was made by a prolific manufacturer that we know through their distributor, Moise Konstam (MOKO). The 30mm figures are from John Hill's Coronation set.

FIVE

THE THREE LINES BROS.:
The Story of Tri-ang's Toy Forts

Joseph ("Joe") Lines was a toy manufacturer from the mid-1870s to the day of his death in 1931. He started in partnership with his brother George, operating as G. and J. Lines Ltd and specializing in the production of rocking horses. As the business flourished, their production was extended to include a wide variety of wooden and metal toys in many sizes – but not toy forts. Eventually, in 1903, he bought out his brother and continued in the same business, assisted by his four sons.

All this may be very interesting, but, in fact, Joe Lines's only relevance, as far as this story is concerned, is that he introduced his sons to the toy industry, and three of them went on to create the great Tri-ang brand name.

In 1919, after service in the "Great War," these three, Walter, Arthur, and William, found that working in the family tradition was too irksome. They started their own toy manufacturing company, which they named Lines Bros. Ltd. The abbreviation "Bros." was used from the start – "brothers" never came into it.

Their trademark was a triangle, which, being a figure formed by three lines, must have appealed to the brothers' sense of humor. They used the brand name Triangle Toys initially, but soon reduced it to Triang Toys and, by 1928, to just Tri-ang, which they finally registered in 1931. Triangtois was also used – probably in that same formative period, but the evidence is not available to give it a precise date.

They started producing toy forts in 1931 or 1932, and continued, with a break for the Second World War, until they went under in 1971. They updated the production every two or three years until the war, although their style of production did not vary much until 1958. Then, in response to the growing threat of plastics, they changed, with some overlap, to a completely new style. In about 1960, they changed again, this time as a reaction to their purchase of another company that produced rubber goods.

Having resisted the onslaught of plastics, they finally gave in to the inevitable, in a half-hearted way. Consequently, all of their forts, from 1960 to the end, had some parts in plastic – usually the more complicated, operating parts. They never really embraced the new material as did some of their rivals.

The end came after a decade of buying anything that came up – Dinky, Hornby, Meccano, Scalextric, Sindy, and many others. Indeed, they were the largest toy manufacturer in the world, but they had over-stretched themselves in the belief that anything was possible. In 1971, it was just too much.

Entry into the Toy Forts Market

The numbering system for their forts, as for all their toys at the outset, was the ultimate in simplicity. The first model introduced was given the number 1. Larger versions became 2, 3, 4, and so on. When smaller versions became necessary they were given 0, 00, 000 and so on. When variations on the same size of fort had to be introduced, letters of the alphabet were used to differentiate them, ie: 1A, 1B, 1C, etc.

The earliest available firm evidence of Tri-ang's existence in the toy fort market comes in their catalogue for 1933/34. Naturally this does not preclude the possibility that they entered the market earlier – they almost certainly did. For example, there are toy forts identified by use of a metal disc with "Triangtois" enamelled on it that could well be taken to imply that they were in production before the registration of the name "Tri-ang."

The 1933/34 catalogue identifies five forts, numbers 1, 1A, 2, 3, and 4. Using the Richard Lines numbering system, it is possible to establish a probable sequence of development. Two scenarios present themselves. Either they first produced Nos.1, 2, 3, and 4, and then No.1A; or they produced No.1 and No.1A, and then Nos.2, 3, and 4. In any case, they all ended up in the 1933/34 catalogue, making it likely that they were introduced in 1931 or 1932.

TRI-ANG TOY FORTS: First Series (First Version)
c1932 to c1939

NO.	DESCRIPTION	DATE	DIMENSIONS	DISTINCTIVE FEATURES
1 (5-005)	**smaller of this series** (illustrated in Tri-ang's 1932-39 catalogues) eg: Allen Hickling Toy Forts	1931/ 1932	12"x12"x10" 305x305x255mm	• built-in ramp to dbridge & gateway • walled court w/small sq corner tower • main building & two square towers • electric light

c1932 to c1958

2 (5-003)	**larger of this series** (illustrated in Tri-ang's 1932-58 catalogues) eg: Allen Hickling Toy Forts	1931/ 1932	22"x17"x10¼" 560x430x260mm	• built-in artificial moat & double ramp • dbridge & gateway & two 'turret' guns • walled courtyard & 4 sq towers • main building w/electric light

Two different series can be easily recognized on the basis of the number of common components used in each and the scale to which they were built. The first series was quite small both in scale and size – broadly to a scale suitable for 25–30mm figures. Those of the second series were of a different design and much larger – broadly to a scale compatible with 40–45mm figures. In fact, Lines Bros. probably intended these to be for the then current production of toy soldiers, i.e., 40mm and 54mm.

Those of the first of the two series, which made up this offering, shared the same main building, gatehouse, short and tall solid square towers, and some battlement pieces. Of these, the No.2 Fort was significantly different. Not only was it much larger, providing a large parade ground in the middle, but it was also the first of the very few Tri-ang produced with an integral artificial moat.

TRI-ANG TOY FORTS: Second Series (First Version)
c1932 to c1939

NO.	DESCRIPTION	DATE	DIMENSIONS	DISTINCTIVE FEATURES
3 (5-004)	**smaller of this series** (illustrated in Tri-ang's 1932-39 catalogues) eg: Allen Hickling Toy Forts	1931/1932	17"x15¼"x15" 430x385x380mm	• separate ramp to dbridge & gatehouse • court w/3 turret guns & one sq tower • main bldg w/1 lg sq flanking tower • red elec lts & gunfire noise (to 1940)

c1932 to c1958

4 (5-002)	**larger of this series** (illustrated in Tri-ang's 1932-58 catalogues) eg: Allen Hickling Toy Forts	1931/1932	29"x16½"x20½" 735x420x520mm	• separate double ramp to db & gatehse • crtyd w/4 turret guns & sq towers • main bldg w/2 lg sq flanking towers • red elec lts & gunfire noise (to 1940)

The second series (the Nos.3 and 4) was of a different design and considerably larger in size and scale. The towers and the gatehouse were fully three-dimensional, as were the main buildings, although these were a little on the skinny side by comparison. 54mm figures do not look too out of place on them – especially the pre-war forts which had deeper "wells" in the tops of the towers to accommodate standing troops. In the case of No.4, the separate ramp was of the double-sloped variety.

All the first forts were *"Fitted with electric light, but without batteries."* In Nos. 1 and 2 this meant a lone light bulb installed in the rear of the main building and operated by a simple pendulum switch on the back. In the case of Nos. 3 and 4, it was a much more complicated arrangement altogether. These were claimed to be *"Fitted with flashing red electric lights in hollow towers."* Indeed, while light bulbs were not installed in the main building, they were in all the towers and the gatehouse as well. The red light was achieved by covering the embrasures (they were too narrow to be called windows and too wide for arrow slits!) with red cellophane on the inside, or by using red-colored light bulbs.

There was only one component that the two series shared. This was a spring-operated "turret" gun and its emplacement (a simple block of wood) fixed to a battlement piece. It has been described as looking like an upside-down saucepan and was a well-loved characteristic of Tri-ang forts for well over thirty years. This is an example of Lines Bros. use of the metal presses, in which they had invested when they moved into their new factory.

THE TOY FORTS PAGE IN TRI-ANG'S CATALOGUE

Many of the same principles that were outlined in the chapter on Moritz Gottschalk also apply here. For example, the toy fairs were no different; in fact the English versions copied the German practice. In the beginning the German toy fairs, the one at Leipzig in particular, were attended by everyone involved with toys in the Western World.

So all the pressures around dates were the same. First came a panic to get the new models out in time for the January/February toy fairs, and then a panic to get the product into the shops in good time for the Christmas rush. And that was in Britain. If you then consider the international trade, everything had to be brought forward by about two or three months.

And all of this had to do with production of the catalogue, which was the main sales item in the first part of the year.

Tri-ang seems to have gone to some trouble and expense to produce its catalogues, making them as tempting as possible to the potential buyer. They were partly full-color printed on quite good paper and would have been impressive in the range of goods on offer. One, or most of one, page, was usually devoted to toy forts. Most of the current range would be illustrated – and any which were not were described next to a similar one.

Strangely, before the 1939–1945 war, not all the forts illustrated were in color. This would have provided no saving on the actual printing cost because the page would have had to run through the presses four times anyway. We can only surmise that there was a saving in production of the original artwork. In fact, the saving would have been minimal, which indicates that Tri-ang were extremely cost conscious in a very competitive market.

Nonetheless, Tri-ang's attitude to the actual production of catalogues was much the same as everyone else's – i.e., keep the cost down wherever possible. Printing, especially color printing, could be expensive – and the most expensive part is in the "origination." This included all the start-up processes such as original art, graphic art (drafting, layout, typesetting, color separations,etc.) and the making of the plates – usually by photography. Consequently, once the origination for an item was completed – such as the illustration of a toy fort – it did not get changed even if the item was modified or up-dated.

Examples of this include their Fort No.1, which continued to be illustrated with an integral ramp after the later version with a separate ramp came out. Similarly, the "Z" fort was brought out with a re-entrant ramp and four sentry boxes before the second World War, and the illustration of it was still being used in 1956, even though the design was changed when production started up again after the war.

Unfortunately, we have no earlier evidence of Tri-ang's approach than their catalogue for 1934, which would have come out just after Christmas 1933. In this, the information is clearly aimed at retailers, in that details are provided not only of the product as it would be on display or in use by the end-user, but also as it would be packaged for transport or storage. For toy forts, this meant their packaged size and weight, as well as their size and appearance when fully erected.

In addition, "point-of-sale" support in the form of end-user focused catalogues was needed. These catalogues would have been published on different time schedules, such as September for the Christmas shoppers. They are of particular interest because, unlike the catalogues for retailers, they contain prices. For example, in 1937 Tri-ang produced a two-sided, four-color printed leaflet poster (16½" x 22" (420 x 560mm) folded three times down to 8½" x 5½" (225 x 140 mm)). In terms of paper size, long before Europe converted to "A" sizes, this was known as "Half Imperial."

It contained examples from their whole range of toys, so there was only space for one toy fort. From the nine they had on offer, they chose their No.3 Fort which was priced at 18/11 (eighteen shillings and eleven pence). Other models are mentioned, but not specified – priced at 7/6, 9/6 and 25/6. The only other available example comes from 1968, in which a Chatham Fort is featured at £1.18.6d (one pound eighteen shillings and sixpence).

Tri-ang's catalogue for 1937
Note some of those illustrated are in black and white, and some are not illustrated at all.

1931-1932

5-002

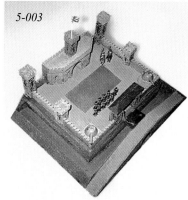

5-003

5-004

5-002 **Tri-ang second series No.4 Fort** *(first version)*
5-003 **Tri-ang first series No.2 Fort** *(first version)*
5-004 **Tri-ang second series No.3 Fort**

The difference in size and scale between series 1 and series 2 can be readily seen. The figures are 40mm by Elastolin.

Up until just before the Second World War, Tri-ang forts were painted either white or a very light grey, covered with a generous sprinkling of red, yellow, and green dots, which simulated vegetation in the form of flowers and grass. A pattern reflecting their construction with stone blocks was represented by pressed indentations.

Ground surfaces were covered in a texture provided by sand painted with paths and green grass. The sides of the box were green with dry brushed yellow and red patches.

But just why these guns should have been so well loved is a bit of a mystery. They were extremely difficult to aim with any accuracy. Their bent metal construction left an open slit down the length of the underside of the barrel, through which one's matchstick ammunition would frequently fall.

The two forts of the second series also boasted *"imitation gunfire noise devices,"* which were created by a simple cranked handle flicking a flat metal spring clapper onto the frame inside the base as it was turned. The flashing effect of the lights was achieved by linking the electric circuit to the spring clapper of this gunfire device.

The first supplementary type came in 1933. The No.1A extended the range of the first type in size, fitting neatly between Nos.1 and 2, and provided a fort with one "turret" gun. One assumes they had perceived a gap in the range and now could offer forts with one to four guns. All the main buildings, towers, and gatehouse were exactly the same as the first type, so there was no extra cost in tooling up, etc.

TRI-ANG TOY FORTS: First Series (First Version)
1933 to c1959

NO.	DESCRIPTION	DATE	DIMENSIONS	DISTINCTIVE FEATURES
1A	**smallest with turret gun** (illustrated in Tri-ang's 1933-58 catalogues) eg: SOFIA Foundation, CY	1933	16½"x13½"x9" 420x340x225mm	• separate ramp to db & gateway • walled crtyd w/one turret gun • three corner & one central sq tower • main building w/electric light

5-005 Tri-ang first series No.1 Fort *(first version)*
Initially, this was the smallest in the range. Note the integral ramp.

5-006 Tri-ang first series No.1A Fort *(first version)*
Tri-ang No.1A was brought out to fill a gap in the range – for guns and size. This was the smallest in the range to have a "turret" gun. Note the juxtapositioning of the almost domestic style of the gate, and the militaristic nature of the gun emplacement.

TRI-ANG'S ELECTRICAL WIZARDRY

Tri-ang were very proud of the lighting in their forts. They put two different systems in their first forts. In their Nos.1, 1a, and 2 Forts it was a quite primitive system, but in their No.3 and 4 Forts it was a much more complicated arrangement. Both systems were powered by batteries.

The wiring was lightly sheathed and fixed to the inside of the box. It wound its way around from tower to tower, where it was linked directly to the bulbs. It had the effect of guns being fired from the fort. This arrangement needed two 4.5-volt batteries to power it.

Taking the simple system first; this was a single bicycle or flashlight bulb mounted on the back wall of the main building, which needed one 4.5-volt battery, mounted in the same building. The switch, on and off, was a pendulum device on the back wall, which permitted easy access for the operator. The wiring was a simple, uncovered wire on the surface. The effect, best seen at night, was merely one of occupation.

The second, much more complicated system was found on the No.3 and No.4 Forts. Not only did it light many more locations and flash red, it was also linked to simulated gun noise devices. These provided the noises and the means of flashing the lights. All towers and the gateway were lighted, but not in the same way as the other system.

About thirty-five years after they pulled the plug on electric lighting, Lines had one more try. About five years before they finally folded, they brought out a Tintagel Castle, which boasted, in quite a low key way – *"battery operated tower light,"* to quote the catalogue. It was a simple system. Batteries connected to a bulb with a switch in between. The bulb was the same as they had used before, powered by two 1.5-volt batteries.

TRI-ANG TOY FORTS: First Series
c1934 to c1937

NO.	DESCRIPTION	DATE	DIMENSIONS	DISTINCTIVE FEATURES
00 (5-018)	**smallest of this series** (illustrated in Tri-ang's 1934 catalogue, described 1937) eg: no known example	1934	10"x9"x8" (estimated)	• built-in ramp to drawbridge • unique crenellated gatehouse • walled crtyd w/sm sq corner tower • 3-tower main building
0 (5-019)	**2nd smallest of this series** (illustrated in Tri-ang's 1934-37 catalogues) eg: SOFIA Foundation, CY	1934	12"x10"x8½" 305x255x220mm	• separate ramp to db & gateway • walled crtyd w/sm sq corner tower • 3-tower main building

In 1934, a new catalogue was published with further supplementary types, both smaller. In it, the Lines Bros. offered seven forts for sale. They used many of the same elements that were in production already, but the main building was too big, so they made do with some walls. This meant that there was no place for the electric light feature, which they did not offer in these forts. For some reason No.00 had a crenellated gatehouse, which was completely different from any of the others.

For the first time, they produced a new version of an existing fort in 1934. They offered it in the catalogue, but did not change the image. This is a comparatively rare occurrence, because they generally preferred to only change something when they absolutely had to. In this case, it concerned the No.1 Fort, for which they decided to make the ramp separately, probably for manufacturing reasons.

TRI-ANG TOY FORTS: First Series (Second Version)
1933 to c1939

NO.	DESCRIPTION	DATE	DIMENSIONS	DISTINCTIVE FEATURES
1 (5-017)	**smaller of this series** (illustrated in Tri-ang's 1934-38 catalogues) eg: SOFIA Foundation, CY	1934	12"x12"x10" 305x305x255mm	• separate ramp to db & gateway • walled crtyd w/sm sq corner tower • two square flanking towers • main building w/electric light

This brings us to the end of Tri-ang's initial attack on the toy forts market. It was two or three years before the catalogue was to change.

Developments Up to the Second World War

This was the period of the "recession" in Britain (called the "Depression" in the US), but it did not seem to have much of an effect on Tri-ang's growth. As far as the toy forts were concerned, they continued to bring out new models at regular intervals.

The firm evidence for the emergence of a completely new series, and coincidentally a new identification system, first came in a price list for 1936, and then in the catalogue for 1937/38, where they were illustrated. Numbers went out and letters of the alphabet came in, with the arrival of their "A" and "B" Forts.

This seems like a retrograde step – the alphabet has a finite number of characters, which means that sooner or later it was going to have to be changed again. In fact, Tri-ang themselves seem to have been a bit confused about it, because the forts were identified in the catalogue as No.'A' and No.'B'!

This innovation was undoubtedly associated with the appearance of a similar fort in Littlewood's Mail Order Catalogue (September 1937), as part of their *"Fort with Soldiers"* set. This was item number GXA117, which claimed to be *"The Ideal Gift for Every Boy."*

It was described as being *"...strongly made, with turrets, ramp and drawbridge. Realistically painted in stone color and moss green."* Although it was not identified as Tri-ang, it is easily identifiable as such, if only because it incorporated one of their unique "upside-down saucepan" turret guns. It was Lines Bros. Ltd. policy not to label their products in any "own brand" deal such as this, and those they had with the likes of Hamley's and Gamage's.

From the rather small illustration, it included what appears to be Johillco figures described as follows: *"...two cannons, two machine guns with gunners, eight Light Infantry with rifles, five mounted Life Guardsmen and a dispatch rider on a motor-cycle."* The parts were not supplied separately, and the set was offered for 10/- (ten shillings) complete.

In terms of size, they fitted in the middle of the range. Compared to Fort No.1A, the "A" fort was slightly smaller, and the "B" fort slightly larger. They both had an integral ramp, unlike the 1A, but similar to the original numbers 00 and 1. But there the similarities stop – otherwise they were very different.

In terms of overall design, they had more towers and were considerably more complex than any of the previous types. This meant that, compared with their other forts of similar size, they had to be built to a somewhat smaller scale – probably compatible with 30mm figures. They also featured a portcullis (for the first and only time) and steps from the courtyard to the upper battlements, previously reserved for the much larger forts of the second series (No.3 and No.4 Forts).

5-017

1934

5-018

5-017 Tri-ang first series No.1 Fort
(second version)
5-018 Tri-ang first series No.00 Fort
(catalogue)
5-019 Tri-ang first series No.0 Fort
   The Tri-ang No.1 Fort (5-017) had to be modified so that the ramp could be made separately.
   These are the supplemental forts to Tri-ang's first offering. They are all part of the first series. Nos.0 and 00 (5-018 & 5-019) were brought out to fill the bottom of the range. The illustration of the No.00 Fort is taken from the catalogue. The finishes were consistent with Nos.1-4.

5-019

TRI-ANG'S PRODUCT STRATEGY: TOY FORTS

The term "product strategy" did not exist when the three Lines brothers were active. However, they must have had one, albeit at an intuitive level. There is no doubt that they thought about what they were doing and that is all one needs to do to develop a strategy.

Some time in the early to mid-1920s, when Tri-ang's designers first sat down to design a toy fort for production, they probably asked themselves, "What were the essential characteristics of a fort? What would a child expect, and be excited by?" As a result, they came up with their so-called No.1 Fort.

The style of fort that they chose to depict was defiantly militaristic. This seems to have been a choice made right at the outset. If so, it was a clear example of differentiation in the marketplace – their forts being significantly different from the offerings of Gottschalk and Hausser, who were the main competition at the time. Gottschalk had always pursued the fortified mansion as a theme, much of it baroque in style. Hausser, on the other hand, had elected to go for a decidedly medieval hill-top settlement type of fort, also much more domestic in style; only later did they produce more fortress-like buildings.

It is likely that they were thinking of the grim grey stone, towers, crenellated curtain walls, ramps, and drawbridges one associates with the sort of castle built by Edward II in his campaigns to subdue the Celts in North Wales. If this were the case, the style of the gatehouse must have hailed from a somewhat earlier period because it is noticeably more domestic in character. It would not have been out of place in the stockade around an old motte-and-bailey castle.

A product strategy includes more than just its appearance however, and the designers must have been wrestling with a number of other factors at the same time. For example, how large should they be – not only from the end-user's point of view but also in terms of manufacture, transport, and storage? Sensibly they started quite small, meaning less cost in every respect and less demand on factory space, which was at a premium in the early days. Richard Lines writes:

In pre-computer days, a very careful analysis was maintained of the number of every item actually manufactured and despatched. With the enormous variety of items on offer, the factory could get in a mess without strict control. My father, Arthur, was responsible for this.

Thus, every week he would have a census of the previous week's activity – production and sales. These figures were set alongside the previous year's performance, and Arthur juggled all these figures to issue the factory with its "Making Order" for the next month. By comparison, it could be clearly seen which items were doing better than before and which were doing worse.

There were specific meetings in the boardroom for each main category of products. Thus, while the meeting was dealing with forts, there would also be dollhouses, nursery furniture, etc. The meeting might conclude with a variety of decisions about action to be taken, quite likely to redesign, or perhaps to delete an item for the next year. It was a sort of on-going process.

In the early days, they found it necessary to develop a series that was much larger in both size and scale. This was possibly another response to the 54mm size adopted by so many toy soldier manufacturers. Alternatively, it may have been merely that, with the move to the new factory at Morden Road, there was at last enough space.

Tri-ang's "turret" gun
This gun, which was fixed in one place, could only be used for defensive purposes. One wonders how they explained the anomaly of having guns like these alongside archers and knights in armour.

The one serious anomaly is the ubiquitous "turret" gun. It appeared together with the first forts, but it was not on all of them – the No.1 missed out. In any case it became one of the most characteristic features of their toy forts for very many years. Maybe they were trying to make the forts more consistent with the majority of toy soldiers being produced in Britain at that time.

It seems a pity they did not pay attention to their design. As it is, if one is using matchsticks as ammunition, they tend to fall down the slot in the bottom of the barrel and get stuck there. Of course, if one is using dried peas as ammunition, that is a different story. Then there is the question of aim. The direction one shoots in is fine, but the range is set by the fixed elevation of the gun, so that the only control is in how far back one pulls the spring.

The guns are more the sort of armament one associates with the defense of seaports from the 17th century until not so very long ago. Seen in this light, the buildings could well be based on those from that period. This, then, makes one wonder what the designers had in mind. Is this why they called them "forts" and not "castles?"

Another related issue would have had to do with materials. Tri-ang had invested in all the machinery necessary for industrial metal-working, so by the time they were designing their forts they would have had the option of metal.

As it happened, they chose wood again – probably because that was what other manufacturers tended to use. Anyway, they had started that way, and a workforce with the relevant skills was already in place. In any case, wood provides the possibility of making relatively large toys with a minimum of capital expenditure – a significant consideration for a business just finding its feet in a recession.

TRI-ANG TOY FORTS: Third Series
1936 to 1939

NO.	DESCRIPTION	DATE	DIMENSIONS	DISTINCTIVE FEATURES
A (5-021)	**smallest of this series** (described in Tri-ang catalogue 1937) eg: Musée du Jouet, Bxl, B	1936/ 1937	14"x12½"x12" 355x315x305mm	• built-in single slope ramp • 90° left turn to drawbridge & gate • square corner tower & steps up • two small & one large sq towers
B (5-022)	**largest of this series** (illustrated in Tri-ang catalogue 1937) eg: SOFIA Foundation, CY	1936/ 1937	17¾"x13"x14½" 450x330x370mm	• built-in single ramp to 90° right turn • db & gate to crtyd w/sq corner tower • steps up to high level walkway • thru lg rect tower to sm sq tower
C? (5-024)	**Littlewood's Mail Order (?)** (September 1937 – no Tri-ang catalogue entry known) eg: no known example	1936/ 1937	18"x13"x13½" 455x330x345mm	• built-in single ramp to 90° right turn • db & gate to crtyd w/turret gun • steps up to high level walkway • thru two large rectangular towers

One of the detail differences was in the battlements. Here the proportions of the crenellation were changed so that instead of the ratio of crenel to merlon being 1:1 it became 1:4. For those unfamiliar with these terms – the crenel is the cut out bit through which the shooting was done, and the merlon was the solid bit behind which one sought protection while re-loading. This meant 75% fewer saw-cuts, with a much reduced probability of splits in the wood during manufacture and breakage in handling afterwards – altogether a much more robust design.

Perhaps even more significantly, a development in their construction appeared. Wood-blocked cardboard, or very thin plywood, came to be the material for the towers. In this case it permitted the upper battlements to be linked through the building. This could have been the forerunner of the ubiquitous "W," "X," "Y," and "Z" Forts that dominated the scene after the war and through to the mid-1960s.

TRI-ANG TOY FORTS: Third Series
1938 to 1940

NO.	DESCRIPTION	DATE	DIMENSIONS	DISTINCTIVE FEATURES
D (5-023)	**second largest of the series** (illustrated in Tri-ang's 1940 catalogue) eg: no known example	1938	??"x17"x??" ??x430x??mm	• re-entrant double ramp • drawbridge & gate with portcullis • three small sq towers & main bldg • electric searchlight on roof

In 1938, having just launched the "A," "B," and "C" Forts, they introduced a "D" Fort. This was clearly an intermediate size of the third series. It had one particular exciting added feature – a *"movable electric searchlight"* mounted on top of the main building.

Otherwise, its only notable aspect was an integral "re-entrant" double ramp. Double re-entrant ramps are unusual, but one that rises from ground level between its upper level and the main body of the fort is extremely rare indeed. It is an attractive arrangement, which, in spite of the difficulty in its manufacture, was a fore-runner for the No."Z" Fort that was to come.

5-021 **Tri-ang third series No."A" Fort**
Identification of the Tri-ang No."A" Fort above is almost certain. It has all the right dimensions and characteristics, although the drawbridge and a piece of the battlements in front are missing.
The "A" Fort is one of the three that made up the third series at this time. A fourth, Tri-ang No."D" Fort, was added to the series later.

5-022

1936-1938

5-023

5-024

5-022 Tri-ang third series No.“B” Fort
5-023 Tri-ang third series No.“D” Fort *(catalogue)*
5-024 Tri-ang third series No.“C” Fort (?) *(advertisement)*

These are three of the four forts that made up the third series. Identification of the Tri-ang No.“B” Fort (5-022) is without question, when one compares it with the catalogue illustration. The whole gateway area and the “walk-through” tower above were significant innovations.

In terms of construction and painting, the Tri-ang No.“D” Fort (5-023), brought out in 1938, appears from the catalogue illustration to bear more characteristics of the fourth series than

the third. Note particularly the sloping sides to the base and the very large gateway, in addition to the searchlight on the roof of the main building.

The Tri-ang No.“C” Fort (5-024) is more uncertain. This is taken from Littlewoods Mail Order catalogue for 1937. It was never featured in any Tri-ang catalogue and no other alternative has yet emerged. It looks remarkably like the “B” Fort. The only difference was in the provision of a second main tower and the all important “turret” gun. It seems unlikely, therefore, that Lines intended to offer it alongside the other two.

TRI-ANG TOY FORTS: Fourth Series (First Version)
1939 to c1966

NO.	DESCRIPTION	DATE	DIMENSIONS	DISTINCTIVE FEATURES
W (5-027)	**smallest of this series** (illustrated in Tri-ang 1939-61 catalogues & described 1965) eg: no known example	1939	10½"x8"x8" 265x205x205mm	• separate single slope ramp • red metal drawbridge to gateway • walled crtyd w/small sq corner tower • main rect building w/small sq tower
X (5-025) (5-028)	**third largest of this series** (illustrated in Tri-ang catalogue 1939) eg: Allen Hickling Toy Forts	1939	12"x10"x9" 305x255x230mm	• separate single slope ramp • red metal drawbridge to gateway • walled crtyd w/small sq corner tower • main rect building w/2 sm sq towers
Y (5-026)	**second largest of this series** (illustrated in Tri-ang catalogues 1939-65) eg: SOFIA Foundation, CY	1939	14½"x12"x9½" 370x305x240mm	• separate single slope ramp • red metal drawbridge to gateway • walled crtyd w/2 sm sq corner towers • main rect building w/2 sm sq towers
Z (5-029) (5-030)	**largest of this series** (illustrated in Tri-ang catalogues 1939-65) eg: SOFIA Foundation, CY	1939	18"x14"x12" 455x355x305mm	• re-entrant ramp to red db & gate • walled crtyd w/2 sm sq corner towers • two 'turret' guns / four sentry boxes • 2 lg circ towers & rect main bldg

5-026

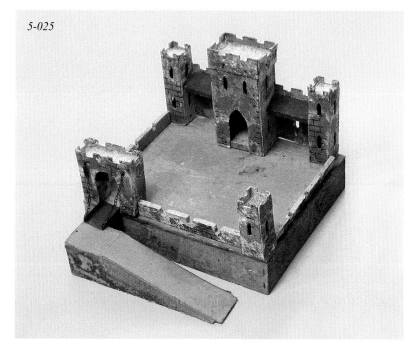

5-025

5-025 **Tri-ang fourth series No."X" Fort** *(first version)*
5-026 **Tri-ang fourth series No."Y" Fort** *(first version)*

   This series represents a major breakthrough in terms of the construction of toy forts. The use of cardboard, or very thin plywood, wrapped around wood formers became Tri-ang's modus operandi for twenty-five years. It allows quite large pieces to be made, while not weighing a lot – all of which made for considerable savings in transport costs,

   The Tri-ang No."X" Fort (5-025) and the Tri-ang No."Y" Fort (5-026) were pretty much the same – except for size. The No."Y" became the most popular, probably because it had a more three-dimensional main building and two sentry boxes.

1938-1939

5-027

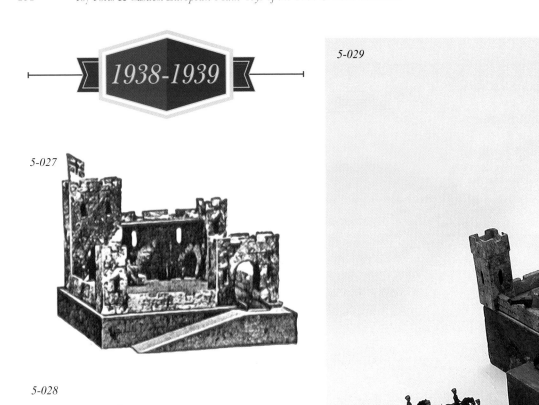

5-028

5-029

5-027 Tri-ang fourth series No.“W” Fort (catalogue)
5-028 Tri-ang fourth series No.“X” Fort (catalogue)
5-029 Tri-ang fourth scrics No.“Z” Fort (first version)
   These are three of the four forts that went to make up the fourth series. There is no known example of the “W” Fort.

Note the painting, which is quite camouflage-like and would have been appropriate given the imminent hostilities. Out goes the vegetation and in come slashes of drab pink and green on a greyish background.
   There appears to be considerable sharing of components, but this is an illusion – they are not exactly the same. When examined closely the only parts that are exactly the same are the battlements around the courtyard, the gateway, and the sentry boxes.

In 1939, Tri-ang launched a new series, the famous "W," "X," "Y," and "Z" Forts. In both style and construction, they had much in common with the "A" and "B" Forts, and the "Y" and "Z" Forts were exactly the same size. So, when this new series was introduced in the 1939 catalogue, something had to go. It was naturally the "A" and "B" Forts, which, being more complex and difficult to make, had to give way to the new range.

At the same time, Nos.0 and 00 Forts disappeared – almost certainly because they were the same size as the new "W" and "X" Forts and there would have been too much duplication of sizes. Interestingly, they decided to keep the "D" Fort – presumably because the searchlight offered something different.

As far as the painting was concerned, Lines was caught in a bind. First, it wanted the new range to be bright and cheerful, but the looming hostilities called for a more subdued approach. So, in fact, Lines used two schemes – one quite light, but the other with dull colors, distinctly reminiscent of camouflage.

5-030

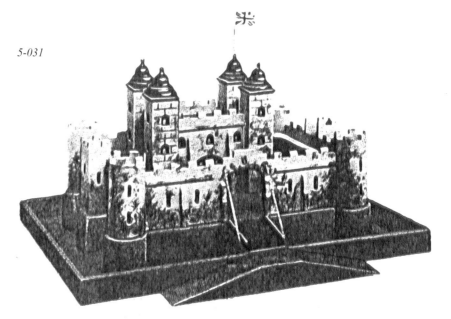

5-031

5-030 **Tri-ang fourth series No."Z" Fort** *(first version)*
 This Tri-ang No."Z" Fort is an early version with brighter colors, probably painted when the war was still a few months away. It was only when the war became a reality, perhaps even as late as 1940, that they changed to the "camouflage" version.

5-031 **Tri-ang's Tower of London** *(catalogue)*
 Tri-ang's Tower of London fort shows a passing resemblance to the real Tower of London, but it could not be described as a model.
 It is symmetrical and, therefore, has two of most things – ramps, gateways, etc. It is made of wood, although the round corner towers were probably of cardboard. The painting is not like Tri-ang, bearing in mind the multi-colored dots on white livery of the earlier forts and the camouflage like later ones. Was it made by another manufacturer? It may have been suitable for 54mm figures.

TRI-ANG'S USE OF TRADEMARKS

In the antiques business, the use of trademarks has long been used as the most reliable means of authentication. China and silver are two of the best known examples. What is interesting here is that they are also used as a source of information when dating old or antique objects – and this includes toy forts.

But it was not until the coming of plastic as a viable material for toy forts that trademarks could be easily made an integral part of the product. Prior to that, something had to be attached to them. Over the years Tri-ang usually used a label of some sort.

Unfortunately for the historian, Tri-ang's attitude to labelling was somewhat devil-may-care. Whatever was to hand would do – and if nothing was to hand, as was often the case in the early years, that would have to do just as well! Marion Osborne told me, by way of an example, that she has come across at least one Tri-ang dollhouse with a Pedigree Prams label.

Richard Lines, the son of Arthur, has himself said that the use of their trade names and labels was treated in such a relaxed way that they provide unreliable evidence of dates. Apparently, if a section of the factory ran out of labels, they would just borrow some from the nearest source, usually the neighboring section, which may have been producing something completely different.

However, we can deduce some general trends. For example, the little circular enamelled metal discs inscribed with the "Triangtois" name were used only in the late 1920s or early 1930s. Thereafter they used mechanical image transfers – or, as we tend to call them, simply transfers – and, much later, adhesive labels.

The first was the gold triangular version that is considered by many to be the classic. It was used for many years and came in various forms. It was not until the early 1950s that the first of the new labels made an appearance. There

were several of these, in particular the "puffy white," the "bold red," and the "warped rectangular" ones. All display the fashionable graphics of their day.

Tri-ang's practice in the location of their trademarks can also give us clues. For the first twenty years, their policy was reasonably consistent – the mark being always placed on the box base. The metal Triangtois discs were nailed to the outside face of the back piece. When they changed to transfers, they were still located on the back piece, but now on its inside face. This was simply because all the outer faces were roughly textured and transfers would not "take" on them. This rough textured finish was a characteristic of Tri-ang forts – except their rubber ones. It was made by mixing sawdust in the paint for the vertical surfaces, and sand for the courtyards.

After the war there seems to have been a change of policy – if, indeed, there was any policy at all. The inside face of the back piece was retained as the favored spot for Nos. 2, 4, and "Z" Forts, but for the No.1a, the "W," and "Y" Forts, a position under the ramp was chosen (the No."Z" Fort's ramp was too narrow for this).

It is true that this under-the-ramp position was quite well protected, but it seems to have been a strange choice if the aim was to keep the brand name in sight for as long as possible. The ramp appears to have been one of the more easily lost or damaged components – whereas the one piece which could be almost guaranteed to survive was the base.

Without a doubt there were simple production process reasons for it. For example, it would have been much easier to line up a large number of ramps to enable the speedy application of transfers – it might even have been possible to apply them to the cardboard before it was shaped over its wood formers.

Much later, with the introduction of labels and then the "castle" series in the late 1950s, the labels were located on the underside of the small, red, painted metal drawbridge which, since 1939, had become almost as much a feature of Tri-ang forts as their turret guns.

Another notable innovation was the introduction of the red metal drawbridge which continued in use until about 1965. It was simply a sort of tray with turned-up sides. What is surprising is that they persisted with its use, despite the fact that fitting it to the inside of the gateways so that it was hinged must have been very difficult.

Another totally new type of fort was also introduced at this time – the so-called Tower of London fort. This was described as a "realistic model" – and so it was, compared to all the others. Not only was it based on a real building, displaying some of its more recognizable architectural characteristics, but all the components seem to have more realistic proportions. It featured two ramps – one each front and back – with drawbridges spanning an integral "dummy moat," somewhat like the No.2 Fort. At a width of 30½" (775mm) it was to remain the largest, if not the tallest, fort Tri-ang ever produced, though their 1959 version of the Tower of London ran a close second.

TRI-ANG TOY FORTS: Stand-alone Extra
1939 to 1940

NO.	DESCRIPTION	DATE	DIMENSIONS	DISTINCTIVE FEATURES
unknown (5-031)	**The largest fort ever made** (illustrated in Tri-ang's 1939 catalogue) eg: no example known	1939	30½"x??"x??" 775x??x??mm	• 2 double slope ramps + gateways • built-in dummy moat • bastions & towers • one electric light

And so, the first decade of Tri-ang's production came to an end on a note of continuing growth and innovation – just at the time that the world went to war in a big way for the second time in twenty-five years. The business of making toy forts continued for about a year, but it was not long before all industrial capacity was redirected towards the war effort.

Some Anomalies

Before moving on to what happened after the Second World War, it is opportune to consider some forts that were made in the period leading up to it, but which never appeared in the Lines catalogues. Three such forts have come into my hands.

The first fort was probably made about 1935. It bears stylistic characteristics of Lines and one other fort that I do not know except that it was distributed by

Manufacturers Accessories Co. Ltd. of London, known as MAC. A number of scenarios present themselves:

1. A take-over is one possibility – if so, it is most likely that Tri-ang was doing the taking-over
2. A merger, although this is unlikely because mergers were not Tri-ang's style
3. Commercial plagiarism is a possibility in that a number of features were adopted

5-038 Tri-Ang / MAC prototype?
The Tri-ang / MAC prototype bears the hallmark of both manufacturers. The most recognizable parts are the towers, the manner of fitting the central turret, and the doors of Tri-ang. Also note the metal drawbridge with its unique connection for the chains, the opening to the storage in the base, and the spacing of the crenellation on the battlements of MAC. It must have been produced about 1935.

5-039

5-040

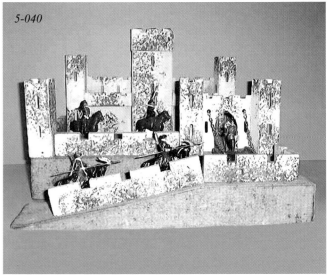

5-039 **Tri-ang prototype?**

  The second was a Tri-ang prototype with pieces that were in production at the time. The recognizable parts are the base from the No.2, two towers from the "A" and "B" series, two "turret" guns, and, finally, the color scheme with its red, yellow, and green dots on white. It must have been produced about 1937. It could have been made as a special for another company – such as Littlewoods.

5-040 **Third series prototype?**

  The third prototype does not fit with any known Tri-ang fort, although it bears some similarity to the No. "A". It is, however, undoubtedly made by them. The figures are 54mm cavalrymen by Britains.

In any case, although it was a bit of a "pigs ear" of a design, it led to several innovations in the third series. Not least of these was the method of joining chains to the drawbridge. The towers were also innovative, as, in particular, was the way of holding the central tower in position. This was achieved by a squeeze fit between the front and back faces of the main building, later to be used in the No."Z" Fort.

The second fort is a bit of a mystery. It shows many of the characteristics of the third and fourth series, but is badly made – see the battlements up the ramp. The finishes are definitely Tri-ang.

The third fort was probably made about 1937. It is quite an elaborate affair based on the "box" of the No.2 Fort. While it has some pieces that are definitely Tri-ang, like the turret guns, there were pieces that definitely were not. These were the gateway and the main building at the back, both of which were quite ornate designs. The towers at the back were of very thin plywood bent around formers, which is like the towers of the fourth series.

The most likely explanation for this is that someone at Lines was playing around with some ideas that might have led to developments. So, while this could have been made for a specific client, such as Littlewoods or Gamages, it seems unlikely.

The Immediate Post-War Period of Austerity

It is not clear from the available evidence just how soon the toy trade started to recover from the war or how quickly it did so. We do know that there was already a significant market operating by Christmas of 1946, in spite of the shortage of labor and, especially, raw materials.

Catalogues were few and far between and those that were produced were of a strictly utilitarian nature – color printing and quality papers were still luxuries! However, Tri-ang had recovered enough by the end of the 1940s to produce fine color catalogues with a good range of toy forts.

Their 1950 catalogue offered six different forts, although there was nothing radically new – all of them were taken from the 1939 range and modified. As might be expected, Tri-ang's immediate pre-war innovations played an important part, and three of the four forts of the fourth series survived – going on to form the core of Tri-ang's toy fort production. The No."X" Fort was the one that fell by the wayside, while the "W", "Y," and "Z" Forts went on for the next fifteen years or more.

TRI-ANG TOY FORTS First Series (Second Version)
c1946 to c1958

NO.	DESCRIPTION	DATE	DIMENSIONS	DISTINCTIVE FEATURES
1A (5-041)	smallest with turret gun (illustrated in Tri-ang's 1950-58 catalogues) eg: SOFIA Foundation, CY	1946/1947	16½"x13½"x9" 420x340x225mm	• integral ramp • one 'turret' gun • main building gate & towers as 2 • simplified finishes
2 (5-042)	largest of this series (illustrated in Tri-ang's 1950-58 catalogues) eg: SOFIA Foundation, CY	1946/1947	22"x17"x10¼" 560x430x260mm	• built-in moat and double ramp • two 'turret' guns • main building, gate & towers as 1A • simplified finishes

TRI-ANG TOY FORTS: Second Series (Second Version)
c1946 to c1958

NO.	DESCRIPTION	DATE	DIMENSIONS	DISTINCTIVE FEATURES
4 (5-043)	larger of this series (illustrated in Tri-ang's 1950-58 catalogues) eg: SOFIA Foundation, CY	1946/1947	29"x16½"x20½" 735x420x520mm	• separate ramp with double slope • four 'turret' guns • buildings as before • now painted terracotta brown

TRI-ANG TOY FORTS: Fourth Series (Second Version)
c1939 to 1966

NO.	DESCRIPTION	DATE	DIMENSIONS	DISTINCTIVE FEATURES
"W" (5-044)	smallest of this series (illustrated in Tri-ang 1939-61 catalogues / described 1965) eg: SOFIA Foundation, CY	1946/1947	10½"x8"x8" 265x205x205mm	• separate single slope ramp • gateway w/red metal drawbridge • walled crtyd w/sm tower as Y & Z • rect bldg & linked med tower
"Y" (5-045)	second largest of the series (illustrated in Tri-ang's 1939-65 catalogues) eg: SOFIA Foundation, CY	1946/1947	14½"x12"x9½" 370x305x240mm	• separate single slope ramp • gateway w/red metal drawbridge • walled crtyd & 2 sm towers as W & Z • rect bldg & 2 linked med towers
"Z" (5-046) (5-047)	largest of this series (illustrated in Tri-ang's 1939-65 catalogues) eg: SOFIA Foundation, CY	1946/1947	12"x18"x14" 455x355x305mm	• separate single slope ramp • gateway w/red metal drawbridge • walled crtyd & 2 sm towers & 2 guns • 2 lg circ towers linked by main bldg

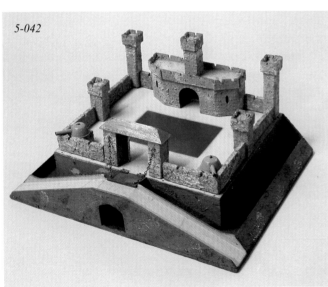

5-041 **Tri-ang first series No.1A Fort** *(second version)*
5-042 **Tri-ang first series No.2 Fort** *(second version)*
5-043 **Tri-ang second series No.4 Fort** *(second version)*
   These are the three survivors of series one and two after the war. Series three did not come through.
   Note the differences in paint style. Most obvious is the change from white to terracotta in their No.4 Fort (5-043). However the absence of sand on the horizontal surfaces is clear in their Nos.1A and 2 Forts (5-041 & 5-042). Also note the distinct grey color of these two.

5-044 Tri-ang fourth series No."W" Fort (second version (?))
5-045 Tri-ang fourth series No."Y" Fort (second version)
   These are two of the survivors from the fourth series to go on for more than fifteen years, forming the core of Tri-ang's offerings.
   Note the grey color of these forts; it was sometimes lighter and sometimes darker.

There were many small changes, mostly to rationalize the production process and simplify the designs. For example, the towers changed in size, very slightly, so that they were all the same. The wings on either side of the main building are narrower and the doorway into the central tower is omitted. Note the sentry boxes are made all in one piece and now are painted green and red.

5-046

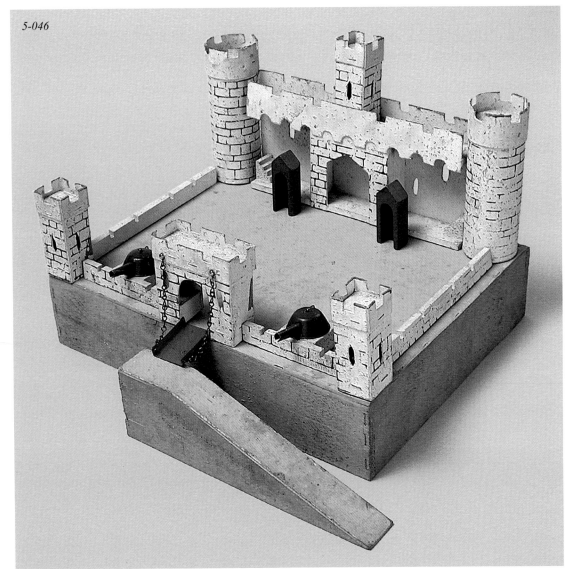

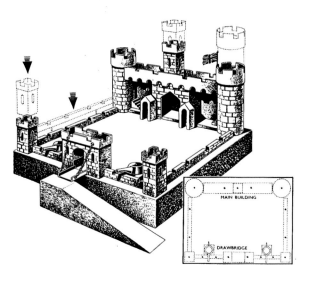

All parts of this Fort peg firmly into the appropriate holes provided and indicated on the plan. The Sentry Boxes are not fixed and may be placed in any position required.

A PRODUCT OF THE LINES BROS GROUP OF COMPANIES

Printed in England

5-048

5-049

5-046 Tri-ang fourth series No."Z" Fort (*second version*)

The most noticeable of the changes in Fort No."Z" were the sentry boxes and the ramp. The color of Fort No."Z" is reminiscent of the more flamboyant of the pre-war schemes.

5-047 Assembly instructions for the "Z" Fort

The assembly instructions, like the one shown, were included with every fort. They do not say much that a reasonably intelligent child could not have worked out for him or herself.

5-048 & 5-049 Green and brown corrugated cardboard packaging

Some packaging is still available from this period. The green packaging (5-049), shown on the right, is rare. It is the "sleeve" style that was by far the most frequently used (the other type was the "shoe-box" style, which is even more rare).

The other packaging is the much more common brown corrugated cardboard type (5-048), in which they retained color by continuing the use of the label. They only made the sleeve type in this material.

Of the first series, only those with the turret guns survived. These were Nos.1A and 2 Forts, albeit with simplified finishes.

Of the second series, only the big No.4 Fort was still there, but now with the buildings painted a bright terracotta red instead of the creamy white of the pre-war version. Lines, wishing to save wherever possible, continued with their pre-war artwork in their catalogue, showing all their first and second series forts colored white.

The third series disappeared altogether, which may have been because of difficulties in the supply of their relatively glamorous accessories, such as the movable searchlight on the No."D" fort. Regretfully, the great Tower of London was never seen again.

Although the range on offer was quite respectable even by their pre-war standards, the quality had had to be severely cut back. To what extent this had to do with the market, in that there was not as much money around, and how much it was due to the austerity program we may never know.

In any case, there were no more sand-textured courtyards or indented stone walls, though, strangely, the complex crenellation of the battlements of Nos.1A and 2 Forts continued, in spite of the lessons of the third and fourth series. The much vaunted electric lighting was also dropped, as were the simulated gun noise devices. Regretfully, these attractive features were never to return, even when things eventually settled down and times became easier.

The fourth series, with its Nos."W", "Y", and "Z" Forts, fared somewhat better. Their overall size, shape, and the disposition of the pieces stayed the same, but, as it was already a relatively economical design, the changes took place in the detail.

There were, in fact, sixteen changes to the No."Y" Fort, but, as some were quite minor, I shall concentrate on the main ones. The central tower in the main building at the back was shortened and the access doorways to the battlements at each side were eliminated. This permitted the support battlements to be slimmer. The corner towers at the front were made slightly bigger, so that they were the same as those on the No."Z" Fort, and the sentry boxes were now routed out of one piece of wood and painted green with red roofs.

The No."Z" Fort had fewer changes. The four sentry boxes were reduced to two of the new sort. The pleasant looking easy-sloped re-entrant double ramp was exchanged for a much steeper single one, though the catalogue still contained this very attractive feature. This would have been much more challenging for the toy soldiers to march up, but it was certainly much less challenging for the workers in the factory who had to manufacture them!

We know little of the No."W" Fort because we do not have an example from before the war, but it seems reasonable to assume that any changes would have been similar to those in the No."Y" Fort.

We now have some post-war examples of the type of packaging Lines provided. The earliest, which may have been in use before the war, used a bright green cardboard to make both a shoe box type (with a lid) and a sleeve type. These were mostly used for the export trade, but a few were used in Britain.

They soon found, however, that it was necessary to economize and they came up with a sleeve made of brown corrugated cardboard. They managed to introduce some color to this by use of the fine labels that they originally used on the green boxes.

Lines had established a range with which they and the market were happy. Having experienced a decade before the war when everything changed all the time, after the war they were able to proceed without change for more than ten years.

The Times They Are A-Changin' – New Models

The late 1950s and early 1960s were exciting times. At last, the austerity program was a thing of the past, and it was possible to think of new horizons. But these new horizons were not always seen to be positive, and the arrival of plastics as a viable alternative material for toy forts was both a threat and an opportunity. It was going to depend on how easily manufacturers could adapt. As it turned out, Lines Bros. Ltd. entered this period circumspectly.

Let us begin with the Castles Series, which came out in 1957 or 1958. Lines Bros. produced four castles, sized to make for a range of value and thus cost, which were numbered 3 to 6. What happened to numbers 1 and 2 in the series is a mystery, and whether the "Rochester" Castle was ever made may never be known.

These models, and I use the term deliberately, were as close as any manufacturer came to producing a genuine copy of an original. The originals they chose were all existing castles, Corfe, Dover, Harlech, and the Tower of London, although Corfe was distinctly ruinous. Thus, they were all totally different, which was quite a change from the "W"/"Y"/"Z" series that, incidentally, they kept on for another seven years. No parts were common, with the exception of the large corner tower on the two larger castles.

Not only were they models, but they used a style of construction which was totally new to them. They used plywood structurally, assembled with simple "sleeved" half joints instead of nails or glue.

TRI-ANG'S APPROACH TO PACKAGING

The fact that there was no physical closure to the underside of any of their forts implies that they must have been sold in boxes from the start – had they not been so, the ensuing muddle when a number of them were accidentally set upside-down, would have been the cause of no little consternation!

But not much survives from before the Second World War, except for the tattered remains of the box for a 1939 No."Z" Fort. This appears to be a conventional "sleeve" box made of strawboard, covered with a very attractive bright green paper. Unfortunately, the board was not very stout for the size of the box, and it did not survive very well.

The finished article was surmounted by a bright spanking new four-color printed label depicting the actual contents, erected and manned by a contingent of toy soldiers. This depiction was (to be polite) somewhat enhanced with a clever extension to the perspective, the addition of a moat, and the use of small-size toy soldiers to make it look like

a quite magnificent edifice. Before being too critical, however, we should remember that this was before the days of the Trades Descriptions Act, and this sort of exaggeration was common practice.

Tri-ang boxes post-war
These were standard packaging for (clockwise from top left) the No."W" Fort, the No."Z" Fort, the No.2 Fort, and the No."Y" Fort.

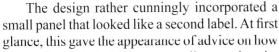

The design rather cunningly incorporated a small panel that looked like a second label. At first glance, this gave the appearance of advice on how to use the fort, but it was actually an advertisement for their Minic toy vehicles! There are some examples of the bright green covering from after the war – mounted on pulp board. There is a No.1A Fort in a "shoe box"

form, as well as a No."Y" Fort and a No."W" Fort in a "sleeve" form. It is not known, however, whether these few examples were for export only.

In the years after the Second World War, Britain was in a period of austerity and it seems that the green paper was a luxury they could ill afford. So Lines developed a more austere brown corrugated cardboard type of packaging. The emphasis was on protecting the contents and the "sleeve" form was chosen. The corrugated cardboard was stamped out in one piece, and, in effect, folded around the contents. Access to the fort inside was through one of the ends. The labels, which were retained, provided color even if the corrugated cardboard

was only a drab brown.

The same materials were used for the new "castle" series in 1958, but now the packaging could no longer rely on the box base part of the fort to contain the pieces. The mass of the fort was made up out of separate pieces of plywood which slotted together for use, and were transported flat – the original "flatpack." So the packaging had to act as a container on its own. This led to a design which lent itself even less than the previous style to being kept by the owner.

Their approach to label design also changed significantly. Now, instead of a different label for each castle – "Corfe," "Dover," "Harlech," and the "Tower of London" – all four castles were depicted on the same label. This had two advantages. In the first place the longer print run that this permitted was an obvious economy measure and, coincidentally, prevented labels being put onto the wrong box. Secondly, and perhaps more importantly, it was an in-built advertisement for the full range of castles on offer.

Then came their rubber-based forts, which were not only produced out of house by another manufacturer, albeit owned by Lines, but required a different sort of packaging. A "shoe box" form was used, with a lid and a tray. The label was of a different character all together.

In the mid-1960s, there was a marked change in the style of production, but it was still a "flatpack" as far as the packing was concerned. The forts, however, were much smaller and could be contained much more easily. The labels disappeared, to be replaced with bold graphics printed directly onto the corrugated cardboard.

The big advantage to this was that Lines Bros. could use what the furniture makers called "flat-pack" production. The parts were produced "knocked down," and the customer did the erection, a system which enabled much larger forts to be made and allowed savings in transportation that were not insignificant.

The only problem appeared where walls came to a corner. This was not new – manufacturers had had to deal with this problem using plywood. The solution was halved joints, which produced ugly results. The four models dealt with the problem in one of three ways. In "Dover," they just let it happen with no disguise. In "Corfe," they were covered by a turret with a cross cut into the base. In "Harlech" and the "Tower of London," much more substantial towers were specially cut to slip over the whole corner, making it look as though it had all been built at one time.

Finishes were very crude, but the scale of the forts allowed one to get away with it. They were painted a basic white, relieved by yellow, green, and red applied with a very dry brush. On top of that, a stonework pattern in black was applied by means of a stencil.

TRI-ANG TOY FORTS: Fifth Series
1958 to c1965

NO.	DESCRIPTION	DATE	DIMENSIONS	DISTINCTIVE FEATURES
1	Not in catalogue			
2	Not in catalogue			
3 (5-058)	**Tri-ang Corfe Castle** (illustrated in Tri-ang adverts 1959 & the 1961 catalogue) eg: SOFIA Foundation, CY	1958	15"x15"x8½" 380x380x215mm	• central building w/2 side buildings • four corner turrets to cover joints • red metal drawbridge and ramp • off-centre gateway
4 (5-062)	**Tri-ang Dover Castle** (illustrated in Tri-ang adverts 1959 & the 1961 catalogue) eg: SOFIA Foundation, CY	1958	17½"x17½"x9" 445x445x230mm	• quite like the actual Dover • two separate buildings • steps up inside building • red metal drawbridge to ground
5 (5-059) (5-063)	**Tri-ang Harlech Castle** (illustrated in Tri-ang adverts 1959 & the 1961 catalogue) eg: SOFIA Foundation, CY	1958	20½"x20"x9" 520x510x230mm	• very much like the actual Harlech • red metal drawbridge and ramp • eight towers • barbican well modelled
6 (5-060) (5-061)	**Tri-ang Tower of London** (illustrated in Tri-ang adverts 1959 & the 1961 catalogue) eg: SOFIA Foundation, CY	1958	28"x23"x13¾" 710x585x350mm	• quite like the real Tower of London • red metal drawbridge and ramp • separate White Tower & chapel

In about 1960, Lines introduced the so-called "King Arthur's Castle," which, it appears, was a one-off unrelated to anything else, except in its materials. It was sited on a high hill made of hardboard on wooden framing. Access was by a built-in ramp, which wound all the way round three sides to end up with a precipitous fall down the back. There was no way to get in without a scramble.

5-058 Tri-ang castle series: No.3 "Corfe"
This is one of the first four castles that went to make up the fifth series.
The difficulty of construction using plywood as a structural element is apparent here. Small towers, little more than turrets, were cross-cut on the bottom to neatly slip over the joint.
The figures are 30mm by Johillco, Britains, and others.

5-059

5-061

5-060

5-059 Assembly instructions for the Castle Series: "Harlech"
5-060 Assembly instructions for the Castle Series: "Tower of London"
5-061 Tri-ang castle series: No.6 "Tower of London"
   This is one of the four castles that went to make up the fifth series.
   The accuracy of the series in replicating the essential characteristics of the castles represented is in little doubt as far as "Dover," "Harlech," and "The Tower of

London" are concerned. There is a question over "Corfe," primarily because the real one is in such a ruinous state.
   The assembly instructions for "Harlech" (5-059) and the "Tower of London" (5-060) were just what was needed. When producing flat-pack products, it was wise to reckon on the recipient needing guidance. They also showed, coincidently, how the system worked.

5-063

5-062

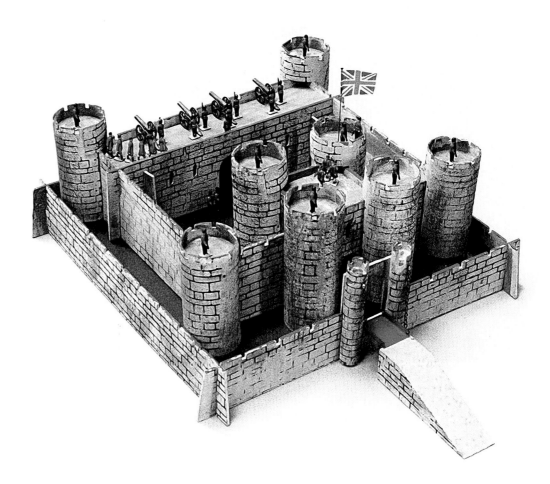

5-062 **Tri-ang castle series: No.4 "Dover"**
5-063 **Tri-ang castle series: No.5 "Harlech"**

These are two of the four castles that went to make up the fifth series.

The difficulty of construction using thin plywood is apparent in "Dover" (5-062). Here they ignored the problem because it occurred only four times and provided a strong corner to the curtain wall. Similar treatment was used for the corners on the outer walls of "Harlech"

(5-063), but all the rest (eight of them) were covered up by sliding "slit up the side" corner towers over them. In the "Tower of London" the halved joints were all covered similarly.

"Harlech" is a good example of how well Tri-ang caught the character of the building. The barbican, in particular, gives the impression of being massive and impregnable, and the double-wall defenses are admirably depicted.

The figures are 30mm by Johillco, Britains and others.

TRI-ANG TOY FORTS : Stand-alone Extra
1961

NO.	DESCRIPTION	DATE	DIMENSIONS	DISTINCTIVE FEATURES
unknown (5-065)	**King Arthur's Castle** (illustrated in Tri-ang's 1961 catalogue) eg: Allen Hickling Toy Forts	1961	21"x15"x??" 535x380x??mm	• high hill type base/box • built-in wrap round ramp (3 sides) • main building centrally located • four circ towers with conical roofs

Described in the catalogue as having *"four towers, each with its imposing spire,"* it was constructed using exactly the same system as the Castles Series. The catalogue went on to add that it *"makes this a most realistic castle."* Seen beside the models of four real castles, this is a bit farfetched. It was probably meant to be more of a fairy castle, which could appeal to the girls.

In 1960/1961, they brought in a new type of fort – a *"Medieval Castle"* made of toughened rubber. This was manufactured by Young and Fogg, which was a small company Lines had bought in 1958. Looking for markets for their product, they had the company make the Landscape and Countryside Series for Scalextric, Spot-on, and Tri-ang Railways. These forts were one such.

TRI-ANG TOY FORTS : Sixth Series
1960 to c1963

NO.	DESCRIPTION	DATE	DIMENSIONS	DISTINCTIVE FEATURES
B (5-068) (5-069)	**Tri-ang Medieval Castle** (illustrated in Tri-ang's 1961 catalogue) eg: Allen Hickling Toy Forts	1961	23¾"x27"x 9½" 605x685x240mm	• traditional layout & base • gatehouse & keep opposite • no ramp or drawbridge • tower at each corner
A1 (5-066)	**Tri-ang Medieval Castle** (described in Tri-ang's 1962 catalogue, illustrated 1963) eg: no example known	1961	16½"x16½"x 9½" 420x420x240mm	• square layout, no keep • gatehouse as "B" • no ramp or drawbridge • tower at each corner
A1 (B1?)	**Tri-ang Medieval Castle** (described in Tri-ang's 1962 catalogue) eg: no example known	1962	16"x17"x 9½" 405x430x240mm	• same as "B" without the base • gatehouse & keep opposite • no ramp or drawbridge • tower at each corner
A (5-067)	**Tri-ang Medieval Fort** (illustrated in Tri-ang's 1963 catalogue) eg: no example known	1963	14"x10½"x??" 355x265x??mm	• imitation rock base • much smaller than the others • five towers on a five-sided plan

There were two forts, although only one made it into the catalogue. The advertised fort was named the "B" castle. It was quite large, with impressive details, and stood on a hardboard base 23¾" x 27" (605 x 685mm). It was claimed to have interlocking separate sections. Quite conventional in its layout, with towers at each corner, a keep, and a gateway, it nevertheless gave the impression, with the instability inherent in the material, of an old and slightly decrepit castle.

The one that was not advertised was much smaller and can only be inferred from hand-written notes on my copy of the catalogue. It was identified as "A1" and cost almost half of the "B."

In 1962, Lines announced two additional models in their catalogue – one without a base, described as "A1," and a smaller one described as "A." It is here, I think, that they got in a bit of a muddle with their numbering system. It seems likely that the smaller fort was "A1," as implied in the hand-written note, and confirmed in the catalogue for 1963 where it is finally illustrated. The "B" castle, without a base, should have been "B1" and not "A1."

In 1963, the larger castle did not appear, but two smaller ones did. One was the "A1" and the other was a yet smaller one identified misleadingly as "A." They failed to make a lasting impact partly because Mr. Fogg left the business. So, despite their attractiveness, they were discontinued.

5-064 **Tri-ang Castle Series "Rochester" Castle** *(catalogue)*
The Rochester extension of the Castle Series was a big disappointment in that there was nothing new – it was merely a re-working of the "Dover" Castle with a larger courtyard and higher wall.

5-065 Tri-ang's "King Arthur's Castle"

This uses the same materials and construction as others in the series, but results in a very different sort of fort. Most noticeable are the box/hill on which it stands and the pointed roofs on the towers.

5-066

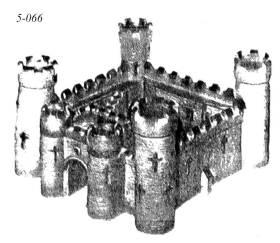

5-067

Tri-ang Medieval
5-066 **FortA1** *(catalogue)*
5-067 **Fort A** *(catalogue)*

It seems that Tri-ang got their numbering somewhat confused about this time. Medieval Fort B was in their 1961 catalogue, although Medieval Fort A1 (5-066) was also available (but not in the catalogue). Then, in 1962, still with only the illustration of Medieval Fort B, Forts A1 and A (5-067) get a mention. Finally, in 1963, Medieval Fort B is dropped and Forts A and A1 are illustrated (see above for copies from the catalogue).

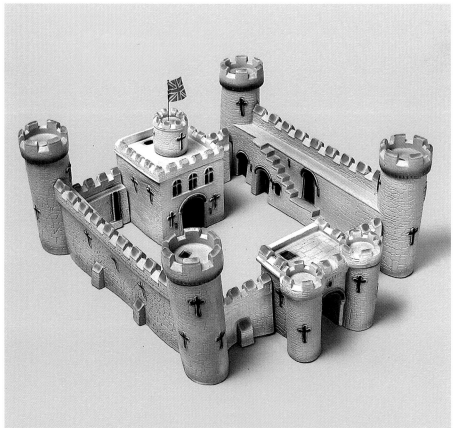

5-068 Tri-ang Medieval Castle B1 *(with base)*

These forts are two of the four that are made of "toughened" rubber, making the sum total of Tri-ang's offering in the material. They were made by Young and Fogg, which was a small company Lines had bought in 1958. They were quite fragile and only one or two remain. The 40mm figures of knights are by Elastolin.

5-069 Tri-ang Medieval Castle B *(without base)*

Medieval Fort B was rather expensive (5-069), but provided much more play value than either A1 or A. The internal detailing is really quite remarkable. The only details missing that are commonly available on other forts are either a drawbridge, a portcullis, or, indeed, both. This is a function of the material, which does not allow the fixing required. The price is probably why Medieval Fort B dropped out of the catalogue.

Tri-Ang's Prices and Pricing Policy for Toy Forts

The earliest indication we have of prices is in the Price List of 13 July 1936, which gives the recommended retail price and some of the trade prices (see table below). These prices, like all of Tri-ang's prices, were in the old coinage. So, for those of us too young to know about such things, before decimalization, a pound was worth twenty shillings, and each shilling was worth twelve pence. Prices could be quoted in pounds, shillings and pence (e.g.: £2/10s/9d), or, as Lines thought best, in just shillings and pence (e.g.: the same amount would have been 50s/9d or 50/9).

	Retail	Trade
No.0 Fort	5/4	—
No.00 Fort	4/–	—
No.1 Fort	6/8	—
No.2 Fort	12/–	8/11
No.3 Fort	16/8	12/6
No.4 Fort	28/–	21/-
No.1A Fort	9/4	6/11
No."A" Fort	4/-	—
No."B" Fort	7/6	—

In addition, "point-of-sale" support in the form of end-user focused catalogues had to be published to different time schedules, such as July / August / September for the Christmas shoppers. These are of particular interest because, unlike the catalogues for retailers, they contain prices. For example, in 1937, Tri-ang produced a two-sided, four-color printed leaflet poster (16½" x 22" (420 x 560mm) folded three times down to 8¼" x 5½" (210 x 140mm).

It contained examples from their whole range, so there was only space for one toy fort. From the nine they had on offer, they chose their No.3 Fort which was priced at 18/11 (eighteen shillings and eleven pence). Other models are mentioned, but not specified – priced at 7/6, 9/6 and 25/6.

Hamley's, in which Tri-ang had taken a majority share-holding in 1931, had the "Tower of London" on offer at a price of 32/6 in 1939.

There is no further pricing information until 1951, when they had two forts on offer – a "Z" Fort for 27/6 and a No.4 Fort for 91/6. (I started work in that year and I earned 10/- a week, so the No.4 was quite a price.) In 1953,

the same two were on offer – the "Z" Fort for 29/3 and the No.4 Fort for 96/3. We have nothing then until catalogues, still from Hamley's, for 1960 and 1961, each of which lists three explicitly Tri-ang toy forts (see table below):

	1960	1961
Medieval Castle "B"	79/11	81/11
Harlech Castle No.5	59/11	not offered
No."Z" Fort	37/11	38/11
No."Y" Fort	not offered	26/11

Tri-ang prices for 1961 also come to us via hand-written notes on a catalogue. These would appear to be recommended retail prices, judging by Hamley's from the same year. I have no idea where they came from. They are listed in the table below.

No."W" Fort	17/9
No."Y" Fort	27/9
No."Z" Fort	39/6
Medieval Castle A1	58/3
Medieval Castle B	83/–
Castle Series Corfe	36/6
Castle Series Dover	38/6
Castle Series Harlech	68/6
Castle Series Tower of London	91/3
King Arthur's Castle	50/9

There is just one fort on offer at Hamley's in 1967, which was the Cambourne Castle retailing at 43/3. In 1968, Tri-ang mentions "Chatham" Fort at 38/6.

There seems to be little one can draw from this, except that the price of forts went up steadily year by year. Having said that, however, they did manage to keep below the £5 threshold (just), which is some sort of achievement, I suppose.

Very little is available on the subject of Tri-ang's pricing policy as such. It would appear that they tried to provide reasonable quality value-for-money toys without going into what might be called the luxury end of the market.

Why, if they could start up a totally new production line, using a plastic-like material like a rubber-based composition, did they not take the logical next step and get into plastics proper? We may never know the answer to this, but they did not. Maybe it had something to do with the fact that the technology and the production were undertaken out of house.

In 1963, the "Rochester" Castle appeared. It was a bit of a let down because it turned out to be only the "Dover" Castle re-branded and given a larger space around it. Admittedly, though, it was a reasonable representation of the real Rochester and it was a more sensible arrangement.

TRI-ANG TOY FORTS : Fifth Series (Supplementary)
1963 to c1966

NO.	DESCRIPTION	DATE	DIMENSIONS	DISTINCTIVE FEATURES
unknown (5-064)	**Tri-ang Rochester Castle** (illustrated in Tri-ang catalogue 1963) eg: no known example	1963	20"x20"x9" 510x510x230mm	• as Dover with larger courtyard • removable tower & side building • central gateway • no ramp

The "Swinging Sixties" – Competing with Plastics

In 1965, a new approach was taken. By this time, plastics were just becoming established, and this is certainly where the competition was focusing. Tri-ang flirted with it – and actually produced or, at least, used some bits and pieces – but, unlike Hausser, they never really embraced it.

Not only was there Kleeware to deal with, but there were now many new competitors. Louis Marx came on strongly, and Tudor Rose, Timpo, and Cherilea came into the market, apparently from nowhere. There may well have been cash flow problems, a shortage of capital, or both, because by this time they had bought just about everything, including Dinky, Hornby, Meccano, Scalextric, Sindy, and many others. You name it, they bought it.

Tri-ang decided to "stick to their knitting," doing things the way they knew best, and buying in any parts they could not produce. They introduced a totally new line using some bits and pieces of plastic, which they bought in. They reverted to their old style of production, assembling a number of forts using a limited range of parts.

These were made of cardboard and hardboard – basically round cardboard tubes for the towers and flat hardboard for the walls. The plastic came in the form of tops for the towers (two sizes) and a gateway incorporating a drawbridge. Clearly, the parts that lent themselves to more detail and were more difficult to make were those for which they used plastic.

The fifth fort in this 1965 offering was No.5 "Arundel." The castle was made up of the more or less standard pieces of the other four forts in the series. This had a plastic base, however, that provided a knobbly rocky area on which the fort stood, with a narrow depression which served as a moat. Almost certainly bought in – probably from France, possibly by Clairbois (7-069) – this was their only venture out of their comfort zone, though it was also used later for "Cambourne" Castle.

TRI-ANG TOY FORTS: Seventh Series
1965 to c1971

NO.	DESCRIPTION	DATE	DIMENSIONS	DISTINCTIVE FEATURES
1 (5-070)	**Hever Castle** (illustrated in Tri-ang catalogue 1965) eg: Allen Hickling Toy Forts	1965	12¼"x9½"x10½" 310x240x265mm	• the smallest in the range • off-center gateway w/drawbridge • no ramp • three towers
2 (5-071)	**Deal Castle** (illustrated in Tri-ang catalogue 1965) eg: no known example	1965	17½"x9½"x10½" 445x240x255mm	• lower middle of the range • gateway with drawbridge • no ramp • four towers
3 (5-072)	**Chatham Castle** (illustrated in Tri-ang catalogue 1965) eg: Allen Hickling Toy Forts	1965	19"x12"x13½" 485x305x345mm	• upper middle of the range • gateway w/drawbridge • no ramp • four towers – two with roofs
4 (5-073)	**Balmoral Castle** (illustrated in Tri-ang catalogue 1965) eg: Allen Hickling Toy Forts	1965	19"x12"x13½" 485x305x345mm	• largest of the range • gateway w/drawbridge w/o ramp • four towers – two with roofs • keep with four turrets
5 (5-074)	**Arundel Castle** (illustrated in Tri-ang catalogue 1965) eg: no known example	1965	15"x17"x14½" 380x430x370mm	• ramp & moat in plastic base • gateway with drawbridge • three large towers

5-070

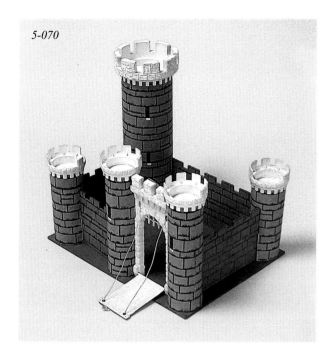

5-073

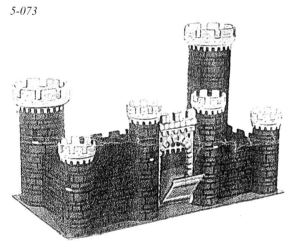

5-074

5-070 **Tri-ang seventh series No.1 "Hever" Castle**
5-073 **Tri-ang seventh series No.2 "Deal" Castle** *(catalogue)*
5-074 **Tri-ang seventh series No.3 "Chatham" Castle**

These are three of the five castles in the initial run of the seventh series in 1965. They are all quite similar in that they are made up with a narrow selection of parts, providing a very limited range of sizes. For example No.2 "Deal" Castle (5-073) is identical to No.3 "Chatham" Castle (5-074), except the towers at the back were on opposite sides and had bright red roofs.

1965

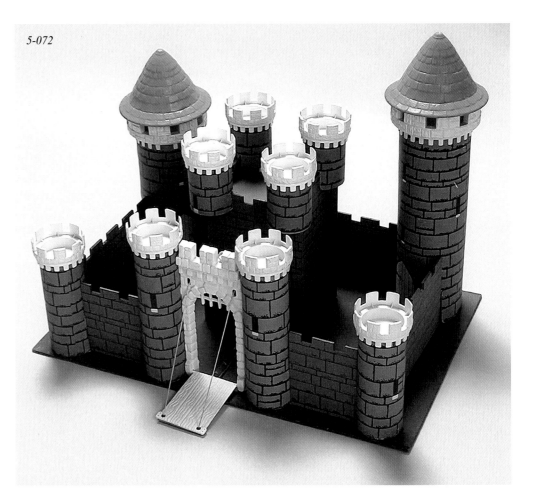

5-072

5-071

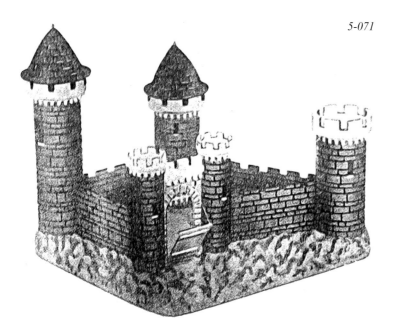

5-071 Tri-ang seventh series No.5 "Arundel" Castle *(catalogue)*
5-072 Tri-ang seventh series No.4 "Balmoral" Castlc
  These are the other two in the seventh series. The increments of growth were minimal. For example the only difference between "Chatham" Castle and "Balmoral" Castle is the central building in "Balmoral."

  Note the plastic base under "Arundel" Castle (5-074), which, given that Tri-ang was keeping out of plastics, may have come from the French firm of Clairebois (7-069), who were using a similar base. They all have battlements made of plastic and the gateway with its operating drawbridge with fancy details is impressive.

5-075

5-075 Tri-ang "Cambourne" Castle

"Cambourne" Castle is a bit of an anomaly. It is more or less the same as "Arundel" Castle, which came out in 1965 with the others in the series. The differences are that the tower at the front is a bit lower, as are the walls front and back, and the towers at the back are minus their conical roofs. It is not known for certain when it came out.

TRI-ANG TOY FORTS: Seventh Series (Supplementary)
c1966 to 1969

NO.	DESCRIPTION	DATE	DIMENSIONS	DISTINCTIVE FEATURES
unknown (5-075)	**Cambourne Castle** (no catalogue evidence for a production date) eg: Allen Hickling Toy Forts	1966/ 1967	15"x17"x14½" 380x430x370mm	• plastic base – like Arundel • gateway with drawbridge • two large towers, one small one • low walls front & rear
unknown (5-076) (5-077)	**Tintagel Castle 1st version** (evidence: production of a second version in 1969) eg: Allen Hickling Toy Forts	1966/ 1967	20"x20"x18" 510x510x460mm	• the largest brought out since 1962 • electric lighting • built-up base and entry ramp • two-level courtyard and five towers

The Tri-ang catalogue of 1965 included "Corfe" and "Harlech" Castles, which were probably the remainder of the stock of the "Castles" series. They also continued to produce the "W"/ "Y"/ "Z" Forts. This may also have been remaindered stock, but it provided a safety net, the well-known and loved forts providing a back-up for the new line should it not succeed.

The series was supplemented in 1966/67 by two offerings. One, "Cambourne," was a reworking of "Arundel," presumably making it cheaper, and the other, "Tintagel," was a completely new fort. Admittedly they used parts of the seventh series, but this was completely different in concept. Nevertheless, there were quite enough similarities to view them as supplementary to the seventh series.

"Cambourne" Castle, the new form of "Arundel," was much less defensible in its new form. Low walls front and rear, a lower tower at a strategic location in the corner, and the towers at the back had no roofs to protect the inhabitants from arrows.

"Tintagel" Castle was large by any standard. It also had a base that was a design in its own right. Made up of three parts, and providing plenty of space, it offered the setting for numerous scenarios. Combined with *"battery operated tower lighting,"* it was something to fire the imagination of any child. This return to a feature abandoned nearly thirty years previously is remarkable. It is not as though the lighting did anything much, unlike the No.4 Fort; it merely provided evidence of occupation. It did not even light the courtyard.

The next evidence I have is a 1969 catalogue that has new forts in it. Two are a continuation of the 1965 line in the form of a second version of "Tintagel" Castle, with its electric lighting still intact, and a "Dover" Castle, which was a very much simplified version. These seem to be aimed at two extreme ends of the market, which implies that Tri-ang must have misjudged it originally.

5-076

5-077

5-077a

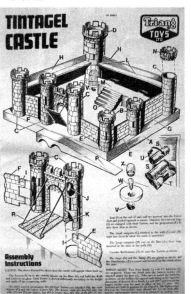

5-078

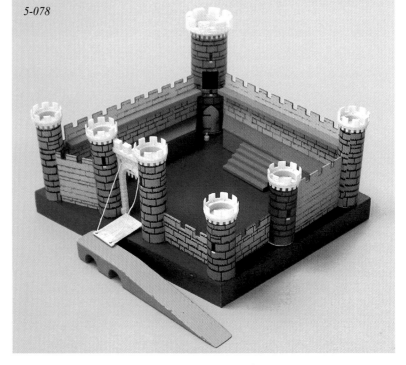

5-076 Tri-ang "Tintagel" Castle *(first version)*
5-078 Tri-ang "Tintagel" Castle" *(second version)*
The first version of "Tintagel" Castle (5-076) probably came out about the same time as "Cambourne" Castle. This marked Tri-ang's taking up the electric light idea again, having dropped it over twenty-five years before. It did no more, however, than demonstrate that the main tower was occupied – or someone had left the light on.

It marked the return to wooden boxes for the fort to stand on, and to provide a suitable tray for the pieces. Also, the courtyard was on two levels. This allowed various settings for the action.

The later "Tintagel" Castle (5-078) was a superior version in nearly every respect. It is true that the lighting could have been more useful but, apart from that, it was a better fort for manufacturer and user.

5-077 Tri-ang "Tintagel" Castle Instructions *(first version)*
5-077a Tri-ang "Tintagel" Castle Instructions *(second version)*
The assembly instructions now served a real purpose. Unlike earlier examples, the fort was quite complicated to put together, with the electric lighting, so the advice proved a wise addition.

Those for the second version were easier to follow (5-077a), mainly because the fort was easier to assemble.

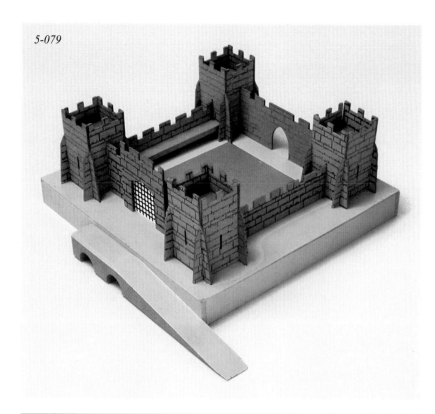

5-079

1968-1969

5-081

5-080

DOVER CASTLE

INSTRUCTIONS

The illustration shows how the castle is built-up.

The cylindrical towers fit on to the circular blocks 'A' attached to the base 'B'.

The short tower 'C' and two of the tall towers 'D' and 'E' are slotted to hold the walls at the corners. The high rear wall 'F' is placed with the platform 'G' on the inside of the castle.

The remaining pair of tall towers 'H' and 'I', are slotted differently to hold the gateway 'J'. The gateway lugs 'K' are inserted into their tower slots 'L' and pushed upward, the projection 'M' engaging in its narrow slot below.

Circular battlements 'N' fit onto the top of each tower.

The drawbridge 'O' is raised and lowered by the winch 'P' above the gateway.

Made in England by
TRI·ANG TOYS LTD. MERTON LONDON S.W.19

SR 16108

5-079 **Tri-ang "Galway" Castle**
5-080 **Tri-ang "Dover" Castle instructions**
5-081 **Tri-ang "Dover" Castle**

"Dover" Castle was the simplest one can imagine (5-081) – even simpler than "Hever" Castle.

The instructions for "Dover" Castle reverted to the obvious (5-080). Apart from the manner of installing the gateway (that is, pushing it), there was nothing

that a five year-old could not figure out for him or herself. The 40mm figures of knights are by Elastolin.

"Galway" Castle was the last to appear (5-079). It is completely different from anything Lines had produced before. Was it the beginning of a new series? The lack of imagination displayed in the design, however, gives the impression of a company "on its last legs."

TRI-ANG TOY FORTS: Seventh Series (Supplementary)
c1968 to 1971

NO.	DESCRIPTION	DATE	DIMENSIONS	DISTINCTIVE FEATURES
unknown (5-077a) (5-078)	**Tintagel Castle 2nd version** (illustrated in Tri-ang 1969 catalogue) eg: SOFIA Foundation, CY	1968	20"x20"x13" 510x510x330mm	• the largest brought out 1968 • electric lighting • simple one-piece base • two-level courtyard & five towers
unknown (5-080) (5-081)	**Dover Castle** (illustrated in Tri-ang 1969 catalogue) eg: SOFIA Foundation, CY	1969	17½"x12"x8" 445x305x205mm	• a simple variant • gateway and drawbridge • off-center gateway • three simple towers

The second version of "Tintagel" Castle was surprisingly like the first, given the changes that were made. These were concentrated on the base, which was lowered and simplified – presumably to keep the costs down. It was now in one piece and of a simpler shape. The upper levels of the courtyard were now created by separate pieces, and the main tower was based on the lower level.

This made it considerably shorter, which was compounded by there being no roof. The walls around the back and sides, which were higher to allow them also to stand on the lower base, now had a walkway around at the higher level.

Taking all this into consideration, it seems that the changes were very sensible and provided a better and cheaper fort for the manufacturer and the user.

The third type, "Galway" Castle (5-079), was completely different. Not only did it have square towers, its construction relied on the slotted technique. It was, in any case, a minimal model using only one plastic piece (the portcullis) with very crude detailing. All together this was a simple model, which gave every appearance of a company dying on its feet.

TRI-ANG TOY FORTS: Stand-alone Extra
c1968 to c1971

NO.	DESCRIPTION	DATE	DIMENSIONS	DISTINCTIVE FEATURES
unknown (5-079)	**Galway Castle** (illustrated in Tri-ang catalogue 1969) eg: SOFIA Foundation, CY	1969	18"x18"x7½" 455x455x190mm	• four towers – one at each corner • long ramp with two arches • platform behind the battlements • plastic for portcullis

Why there should have been so few forts on offer in 1969, at least based on the evidence available to me, is a difficult question to answer. Previously they had had six or more forts on offer at any one time. Perhaps they had over-stretched themselves in their take-overs, now counted in their twenties or thirties. We may never know.

The Dénouement – The Coming of a New World

From about 1965, Tri-ang was in decline. In retrospect, it was clear from the lack of attention being paid to the toy forts. The 1965 new line was their last real roll of the dice. The "Tintagel" Castle was a brave effort, but the end came in 1972, when they went into receivership. Some parts of the company continued under new management and are still manufacturing today, but the toy forts just died out.

SIX

THE REST OF BRITAIN:
How the Brits Played Catch-up

This is a story of the manufacture of toy forts in Britain. It does not include the activities of Lines Bros., or Tri-ang, to give it its erroneous but better known name. That is the subject of a previous chapter. Nor is it a complete story in any other sense. It is more a history based upon my knowledge and experience.

Nothing was produced in Britain until about 1910. Up to that time, the market was satisfied handsomely by the Germans. About 1910, however, there came one C. E. Turnbull, who was the owner of a company calling itself Charterhouse. They did not do much with toy forts, being better known for large boxed sets containing, amongst other things, figures produced by William Britain and Sons. As far as I can make out, these were the first British-made toy forts.

When the First World War broke out, the government provided various incentives to toy manufacturers to try to break the stranglehold of the Germans. This was not very successful, even though a number of firms came and went in the effort. Among these was Chad Valley, who dabbled at it on and off for about twenty years. The only one to show any long-lasting success was A. J. Holladay, the producer of the Skybird range of toys, which started up after the war.

With the world recession of the 1930s, the Germans could no longer maintain their export trade, and an opportunity presented itself. This is when Tri-ang came into the market.

There were several other manufacturers around, but only two who could provide any sort of competition. The name of the first, whose distributor was the Manufacturing Accessories Company of London, is unknown to me. In the early 1930s, they produced a large number of forts, which were of wood and rather poorly made when compared to those of Tri-ang. They were, however, cheap, so they hit a part of the market that was otherwise open. The second, which came out about 1934, was Burnett and Company, which made the UBILDA range of small-scale forts and other toys in metal.

The Second World War put a stop to any ideas anyone may have had for further expansion. After the war, manufacturers, with the exception of Tri-ang, seemed reluctant to get going. There was no real effort until Binbak started in about 1950, closely followed by Elf (later Joy Toys), and Tudor Toys, with their range of Gee-Bee products. Between them, these companies managed to provide Tri-ang with some competition.

By the mid-1950s, plastics had begun to emerge as a realistic alternative material, which was to revolutionize the industry. Leading the way was Kleeware, the well known manufacturer of kitchenware. They decided to diversify and, for some reason unknown to me, they chose to go into toy forts. Their design was so good that it was still being made until about the year 2000, not by Kleeware, but by a wide variety of companies who took it on worldwide.

Many companies saw an opportunity to get into the market, with Timpo and Marx probably being the front runners. Strangely, Tri-ang never took to the new material, maybe because they were too busy buying up other companies to get involved; they went under in 1971.

C. E. Turnbull and Charterhouse

At the end of the first decade of the 20th century, all the toy forts in Britain were made in Germany. There was a well established supply route, based on the toy figure trade and involving manufacturers, exporters, importers, wholesalers, and retailers, which had been in existence for thirty years or more. No one thought twice about it, much less did anything about it.

Until, that is, a very special person by the name of C. E. Turnbull came along. He was a man who "thought outside the box." He was the head of C. E. Turnbull & Co., which operated under the name of Charterhouse or CETANDCO. They produced complete sets, including figures by William Britain & Sons, which represented important military events. These came all in a box that was often quite a large size.

Turnball had the insight that toy forts could be as easily made in Britain as they were in Germany. He set out to produce and market two fairly ordinary forts, and one very big one, something along the lines of the Tower of London. At least those are the ones I know about.

CHARTERHOUSE
c1910 to c1925

NO.	DESCRIPTION	DATE	DIMENSIONS	DISTINCTIVE FEATURES
unknown (6-003)	**the smaller of this series** (identified by an example in the ownership below) eg: Allen Hickling Toy Forts	c1910	21"x11"x13" 535x280x330mm	• box with cork crumb, single ramp • courts on two levels, drawbridge • two 2-D main bldgs & two towers • battlements white & pale blue
unknown (6-001)	**the larger of this series** (identified by an example in the ownership below) eg: SOFIA Foundation, CY	c1910	24"x15¾"x13" 610x400x330mm	• box w/cork, single ramp, 2-D gateway • courts on two levels, drawbridge • two 2-D main bldgs & four towers • battlements ylw, w/red, wht & blk
unknown (6-002) (6-004)	**the largest of all** (identified by an example in the ownership below) eg: SOFIA Foundation, CY	c1910	31½"x28½"x15" 810x730x335mm	• 2 double ramps, two gates w/db • cork box, 3 tanks for moat water • square White Tower, 4 towers • battlements ylw, w/red, wht, & blk

He used wood as the main structural material, and four-color lithographed paper for the covering and details. Most of the buildings were 2-D, relying on the lithography to provide depth. The actual base color of the buildings seems to vary between red and yellow – sometimes red, sometimes yellow, and sometimes a bit of one and a bit of the other.

He covered the outsides with cork, and the battlements and drawbridges were hand painted. In this, he was copying the style of forts from Germany about ten years before. It seems he was unaware of the amazing changes in the industry that were just about to take place there.

The largest example known to me owes much to the Tower of London in its appearance. Of course, it is only surmise that gives this its name, although it is difficult to imagine anything else. The likeness to the White Tower in particular is well depicted.

In this fort, he went for water in the moat. This necessitated the construction of metal trays to hold the water. Maybe the proximity of the Tower to the Thames influenced the choice. All the problems one can imagine were about to take place – soaking playroom floors among them.

There is nothing to tell us how long Turnbull persevered with these forts or how successful he was. It is known that he continued in business until well after the First World War, but not if he continued with the forts. We only have a few examples of his product to go on now.

6-001 **Charterhouse**: *the larger in the series*
  The two-dimensional buildings became three-dimensional in this case because the main building has a space for men to patrol the battlements. The towers have windows and doors cut out from paper used to cover the other buildings. The orange, yellow, white, on a dark green base are typical for Charterhouse, as are the green courtyards.

6-002

6-003

6-004

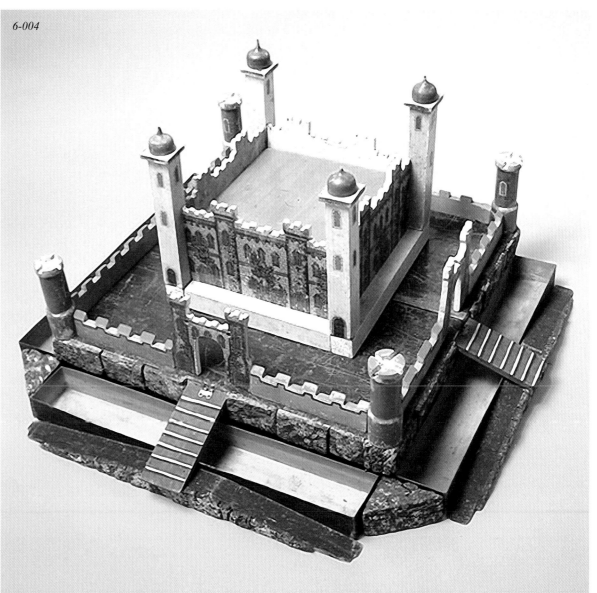

6-002 **Charterhouse**: box of Tower of London
6-003 **Charterhouse**: second in the series
6-004 **Charterhouse**: Tower of London

The Tower of London was the largest (6-004). This fort has been slightly restored in that one drawbridge, the pinnacles on the side tower roofs, and one or two doors and windows on the peripheral towers needed to be replaced.

The smaller in the series (6-003) is missing three bits of battlement and probably a gateway, but is otherwise in good shape.

Johnson Bros. and Chad Valley

There is just one example of another British company trying something before the First World War. That was Chad Valley, which had not formed an official company, so was operating out of Birmingham as a number of separate entities in the ownership of Johnson Bros. In 1914, which in retrospect was not an auspicious year to launch a toy, they came out with "Storming the Citadel."

This was a strawboard fort, quite small, with cast metal, semi-flat figures to defend it, and two guns with which to attack it. The actual fort was not very fort-like in that the sides were left open, presumably to enable it to be folded into a box. Again, the color and detail were provided by the application of lithographed paper. The guns were made of tin and were very fine, but I cannot imagine how they would have had an effect on the fort. It is not clear how they fitted it into the box.

About this time, Chad Valley produced another game based on forts. This was "Shell Fort," which had some very good graphics, but not much else.

CHAD VALLEY
1914 to c1920

NO.	DESCRIPTION	DATE	DIMENSIONS	DISTINCTIVE FEATURES
unknown (6-005) (6-006) (6-007)	**a stand-alone model** (identified by an example in the ownership below) eg: Bonhams Auctions, UK	1914	17?"x9?"x6¾" 430?x230?x170mm	• "Storming the Citadel" • cardboard folded flat • seven "circular" towers • perimeter wall, men and guns
unknown (6-006a) (6-006b)	**a stand-alone game** (identified by an example in the ownership below) eg: Peter Stenning, UK	c1915	unknown	• "Shell Fort" • cardboard folded flat • two "circular" towers • figures and mortars

6-005

6-006

6-005 Chad Valley "Storming the Citadel" *(Courtesy Bonhams, Knightsbridge)*
6-006 Chad Valley "Storming the Citadel": *box (Courtesy Bonhams, Knightsbridge)*

This image (6-005) is claimed to be of the whole set as sold by Chad Valley in 1914. It made for an impressive display even if it did not work very well. Maybe the children had more imagination in those days and were better able to cope with the disappointment of it.

As was par for the course in the days before the Trades Description Act, the box label (6-006) did not show what was actually in the box. It was a work of art by any standards.

6-006a

6-006b

6-007

6-008

6-006a **"Shell Fort"** *The label (Courtesy Peter Stenning)*
6-006b **"Shell Fort"** *The game (Courtesy Peter Stenning)*
   The box label (6-006a) was full of action, but the game did not really live up to the its promise. Of course this was in the days before the Trades Description Act, and anything was possible.
6-007 **Chad Valley "Storming the Citadel:"** *the castle only*
   This may be a part of a smaller version of the one on the previous page. In any case, it shows how manufacturers could use graphics from old forts to make new ones. It makes economic sense after all.
6-008 **The "Chad Valley" Toy Fort No.0**
   This is the first one in the series and is something of an odd one out. It is different from the other four in the series in that it is the only one without a 3-D keep and it does not have a drawbridge.

They used the graphics again after the First World War to make another fort. This time it was much more 3-D and formed part of a series. It was No.0 in a series, numbered 0 to 4, which was called *The "Chad Valley" Toy Fort*. It was the only one in the series using these graphics, but it was in the same style as the others – lithograph-covered strawboard.

CHAD VALLEY
c1920 to 19??

NO.	DESCRIPTION	DATE	DIMENSIONS	DISTINCTIVE FEATURES
6170/0	**the smaller of this series** (identified from a listing on the box of No.1) eg: no known example	c1920	10"x8"x6" 255x200x150mm	• The "Chad Valley" Toy Fort No.0 • lithograph covered strawboard • one small building, four towers • perimeter wall with small towers
6170/1 (6-009) (6-011) (6-012)	**the second of this series** (identified by an example in the ownership below) eg: SOFIA Foundation, CY	c1920	20"x10"x9" 510x255x230mm	• The "Chad Valley" Toy Fort No.1 • lithograph covered strawboard • one keep with four towers • one drawbridge
6170/2	**the third of this series** (identified from a listing on the box of No.1) eg: no known example	c1920	28"x14"x12" 710x355x305mm	• The "Chad Valley" Toy Fort No.2 • lithograph covered strawboard • one drawbridge
6170/3	**the fourth of this series** (identified from a listing on the box of No.1) eg: no known example	c1920	30"x17"x13" 760x430x330mm	• The "Chad Valley" Toy Fort No.3 • lithograph covered strawboard • one drawbridge
6170/4	**the largest of this series** (identified from a listing on the box of No.1) eg: no known example	c1920	50"x20"x15" 1270x510x380mm	• The "Chad Valley" Toy Fort No.4 • lithograph covered strawboard • two keeps, four corner gateways • one drawbridge

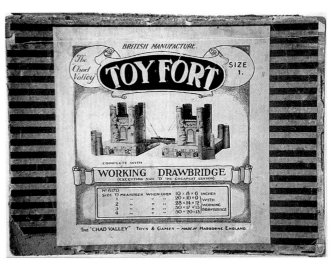

6-009 **The "Chad Valley" Toy Fort**: *box label*
   This is the box for the Size 1 fort. The label, which the manufacturer used for all sizes (note on it the details of each size), actually illustrates Size 4 – probably leading to much disappointment when the purchaser finally opened the box. The shape and size of the label was designed to be exactly the same size as the keep so that it would be hidden beneath the fort when it was set up.

Nos.1 to 4 in the series were essentially towers or keeps of different numbers and heights, depending on the set, which stood four-square on a raised base. All four sides, which were very pretty in the typical English medieval style, were the same, with battlements and arrow slits galore. Shadow effects gave them three-dimensionality, and perspective was cleverly used in the design of the towers to give the impression of greater height.

The larger size(s?) had two keeps, and the very large one was arranged on two raised bases. The larger sizes also had gatehouses located at each corner. All except the smallest boasted a drawbridge. The No.1 is smaller with a single keep (it is just possible that there were originally two keeps, and that one has been lost), but it does have a drawbridge.

In the one hundred years prior to 1960, forts were most commonly made of wood or strawboard and figures were made of metal. This involved two fundamentally different skills and manufacturing processes, leading to two different products being marketed separately. Thus the identification of an exception is notable indeed – and the Chad Valley Company seems to have provided us with just that.

This particular example contains nine hollowcast, 54mm gilt toy soldiers (it is not known if any or all of the other the forts in the range had this feature). They are examples of one of the most common fixed-arm figures of the time – an infantryman on guard with fixed bayonet, in this case wearing a typical British army cap of the First World War.

As Chad Valley did not produce metal figures of any sort, they must have been bought in – as the race horses in their "Escalado" game certainly were. They have no integral identification such as an imprint, nor do they have a label, so their source can only be judged from their style. They could have been supplied by Reka.

It is remarkable that they made no mention of this feature on the label. It being a boxed set, the average customer might never have known that the figures were there. In some ways this is so unusual that it might be prudent to assume that they have been since added to the set.

The packaging, however, is very neatly designed to accommodate them, and all aspects of the various parts – printing, materials, technology, and presentation – appear consistent in style and must be of the same period, probably the very early 1920s.

6-011

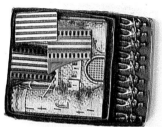

6-012

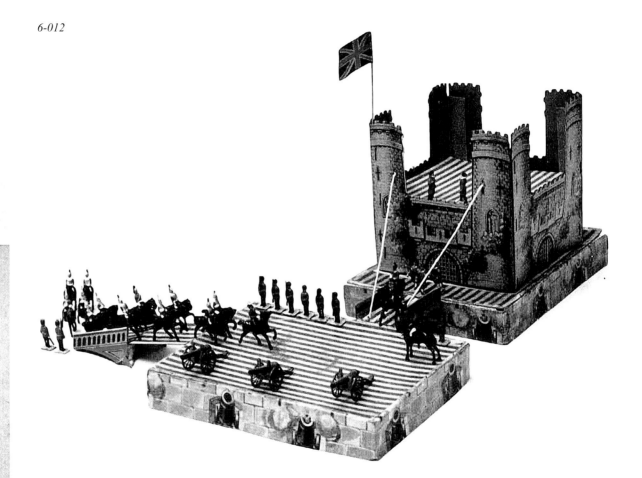

6-010

THE "CHAD VALLEY" GAMES.

Instructions for Erecting the

Chad Valley Toy Forts.

NOS. 1, 2 & 3.

Take the contents out, and place both box and lid flat side upwards on the table.

Place a folding tower upon each, with a centre loose square piece of cardboard inside them, resting upon the supports just below the battlements; these hold the towers firm and form the floors for soldiers to stand on.

Fix the drawbridge in position as shown in the illustration, the flat end being pushed between the upturned box and the tower.

Slip the string with the tin spike attached up through the hole in the floor of the tower, pass it through the hole in the turret and down through the drawbridge, which will then be found to work perfectly, rising and falling at will.

NO. 4.

Turn the containing box and lid flat side upwards, and the two inside blocks likewise upon them.

Place the folding walls around three sides of these blocks (the fourth being left free for the drawbridge), fastening them together by means of the paper fasteners, which should be pushed through the holes in the walls and block and fastened inside the latter.

Complete the erection as above described.

Manufactured solely at Chad Valley Works, Harborne, England.

6-010 **The "Chad Valley" Toy Fort No.1**: instructions
6-011 **The "Chad Valley" Toy Fort No.1**: open box
6-012 **The "Chad Valley" Toy Fort No.1**

These cardboard forts were nicely printed in four colors, but it was not an expensive production. The fort (6-012) was the smallest of four and used the same components. It stands on its own box lid and tray, which have the images of guns in action belching fire and smoke over the battlements. The figures shown are 30mm from Johillco and others. They did not come with the fort.

The "Chad Valley" Toy Fort No.1 open box (6-011) shows how the 54mm figures that came with the set were accommodated.

A. J. Holladay and Givjoy

Of course, Charterhouse and Chad Valley were not the only companies trying to make a go of it during and after the First World War. A number of companies, among them Lord Roberts' Memorial Workshops, Bournemouth Novelty Works, the Emell Toy Manufacturing Co., the Novelty Construction Co., and Compocastles, came and went with disappointing regularity.

But there was one who made a rather better fist of it. This was A. J. Holladay, whose company operated out of London. He started in a small way, in 1919, mainly with Givjoy dollhouse-related products. He gradually expanded his range of products, taking in toy forts on the way to his best known line of Skybird figures and airplanes, which continued in production until about 1960.

The toy forts, which varied substantially over the years, were still in production up to the Second World War. They started rather small and quite cute, but by the end they were in the mix with Manufacturers Accessories Co., even if Lines Bros. and Burnett Ltd. were in a different league as far as quality was concerned.

One recognizes these forts by their quite distinct general style, which varied only a little after the first few years. Apart from the slapdash approach to the paint work, the inside of the base was accessed from the rear as opposed to the underside. The cover was not hinged; there was just a single pendulum catch holding in a loose piece slotted in at the bottom, on which they placed their label.

There is one other characteristic with which they persevered. This was the treatment of the doors. They were outlined by hand in black, with often distinctly bulbous hinges and crude handles, on a thin piece of wood.

The first two forts were small and of the "cute" type. Roofs accurately constructed in metal with a small pennant flying were the best finished pieces, the rest being quite crudely made of wood. Doors and windows were stuck on and the base had a hand-crafted look about it. The scale was small.

GIVJOY: First Series
c1925

NO.	DESCRIPTION	DATE	DIMENSIONS	DISTINCTIVE FEATURES
unknown (6-013)	the smaller of this series (identified by an example in the ownership below) eg: Graham Bailey, UK	c1925	16¼"x7¼"x9" 415x185x205mm	• wood box w/molded composition • single integral ramp to gateway • one tower w/metal pointed roof • main building & side building
unknown	the larger of this series (identified by an example in the ownership below) eg: Allen Hickling Toy Forts	c1925	16½"x10¼"x12" 420x260x305mm	• wood box w/molded composition • single integral ramp to gateway • two towers w/metal pointed roofs • main building & side building

6-013 **Givjoy** *first series: single tower*
This is one of the first with a Givjoy name. It is very small, as is evidenced by the 15mm figures of unknown origin. Note the Givjoy door which appears on all Givjoy forts.

There is almost no doubt about their starting date – about 1925 – as they were mentioned in the magazine *Games and Toys* in 1926. There is, however, no catalogue, as far as I know. The series, and the dates of them, are a little more unreliable, having been established on the basis of my knowledge and some common sense.

GIVJOY: Second Series
c1930 to c1934

NO.	DESCRIPTION	DATE	DIMENSIONS	DISTINCTIVE FEATURES
unknown (6-014) (6-015) (6-015a)	the only one of this series (identified by an example in the ownership below) eg: Graham Bailey, UK	c1930	16½"x12"x16½" 420x305x420mm	• wood box w/molded composition • single integral ramp to gateway • two tall circular towers in centre • main building each side of towers

The second series proved a major departure. Apparently, the base was still hand-crafted, but now the battlements were fixed to it and there were gun emplacements at the two front corners.

A more significant difference was in the buildings. Although they were quite nicely finished, nothing seemed to hang together. The circular towers were very tall with very tall arrow slits to match, and they completely dominated the gateway. If it were not for the traces of a label on the back and the ubiquitous door, there would be some doubt about it being by Holladay at all. We shall probably never know how long it was in production.

GIVJOY: Third Series
c1934? to c1938?

NO.	DESCRIPTION	DATE	DIMENSIONS	DISTINCTIVE FEATURES
unknown	**the smaller of this series** (identified by an example in the ownership below) eg: Allen Hickling Toy Forts	c1934	14"x12½"x11¾" 355x315x300mm	• wood box w/dry moat • double ramp to cent gateway • one central tower • main building & side building
unknown (6-017)	**the second of this series** (identified by an example in the ownership below) eg: Jim Osborne, UK	c1934	unknown	• wood box w/dry moat • double ramp to cent gateway • two corner towers • main building & side buildings
unknown (6-016)	**the larger of this series** (identified by an example in the ownership below) eg: Graham Bailey, UK	c1934	25¾"x16¼"x14" 655x410x355mm	• wood box w/dry moat • double ramp to cent gateway • two corner towers • bowed main building & others

By the time the third series was being manufactured, the forts displayed a much more professional approach. All the buildings seemed in scale with one another and the whole looked to be in harmony. The slapdash paint work was still there, with bright red, green, and yellow, mixed with silver where there was water, and plain grey on the courtyards. Arrow slits were painted on by hand, and the windows and the door were stuck on.

GIVJOY: Fourth Series
c1938? to c1940?

NO.	DESCRIPTION	DATE	DIMENSIONS	DISTINCTIVE FEATURES
unknown (6-018)	**the only one of this series** (identified by an example in the ownership below) eg: SOFIA Foundation, CY	c1938	16"x12¼"x13" 405x310x330mm	• wood box w/textured paint • single integral ramp to gateway • 2 towers each side of main bldg • 3-D main bldg in form of cloister

The fourth series was probably the end of the line for Givjoy. Although Holladay continued in business for some years after the Second World War, it was with his Skybird range. It is unlikely that he produced any more forts.

6-014

6-015

6-015a

6-014 **Givjoy** *second series*
This is an odd one. No other example has circular towers. The figures are 30mm and of a Germanic origin, and the cannon are by Simon and Rivolet of France.
6-015 & 6-015a **Givjoy**: *labeling*
View of the back shows the access door. The remains of a label are just visible, and are reproduced above.

6-016 **Givjoy**: *third series 1*
6-017 **Givjoy**: *third series 2 (Courtesy Jim Osborne)*
6-018 **Givjoy**: *fourth series*

   Givjoy third series 1 is the largest Givjoy fort we have (6-016). In spite of the slap-dash paint, it is very convincing.

   Givjoy third series 2 is a classic example of the later forts in the series (6-017). Only the gateway and the buildings at the back were fixed, including the two gun emplacements.

   Givjoy fourth series is relatively bright and cheerful (6-018). The gatehouse is interesting in its 3-D modeling, as is the cloister walkway. This has brick-patterned paper on the inside wall usually used for dollhouses. Notice the doors on the two towers are not classic Givjoy, but the one in the cloister is.

Eaton & Munby and Burleytoys

In the early 1930s, Mr. C. T. Eaton and Col. A. M. Munby set up a company, unsurprisingly by the name of Eaton & Munby Ltd., located in Burley which is near Ringwood in Hampshire in the UK. They were manufacturers of the "exciting Burleytoys range of 'action' toys." One of these was their "Buster" Toy Fort No 1.

The fort could be bought in the shops for 10/- (ten shillings), which must have been quite expensive during the depression, especially as it was not a large fort. In their trade advertisements they claim: "Packs neatly into box 15½" x 9½" x 4½"." The 4½" dimension seems particularly small, but this was only the height of the base; when erected, the full height was 13", not including the flagpole.

BURLEYTOYS: "Buster" Toy Fort
c1933 to c1937

NO.	DESCRIPTION	DATE	DIMENSIONS	DISTINCTIVE FEATURES
unknown (6-019) (6-021) (6-022)	**the only one of this series** (identified by an example in the ownership below) eg: SOFIA Foundation, CY	c1933	15½"x9½"x13" 395x240x330mm	• single separate ramp to gateway • courtyard w/battlemented walls • two main buildings & cent tower • three rectangular corner towers

Correct assembly was enabled by a numbering system similar to that used by most manufacturers in the early days. Each component was given a number on the underside, which was intended to match up with the same number on the base indicating its "correct" position. These numbers were commonly hand-written in pencil, but, in this case, they were punched into the underside of the components and stenciled onto the base.

It was a rather crude design, robustly constructed of wood and plywood. It was also quite ordinary in its gloss painted finishes – basically a rich cream color, with bright red roofs and healthy, grass green vegetation. Texture for the vegetation was achieved by mixing sawdust into the green paint.

This lack of refinement can probably be explained by the manner in which it was intended to be used (i.e., as a target for toy guns) which could cause it to "blow up" whenever a critical hit was achieved. This spectacular effect was probably equivalent to what one would expect if a real fort received a direct hit in its main ammunition magazine.

The explosion effect was achieved by releasing a large bed-spring tightly compressed into the space under the courtyard. The spring was held down by a strip of wood fixed to the base by a hinge at the front and retained by a bullet-nosed piece of dowel passed through a hole in the back wall. This dowel was set in another strip of wood which stood vertically directly against the back of the central tower.

A direct hit (or perhaps several of them because it was really quite stiff) pushed the tower back, and with it the strip of wood with the dowel retaining pin in it, thus releasing the coiled-up spring and flipping up the retaining strip.

Most of the super-structure was loose, and the courtyard formed in two sections – so the effect was one of the courtyard bursting open throwing all the pieces up in the air. It was all very satisfactory if you were doing the shooting – and if you were the manufacturer of the fort's complement of lead toy soldiers, which would almost certainly have suffered severe damage in the process.

6-019 **"Buster" Fort No.1**
The "Buster" Fort No.1 all set up and ready for action. There is not a hint of anything untoward about to happen. The figures are 30mm Johillco and one or two others of unknown origin.

6-020

HIT
THE
TOWER
AND
UP GOES
THE
FORT

THE "BUSTER" FORT

BOYS, you get a realistic explosion when the tower of the " Buster " Fort is hit by gunfire. A gun complete with shells is supplied with each fort.

Obtainable at most toy shops and big stores.

Price 10'-

EATON & MUNBY LTD., BURLEY, HANTS.

6-020 The "Buster" Fort No.1: *advertisement from the Meccano Magazine of December 1933.*
6-021 The "Buster" Fort No.1: *the spring primed.*
6-022 The "Buster" Fort No.1: *the denouement.*

An interesting consequence of this concept was that the designer(s?) had to develop a new construction of the drawbridge. The "exploding" effect would have been severely hampered, and the drawbridge itself too easily damaged if it were attached to the base in the then conventional manner. It was therefore made as an integral part of the gatehouse.

Even so the drawbridge hinge had to be much stronger than normal. A metal rod was inserted through one side wall, across the opening, and through the other side wall of the gateway. This provided a strong hinge pin around which a metal plate was wrapped to create the hinge plate. Unfortunately, this createde a considerable step down into the courtyard from the drawbridge, although this was no worse than the step down from the drawbridge going out onto the top of the ramp, which was a feature common to all drawbridges made of wood. Later Tri-ang and Elastolin solved this by making their drawbridges out of pressed metal.

In design terms, all of this had a "knock-on" effect in that, in order for the drawbridge to operate, the gatehouse (unlike all the other buildings) had to be somehow fixed to the base. The standard "nail-in-the-building-hole-in-the-base" system was used, but, in order to make it strong enough to withstand the "explosion," the nails were substituted with wood dowels.

A quite powerful gun would have been necessary, and Eaton & Munby were thoughtful enough to offer just that in their Burleytoys range. This is a classic example of simple design to a precise design brief. It was nothing but a block of wood with a ⅜" hole drilled through it, and a tube of the same diameter attached to form the barrel. A strong elastic band wrapped around it provided the propulsion. The ammunition was ⅜" wood dowel cut to 4½" lengths. This delivered enough weight on target as a point load, to move the target building back and release the spring.

6-021

6-022

Burnett Ltd. and 'UBILDA'

In the late 1920s, Burnett Ltd., a toy company located in London, was well known for its mechanical motor cars, omnibuses, toy cannon, and the like. On another front, they were established suppliers of cash and paint boxes. They were somewhat less well known for their concern with constructional toys. It was not until 1932 that the first advertisements for the UBILDA system appeared, and 1935/1936 before the catalogue in my possession came out.

The system was comprised of sets for making a variety of models, including toy forts. The components in the sets were made of sheet metal which was printed on, using a form of silk-screening. The components were to be bolted together – using Meccano-type nuts and bolts – although some low wall pieces were slotted together at the corners, and connected to the towers with simple wire clips.

Burnett's UBILDA: (Pre-World War ll)
c1935 to 1939

NO.	DESCRIPTION	DATE	DIMENSIONS	DISTINCTIVE FEATURES
81/30 (6-023)	**the smaller of this series** (identified by an example in the ownership below) eg: Allen Hickling Toy Forts	c1935	10¼"x8"x7" 260x200x180mm	• single ramp to gatehouse • battlemented courtyard • one central main building • two circular side towers
30/60 (6-028)	**the second of this series** (identified by an example in the ownership below) eg: SOFIA Foundation, CY	c1935	12½"x11¼"x7" 320x285x180mm	• two single ramps to upper levels • gateway & low battlemented walls • terrace & 3-D main building • four circular corner towers
31/90 (6-024)	**the larger of this series** (listed in Burnett catalogue 1935/1936) eg: no known example	c1935	21"x12"x7" 655x305x180mm	• two single ramps to upper levels • gateway & low battlemented walls • terrace & 3-D main building • six circular corner & side towers

Burnett did not manufacture all of their products themselves. They bought in many of their lines, and the UBILDA range was one of them. The actual production was undertaken by a well-established metal toy manufacturing company – Barringer, Wallis and Manners, of Mansfield.

The components of the series were impressive, the thicker layers of paint used in the silk screen process providing a feeling of solidity. The walls were two different tones of brown with light beige highlights and detailing around the openings. Black was used for the openings themselves and stonework details. This was set off by the use of red for the door and portcullis, with green for the vegetation.

The boxes were well illustrated and, having a covering of stonework paper, provided the base for the fort. On them, rather more amusingly, Burnett made vastly exaggerated claims about the contents (e.g., "48 parts to build a fort," when I counted 24, including the nuts and bolts – not separately), but this was before the Trade Descriptions Act. Not only did 1939 mark the start of the Second World War, but also the fact that Barringer, Wallis, and Manners were taken into the Metal Box empire. Burnett disappeared from the scene not long after. And that was that for the duration of the Second World War.

6-023 **UBILDA**: 81/30

This was the smallest of the range. As such, it is very small and does not make much of a fort. It seems likely that No.30/60 proved more popular, which may account for there being more of them around today.

The gatehouse rather dwarfs the castle. With its operating portcullis, it justified Burnett's claim that the box contained a "Working Model of a Fort."

Assembly was a tricky business. The parts were small, as were the nuts and bolts, making its assembly a challenge to anyone's dexterity, and very frustrating if you were eager to start a game in which it was to play a role.

c.1935

6-024

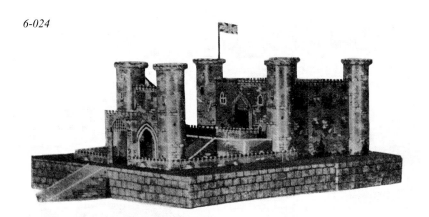

6-025

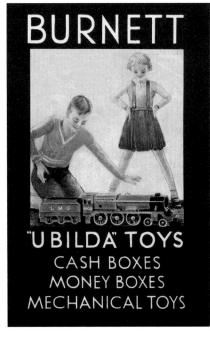

6-026

6-027

6-028

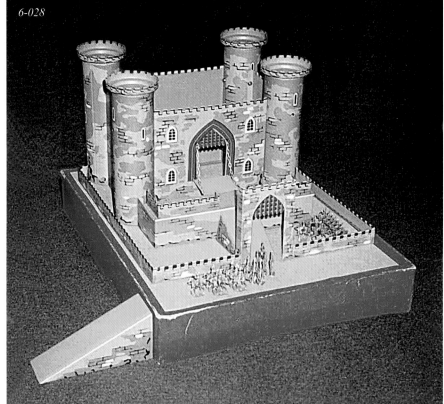

6-024 **UBILDA**: *31/90 (catalogue)*
6-025 **UBILDA**: *catalogue 1935/1936*
6-026 **UBILDA**: *instructions*
6-027 **UBILDA**: *box*
6-028 **UBILDA**: *30/60*

UBILDA 31/90 (6-024). This is the only image we have. It has no new pieces and can be made up out of the other two sets plus one or two bits.

UBILDA 30/60 (6-028). This is the regular fort in the middle of the range. It has

a red box. The figures are 25mm semi-flat cavalry of unknown origin.

The UBILDA catalogue (6-025) for 1935/1936. This covers the whole range of UBILDA – not just forts.

The UBILDA instructions (6-026) came stuck inside the lid of the box. In fact, they are not so much instructions as suggestions for layout.

The UBILDA box lid (6-027) is where they made extravagant claims about size.

Chad Valley and "UBILDA"

After the war was over, Burnett Ltd. did not come back, so Chad Valley, operating out of Birmingham, seized the opportunity to start producing toy forts again. In 1946, they took over all of Burnett's interests, including the tools for some of Burnett's mechanical and non-mechanical toys, which were still at Barringer, Wallis and Manners.

Chad Valley immediately took up the UBILDA concept, and asked Barringer, Wallis and Manners to produce one fort set for them. This was No.10009, which was very similar in composition to Burnett's No.30/60. The only major structural change they made was to omit the terrace at the front of the keep. They also left out the flag.

Chad Valley's UBILDA: (Post-World War II)
1946 to 1949

NO.	DESCRIPTION	DATE	DIMENSIONS	DISTINCTIVE FEATURES
10009 (6-029) (6-030)	the only one of this series (identified by an example in the ownership below) eg: Allen Hickling Toy Forts	c1946	12½"x11¼"x7" 320x285x180mm	• two single ramps to upper levels • gateway & low battlemented walls • 3-D main building • four circular corner towers

The number of colors was also reduced. Only one brown was used for the main walls and the light beige was replaced with a sharper, lighter color – a sort of cream. The red of the portcullises was replaced with the same green as the vegetation. Though the result was rather monochromatic, the contrasting tones made for a slightly disturbing "jazzy" effect.

Some of the printing was redesigned. It was simplified, notably along the battlements, and some of the detailing was cruder. Such changes may have been necessary because the original screens decayed or got damaged during the war. Alternatively, they may have been lost in the changeover to Chad Valley, or it may have simply been a question of economics.

The boxes were made of a utilitarian grey card, but they used more or less the same graphics on the label including, at first, Burnett's extravagant claims. These were soon replaced with a wiser "all parts to build a fort."

Chad Valley priced the forts at "143s/doz" in 1946 (that is £7.15 in today's money). This works out at 11/11 each (eleven shillings and eleven pence), but

it is not clear whether this was wholesale or a retail price. They probably quoted the retail price and then gave a discount to their wholesale buyers.

They were brought out for the Christmas trade in 1946 and the last year of production was 1949. The tools were finally scrapped on 31 October 1951.

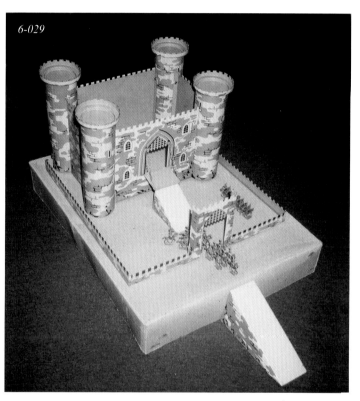

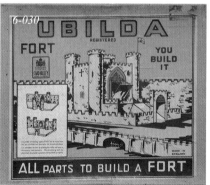

6-029 **UBILDA No.10009**
6-030 **UBILDA No.10009**: box
  UBILDA No.10009 (6-029) was the only version to be brought out by Chad Valley. Various changes had to be carried out to make it a feasible proposition. The main one was the omission of the terrace at the front of the keep.
  The figures are 25mm, semi-flat cavalry of unknown origin. If one wished to use the fort with anything larger, it was probably best to keep it in the background as a sort of scenery.
  The UBILDA box (6-030) was one of the later ones – after Chad Valley had to water down their claims about the contents.

William Britain & Sons and Their Model Fort

Britains were producing toys in London about 1855, if not before, but, his son William Britain Junior started making hollowcast figures in 1893. He soon became famous for his 54mm toy soldiers. These were probably the first hollowcast figures on the market; certainly they were the first commercially successful ones. In spite of this, and the vast array of soldiers needing somewhere to live, he did not get into making forts until 1935.

When he did so, he really only dabbled at it. The chosen material was strawboard, and the fort was sold folded flat in a paper envelope or as an added feature to two different sets of soldiers. When sold separately it was called a Model Fortress, and when it was sold as an accompaniment in a box it was called a Model Fort.

It was really only one façade of a fort, and even that was hardly complete in that the towers were only two sides of a tower. Moreover the courtyard in front was barely big enough for more than a dozen Britains toy soldiers.

BRITAINS: Model Fort
1935 to 1939

NO.	DESCRIPTION	DATE	DIMENSIONS	DISTINCTIVE FEATURES
1391 1394 1397	**the only one of this series** (identified by an example in the ownership below) eg: Rob Wilson, UK	1935	unknown	• front of the fort only • steps up to gateway • courtyard with crenellated walls • two square towers & main building

They did eventually try again in 1977, again with cardboard, which was not very successful. It was a cut-out, do-it-yourself sort of production that was not a commercial success and went out in the next year.

The cardboard used was too thin for what it was intended to do. Consequently the walls were unstable and the whole structure did not give the impression of a castle.

BRITAINS: Make-up Card Model
1977

NO.	DESCRIPTION	DATE	DIMENSIONS	DISTINCTIVE FEATURES
4752 (6-033) (6-034)	**Knights Castle–** (identified by an example in the ownership below) eg: Allen Hickling Toy Forts	1977	unknown	• make-up card model • no ramp, entry through gatehouse • courtyard with crenellated walls • chapel with large circular tower

6-031

6-032

6-031 **Britains Model Fort**: *The fort erected. (Courtesy Rob Wilson)*
6-032 **Britains Model Fort**: *The box. (Courtesy Rob Wilson)*
    This fort was in production at Britains for about seven years. Its play value was severely limited in that it was hardly a fort at all – it was barely more than a bit of two-dimensional scenery. Having said that, it was a clever bit of marketing. The 54mm figures are Britains' red coats and Scotsmen.

6-033 **Britains** *make-up card model: the complete set*
6-034 **Britains** *make-up card model: illustration*

    Britains first attempt at re-entry into the forts market was a failure. Their attempt to get the children making their own fort just did not catch on.

    This was in spite of the fact that the forts were really quite realistic. Probably it was because they did not stand up to much in the way of rough play.

6-033

6-034

It was not until the 1980s that they produced anything like a sensible toy fort. In about 1985, they produced the Knights Sword series. This was composed of a flat-pack fort and two vacuum-formed forts. These were more successful, appearing in the catalogue for some time.

BRITAINS: Knights Sword Series
1985 to present

NO.	DESCRIPTION	DATE	DIMENSIONS	DISTINCTIVE FEATURES
7791 (6-035)	**Castle Set** (identified by an example in the ownership below) eg: Allen Hickling Toy Forts	c1985	16½"x16½"x9" 420x420x230mm	• gateway with portcullis • crenellated courtyard • four triangular corner towers • open backed towers
7792 (6-037)	**Lion Castle** (identified by an example in the ownership below) eg: Allen Hickling Toy Forts	c1985	18"x18"x4½" 450x450x115mm	• small narrow moat • gateway + portcullis & drawbridge • crenellated walls round courtyard • four square corner towers
7793 (6-036)	**Sword Castle** (identified by an example in the ownership below) eg: Allen Hickling Toy Forts	c1985	18"x23½"x8" 450x600x200mm	• gateway + portcullis & drawbridge • crenellated walls round courtyard • courtyard over undercroft • four square corner towers

The vacuum-formed forts represent Britains' one and only use of 100% plastic in their fort production. The Sword Castle (6-036) was in two parts. One part sits on the other to make a second storey. The top piece has four corner towers and a courtyard, while the lower piece comprises the undercroft.

The gate is an ingenious combination of a portcullis and a drawbridge – when the portcullis is down, the drawbridge is up, and vice versa. All is enhanced with colorful flags and labels.

The Lion Castle (6-037) is in effect the upper part only of Sword Castle with a moat attached. It did not provide much protection. The gate is exactly the same as for the Sword Castle, as are the flags and labels.

They also produced a variation of this one in white.

In the case of the flat-packed fort (6-035), the walls and walkways were of medium-density fiberboard (MDF). The crenellation was of plastic. The portcullis was the same as Sword Castle without the drawbridge. All was again enhanced with colorful flags and labels.

6-035

c.1985

6-036

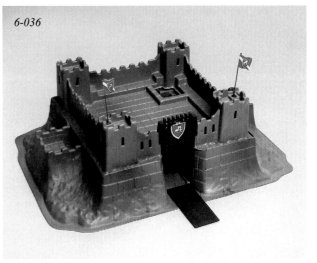

6-037

6-035 **Britains Knights Sword series 7791**: *Castle Set*
6-036 **Britains Knights Sword series 7793**: *Sword Castle*
6-037 **Britains Knights Sword series 7792**: *Lion Castle*
   This Knights Sword series was commercially successful, unlike the other series Britains produced.
   One of them (6-035) was constructed using more or less conventional materials. Medium-density fiberboard was the material mostly used, which led to unrealistic, but eminently play worthy, features such as open-backed towers. The 54mm knight figures are by Britains.
   Two of them (6-036 & 6-037) represented their first 100% use of plastic, which used the vacuum-forming technique.

Manufacturers Accessories Co. (MAC)

Manufacturers Accessories Co., or MAC as they were known, seem to have been around for ages. They claim in their catalogues to have been established in 1882, and there is some evidence of their being around about 1910. We have catalogues from 1930 through to 1958, although we do not know how long after 1958 they carried on.

Really little is known about them other than, in the early 1930s, they were marketing many things from electrical goods to sewing machines and mangles. In between all of these, they sold Britains toy soldiers and, more importantly here, a range of four toy forts. These would appear to be almost certainly of German origin; at least they did not claim them to be British as I am sure they would have done if they had been.

Then, by the mid-1930s, with the Germans no longer exporting because of the world depression, they were selling forts made in Britain. These are the ones of which we have examples, although it is difficult to match up the forts with the claims made for them in their catalogues.

MAC (British-made Forts from the Catalogue)
1937

NO.	DESCRIPTION	DATE	DIMENSIONS	DISTINCTIVE FEATURES
S7995 /300	**the smallest of the series** (listed in Manufacturers AC catalogue 1937/1938) eg: no known example	1937	13"x12"x14" 330x305x355mm	• strongly constructed & collapsible • colored and very attractive • neatly packed away in base
S7995 a/506	**the second of the series** (listed in Manufacturers AC catalogue 1937/1938) eg: no known example	1937	15½"x13"x11" 395x330x280mm	• sturdy construction & collapsible • realistic model of old-time outpost • drawbridge & moat • electric lighting
S7996 /700	**the third of the series** (listed in Manufacturers AC catalogue 1937/1938) eg: no known example	1937	16"x14"x15½" 405x355x395mm	• sturdy construction & collapsible • realistic model of old-time outpost • drawbridge & moat • electric lighting
S7998 /900	**the largest of the series** (listed in Manufacturers AC catalogue 1937/1938) eg: no known example	1937	19½"x15½"x15" 495x395x380mm	• strongly constructed & collapsible • realistic in attractive shades • drawbridge & slope • electric lighting

We do not know who made them; maybe it was MAC themselves, but I doubt it. Whoever it was, they knew their market very well. They did not try to compete with Tri-ang, who produced forts with a superior finish. They aimed for the cheaper end of the market, which accounts for the rather slapdash approach to design.

The main characteristics of all these forts, apart from their rough and ready construction, are to be found in the drawbridges. Here the designers came up with the novel use of sheet metal for the bridge itself. This gave the distinct advantage of providing no step up onto them as is the case with wooden ones. This meant, however, that it was necessary to come up with an equally novel way of joining the chains to them. This they did with a simple slot device into which the links of the chain fitted.

MAC (British-made Forts)
c1933 to c1940

NO.	DESCRIPTION	DATE	DIMENSIONS	DISTINCTIVE FEATURES
unknown (6-039)	**smallest of these castles** (identified by an example in the ownership below) eg: Allen Hickling Toy Forts	c1935	11½"x12"x11" 295x305x280mm	• integral ramp to metal drawbridge • gateway & low battlemented walls • 2 square towers & main building
unknown (6-038)	**the second of these castles** (identified by an example in the ownership below) eg: Allen Hickling Toy Forts	c1935	12"x12"x12" 300x310x300mm	• integral ramp to terrace level • metal drawbridge & gateway • court with low battlemented walls • square & separate circular towers
unknown (6-040)	**the third of these castles** (identified by an example in the ownership below) eg: SOFIA Foundation, CY	c1935	16½"x14"x13½" 420x360x340mm	• 1 separate ramp to main level • 2nd ramp to drawbridge & gateway • square tower & main building • separate circular & corner tower
unknown (6-041)	**the largest of these castles** (identified by an example in the ownership below) eg: SOFIA Foundation, CY	c1935	35½"x20"x21½" 900x510x550mm	• two single ramps to upper levels • 2 gateways & 1 metal drawbridge • three towers & 4-arch building • electric lighting

There was one other distinct characteristic. The roofs of the gateways were not crenellated, but were simple half-round pieces of wood painted red with white stripes across. This form of decoration found its way into other parts, such as the pinnacles attached to towers, adding to the jolly appearance of the castles.

Before moving on, mention must be made of their electric lighting. This seems a bit sophisticated compared to their other finishes. It was, of course, very simple, operated by a "pocket lamp battery." In the only example we have, the largest tower, the main building, and the other square tower on the back were provided with lighting. It is not clear where the batteries were stored or where the switches, if any, were located.

After the break for the war years, MAC moved their premises from the east of London to Weybridge in Surrey.

By the mid-1950s, they were still selling toy forts, but were now allied to the Tudor Toy Co. and Kleeware. These forts will be discussed later; suffice it to say that these forts were more sophisticated than their previous pre-war supplier could manage.

6-038

6-039

6-040

6-041

6-038 **MAC second**
6-039 **MAC smallest**
6-040 **MAC third**
6-041 **MAC largest**

MAC's smallest and second smallest forts (6-038 & 6-039) display their chunky, self-confident nature. Both have the characteristic metal drawbridges and the white-striped red roofs of the series. The colorful appearance is achieved without losing a sense of reality. The figures are 30mm flats from Germany on the one on the left, and 30mm figures from the coronation set by Johillco on the right.

The second largest of the series (6-040) can be seen as a small fort on a base. This makes for an impressive fort without the production of many parts. It is not known whether this example is an early one or a late

one. It has a wooden drawbridge, a crenellated gateway, and a separate ramp, which could be either early or late. The color scheme, however, appears the same as the smaller one above left. The tops of the two towers seem to have been nibbled by a dragon.

MAC's largest fort (6-041), in our possession, is large indeed. The color scheme gives some reason to doubt its origin, but such doubts are easily dispelled by the metal drawbridge and the white-striped red roof on the gateway. There are many pieces on this fort that are unique, including the large fortified gatehouse, the large hollow towers, and the balcony on the main building. The electric lighting can be seen on the backs of the buildings and in the bulb sockets in them, but there is no provision for storage of the batteries. The 54mm figures on this one are from Britains Deetail range.

Jack Binns & Bill Baker were "BINBAK"

Jack Binns and Bill Baker knew each other before the Second World War, when they were apprenticed to a firm of sign-writers. They came together after the war to form a company producing the well known brand of toys with the trade name of Binbak Models.

In the beginning, they relied on their strengths – woodworking and painting. They had a policy of producing top quality toys, which never changed; they insisted on making toys that would last. They started with garages, but soon got into making dollhouses, farms, zoos, shops, and, of course, forts.

At the outset, the forts were a little on the naïve side in design terms, and owed much to the world of fantasy. One of the first (6-042) was basically a white affair with many red roofs, and was quite a challenge to make.

BINBAK: First Series
c1950 to c1953

NO.	DESCRIPTION	DATE	DIMENSIONS	DISTINCTIVE FEATURES
unknown (6-042)	**the only one of this series** (identified by an example in the ownership below) eg: David Baker, UK	1950	19"x17½"x9½" 485x445x240mm	• fort in one-piece construction • ramp, moat, drawbridge & gate • five flat towers • back piece w/various buildings

Their next development was, not surprisingly, simpler to make. They produced four forts, all using essentially the same parts, in two different sizes and two different paint styles. The towers were not very realistic, but there were more of them – seven on the big model and six on the smaller one.

The forts were all more or less the same size, the difference between the sizes being mostly in the water feature in front. The bigger model had a virtual lake, while the smaller one had a more conventional moat.

All four forts had landscaping in the form of trees made up by a Christmas tree manufacturer working in the off season, and, at least in the later models, flocking was added. This looked very good, but protecting the trees, which were particularly vulnerable, was a problem they never really solved, hence the lack of vegetation on those that we have. Of course, the trees were wildly inaccurate in terms of defense, which required the clearance of all trees in the vicinity.

The painting of the two types was significant. The first type was a throw back to the first series in that the buildings were mostly white with red trim. This type could be called a fairy castle or princess's castle – it was certainly more romantic. The second type was much more realistic in that the walls were more

stone-like, looking much more defensible. This was much more likely to house knights of the realm.

BINBAK: Second Series
c1953 to c1960

NO.	DESCRIPTION	DATE	DIMENSIONS	DISTINCTIVE FEATURES
unknown (6-043)	**the small fairy castle** (identified by an example in the ownership below) eg: Allen Hickling Toy Forts	c1953	18"x17½"x8½" 455x445x215mm	• one-piece construction (white) • ramp, moat, drawbridge & gateway • six thin towers (two by gate) • naïve style back buildings
unknown	**the large fairy castle** (identified by an example in the ownership below) eg: Jeff Scott, US	c1953	17¾"x23½"x8½" 450x595x215mm	• one-piece construction (white) • ramp, lake, drawbridge & gateway • seven thin towers (two by gate) • naïve style back buildings
unknown	**the small knights' castle** (identified by an example in the ownership below) eg: David Baker, UK	c1953	18"x17½"x8½" 455x445x215mm	• one-piece construction (brown) • ramp, moat, drawbridge & gateway • six thin towers (two by gate) • naïve style back buildings
unknown (6-044)	**the large knights' castle** (identified by an example in the ownership below) eg: Jack Binns estate, UK	c1953	17¾"x23½"x8½" 450x595x215mm	• one-piece construction (brown) • ramp, lake, drawbridge & gateway • seven thin towers (two by gate) • naïve style back buildings
unknown (6-045)	**the large transition castle** (identified by an example in the ownership below) eg: Jack Binns estate, UK	c1953	unknown	• one-piece construction (brown) • ramp, moat, drawbridge & gateway • two thin towers by gate • robust 3-D back buildings

There is one fort I have put into this series that was more of a transition piece. By the gate, it had two of the thin towers, which were typical of the second series, but it also had a robust square tower at the back as part of the main buildings.

With the next series they really "took the bull by the horns" in making it realistic; this style lasted a long time. The buildings were more substantial, and the towers, in particular, were more convincing. To accommodate the increased bulk of the forts, the landscaped area became less of a feature.

They also began to pay attention to how access was achieved from one level to the other, so the modeling of their staircases was really quite intricate, with steps cut to a sensible scale. The application of small shields attached to the walls in strategic locations also added to the attraction of the forts.

In addition, the forts were artistically rendered to express natural traces of weathering and patterns of heavy use. The clear exception to this was in the blue they used to represent water. Although fine in connection with their fantasy castles, it was a bit of an anomaly in the medieval context. The only explanation seems to be that it made them look attractive to the buying public.

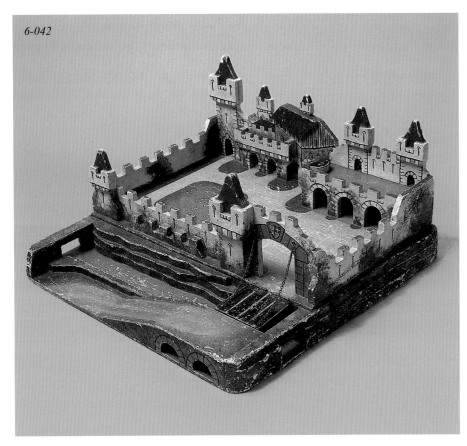

6-042

c.1950-c.1955

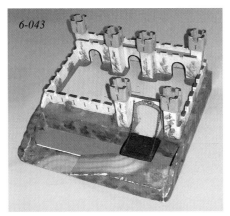

6-043

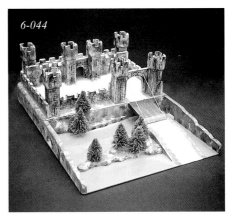

6-044

6-045

6-042 **Binbak: first series**
6-043 **Binbak: second series** – *small Fairy Castle*
6-044 **Binbak: second series** – *large Knights Castle*
6-045 **Binbak: transition**

The Binbak first series was the start of it all (6-042). One can see how Binns and Baker got carried away with enthusiasm, not thinking of the practicalities. Apart from the number of pieces required, the painting was extremely complex. There was no landscaping in the form of trees.

The Binbak second series began to get the hang of it (6-043 & 6-044), but lost sight of their aim to produce forts that really looked believable. This was alright as long as they concentrated on the Fairy Castle painting option, but failed miserably with the Knight's Castle. The landscaping took off here, although its fragility is evidenced in the Fairy Castle where there are parts of trees still left by the front wall and the gateway.

The transition model (6-045) is included here because it has the gateway of the second series and the beginnings of their later three-dimensional buildings with a square tower. There are no staircases yet and the square tower does not have the sophistication of later models. The landscaping in front shows some more care being taken.

BINBAK: Third Series
c1960 to c1970

NO.	DESCRIPTION	DATE	DIMENSIONS	DISTINCTIVE FEATURES
unknown (6-047)	**the smaller fort in the series** (identified by an example in the ownership below) eg: Allen Hickling Toy Forts	c1960	17½"x24"x8½" 445x610x215mm	• one-piece construction • ramp, moat, drawbridge & gatehouse • gatehouse with two square towers • long building & two square towers
unknown (6-048)	**the larger fort in the series** (identified by an example in the ownership below) eg: Jack Binns estate, UK	c1960	17¾"x24"x8½" 450x610x215mm	• one-piece construction • ramp, moat, drawbridge & gatehouse • gatehouse with two square towers • long building & two square towers
unknown (6-049)	**complex 1 fort in the series** (identified by an example in the ownership below) eg: Allen Hickling Toy Forts	c1960	18"x17½"x8½" 455x445x215mm	• one-piece construction • ramp, moat, drawbridge & gate • three towers (one by gate) • back building with porch
unknown (6-050)	**complex 2 fort in the series** (identified by an example in the ownership below) eg: Allen Hickling Toy Forts	c1960	17¾"x17¾"x8½" 450x450x215mm	• one-piece construction • ramp, moat, drawbridge & gatehouse • three towers (one in gatehouse) • steps up to roof of back buildings

Although different series representing developments in Binbak's approach to toymaking can be identified, and such developments indicate progress, this does not mean that production followed a step-by-step sequence. The series overlapped in time. For example, the white and red fantasy range of the first series continued in production well into the 1970s.

The move to their fourth series was marked by a bold move away from the rectangular courtyard format, and a significantly more realistic layout, including the introduction of towers at the front of the courtyard. This meant further reduction of the landscaping with minimal water features.

A further development had not so much to do with design as with marketing. There must have been pressure from the retailers to produce something smaller and, presumably, cheaper. The results were much smaller models.

BINBAK: Fourth Series
c1965 to c1975

NO.	DESCRIPTION	DATE	DIMENSIONS	DISTINCTIVE FEATURES
unknown (6-051)	**the small fort in the series** (identified by an example in the ownership below) eg: Jack Binns estate, UK	c1960	unknown	• mainly one-piece construction • gatehouse with gates • one demountable tower • minimal landscaping
unknown (6-046)	**Super Fort in the series** (identified by an example in the ownership below) eg: Jack Binns estate, UK	c1960	unknown	• one-piece construction • ramp, moat, drawbridge & gatehouse • four towers + two part of gatehouse • extensive 3-D back buildings

It is known that Binbak produced specials from time to time, and that they were happy to make items to order.

From the stock records "super" forts appear a few times a year. These records are seriously incomplete, so it is difficult to know what these so-called "super" forts were. The most likely candidate (6-046), which has four towers, a substantial gatehouse, and many stairways, shows characteristics of the second, third, and fourth series. Its size can only be estimated, but was probably over four feet (1.2 metres) across.

Another form of special was a standard second series model, made special with a dungeon built in under the front corner of the courtyard. It had a trap door, with steps leading down and a small barred window looking out low over the moat at the front.

Two large one-offs are known to have been made. There was a model based on Windsor Castle, which was the one made for the royal family. It was extremely large and had a special moving belt on which toy soldiers could be made to march up and down.

***6-046* Binbak: Super Fort**
Super Forts were made in very small numbers quite regularly. It is said that they were intended for display in shops, but there is no evidence for this. Equally possible is that they may have been made to special order, as they had a reputation in this respect.

6-049

6-050

c.1965

6-047 **Binbak: third series** (smaller)
6-048 **Binbak: third series** (larger)
6-049 **Binbak: third series** (complex 1)
6-050 **Binbak: third series** (complex 2)
6-051 **Binbak: fourth series** (small)

   Binbak's third and fourth series represent their move towards realism. The more robust towers and a conscious effort with staircases as a means of getting to the upper levels are indications of this. These formed the basis of their fort production for ten years.

   In the fourth series, the move away from waterscapes is noticeable as is the tendency to produce smaller forts for the first time. The tower may have been demountable.

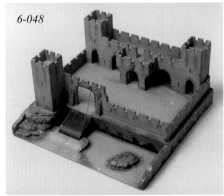

6-048

6-051

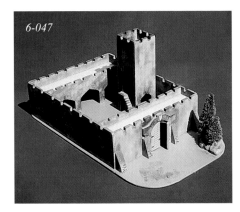

6-047

The other was a model based on Leeds Castle in Kent – a very Binbak sort of castle with a very large expanse of water around it. It took a long time to make – coordinating its production with their regular orders – and the customer did not want it when it was finished. So they took it to London where it was bought by the first shop they offered it to.

In 1972, when Bill Baker left the company, the workshops were moved from Bradford to Batley. It was from there that the fifth series was launched.

This fifth series was developed in response to the business, which expanded internationally, particularly to the USA. The principle changes involved reducing the waterfront feature, yet again, to just enough water for the drawbridge to span, and making the buildings interesting with changes of level and more complex staircases to match. The series was also marked by the introduction of the occasional taller tower.

Binbak also began experimenting with demountable pieces. These had clear advantages in terms of storage and transportation. One might expect this development to have found a place in their product strategy somewhat sooner, but these strategies were a bit on the rough-and-ready side, and it probably seemed like too much trouble.

BINBAK: Fifth Series
c1975 to 1991

NO.	DESCRIPTION	DATE	DIMENSIONS	DISTINCTIVE FEATURES
unknown (6-054)	the small fort (identified by an example in the ownership below) eg: Steve Sommers, USA	c1975	unknown	• one-piece construction • doors & gateway • two square towers at front • one large building
unknown	the small fort with tower (identified by an example in the ownership below) eg: Allen Hickling Toy Forts	c1975	14½"x14½"x10½" 370x370x265mm	• two-piece construction • moat, drawbridge & gateway • 3-D buildings down both sides • one demountable tower
unknown (6-052)	the long narrow fort (identified by an example in the ownership below) eg: Allen Hickling Toy Forts	c1975	23"x15"x11" 585x380x280mm	• two-piece construction • moat, drawbridge & gateway • single storey buildings on 3 sides • one demountable tower
unknown (6-055)	the Sir Lancelot Castle (identified by an example in the ownership below) eg: SOFIA Foundation, CY	c1975	18"x18"x9" 460x460x230mm	• one-piece construction • moat, drawbridge & gateway • wide gate & two square towers • 3-D buildings & two square towers

The sixth series was probably the most interesting. Stimulated by the growth of the company's export trade to America, which made shipping a much more serious consideration, Jack embarked on what was, for him, a completely new

style of toy fort (6-056). He designed some parts to be demountable. This allowed him, for the first time, to make the forts even more realistic. They were bulkier and more three-dimensional, which enabled more accurately represented crenellation and stone detailing.

BINBAK: Sixth Series
c1980 to 1991

NO.	DESCRIPTION	DATE	DIMENSIONS	DISTINCTIVE FEATURES
unknown	the Camelot Castle (listed in a US distributors catalogue 1980) eg: Peter Clark, US	c1980	18"x20"x9" 460x510x230mm	• one-piece construction • moat, drawbridge & gateway • wide gate & two square towers • 3-D buildings & two square towers
unknown (6-056)	the Greystone Castle (identified by an example in the ownership below) eg: Allen Hickling Toy Forts	1980	15"x18"x9½" 380x460x240mm	• three-piece construction • moat, drawbridge & gateway • two demountable towers • robust 3-D back buildings

By this time, the British laws with respect to child safety had changed and Binbak had to invent alternatives to the "spike-in-the-hole" system of locating the loose parts. This challenge brought out the best, resulting in some ingenious yet practical features, which produced some very convincing models. In all cases, it was difficult to detect where the separate part joined the main body.

Jack Binns died in 1987, and the company closed for business in 1992.

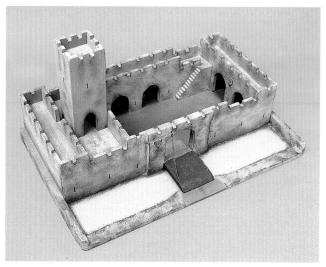

6 052 **Binbak: fifth series** *(long narrow fort) The complexity of the layouts became more apparent in the shape and levels, and the trees were out.*

6-054

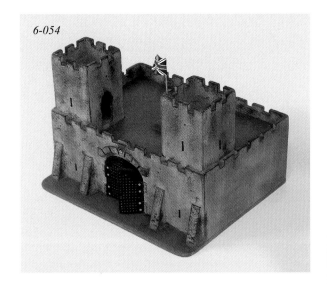

6-055

6-056

6-054 **Binbak: fifth series** *(small/tower)*
6-055 **Binbak: fifth series** *(Castle Lancelot)*
6-056 **Binbak: sixth series** *(Greystone Castle)*

Binbak's fifth series was characterized by experiments with demountable towers, doors instead of drawbridges on the smaller items, complicated shapes, and an ever decreasing attention paid to water. The smallest (6-054) is unusual in that it has no courtyard. The resulting space would have been very dark without windows, but it would have been easily defensible.

The larger fort illustrated here (6-055) is in some ways more conventional. The low walls around the courtyard give a feeling of vulnerability, although with four towers a reasonably

strong defense could have been mounted. Note how the three staircases (one is behind and above the entrance) gives a sense of reality.

Binbak's sixth series was just getting off the ground when Jack Binns died. We only have the one example (6-056), which shows all the latest refinements. The stone detailing, especially the crenellation, is quite wonderful in its simplicity, while retaining its credibility. The two towers are both demountable, and lie comfortably in the courtyard when the fort is in transit.

The Hall Family Was Elf Toys and Joy Toys

In about 1955, Fred Hall and Fred Elford started making toy forts. They had been in business since 1948 making bobbins for the carpet industry, mounting blocks for electric switches, and a few toys. Now they wished to focus their activities, so they set up a company called Elf Toys. Over the years, they produced garages, farms, zoos, dollhouses, Wild West forts, and Medieval Castles. Of these, we are only interested in the Medieval Castles.

They started out with relatively robust plywood, glued together "box" construction in a relatively sober style. Although realistic in concept, the detail was slightly crude. On the castle (6-058), of which only one model is known to me, the stonework is quite realistically enlivened with silkscreen details, although the windows were only stenciled on.

ELF TOYS: Smaller Medieval Castles
1955 to c1980

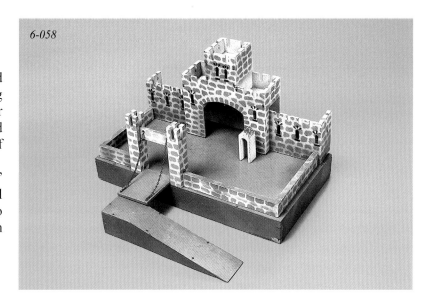

6-058

NO.	DESCRIPTION	DATE	DIMENSIONS	DISTINCTIVE FEATURES
unknown (6-058)	the small-medium fort (identified by an example in the ownership below) eg: SOFIA Foundation, CY	c1955	18"x18"x9" 460x460x230mm	• one-piece construction • ramp, drawbridge & gateway • three-storey rear buildingt • sentry box
unknown (6-059)	the small-medium fort (identified by an example in the ownership below) eg: Allen Hickling Toy Forts	c1965	unknown	• flat pack construction • ramp, drawbridge & gateway • three-storey rear building
unknown (6-060)	the small-medium fort (identified by an example in the ownership below) eg: Allen Hickling Toy Forts	c1970	18"x18"x9" 460x460x230mm	• two piece construction • drawbridge & gatehouse • one piece two-storey building
unknown	the small-medium fort (identified by an example in the ownership below) eg: Allen Hickling Toy Forts	c1980	18"x18"x9" 460x460x230mm	• two piece construction • drawbridge & gatehouse • two small square towers at front • single storey main building

6-059

The business was taking off and more help was needed in the workshop. As a result, much of the work, especially assembly and finishing, was "farmed out" to the rehabilitation workshops at the local psychiatric hospital.

By the end of the decade they had been joined by Philip Hall (Fred's half-brother), who became the designer. In 1964, Ted (Fred's son) entered the business straight from his apprenticeship as an industrial machine engineer.

6-058 **Elf Toys: first smaller Medieval Castle**
6-059 **Elf Toys: second smaller Medieval Castle**
Elf Toys' first smaller Medieval Castles (6-058) was their first attempt at a castle. It was simple in its concept and its construction, as were the simpler efforts of their competition. Note how the main theme of their castles stayed the same for many years.
Their second smaller Medieval Castle (6-059), which came about ten years later, demonstrates their concern with "flat pack" construction, although only partial at this stage.

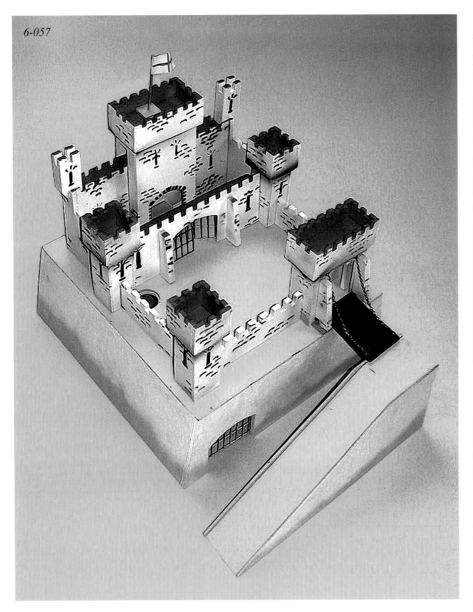

6-057

6-057 Elf Toys: King Arhur's Castle
This castle (6-057) represents Elf Toys' first attempt at a large fort. It is really quite involved with its working drawbridge, its dungeon accessed from two levels and its several working gates. Note the move towards "flat pack" construction.

The product line went through a number of changes, the most important of which was the beginning of the evolution of the slot-together system. This flat pack system eliminated assembly, saved warehouse space, and promoted cheaper shipping and easier storage for the retailer.

The medieval fort (6-059) also went through a color change to white with an orange representation of stonework, and the gateway was moved to the center. More significant was the introduction of King Arthur's Castle (6-057), which was a much larger and far more elaborate affair, with towers, two courtyards, a dungeon, and a far more cheerful color scheme.

ELF TOYS: King's Castles
c1965 to c1975

NO.	DESCRIPTION	DATE	DIMENSIONS	DISTINCTIVE FEATURES
44 (6-057)	**King Arthur's Castle** (identified by an example in the ownership below) eg: SOFIA Foundation, CY	c1965	18"x18"x16¼" 460x460x410mm	• box w/separate ramp to gatehse • 3 towers to forecourt w/dungeon • wall w/gate to inner courtyard • main building with side turrets
66 (6-062)	**King William Castle** (listed in manufacturers catalogue c1964) eg: no known example	c1975	18"x16"x10½" 460x405x265mm	• drawbridge & gatehouse to court • 2 towers & wall w/gate to court • inner courtyard with main building

By the mid-1960s the company was well established and running smoothly.

In 1967, Fred Elford chose to retire and Elf Toys was sold to two chicken farmers cum businessmen. They had no experience of the toy industry and must have seen Elf as what market analysts call a "cash cow;" that is, a well-established business with a well-defined market, which could continue to make money with little or no further investment needed for development.

The Elf Toys name was retained and the Hall family was invited to continue managing the business – subject to the new owners' ideas, of course. After eighteen months or so, Fred and Ted were told that their services were surplus to requirements and they were asked to leave.

Fred and Ted Hall were joined by Ted's half-brother, John Cartwright, and together they set up Joy Toys and Woodcrafts, using the trade name Joy Toys, in a new workshop in Upton-on-Severn. Fred was Works Director and Chief Designer; Ted was Production Manager; and John took over Sales and Finance.

The Early Learning Centre, which was just beginning to become a force on the high street, was having trouble with Tiger Toys, their original suppliers. Eventually Tiger Toys went bankrupt and Joy Toys stepped in. They were soon operating very successfully, producing 5000 Wild West forts per year with television-related marketing.

JOY TOYS: Larger Medieval Castles
c1975 to c1985

NO.	DESCRIPTION	DATE	DIMENSIONS	DISTINCTIVE FEATURES
unknown (6-061)	**Castle with slim towers** (identified by an example in the ownership below) eg: Ledbury Toy Museum, UK	c1975	22"x18"x13" 560x455x330mm	• flat pack construction • drawbridge & gatehouse • two square towers at rear • one long low building at rear
60 (6-063)	**Castle with good defenses** (identified by an example in the ownership below) eg: SOFIA Foundation, CY	c1985	22"x18"x13" 560x455x330mm	• flat pack construction • drawbridge & gatehouse • two square towers at rear • one long, low building at rear

The products went through several makeovers during this time. The original medieval fort was simplified and given a substantial gatehouse. King Arthur's Castle got some turrets, a flag, and a new stencil for the stonework, and was given the number 44. An all new model was introduced, which was a Medieval Castle and given the number 60 (6-063). The clever bit of design in this model was the simple depiction of an inner courtyard through the arch at the back.

About 1975, things were going so well that they opened a new larger workshop in Malvern.

They were using management and production techniques similar to those they had when they were operating as Elf. They "outsourced" much of the assembly and finishing to the rehabilitation workshops in the open prison at Sudbury. This had the added advantage because Sudbury made packing cases for the Ministry of Defense, and Joy Toys used their off-cuts for the forts.

By now, their use of the "flat pack" self-assembly system was in full swing. The medieval fort given the number 60 underwent a considerable overhaul. Not only did the color and windows change, but the crenellation was much more substantial. King Arthur's Castle, now also a dark color, was reduced in size and complexity to become King William's Castle numbered 66. There was also a simplified version of the smaller Medieval Castle.

In 1985, Fred Hall died. If this were not bad enough, John Cartwright left in 1986 to follow a different career. This meant that all of their workloads had to be taken on by Ted doing three full-time jobs – Works Director and Chief Designer, Production Manager, and Sales and Finance – and, in 1987, he had a heart attack. So, not surprisingly, things had to change.

He sold out to TP (Tube Plastics) Activity Toys – industrial friends and neighbors from their Elf Toys days in Stourport-on-Severn, who had often expressed an interest in the fortunes of the Halls. They were well known for the production of outdoor equipment (swing sets,etc.), and, presumably, they thought that they would benefit from an extended product range, as well as helping out old friends.

They retained the name Joy Toys, although prefixed by the use of TP, and things continued much as before. Ted, with considerable help, recovered from his heart attack and continued to run the production side of things. They carried on in the old workshop in Malvern, though the owners were now located with Activity Toys in Stourport-on-Severn.

This was a quite successful arrangement. In 1990, the operation was joined by Ted's son Rob and between them they saw the market for their toy forts begin to change, with a stronger emphasis on the younger user. The design changed accordingly.

6-060 **Joy Toys: small Medieval Castle** *3rd version*
The smaller Medieval Castle pictured here shows how the design became simpler over the years. This represents a sort of transition from the early form (6-058 & 6-059) to the later forms (6-061 & 6-063).

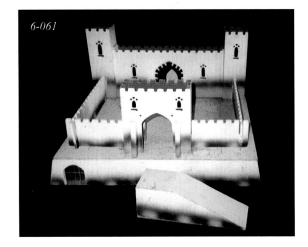

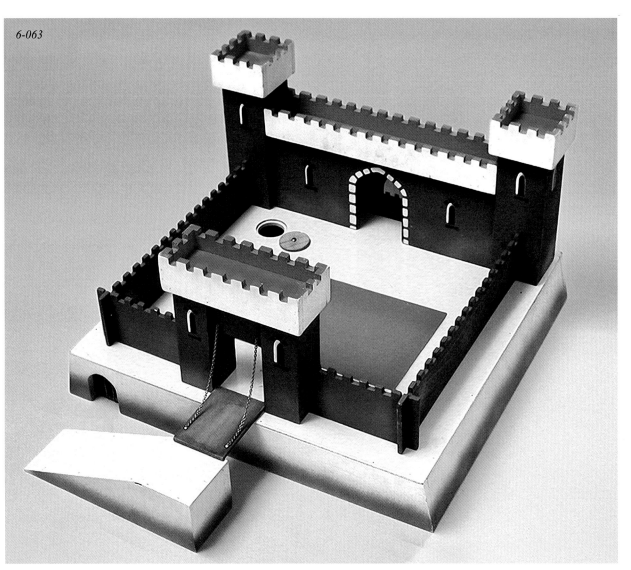

6-061 **Joy Toys: Larger Medieval Castle** *1st version*
6-062 **Joy Toys: King William Castle**
6-063 **Joy Toys: Larger Medieval Castle** *2nd version*

The first version of the larger Medieval Castle (6-061) demonstrates how a bigger format with a few extra pieces can work. This castle has a shallow plinth, which contains a dungeon, and two towers attached to the building behind.

The second version of the larger Medieval Castle (6-063) is essentially the same as the first. It is exactly the same size, but the crenellation is treated quite differently, giving the impression of a more rugged fort. The clever use of the far wall in the arch to give an impression of size is the same for both forts, but it appears differently when it is set in a smart, dark wall. The windows are more realistic also.

King William Castle (6-062) used King Arthur's Castle (6-057) as a basis. The height of the base was cut down and the dungeon disappeared along with the ramp. The inner courtyard remained, but the buildings at the back of it were much reduced. The gateway was moved to the center. All the trimmings were gone and the color changed to a sober very dark grey.

The medieval castles were reduced to one – numbered 67 and later called Knight's Castle (6-064) and then New Knight's Castle numbered TP567. This was really colorful and began to hark back to the basic shape, at least in the main buildings, of twenty years before.

TP ACTIVITY TOYS: Knights' Castles
c1988 to c1998

NO.	DESCRIPTION	DATE	DIMENSIONS	DISTINCTIVE FEATURES
67 (6-064)	**Knights' Castle** (identified by an example in the ownership below) eg: Allen Hickling Toy Forts	c1988	18"x21¼"x9¾" 460x540x230mm	• flat pack construction • drawbridge & gatehouse • two square towers at front • one large building at rear
TP567	**New Knights' Castle** (listed in manufacturers catalogue c1994) eg: no known example	c1994	16"x16"x?" 410x410x?mm	• flat pack construction • drawbridge & gatehouse • two square towers at rear • one low building at rear
JT30	**Sir Lancelot's Castle** (listed in manufacturers catalogue c1997) eg: no known example	c1997	21½"x18"x13½" 555x460x345mm	• flat pack construction • drawbridge & gatehouse • buildings raised on plinth • one med-high building at rear
JT31	**Sir Arthur's Castle** (listed in manufacturers catalogue c1997) eg: no known example	c1997	19"x15¾"x8" 480x400x200mm	• flat pack construction • drawbridge & gatehouse • one small building at rear
JT32	**Medieval Castle** (listed in manufacturers catalogue 1990) eg: no known example	c1998	19"x15¾"x8" 400x400x200mm	• flat pack construction • drawbridge & gatehouse • one med-high building at rear

The old client base of small retail shops in the UK was disappearing fast, with the retail giants, like Toys-R-Us, the Early Learning Centre, and others buying cheaply from the Far East and putting them out of business.

TP could see the writing on the wall, recognizing that their market share could not support a larger organization. Consequently, in 1997, after ten years, they closed down the Joy Toys operation and ceased production of their toys, although continuing with their outdoor range.

Ted and Rob Hall were then asked by a venture capitalist to continue production under the new name of Joy Toys and Woodcrafts Ltd – which they did, still operating out of the workshop in Malvern.

Operations were slimmed down into smaller premises and production became much more automated, using very modern machinery and methods, with virtually no employees. All assembly and finishing was now done in-house.

The medieval castle became even more basic with appeal to the younger market. Three slightly different castles were produced in as many years. But the venture capitalist withdrew in 1999, at which time Ted, Rob, and Geraldine Henning formed Joy Toys (Malvern) Ltd. Ted was responsible for design, Rob handled production, and Geraldine looked after sales and administration.

The business continues to this day, but the world has changed and the company has changed with it. All of their toys are now produced in China and are made for a much younger market. Although they are still designed by Ted, the forts are reduced to one – the Castle of Legends. But this has been the story all along. It is a company that changes itself in response to market trends – and very well at that.

6-064 TP Activity Toys 67: *Knights Castle*
This was the first of a number of versions coming out in the late 1980s or the 1990s. Apart from the towers at the front, this is almost the same as the Medieval Forts that they produced twenty-five years or so previously. Of course, the colors are more jolly, the courtyard is more interesting, and the windows more realistic, but its ancestry is clear.

The Crescent Toy Co. and Their Fortresses

The Crescent Toy Co. had been in existence since about 1920, but did not produce forts until about 1950. They had been involved in the production of hollowcast figures and had played the role of cleaning up where others had not made the grade. Consequently, their history is not all that clear.

Crescent's forts were not like that. They came after the Second World War, when the company tried to put some sort of order to their activities. They were an original design. Made of metal, they were very small (6-065 & 6-066), and came in boxes, in some cases together with 48mm figures, which were seriously incompatible (6-067). The boxes were covered in different cuttings of the same label.

CRESCENT: Fortresses
c1950 to c1960

NO.	DESCRIPTION	DATE	DIMENSIONS	DISTINCTIVE FEATURES
unknown (6-065)	**Crescent Fortress (small)** (identified by an example in the ownership below) eg: SOFIA Foundation, CY	c1950	box 12¼"x3½"x1¾" 310x90x45mm	• gatehouse with drawbridge • six small square towers • seven sections of curtain wall
unknown (6-066)	**Crescent Fortress (large)** (identified by an example in the ownership below) eg: SOFIA Foundation, CY	c1950	box 18½"x3½"x1¾" 470x90x45mm	• gatehouse with drawbridge • 4 circular & 4 small sq towers • nine sections of curtain wall
unknown (6-067)	**Crescent Fortress (figures1)** (identified by an example in the ownership below) eg: Allen Hickling Toy Forts	c1950	box 12¼"x7"x1¾" 310x180x45mm	• gatehouse with drawbridge • six small square towers • seven sections of curtain wall • six knight figures
unknown	**Crescent Fortress (figures2)–** (identified by an example in the ownership below) eg: Allen Hickling Toy Forts	c1950	box 18½"x7"x1¾" 470x180x45mm	• gatehouse with drawbridge • 4 circular & 4 small sq towers • nine sections of curtain wall • seven knight figures (1 mounted)

They kept it very simple. They made a small square tower, a circular tower somewhat larger, a flat piece of wall, and a gateway. The flat piece of wall had hooks that fit into slots, which looked remarkably like windows, in either of the tower types. The gatehouse was made up of a gateway with a drawbridge fixed between two of the circular towers. And that was it. There were no buildings to provide accommodation, and no hill for them to stand on – they stood on the floor any which way.

In fact, they made only two forts – one small, the other large (6-068 & 6-069), although these terms are relative to the size of the components. They were actually both quite small, probably suitable for 25mm figures. They could be assembled in various ways to make a fortress, and this could be quite spectacular, especially if one had more than one set. They made fine companion pieces to the UBILDA range being produced by Chad Valley (6-070).

6-065

6-066

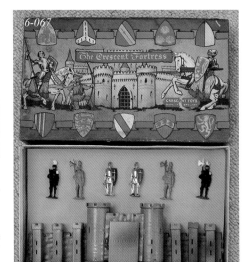

6-065 **Crescent Fortress (small)**: *box*
6-066 **Crescent Fortress (large)**: *box*
6-067 **Crescent Fortress (small)**: *with figures*

Crescent had two basic sets – large and small. They were both made up of the same parts, which was good for mass production – the large one had self-standing circular towers.

Theoretically they could be assembled in any way the person doing the erecting wanted, but this was only really true if one had multiple sets.

In the sets with figures, there were six standing knights, with an extra horseman in the larger one.

In the examples shown, one can see how the various boxes all had labels cut from the same original. The two basic sets sometimes had the shields wrapped around the box, but at other times it was a true label and the sides were left a plain red.

6-070

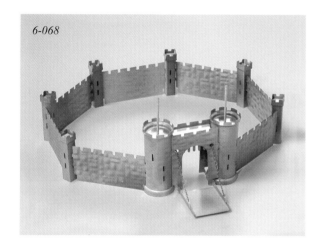

6-068

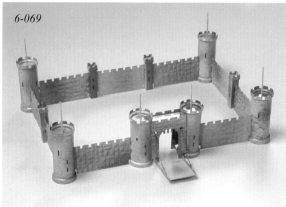

6-069

6-068 **Crescent Fortress (small)**
6-069 **Crescent Fortress (large)**
6-070 **Set up combining UBILDA and Crescent**

The two Crescent Fortresses (6-068 & 6-069) are made up of the same parts. The only difference was that the large one had four circular towers. Both are remarkably small and could serve as little more than background.

The set up (6-070) shows the similarity of the UBILDA and Crescent forts in terms of scale. It also demonstrates how effective the two go together when you have several sets – in this fort, there are three sets of both UBILDA and Crescent (it would have been better with four of Crescent). The roofs of the two UBILDA forts are made of cardboard – they would have been open in normal circumstances. The figures are 30mm German-made flats and semi-flats from different regiments, together with a few of John Hill and Co.

The Tudor Toy Co. and GeeBee

The Tudor Toy Co. was located in Hull, England, and produced a variety of toys. We, however, are concerned with their forts, which they began producing about 1950. We know this from various advertisements and catalogues of a distributor – Pointer's (Dolls) Ltd. Mr Pointer was the Managing Director of this and the Tudor Toy Co.

They seem to have called nearly all of their products by the same name, the GeeBee "Tudor" Fairy Castle Fort, which was a sort of group name, but not helpful for identification. The Castle Fantasia was the only exception.

It is difficult to say how they started. From the evidence of the forts in my possession, it appears that they started with a rather tall castle that had no known number (6-071). It broke down into three parts, which, when the top two were turned upside down, nested in the base for storage. This base, the cubic part at the bottom, was made of fiberboard, which was used as insulating material in the building trade at the time. This was based on some light wood framing to hold it all together. The upper parts were mostly made of hardboard.

After about five years, they produced a second version, which was much lower and compact, but still in three-part, fold-away sections. This they called Castle Fantasia and they gave it a GeeBee number – F/4 (6-073). It was in production for about fifteen years.

GEE-BEE Fortresses: F/4 Series
c1950 to c1980

NO.	DESCRIPTION	DATE	DIMENSIONS	DISTINCTIVE FEATURES
unknown (6-071)	**"Tudor" Fairy Castle Fort** (identified by an example in the ownership below) eg: Allen Hickling Toy Forts	c1950	15¼"x15¼"x27" 390x390x690mm	• large base with ramp to gatehouse • 3-storey main bldg with tower • 8 various turrets & pinnacles • strong representation of vegetation
F/4 (6-073)	**Castle Fantasia** (identified by an example in the ownership below) eg: SOFIA Foundation, CY	c1955	21"x17"x20" 530x430x510mm	• ramp to gatehouse w/dbridge • 2-storey main building with tower • stair from courtyard to first floor • 2-D background
F/4 (6-082)	**Medieval Fort** (identified by an example in the ownership below) eg: SOFIA Foundation, CY	c1970	18½"x7"x1¾" 470x180x45mm	• true flat pack construction • square plan, no ramp & gatehouse • four square corner towers • walkway all round at 2-floor level

Of course, making it more compact was not the only improvement. The main one was that construction now avoided the use of fiberboard and everything was made of hardboard. Other changes were a wider ramp, the installation of a staircase, the provision of a corner tower, the addition of a built-in sentry box by the dungeon, and some two-dimensional scenic effects behind it all.

6-071 Gee-Bee "Tudor" Fairy Castle Fort *(Courtesy Ed Poole)*
This is the first of the Tudor Toy Company's toy forts. The base, which is the square part at the bottom, was made of fiberboard, which was used as insulating material in the building trade at the time, based on some light wood framing. The upper parts were mostly made of hardboard, which divides horizontally into two and, when inverted, fits neatly into the base.
This model was sold under contract to the Conway Toy Company, who produced a version with a turntable in the courtyard on which marched 54mm figures into and out of the building (6-072). The figures are Britains 54mm guardsmen and a lone charging Scot.

They also supplied these under a contract with the Conway Toy Co., who made a slightly different top section (6-072) incorporating a clockwork-driven turntable section on which soldiers marched in and out of the main building through two arched doorways. It is not known if the Tudor Toy Co. installed the clockwork mechanism or not.

CONWAY VALLEY Series
c1950 to c1955

NO.	DESCRIPTION	DATE	DIMENSIONS	DISTINCTIVE FEATURES
unknown (6-072)	**Conway Valley Series** (identified by an example in the ownership below) eg: Allen Hickling Toy Forts	c1955	15¼"x15¼"x27" 390x390x690mm	• large base with ramp to gatehouse • 3-storey main bldg with tower • eight various turrets & pinnacles • clockwork turntable in courtyard

At the same time as the Castle Fantasia came on stream, they produced a smaller companion fort which they called the GeeBee Fairy Castle Fort small size, with the GeeBee number F/2. This appeared in a number of versions over the ensuing years.

GEE-BEE Fortresses: F/2 Series
c1955 to c1980

NO.	DESCRIPTION	DATE	DIMENSIONS	DISTINCTIVE FEATURES
F/2 (6-074)	**Small Size (first version)** (identified by an example in the ownership below) eg: Allen Hickling Toy Forts	c1955	14½"x12¼"x14¼" 370x310x365mm	• wide ramp to gateway • 1-piece main building • red tops to turrets & pinnacles • strong depiction of vegetation
F/2 (6-075)	**Small Size (early version)** (identified by an example in the ownership below) eg: Allen Hickling Toy Forts	c1965	15"x14¼"x12¼" 385x365x310mm	• no ramp to gateway • 1-piece main bldng w/staircase • red tops to turrets & pinnacles • strong depiction of vegetation
F/2 (6-076)	**Small Size (late version)** (identified by an example in the ownership below) eg: Allen Hickling Toy Forts	c1970	15"x14½"x11¾" 385x370x290mm	• no ramp to gateway • 1-piece main bldng w/staircase • red tops to turrets & pinnacles • strong depiction of vegetation
F/2 (6-077)	**Small Size (last version)** (identified by an example in the ownership below) eg: SOFIA Foundation, CY	c1975	14½"x14½"x11¾" 375x375x290mm	• no ramp to new model gateway • 1-piece main bldg (no stair) • red tops to turrets & pinnacles • strong depiction of vegetation

It all started with one quite like the Castle Fantasia (6-074). Of course, it was much smaller, but it had a ramp up and many features in common with the larger castle. As the castle re-invented itself through the versions (6-075 & 6-077), it lost its ramp and eventually its battered side walls. It did gain a staircase

only to lose it again. The most interesting innovation introduced on the second version, which it retained to the end, was the simple lever-operated gate.

There was another series they produced that bore the number F/1. It seems likely that this, which was called the GeeBee Fairy Castle Fort medium size, was brought out at a similar time as the small size.

The trouble is that the one I have in my collection (6-080) is very early, and maybe not one at all. It has many of the characteristics of the series and the same sort of main building, but it is very poorly made by comparison and the materials used are unusual. It could be a "one-off" copy made by someone else.

GEE-BEE Fortresses: F/1 Series
c1950 to c1980

NO.	DESCRIPTION	DATE	DIMENSIONS	DISTINCTIVE FEATURES
F/1 6-080)	**Medium Size (early version)** (identified by an example in the ownership below) eg: Allen Hickling Toy Forts	c1950	15"x10¼"x12¼" 380x260x320mm	• ramp to gateway • 2-piece main building • red tops to turrets & pinnacles • strong representation of vegetation
F/1 (6-081)	**Medium Size (late version)** (identified by an example in the ownership below) eg: SOFIA Foundation, CY	c1970	unknown	• small wide ramp to gatehouse • staircase to first level • dismountable main bldg & gate • strong representation of vegetation

The last model they produced was a truly flat-pack version of the Castle Fantasia, even taking on its number F/4, and called Medieval Fort (6-082). This was a major innovation in that all their previous productions had made use of large pre-assembled sections.

This Medieval Fort was really quite impressive given the limitations on size and complexity. It had four towers, one at each corner, and a walkway all around at first floor level. The number of different parts was minimal. It was surprisingly rigid, given the flat-pack construction.

6-072 Conway Valley Series
This is an example of the way the Conway Toy Co. took the GeeBee model (6-071) and adapted it to include a clockwork turntable on which the soldiers could march around.

Apart from the remodeling of the main building to accommodate the two arched doorways for the soldiers to march through and the increased depth of the courtyard to take the mechanism, there was no alteration to the original.

The Conway Valley Series label can be seen just in front of the dungeon door.

6-073

6-074

6-075

6-076

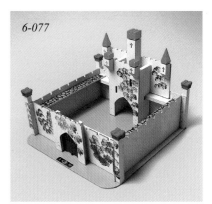

6-077

6-073 GeeBee Castle Fantasia F/4

   The F/4 Castle Fantasia (6-073) is a more compact version of the "Tudor" Fairy Castle (6-071). It has a back building in two halves, which, with the scenery, store comfortably in the base. The main improvement was that construction now avoided the use of fiberboard, and everything was made of hardboard. Other changes were a wider ramp, the installation of a staircase, the provision of a corner tower, the addition of a sentry box by the dungeon, and some two-dimensional scenic effects behind it all.

6-074 **GeeBee Fairy Castle F/2**: *small size c1955*
6-075 **GeeBee Fairy Castle F/2**: *small size c1965*

6-076 **GeeBee Fairy Castle F/2**: *small size c1970*
6-077 **GeeBee Fairy Castle F/2**: *small size c1975*

   These four F/2 castles represent about twenty-five years of production and the changes that took place over that time. This was clearly a best seller. The Tudor Toy Company actually produced at least four different versions, the last being the one at the bottom right. They were all made of hardboard. In true GeeBee style, the whole of the central back section comes off and fits into the space underneath or, in later versions, into the courtyard.

6-078 **Conway Toy Co. Label**
Used to identify Conway Valley Series items.

6-079 **Tudor Toy Co. Label**
Used to identify GeeBee items.

6-080

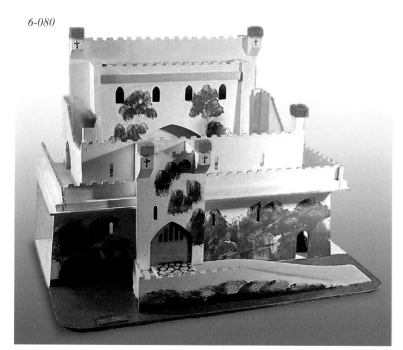

6-082

6-081

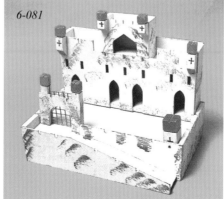

6-080 **GeeBee Fairy Castle F/1**: *late medium size*
6-081 **GeeBee Fairy Castle F/1**: *early medium size*
6-082 **GeeBee Medieval Fort F/4**

The two GeeBee F/1 Fairy Castle Forts, medium size, are the only two examples available to me. The very early one (6-081) may not be a GeeBee, although it has many of the characteristics of one. It is poorly made, partly

with materials GeeBee did not use. The saw cuts in the red tops of the towers are also unlike their later efforts.

It does have, however, the typically GeeBee white walls, with crudely represented vegetation. It also has the main building that disassembles in two parts, towers and pinnacles with red painted tops, and painted arrow slits in the form of a cross. The later version (6-080), and a very attractive gatehouse c1970, is much more typically GeeBee. It has a staircase to get up to the first level.

The last model to come out was the GeeBee F/4 Medieval Fort (6-082). This was truly a flat-pack version. It was a complete change in philosophy for the designers. Up to this time, their unique selling point had been that the forts were completely constructed – the loose parts were few and large, with no fiddly bits which could get lost. All that remained of the old order were two crudely painted trees on the front

O. & M. Kleeman and the Crusaders Castle

In the early 1950s, O. & M. Kleeman Ltd, a company based in Aycliffe, County Durham, in the north of England, was manufacturing plastic kitchen utensils, providing competition for the traditional wood and metal implements. It was then that they decided to use the technology to do the same for traditional wood and metal toys. The idea seems simple enough now, but it had not been done before. Indeed the technology had existed for only a very short time.

Harry Kleeman, son of one founder and nephew of the other, recalls that, in the mid-1950s, he asked their design team to develop a plastic toy fort. This was clearly a visionary idea, but did he have any idea that it would be taken up, manufactured, and sold by numerous companies in many countries worldwide? And what do you think the designer, Gordon Manning, would have thought if he had known that his design, and its derivatives, would be a source of wonder and joy for millions of children for more than fifty years?

At the outset, the toy fort, along with other toys, was manufactured using their brand name *Kleeware*. It was distributed initially by E. Weston & Sons Ltd of Sheffield, but many others, including Manufacturers Accessories Co. Ltd of Weybridge, followed suit.

There were two versions: one was molded in a gray/khaki plastic and named "Crusaders Castle" (6-083); the other, molded in white, was named "The Little Princess Castle." The selected architectural style was medieval – mostly English, although one or two decorative details might have been French or Italian. There were four towers on the curtain wall, a formidable barbican protecting the entrance, and a keep surmounted by a circular tower.

The main body of the castle was made of "tough high impact polystyrene." The flag was printed on paper. The tray of the cardboard box was used as the "hill"/base on which the whole thing stood – suitably printed with a rock-face or paved courtyard pattern in green (or dark blue). The ramp to get up to it was made of the same cardboard.

KLEEWARE: Fortresses
c1955 to c2005

NO.	DESCRIPTION	DATE	DIMENSIONS	DISTINCTIVE FEATURES
2350 (6-083)	**Crusader's Castle** (identified by an example in the ownership below) eg: Allen Hickling Toy Forts	c1955	17"x23"x15½" 430x585x395mm	• ramp to gatehouse & drawbridge • 3-D keep w/tower on housing • 4 ½-circular towers on curtain wall • mottled khaki color
unknown	**Little Princess Castle** (listed in manufacturers catalogue 1955) eg: no known example	c1955	17"x23"x15½" 430x585x395mm	• ramp to gatehouse & drawbridge • 3-D keep w/tower housing • 4 ½-circular towers on curtain wall • white color

It was presented in a box, 23" x 17" x 4", with an impression of the castle on the top. The sides showed all the parts, and advertised "HOURS OF FUN put it together – take it apart," which was easier said than done.

6-083 Kleeware: Crusaders Castle
This was the first all-plastic fort. It served as a model for many others all around the world, and influenced, amongst others, Ideal, Tudor Rose, Georg Brohm, Debrez Freres, unknown Italian and Belgian makers, Timpo, Accurate, CTS, and Imex. It was still being produced about 2005.

The balance between realism and playability was very finely struck. The level of detail was amazing for the time, a time when wood was the basic material used by other manufacturers. The design of the corner connections, using the open-backed towers to hold it all together, was a masterstroke – even if it provided a source of possible breakages.

It is a fine example of a trend-setting model.

Kleeware Derivatives

The Kleeware castles were an immediate success, and it was not long before other manufacturers were expressing an interest in them – not only in the UK. So, in order to expand their market, O. & M. Kleeman licensed the design to the Ideal Toy Co. for manufacture in the United States.

Exactly how and when the next developments came about is unclear. Precisely the same fort – with different colored plastics – has been manufactured by Georg Brohm in Vielbrunn, Germany, as well as unidentified manufacturers in Italy and Belgium. Debrez Frères of Comines (Nord), in France, used most of the parts, with a cunningly reconstructed entrance piece suspiciously like the Timpo one, to manufacture a simplified version. Most of the moldings are almost exactly as the original, so that one has to really hunt for the variations. For example, the packaging of the Georg Brohm version consists of a box almost identical to Kleeware's, but sporting artwork that is a reversed image of the original. Harry Kleeman thinks that it is possible that some sort of deal was done with these firms, but it is quite likely that most copies were pirated.

In the UK, it seems that Rosedale Manufacturing, operating with the trade name Tudor Rose, had been closely involved, and some of their figures of toy knights turn up in the box from time to time. In any case, in 1959, when Harry Kleeman finally wanted to give up manufacturing the fort, he sold the design and the molds to Rosedale and it became a Tudor Rose product. It is interesting to wonder how they dealt with the fact that their toys had always been made of soft polythene, whereas their newly purchased toy fort was designed to be made of rigid polystyrene.

The old Rosedale-owned molds turned up at a molding works in the early 1990s, and the castle was remolded and marketed by Accurate Figures Ltd of Surrey in the south of England. Peter Reading of Accurate seemed to have the same idea that Toyway had had with Timpo (see below), even having the boxes made. However this version ended up being sold in the USA by Classic Toy Soldiers (CTS), logically as the "Ideal castle remold." Accurate is now wholly owned by yet another American company, Imex, and the fort is no doubt part of their range. It is probable that some of these were marketed, in handsomely embellished form, by Galena Toy Soldier and Hobby (GTSH) from Illinois.

6-084 Georg Brohm's "Ritter-Burg"
Whether this fort (6-084) was made under license or not is an open question, but it is difficult to imagine how the parts could be manufactured so identically without one. It is, in fact, identical to the Kleeware example (6-083) with the exception of the color of the plastic and the graphics on the box and ramp. The color scheme is very fine with the red trim, but the box graphics leave much to be desired.
The figures are 40mm Landsknechts made by Elastolin.

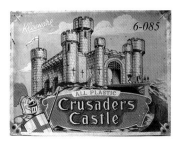

6-085 The original Kleeware box
6-086 Georg Brohm's mirror image copy
This is an example of how any laws about copyright were overcome. If you change something just enough they cannot touch you. The artwork of the Georg Brohm box is based on a mirror image of the Kleeware box, with one or two graphic tweaks.

c.1965-c.1995

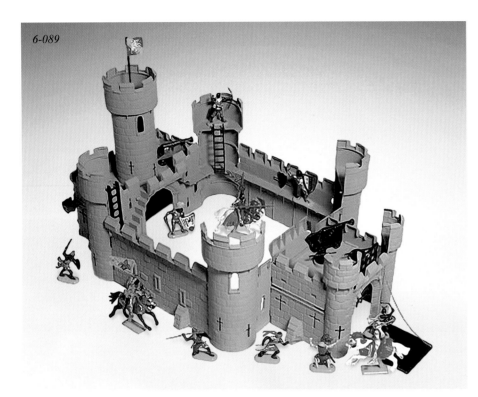

6-089

6-087

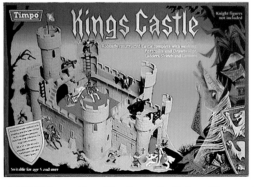

6-088

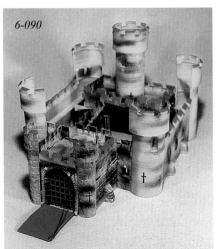

6-090

6-091

6-087 **Château-Fort Plasticque by Debrez Freres:** *the box*
6-088 **The Kings Castle by Timpo:** *the box*
6-089 **The Kings Castle by Timpo**
6-090 **The Italian or Belgian version**
6-091 **The Debrez Freres" fort**

   The Debrez Freres variation (6-087 & 6-091) is much smaller than the Kleeware original (6-083); it has an entrance quite like the one used by Timpo. The building at the base of the central tower was made of printed cardboard, but this is a reproduction.

   The castle above (6-090) is by an unknown Italian or Belgian manufacturer. The colors are more suitable for a fairy castle than anything else.

   Finally, the example attributed to Timpo (6-088 & 6-089) is a recent castle. Timpo picked up the original Kleeware molds, or copies of them, and named it Kings Castle. It is identical (except for color) in every respect.

Toy Importers (Timpo) and Its Many Guises

Toy Importers, otherwise known as Timpo, were doing business in a big way after World War II. As far as their military output was concerned, they concentrated first on figures in metal, borrowing from various sources. When plastics came along, they really branched out into all sorts of original figures including many and varied play sets. These included a variety of forts.

About 1960, Timpo got hold of the Kleeware's design idea and developed a similar castle. They produced it as an item by itself, using different colored plastic in "Medieval," "Desert," and "Wild West" versions, and in other guises in various play sets. Using ingenious design, they managed to make them all look different with minimal change to the parts.

It was not exactly the same as the Kleeware original, although the overall concept was and the very clever way of joining the towers to the walls most certainly was. There are also details which are so suspiciously similar that "outright plagiarism" is a phrase that comes to mind! – though that was hardly novel in the toy industry, then as now.

When Timpo failed as a company, a chain of derivatives started up. The molds were bought from Wisbeach (Timpo's molders) by Toyway of Letchworth, who went on to market the fort in exactly the form that Timpo had, making a feature of it by claiming "original Timpo" on their boxes. They were able to do this because, when they took over from Timpo, they inherited a vast stock of already molded parts, which they used in their boxes and, with great foresight, they cheekily registered the name *Timpo* as their own trademark.

6-092

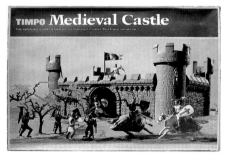
6-093

6-094

6-092 **The original Timpo fort**
6-093 **The original Timpo fort:** the box
6-094 **The box of the Toyway version when Timpo failed**
   The original Timpo version, which was in production from about 1960 until Timpo went under, was a classic of sorts. It formed a natural part of their play sets, in which their figures and scenery played a major role.
The Toyway version was identical, using some genuine Timpo parts.

Some Other British-made Forts (1930–1955)

6-095 **Ford's of Bristol** *(c1955)*
6-096 **Playtime** *(c1930)*
6-097 **J R S "Tower of London"** *(c1935)*
6-098 **Rochester Castle No.3** *(c1938)*
6-099 **Welcom Fort** *(c1950)*
6-100 **Amersham Toys** *(c1950)*

Three of these are made of cardboard, in a precut, assemble-it-yourself format. Two of them (6-095 & 6-099) use a thick, strong card, which makes a stable fort, capable of taking lead toy soldiers. A third (6-096) is more ephemeral in nature, using less robust material, and is more for girls than boys.

The other three are of more traditional construction, which is basically wood. The first, by J R S of London (6-097), is a large fort with a base that would allow extensive parades to take place. The less said about its relationship with the real Tower of London the better.

The other two are more conventional in form as well as materials. The Rochester Fort No.3 (6-098) is the more realistic, but the one by Amersham Toys (6-100) is perhaps the more appealing in the market place.

6-095

6-096

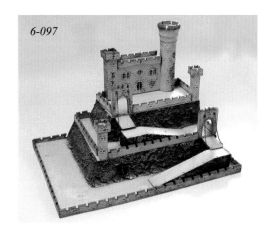

6-097

6-098

6-099

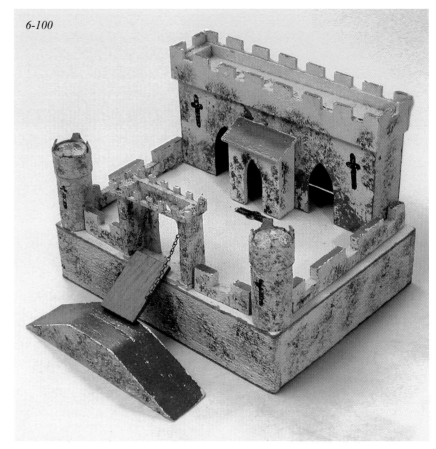

6-100

6-101

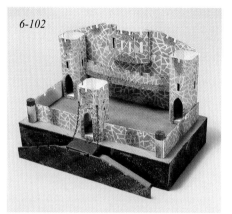

6-102

6-103

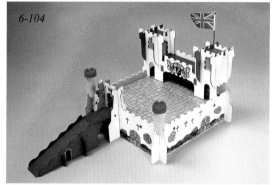

6-104

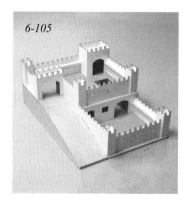

6-105

Some More British-made Forts (1955–1975)

6-101 **Belinda "Giant Castle"** *(c1960)*
6-102 **Basildonia No.2** *(c1955)*
6-103 **Cherilea Toy Castle Set** *(c1965)*
6-104 **Gaytoy "Packaway Fort"** *(c1970)*
6-105 **Debtoy's Desert Fort** *(c1975)*
6-106 **Tiger Toys No.T.575 "King William's Castle"** *version 2 (c1965)*

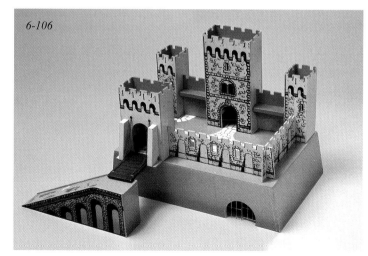

6-106

The Belinda "Giant Castle" (6-101) was a fine example of a toy fort. It has deep wells in the towers allowing soldiers to stand in them without exposing themselves, "walk-throughs" at battlement level, and effective walkways behind the battlements with enclosed spaces beneath them. It was copied by others and was still on sale, with minor changes, in the 1990s, distributed by Tridias. The figures are 30mm by mostly British manufacturers.

Three of the others are more conventional in form and construction. The Tiger Toys fort (6-106) is perhaps the most sophisticated, but they went out of business in the early 1970s. The bright and cheerful Basildonia No.2 (6-102) was the earlier, and Gaytoy's "Packaway Fort" (6-104) was the later, showing the trend towards the younger child.

Debtoy's Desert Fort (6-105) shows the potential of working with hardboard or medium-density fiberboard (MDF).

Cherilea's plastic toy castle play set (6-103), which had figures with it, was also a trendsetter. Not only were there different versions in Britain, but there was considerable activity, probably under license, in other countries (Tibado, Italy, for example).

SEVEN

THE REST OF EUROPE:
The Role of Countries Other than Germany and Great Britain

If you take Germany and Great Britain out of the equation, there were, in my experience, only three countries producing forts and castles in any quantity. They were France, Belgium, and Denmark and they are dealt with in that order here.

The French were, I think, the earliest of these to make toy forts and castles, notably the firm of CBG. Principally a toy figure manufacturer, about 1885, they produced boxes inside of which was a sort of diorama, the figures being set off against the background of a fort.

Much later, in the period leading up to the Second World War, under the trade name Jouets Lilliput, they again produced toy forts. These were made of *Blanc de Meudon,* which was plaster, ground up pumice stone, and water, poured into molds and allowed to dry; the resulting buildings were suitable for quite small figures.

About 1885, another form of fort was produced. This was much larger and was made of wood. It again took the form of a box, with the fort (or part of one) built inside. It had a hinged front that came down to form the foreground. These came to prominence about 1895 through sales in the *Grands Magasins* of Paris and the other big cities. The leading manufacturer was the firm of Villard and Weill (or Bon Dufour?), although there were others. They were made after the First World War, but they disappeared about 1940.

After the Second World War there were two main manufacturers in France, La Hotte aux Jouets and Starlux, but, of course, there were a number of others.

The first was quite small and we do not know the name, but they were the first to manufacture the typical French style of fort. This was a one-piece affair, basically all in white, which sat on a flat base, thus doing away with the need for a ramp.

The firm of La Hotte aux Jouets, founded in 1962, was the first large producer, and they dominated the market for about fifteen years – still making more or less the same sort of fort, although they tended to be larger.

At the same time there were two smaller manufacturers. One made interesting, well-designed forts, while the other produced what can only be seen as the forerunner of the next major manufacturer, Starlux.

Starlux was launched by Pierre Beffara in 1945, based on an earlier company that made primarily figures. They did not start making forts until the mid-1970s. The forts were an immediate success, and Starlux became the main source of toy forts in France until they ceased trading in 2003.

In Belgium, there were several manufacturers, of which two stood out. Nazaire Beeusaert, which could be called the market leader, was formed in 1921, and ceased as a manufacturer about 1975. They did not make forts until 1952, but then were quite active for twenty years.

We have no idea who the other one was. They were considerably prolific, and we have many examples of their production. We have no evidence apart from that, however, no labels, numbers, catalogues, etc.

In Denmark, the leading manufacturer was not a real manufacturer in the commercial sense. The forts were made in the prisons by the prisoners working separately in their cells. There was a quite limited range of designs from which they worked, but allowance was made for the individual skills and tastes of the makers.

They were marketed from about 1905 to 1971 and, needless to say, without any labor costs, there was little competition. Initially, it was a fairly informal organization, but it came together as a company under the name of Dansk Legetøjsfabrik when a businessman took control in 1916.

—FRANCE—

CBG Mignot Were the Early Manufacturers

CBG (or Cuperly, Blondel, and Gerbeau, to give them their proper names) were probably the first in France to manufacture toy forts, although, let it be said, these toy forts were not as complete as the German ones of the same era. The history of fort production in France is shrouded in uncertainty, so this account will, of necessity, be brief.

Initially, CBG carried on the tradition that they had inherited from Lucotte, which they had taken over in the first half of the 19th century, of making toy figures, mostly soldiers. Some time around 1880, they took to presenting the figures in boxed dioramas – dioramas that quite often included a fort, or at least part of a fort. Because they were built inside a box, they were partial sections of forts, rather than complete ones.

The forts varied in style according to the period represented by the soldiers' uniforms, so they ranged from medieval types right up to the sort typical of the First World War. Each required a different approach to construction, being mostly of mixed materials, but there was still much metal, owing to their expertise in making metal figures.

CBG MIGNOT: Metal Forts in Boxes
c1880 to c1930

NO.	DESCRIPTION	DATE	DIMENSIONS	DISTINCTIVE FEATURES
unknown	**a typical box in this series** (identified by an example in the ownership below) eg: Burtt Ehrlich, US (dec'd)	c1880	unknown	• medieval diorama: a siege • gateway and drawbridge • walled courtyard with circular towers
unknown	**Jeanne d'Arc** (identified by an example in the ownership below) eg: Burtt Ehrlich, US (dec'd)	c1885	unknown	• Jeanne d'Arc on two levels • lower level: battle outside the walls • upper level: victory parade inside
unknown (7-002)	**a typical box in this series** (identified by an example in the auction below) eg: Noel Barratt, US	c1900	unknown	• crossing the river to attack • no castle, more a fort • two-arch bridge & 3 pontoon bridges
unknown (7-001) (7-004)	**a typical box in this series** (identified by an example in the ownership below) eg: Rob Wilson, UK	c1910	28½"x20½"x23¾" 725x520x605mm	• 1900s fort w/gun emplacement on top • neo-medieval main gateway
unknown (7-003)	**a typical box in this series** (identified by an example in the auction below) eg: Lyon & Turnbull, UK	c1910	unknown	• 1900s fort with gun on top • neo-medieval main gateway

So this was the beginning. Sometime in the first quarter of the 20th century, Henri Mignot joined the firm, continuing the tradition of dioramas in boxes. It is not known when they discontinued them.

About 1930, CBG Mignot, as it has become to be known, launched a new type of fort under the trade name of Jouets Lilliput. These were made of *Blanc de Meudon*, which was a sort of porridge made of plaster, ground up pumice stone, and water, poured into molds and allowed to dry. The result was hard but quite brittle, not unlike china. This mixture molded well, in that it took very fine detail from the molds, but keeping its shape was quite a challenge.

The forts were of the modular type that could, theoretically, be assembled in different ways. There were two sets (there may have been more, but I have no evidence for it), but there was only one tower, serving as a keep, which stood in the middle of defenses formed of the battlement pieces.

There was an outer wall, which came in straight pieces, one with a gate and a drawbridge. There were two types of corner. One was the simple 90° type, and the other a sort of expanded version of the type usually associated with bastions, which did not fit so well with the wall.

It required some measure of imagination to get away from the standard layout, although there were several pieces which made for slight variations.

The forts were made to a small scale, suitable for 40mm figures, and came in two color schemes. One was painted a bright red and green, with beige crenellation, while the other was painted a mixture of the two colors, which made a more realistic khaki effect. It is difficult to tell what the first scheme was supposed to represent, or what it could be used for.

This form of toy fort was probably in production until the outbreak of the Second World War.

CBG MIGNOT: Forts of *Blanc de Meudon*
c1930 to c1940

NO.	DESCRIPTION	DATE	DIMENSIONS	DISTINCTIVE FEATURES
1 (7-010 to 7-013))	**the small set in this series** (identified by an example in the ownership below) eg: Peter D Clark, US	c1930	unknown	• set of pieces to make the following • one tower/keep & four pieces of wall • one gateway and drawbridge • walled courtyard with corner pieces
2 (7-008) (7-009)	**the large set in this series** (identified by an example in the ownership below) eg: SOFIA Foundation, CY	c1930	21¾"x21¾"x9¾" 545x545x259mm	• set of pieces to make the following • one simple tower/keep • one gateway and drawbridge • walled courtyard with corner pieces

7-001

c.1880-c.1930

7-002

7-003

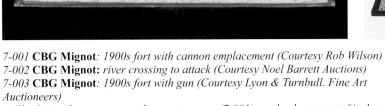

7-001 **CBG Mignot**: *1900s fort with cannon emplacement (Courtesy Rob Wilson)*
7-002 **CBG Mignot**: *river crossing to attack (Courtesy Noel Barrett Auctions)*
7-003 **CBG Mignot**: *1900s fort with gun (Courtesy Lyon & Turnbull. Fine Art Auctioneers)*

The fort with a cannon emplacement on top (7-001) can be drawn out of its box to some extent. This makes it into more of a conventional toy fort. The gateway is a bit of whimsy. I am not sure how it would have been used.

The river crossing (7-002) is probably the oldest of these but there is no certainty about it. It appears that the creator of this piece was having something of a brainstorm, or more likely was letting his desire to show off many figures take over. There are two fortified hills, one at each side of the two-arch bridge in the background. The attackers appear to have their work cut out. It makes for a splendid set up.

The fort with the gun (7-003) is somewhat easier to use, but nonetheless would have to remain in the box.

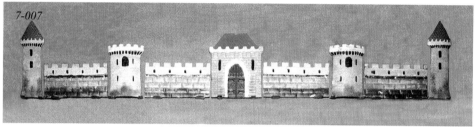

7-004 **CBG Mignot: Typical label** *(Courtesy Rob Wilson)*
7-005 **CBG Mignot: Jeanne d'Arc**
7-006 **CBG Mignot: Medieval diorama**
7-007 **CBG Mignot: The castle taken from Medieval diorama** *(Courtesy Marc Azzini)*

The label is typical of CBG Mignot and could have been on any of these forts.

The primary use of these forts was as boxes to house figures, but they also served to fire the imaginations of potential buyers. They contained parts of castles that could be used separately in play.

The medieval diorama (7-006) is the easier to understand, even though the figures are a bit bunched together for display purposes. The castle segment can be taken out and used, theoretically, to make various combinations of castle, as can be appreciated from the pieces below (7-007) – the striking limitation being the few pieces available.

7-008

7-010

7-011

7-012

7-008 CBG Mignot: Jouets Lilliput No.2: Mon Donjon
7-009 CBG Mignot: Jouets Lilliput No.2: *box label.*
7-010 to 7-013 CBG Mignot: Jouets Lilliput – *pieces of the red and green version (Courtesy Rob Wilson)*

Above (7-008) is a complete layout of the No.2 set in a sort of brown/camouflage version. This configuration of the parts is exactly the one on the box label (7-009), and it required a feat of imagination to come up with another.

The images to the right are of a red and green version (7-010 to 7-013). I do not know if they were sold in a set. Note the different type of gate and the wall section with a tower. These would have allowed some differentiation in layout.

7-009

7-013

Villard & Weill (or Bon Dufour?) Also Made Forts in Boxes

Sometime about 1885, a new concept in toy forts appeared in France: building a fort, or more often a part of a fort, in a box. The idea probably came from CBG's range of forts used to set off soldiers in a context, but this was different. The forts were made of wood and were much larger – mostly to scale with 54mm figures or larger. These forts were really meant to be played with.

Who was first into the field is difficult to judge, but Villard & Weill (or Bon Dufour?) was by far the most prolific. Others were E. F. Lefevre, and SFBJ – there may have been more but I do not know of them. The amazing thing is that they all used the same sort of box. This, of course, makes identification of the manufacturer extremely difficult, especially as I have hardly any access to catalogues.

They were particularly active during the twenty years prior to the First World War. Apart from a few specials, they concentrated on two styles – medieval times in Western Europe, and the colonial years in North Africa and the Far East. Exactly how long they continued after the First World War is not at all clear, but it is reasonably certain that they had fallen by the wayside by about 1935.

VILLARD & WEILL (or Bon Dufour?): European Medieval in Boxes
c1885 to c1940

NO.	DESCRIPTION	DATE	DIMENSIONS	DISTINCTIVE FEATURES
unknown (7-021)	a typical box of this type (identified by an example in the ownership below) eg: Musée du Jouet, Bxl, B	c1895	17¾"x6"x13½" 450x155x340mm	• front flap (missing?) no ramp • castle in 2 parts w/background of bridge • main gateway with two circular towers • 2nd part with one circular tower
unknown (7-023)	a typical box of this type (identified by an example in the ownership below) eg: Musée du Jouet, Bxl, B	c1895	27½"x6¾"x17¾" 700x170x450mm	• separate ramp to drawbridge (missing) • castle in 2 parts w/backgd of bldg & lake • gateway w/2 circ towers w/blue roofs • 2nd part w/2 circ towers w/blue roofs
unknown (7-014)	a typical box of this type (identified by an example in the ownership below) eg: Allen Hickling Toy Forts	c1895	28¼"x7¾"x18" 720x195x460mm	• separate ramp (missing) to drawbridge • castle in 2 parts w/backgd of bldg & lake • main gateway with two circular towers • 2nd part w/2 circular towers w/red roofs
unknown (7-022)	a typical box of this type (identified by an example in the ownership below) eg: Musée du Jouet, Bxl, B	c1895	31¾"x8"x21" 805x200x530mm	• separate ramp (missing) to drawbridge • castle in 2 parts backgd of bldg & lake • gateway w/2 large circular towers • 2nd part w/2 circular towers w/red roofs

unknown	a typical box of this type (identified by an example in the ownership below) eg: SOFIA Foundation,CY	c1925	47¼"x12"x23¾" 1200x305x600mm	• landscaped flap, no ramp, balanced db • castle in 2 parts w/background of lake • entrance tower w/2 doorways each side • 2-arch bridge to 2nd part
unknown (7-020)	a typical box of this type (identified by an example in the ownership below) eg: Collectoys Auctions, F	c1930	unknown	• simplified version with no ramp • buildings much simplified • background of modern city with plane

The most striking feature of these forts was the way the inside of the box was painted as a backdrop providing the setting. These were portrayed on canvas or paper stuck to the inside back of the box, and painted, with no little skill. They achieved a great sense of depth behind the castle itself, giving the whole a feeling of realism. The settings often included a view over a lake, and usually had some buildings in the middle distance.

7-014 Villard & Weill (or Bon Dufour?): *typical medieval fort*
This is a good example of the genre. It is missing its ramp and three of the roofs over the circular towers are gone – with one of them having a paper replacement. It does have its drawbridge, however, which is normally one of the first candidates for damage. The background, on canvas, is a very well painted scene of a lake with an extended wing of the castle.

THE BOXED FORTS OF VILLARD & WEILL (OR BON DUFOUR?) AND OTHERS

This was the chosen format for toy forts in France for about thirty years. It was a wooden box, of the approximate proportions (length:breadth:height) 4:1:3. This was left open on one long side, with the tops of the sides cut sloping slightly towards the open long side. This side had a hinged flap on it, which folded down when the fort was in use to form an extended apron, sometimes with landscaping on it. They had no top.

7-015 and 7-016
    These two images show the fort stowed as it would have been in storage. One can appreciate the advantages of the box-like form in this context. The only drawback is the lack of complete closure, which would have been a protection against dust and would have permitted storage on top.

This format had the advantage of easy storage when not in use, and speed of erection when brought out to play. Compare this to typical German or British approach. With all their different pieces tucked away inside, leaving an irregular lump, often with fragile pieces like drawbridges left hanging out, this still provided a magnificent dust trap. Although, if this was really a concern, one wonders why they did not put a top on it.

Inside the box there was a painted background of the setting of the fort, usually on canvas stuck to the back inside of the box, but sometimes on paper. They were painted by quite talented artists. The settings varied from town to rural scenes often with a lake. These also varied according to the style of fort. Although

7-017
    The paint shop at Villard, Weill & Cie in Lunéville about 1910.

they seemed to concentrate on medieval forts of western Europe, they also produced many with a North African or Oriental theme.

The one major problem with this design was the vulnerability of the hinge-down front piece on the bigger forts. This was clearly a difficulty, witnessed by the number today without their apron. It is quite understandable when you consider the size of the flap, and the difficulty of finding adequate fixing for hinges. There are some forts which may have been designed without a flap – usually the smaller ones.

One limiting factor in play was the fact that the design of the toy fort meant it had to be placed against a wall or some such. This meant that it was virtually impossible to extend the context all around, thus constraining the creative abilities of the child. The action was focused on the fort itself, rather than the battle around it.

7-018 **Villard & Weill (or Bon Dufour?) c1925**.
    This is the fort in play with the flap down. The figures are Britains 54mm Deetail knights.

c.1895-c.1930

7-019

FORT en bois, intérieur en cartonnage artistique,
garni de canons et de soldats en bois comprimé.

Longueurs...	0·40	0·50	0·60	0·70
Prix........	5.90	7.90	12.50	16.50

7-020

7-021

7-022

7-023

7-019 **Villard & Weill (or Bon Dufour?)**: *catalogue illustration (Grand Magasin)*
7-020 **Villard & Weill (or Bon Dufour?)**: *a later version c1930*
7-021 **Villard & Weill (or Bon Dufour?)**: *typical medieval fort with no flap*
7-022 **Villard & Weill (or Bon Dufour?)**: *typical medieval fort missing flap*
7-023 **Villard & Weill (or Bon Dufour?)**: *typical medieval fort*

The catalogue illustration (7-019), which is taken from a catalogue dated 1906, provides evidence for the sales strategy being used, as well as the range of available sizes and their costs. It also tells us of the materials being used, and the fact that there were soldiers and cannon making up the set.

The later version (7-020) never had a ramp or a drawbridge. The background is definitely modern, while the buildings are clearly medieval (neo-medieval?). The figures are typical papier mâché, pâte or bois comprimé, representing French troops.

There is doubt whether the small one (7-021), with the bridge on the backdrop, ever had a flap. It certainly had no ramp or drawbridge (there is no access point through the castellation).

The two medium-sized castles (7-022 and 7-023) have similarly painted backgrounds of a lake and buildings that may, or may not, be parts of the castle. The one with blue roofs has lost its drawbridge, while the one with red roofs has lost its drawbridge and its front flap. They still retain their distinctly medieval character.

The structures, which formed the foreground, were made of wood framed up in box form that provided the bulk of the buildings, which were to be parts of the fort. Details, such as round towers, conical roofs, windows and so on, were of *papier mâché*, *pâte* or *bois comprimé* (I am not sure if there is a difference in fact), heavily impressed to represent stone. They were then attached to the basic wooden boxes.

The doorways, which always seemed somewhat large, were cut out of the areas of flat wall between the towers. Paint was then applied to provide color and to accentuate the detail.

They were sold through the *grands magasins* (department stores) of Paris and other major cities. It is from the sales catalogues of these establishments that it is possible to determine that Villard & Weill (or Bon Dufour?) produced a range of sizes for each model. For example, in a sales catalogue of the *Au Bon Marché* in Paris, the one model they had came in six sizes, varying from 42cm to 82cm across the front.

They also made soldiers out of *papier mâché*, *pâte* or *bois comprimé*. These were necessarily of naïve quality, because of the instability of the material, but they made a good show *en masse*. They sold them in combination with the forts.

7-024 Villard & Weill (or Bon Dufour?): *typical oriental fort (Courtesy Musée du Jouet, Brussels)*
This fort has lost its front flap and its ramp, but it still has its drawbridge and most of its Oriental character. The Eastern nature of the buildings shows up particularly in the buildings behind on the right, and in the towers flanking the doorway on the left. The buildings on the backdrop, especially the towers on either side of the gate, display a Moorish touch.

VILLARD & WEILL (or Bon Dufour?): Oriental Forts in Boxes
c1895 to c1930

NO.	DESCRIPTION	DATE	DIMENSIONS	DISTINCTIVE FEATURES
unknown (7-029)	**a typical box of this type** (identified by an example in the ownership below) eg: Galerie André auction, B	c1895	unknown	• no front flap, no ramp, no drawbridge • 2 parts w/painted backgd of bldg & lake • main gateway w/one circ domed tower • second part with one circ domed tower
unknown (7-028)	**a typical box of this type** (identified by an example in the ownership below) eg: Musée du Jouet, Bxl, B	c1895	unknown	• front flap, ramp & dbridge (all missing) • 2 parts w/printed backgd of eastern city • main gateway w/one circ domed tower • second part w/one circ domed tower
unknown (7-027)	**a typical box of this type** (identified by an example in the ownership below) eg: Toy Museum, Baden, CH	c1895	unknown	• separate ramp to drawbridge • 2 parts w/paintd backgd of lake w/island • main gateway w/one rect domed tower • second part with tall square tower
unknown (7-024)	**a typical box of this type** (identified by an example in the ownership below) eg: Musée du Jouet, Bxl, B	c1895	unknown	• missing front flap & ramp to drawbridge • 2 parts w/print backgd of eastern town • main gateway w/two circ domed towers • second part with two hexagonal towers
unknown (7-030)	**a typical box of this type** (identified by an example in the ownership below) eg: Allen Hickling Toy Forts	c1925	12¾"x4½"x9" 325x115x230mm	• simplified version with no ramp • buildings much simplified (one missing) • background of eastern village

Little is known about E. F. Lefevre, one of the several producers of forts in boxes, who conducted his business in Paris. Most noticeable is the attention he paid to the buildings in the early days, and how little attention he paid to the background.

E. F. LEFEVRE: European Medieval Forts in Boxes
c1895 to c1915

NO.	DESCRIPTION	DATE	DIMENSIONS	DISTINCTIVE FEATURES
9 (7-034)	**a typical box of this type** (illustrated in E. F. Lefevre catalogue c1900) eg: no known example	c1900	unknown	• no ramp or drawbridge necessary • gateway w/two turrets & curtain wall • substantial buildings behind wall
10 (7-033)	**a typical box of this type** (illustrated in E. F. Lefevre catalogue c1900) eg: no known example	c1900	unknown	• no ramp or drawbridge necessary • large defensible gateway & curtain wall • substantial buildings behind wal
11 (7-032)	**a typical box of this type** (illustrated in E. F. Lefevre catalogue c1900) eg: no known example	c1900	unknown	• no ramp or drawbridge necessary • massive gate w/2 turrets & curtain wall • substantial buildings behind wall
unknown (7-035)	**a typical box of this type** (identified by an example in the ownership below) eg: Musée du Jouet, Bxl, B	c1910	unknown	• front flap& ramp (both missing) • db (broken) & entrance w/2 circ towers • crenellation on two levels • retaining wall at lower level

c.1895-c.1930

7-025

Nº 19120. **FORT ORIENTAL** bois et
cartonnage décoré, garni soldats pâte et canons.
0ᵐ42 **5.90** 0ᵐ47 **6.90** 0ᵐ54 **9.50** 0ᵐ62 **13.50**
0ᵐ72 **17.75** 0ᵐ82 **23.—**

7-026

7 — 226 **FORT** en bois et cartonnage
décoré, soldats bois comprimé, canons
métal.   Longueurs :
0ᵐ62   0ᵐ52   0ᵐ42   0ᵐ38   0ᵐ30

| 16.90 | 11.90 | 7.50 | 4.90 | 2.45 |

7-027

7-028

7-029

7-030

7-025 Villard & Weill (or Bon Dufour?): *catalogue
illustration (Grands Magasins)*
7-026 Villard & Weill (or Bon Dufour?): *catalogue
illustration (Grands Magasins 1913)*
7-027 Villard & Weill (or Bon Dufour?): *typical oriental fort*
7-028 Villard & Weill (or Bon Dufour?): *typical oriental
fort (Courtesy Musée du Jouet, Brussels)*
7-029 Villard & Weill (or Bon Dufour?): *typical oriental
fort without front flap*
7-030 Villard & Weill (or Bon Dufour?): *a later version c1925*

The catalogue illustrations (7-025 and 7-026) provide
information on the construction, sizes, costs, and composition
of sets, as well as an indication of the sales strategy in use.

Of the three typical forts, the one to the bottom left
(7-027) is complete, even to its complement of figures which represent both sides of the battle.
These are of papier mâché, pâte, or bois comprimé, representing English (French?) and Arab
troops. It is a fine example of the genre.

Both of the other two older forts (7-028 and 7-029) have lost their front flap, and it is very
doubtful if they ever had a ramp and drawbridge. One (7-029) does, however, have soldiers of
papier mâché, pâte or bois comprimé, representing French troops to man it.

The last (7-030) is a later version. Produced about 1925, it is simplified to an extreme,
probably in an effort to keep the company going. They stopped about 1930.

7-031

7-032

7-035

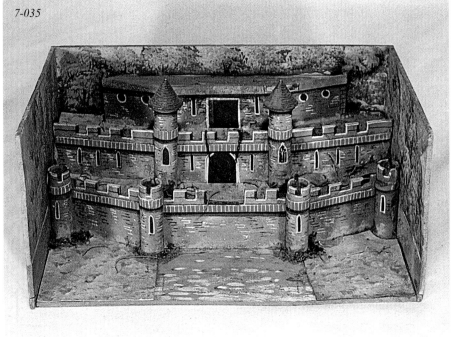

7-033

7-034

7-031 **E. F. Lefevre**: *label*
7-032 **E. F. Lefevre No.11**: *a typical larger fort (catalogue)*
7-033 and 7-034 **E. F. Lefevre Nos.9 & 10**: *typical smaller forts (catalogue)*
7-035 **E. F. Lefevre**: *a typical later fort (Courtesy Musée du Jouet, Brussels)*

When one compares Lefevre's production with that of Villard & Weill's (or Bon Dufour's?), one thing is immediately clear – Lefevre's backgrounds are much less informative. In fact, they are no more than trees. The buildings, though, are considerably more fully developed, at least in the case of the early forts.

They are reproduced at the left (7-032 to 7-034) in more or less relative size, although I cannot be certain of that because the actual sizes are not available to me. However, judging by the size of the figures, the largest was indeed very large.

The fort above (7-035) was produced somewhat later, probably about 1910. It is certainly less attractive than the earlier ones, but had the advantage that there were fewer pieces that could be broken off. The central drawbridge has only its chains left The lack of attention given to the background is manifest here.

7-036   7-037   7-038   7-040

7-039

7-041

Various French "Boxes" of Unknown Origin

(7-036, 7-038, & 7-041 are by courtesy of Musée du Jouet, Bxl)
(7-037 is by courtesy of Rob Wilson)

Here are a number of forts in boxes about which I have no knowledge. Nonetheless, they were colorful and imaginative, and provided great play value. The three at the top (7-036 to 7-038) were very small indeed, probably not Villard & Weill (or Bon Dufour?), while the one below them (7-039) is quite large. The two on the right are of medium size and are interesting in different ways. The one above (7-040), which has been extensively restored, is a later example, probably about 1925. The one below (7-041) has almost lost its drawbridge and has lost its chains, but considerable effort was put into the oriental detailing. The figures are 40mm in the lower left (7-039), Heyde supplied the 45mm figures in the upper right (7-040), and the others are the standard *bois comprimé*.

An Unidentified Manufacturer Starts a Trend

There seems to be much confusion about what happened on the toy forts front in France after the Second World War. There are a number of possible manufacturers, all of whom produced forts along much the same lines. Consequently, they often get attributed incorrectly.

Such confusion is easily understood when one considers the similarities in the products of the various manufacturers. One common feature, which they all share, is that they were all white. There was no depiction of stone or other building material. This, combined with the typical French characteristic of conical roofs on the circular towers, makes identification very difficult.

Another common feature is the lack of a "hill"/box on which the fort stands. This may have been inherited from Villard & Weill (or Bon Dufour?), whose "boxed-in" forts did not lend themselves to such treatment. Anyway, the result was an entrance at ground level, thus doing away with the need for a ramp. A piece of hardboard or similar material laid flat represented the ground, and provided a base for the fort.

A side effect of this was that there was no box to keep the pieces in. This led to the logical conclusion that, to avoid pieces getting lost, it was necessary to make the forts fixed in one position – erect. Later they developed the idea of leaving the center of the fort open to represent a courtyard. Coincidently, this left a space where odd pieces, such as roofs, figures, flags, and so on, could be placed inside for storage.

UNIDENTIFIED MANUFACTURER: Small Forts
c1955 to c1965

NO.	DESCRIPTION	DATE	DIMENSIONS	DISTINCTIVE FEATURES
unknown (7-045)	**a small fort** (identified by an example in the ownership below) eg: Marc Azzini, Jambes, B	c1955	19¾"x11¾"x14½" 500x300x370mm	• db over moat (renovated) to gateway • one large square tower w/metal turret • one large circular tower • towers at front – restored base
unknown (7-042)	**a small fort** (identified by an example in the ownership below) eg: Musée du Jouet, Bxl, B	c1955	unknown	• drawbridge to gateway • one large square tower w/metal turret • one small square tower w/metal turret • towers at front
unknown (7-043)	**an average fort** (identified by an example in the ownership below) eg: Marc Azzini, Jambes, B	c1955	21½"x15¾"x9¾" 550x400x250mm	• drawbridge over moat to gateway • three small circular towers (two at front) • one small metal turret at rear
unknown (7-044)	**a transition fort** (identified by an example in the ownership below) eg: Musée du Jouet, Bxl, B	c1960	unknown	• drawbridge over moat to gateway • three small circular towers (two at front)) • one large square tower w/metal turret • structure w/a monopitch over gateway

There were at least five recognizable manufacturers, or groups of them, producing similar toy forts. The first, whose name is unknown, seems to have been early on the scene, although exact dates are difficult to establish. They produced forts with a distinctive pressed metal turret. These forts may have been an early version of one of the other manufacturers. They are easily recognized both by the turrets and a particularly unusual pattern of arrow slits in pairs, one slightly higher than the other.

There are other, less obvious, distinguishing features. First is the doorway, which had a slightly pointed head; second are the strange circular holes in the walls of the circular towers; and third is the use of some unique crenellation, in which every other merlon was projecting.

7-042 **Unidentified manufacturer**: *a small fort (Courtesy Musée du Jouet, Brussels)*
This is one of this unidentified manufacturer's very first forts. It displays some of the distinctive features of this production – the metal turret; the slightly pointed doorway; the arrow slits in pairs; and the oddly projecting crenellation. It shows its early date by the two incomplete square towers, the use of two metal turrets instead of one, the lack of a water feature, and the manner of representing vegetation on the walls. These changed soon after the start of production.

c.1955–c.1965

7-043 **Unidentified manufacturer**: *a medium fort (Courtesy Marc Azzini)*
7-044 **Unidentified manufacturer**: *a transition fort (Courtesy Musée du Jouet, Brussels)*
7-045 **Unidentified manufacturer**: *a small fort (Courtesy Marc Azzini)*

These three forts are also from the same unidentified manufacturer's production.

The fort above (7-045) bears the distinguishing features of the range: the metal turret; the head to the doorway; the arrow slits in pairs; the projecting crenellation; and the holes in the circular towers. This is a later one, in that the courtyard is open. Note also the method of representing vegetation on the walls. The base has been repainted. The figures are Belgian (Wetthra).

Above left (7-043) is a medium fort that shows evidence of the paint work on the base having been damaged. However it is complete. It also bears all of the distinguishing features.

The lower castle (7-044) shows features of a later series, in particular the last vestiges of vegetation on the wall (a smear of dried up glue) similar to those of La Hotte aux Jouets. It has a general configuration of parts somewhat similar to that of forts at the time of Starlux's production. The river or moat around the front and the structure over the entrance also appeared later. There is some interesting experimentation with plastic crenellation, which did not appear again.

7-043

7-044

7-045

A New Manufacturer Opens Up

This new manufacturer's production was a series of what appears to be small to medium forts. However there were no manufacturer's marks of any sort. They were all white, as was the style of the time in France. Otherwise, they were much like the forts that followed, except for their crenellation, which was much closer together, and the roughcast type of finish.

One feature, which made them clearly identifiable, was their base. This was a simple piece of square or rectangular board, painted a dark blue to represent water and a sandy cream color with large green patches, presumably to represent grass. The fort, with or without a base of its own, sat on the "water" areas, thus creating a moat.

Finally, they used real foliage to represent vegetation growing up the walls. It was quite sensitively done, but, as might have been expected, it did not last long with rough treatment in the playroom, leaving just a trace of glue where it had been.

UNIDENTIFIED MANUFACTURER
c1960 to c1965

7-046

NO.	DESCRIPTION	DATE	DIMENSIONS	DISTINCTIVE FEATURES
unknown (7-046)	**triangular two-tower fort** (identified by an example in the ownership below) eg: Marc Azzini, Jambes, B	c1960	19¾"x9¼"x11¾" 500x250x300mm	• drawbridge over moat to gateway • triangular building with roof • one large circular tower (squat) • one regular circular tower
unknown (7-047)	**triangular three-tower fort** (identified by an example in the ownership below) eg: Marc Azzini, Jambes, B	c1960	19¾"x9¼"x11¾" 700x330x250mm	• separate ramp to drwbrdg & gateway • twin flanking regular circular towers • entry yard w/1 sq tower (squat)

7-046 **Unidentified manufacturer:** *triangular two-tower fort (Courtesy Marc Azzini)*
7-047 **Unidentified manufacturer:** *first series – triangular three-tower fort (Courtesy Marc Azzini)*
These are the only two we have of the series, although I have seen two others, both somewhat larger.

Forts by other makers, which were to come later, were not that different. There were differences however. The creation of as ramp was one such. The fact that the towers at the rear only butted up against the body of the fort, rather than fitted in, was another. The crenellation was much closer together than that of other manufacturers. And the roughcast type of finish was quite distinctive.

The example with the access ramp (7-047) has two non-original conical roofs. It did have such roofs, but with more of an overhang as on the smaller example (7-046). Also, the square tower on this one originally had a small turret at the rear, now only visible by the missing crenellation. On both examples, note the traces of glue from the fixing of the vegetation; it was originally applied with a broad brush and is now vaguely brown colored.

The figures on both forts are a mixture of British (Britains) and Belgian (Wetthra) manufacture.

7-047

La Hotte aux Jouets Came Next

La Hotte aux Jouets is a well-known commercial operation. It still exists today, selling all types of toys, especially toy cars, but not toy forts like this. They were established in 1962.

That they sold these forts in the 1960s and 1970s is not a question, but whether they manufactured them is open to debate. Of course, they may have had them manufactured elsewhere and then sold them on. This was quite a common practice in the toy fort world.

La Hotte aux Jouets stayed with all-white forts in various sizes and configurations. The most identifiable feature was their base, with a river or moat snaking around the front of the fort. They were colorfully spray painted, with a black outline for the banks, providing something for the drawbridge to span.

LA HOTTE AUX JOUETS: Smaller Forts
c1965 to c1975

NO.	DESCRIPTION	DATE	DIMENSIONS	DISTINCTIVE FEATURES
unknown (7-051)	**triangular two-tower fort** (identified by an example in the ownership below) eg: Musée du Jouet, Bxl, B	c1960	unknown	• drawbridge over moat to gateway • triangular building with roof • one large circular tower at front • one regular circular tower at rear
unknown (7-050)	**triangular three-tower fort** (identified by an example in the ownership below) eg: Musée du Jouet, Bxl, B	c1965	24¾"x8¼"x10¼" 630x210x260mm	• drawbridge over moat to gateway • triangular building open courtyard • one regular circular tower • two large circular towers
unknown (7-048)	**stretched four-tower** (identified by an example in the ownership below) eg: Allen Hickling Toy Forts	c1965	24"x13"x14½" 610x330x370mm	• drawbridge over moat to gateway • stretched rectangular fort • two small circular towers at front • two large circular towers at rear
unknown (7-049)	**stretched four-tower** (identified by an example in the ownership below) eg: SOFIA Foundation, CY	c1965	25¾"x15¼"x10½" 650x385x265mm	• drawbridge over moat to gateway • stretched triangular fort • two sm circular towers w/roofs at front • 1 lg circ & 1 lg square tower

They manufactured three basic sizes of fort. The smallest one was based on a triangular building, with or without an open center, but with two or three towers. The middle one was a larger extended type that sported four towers. The third one was considerably more interesting. Not only were they bigger, with an open courtyard, but they used the upper level as well. This one also had a large square tower with steps up to the upper level. This could be used as a keep.

They also introduced plastic conical roofs to fit over the towers, although the evidence for this is scrappy. There is also evidence of two pitched roofs. One was a very steeply pitched roof over the main building. This and the conical ones were made of plastic. Another was an average pitched roof on a building over the gateway, and this was made of wood.

LA HOTTE AUX JOUETS: Larger Forts
c1965 to c1975

NO.	DESCRIPTION	DATE	DIMENSIONS	DISTINCTIVE FEATURES
unknown (7-052)	**fort with steps** (identified by an example in the ownership below) eg: Musée du Jouet, Bxl, B	c1965	24"x19½"x18" 610x495x455mm	• drawbridge over moat to gateway • one sm & 1 lg circ towers at front • one lg circ tower & main bldg at rear • steps to main bldg under steep roof
unknown (7-053)	**fort with steps** (identified by an example in the ownership below) eg: Marc Azzini, Jambes, B	c1965	24"x19½"x18" 610x495x455mm	• db over moat to gateway w/bldg over • two sm circ front towers & 1 lg at rear • large rect main building at rear • steps to top sq tower w/sm circ tower
unknown (7-054)	**fort with steps** (identified by an example in the ownership below) eg: Musée du Jouet, Bxl, B	c1965	26¾"x16½"x18" 680x420x460mm	• drawbridge over moat to gateway • extended triangular fort w/gate at end • one sm circ & 1 lg circ towers by gate • steps to top square tower at rear

7-048

7-048 La Hotte aux Jouets No.740: *four-tower fort*
   This is one of La Hotte aux Jouets's extended forts. It has many of the characteristics of the smaller triangular forts, but it has four towers. Unusually, most of the crenellation is cut directly out of the walls, which is unlike the stuck-on merlons of all our other examples, large and small. It has an open courtyard so that the interior is accessible for play. The conical roof is probably not original. The 54mm Deetail knights are by Britains.

7-049

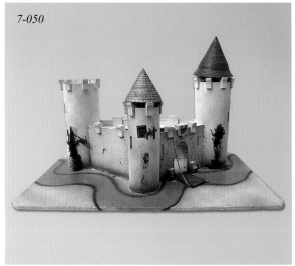

7-050

7-051

7-049 La Hotte aux Jouets: *extended four-tower fort*
7-050 La Hotte aux Jouets No.730: *triangular three tower fort (Courtesy Musée du Jouet, Brussels)*
7-051 La Hotte aux Jouets No.720: *triangular two-tower fort (Courtesy Musée du Jouet, Brussels)*
These are some of the smaller forts of the second series. They are all basically triangular forts with towers.

They all show complete rejection of the distinctive features of the earlier series and all display a robustness which comes from the construction being mostly wood and hardboard.

However the fort top right (7-050) is earlier than the other two. The difference is the open courtyard, allowing play within the walls.

Note that the vegetation on the tower of the fort has lasted well. This is evidence of the practice of applying three-dimensional foliage, which is now only survived by smears of glue on most of the forts.

The figures on the extended fort (7-049) are 54mm Deetail knights by Britains, while those on the fort far right (7-051) are of French manufacture (Starlux).

7-052

7-053

7-054

7-052 **La Hotte aux Jouets**: *large fort with building and steps (Courtesy Musée du Jouet, Brussels)*
7-053 **La Hotte aux Jouets No.751**: *large fort with tower and steps (Courtesy Marc Azzini)*
7-054 **La Hotte aux Jouets**: *smaller fort with tower and steps (Courtesy Musée du Jouet, Brussels)*

These are three of the larger forts in the series. They all admirably show the painting of the moat or river, and the traces of the glue used to fix the vegetation to the walls.

The one above right 7-053 is the most defensible by virtue of its height and its structure over the gateway, both of which were known defensive features. The one below right (7-054) appears equally defensible with all its corners equipped with towers. The one above (7-052) is clearly more domestic in character, but even this one, with its crenellation and towers, could not be taken on lightly. The conical roofs are probably not original.

The 54mm figures on the top right fort are from Britains' Herald series.

Another Manufacturer Enters the Scene

Sometime in the 1960s, another manufacturer entered the market. I cannot find a name anywhere, nor can I find a place or date of origin, but I certainly found some of their forts. It seems that they started with four forts, with one, two, three, and four towers, the first three being in triangular format. I know nothing about how they differentiated between them, other than by counting the towers.

As with all forts produced in France during the post-war period, they were basically white throughout, with no depiction of stone or other building material. Also, the entrance was always at ground level, doing away with the need for a ramp. A piece of hardboard or similar material laid flat represented the ground and provided a base for the fort.

UNIDENTIFIED MANUFACTURER
c1960 to c1970

NO.	DESCRIPTION	DATE	DIMENSIONS	DISTINCTIVE FEATURES
unknown	**triangular one-tower fort** (identified by an example in the ownership below) eg: unknown	c1961	unknown	• drawbridge over moat to gateway • triangular building with roof • one large circular tower
unknown (7-056)	**triangular two-tower fort** (identified by an example in the ownership below) eg: Alain Thomas, B	c1961	12½"x12½"x10¾" 320x320x275mm	• drawbridge over moat to gateway • triangular building with roof • one large & one small circular towers • towers at front
unknown (7-055)	**triangular three-tower fort** (identified by an example in the ownership below) eg: Marc Azzini, Jambes, B	c1961	12¼"x12¼"x10¼" 310x310x260mm	• drawbridge over moat to gateway • triangular building with roof • one large square tower at front • two med circular towers at rear & front
unknown (7-057)	**square four-tower fort** (identified by an example in the ownership below) eg: Marc Azzini, Jambes, B	c1961	19¾"x18½"x12½" 500x470x320mm	• drawbridge over moat to gateway • 1 large & 1 small circ towers at front • one large square tower at rear • one small circular tower at rear

The main difference, when compared to the products of La Hotte aux Jouets, is found in their bases. They both had representations of water around the buildings, but this manufacturer did more than just paint it on. They actually formed a channel for the "water" by using two thicknesses of the base board, so that the moat had "real" banks. This meant that the water was much more clearly defined than anything La Hotte aux Jouets produced.

There was another very noticeable difference. The vegetation was very casually done by flicking green paint around the base and up the walls, as opposed to the elaborate efforts of La Hotte aux Jouets, which used three-dimensional foliage. This painted technique was much more robust, and did not come off in play as did the more realistic efforts of La Hotte aux Jouets.

There are several minor differences as well, but in their general approach there was a strong similarity to the production of La Hotte aux Jouets – and, to some extent, to Starlux.

Consequently, many of these forts have been attributed to Starlux, but they were to come a little later. Starlux was well-known at the time as a manufacturer of figures, but did not get into the manufacture of forts until quite late in their career. The Starlux name is commonly, if mistakenly, attached to these examples, which leads to much confusion.

7-055

7-055 **Unidentified manufacturer:** *three-tower fort (Courtesy Marc Azzini)*
   Coming on at the same time as La Hotte aux Jouet's forts, this manufacturing firm needed to differentiate its products. They were not very successful in this, except for the method of defining the water in front of the buildings, the depiction of foliage, and one or two minor details.
   Note the channelling of the water between "real" banks, which was achieved through using two thicknesses of the baseboard. Note also the slapdash depiction of foliage. The other differences were small indeed, concerned mainly with the shape of the gateway and the rounded end to the drawbridge.

7-057

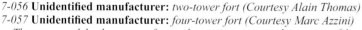

7-056 **Unidentified manufacturer:** *two-tower fort (Courtesy Alain Thomas)*
7-057 **Unidentified manufacturer:** *four-tower fort (Courtesy Marc Azzini)*

These two, and the three-tower fort on the previous page, make up most of the series. Their distinguishing features are few and far between. Apart from the water, the shape of the entrance, it being quite narrow and high, and the drawbridge, with its rounded end being made to fit the gateway, would probably be everything. Of course, the sparse vegetation on the towers is distinctive also.

The two-tower fort (7-056) is missing one of its chains, and the 55mm figures are by Cyrnos in France. The conical roof on the four-tower version (7-057) is not original, and the figures are of French or Belgian origin.

It is interesting to note how these are the forerunners of all the forts that Starlux made later. This is most obvious in the siting of the triangular forts on their baseboard. They also produced four forts, graduated in size, through their various versions. Of course, there are significant differences, not least in the sizes of the towers, and the moat/river feature, but the general disposition of the parts, and the sizes and shapes of the whole are more or less the same.

Starlux Came Late to the Game

In the 1930s, Elie Tarroux was busy in Paris, as he had been for the previous twenty-five years, making figures made of *Blanc de Meudon* and glue. From a very small workshop, with five or six workers, he sold solely in and around Paris. Such a limited market required a real effort to keep the business going.

In 1938, Elie was joined by his son-in-law, Pierre Beffara. Together, they improved their production methods and, subsequently, sales. In 1945, Pierre became the sole proprietor. He established S. A. Starlux, now commonly known just as Starlux. He kept on with the manufacture of figures, but quickly abandoned the *Blanc de Meudon* tradition and substituted plastic, using the new injection-molding technique.

In 1947, he decided to decentralize and chose Perigueux for his relocation. It took three years to get settled, but by then their markets had expanded considerably and they were into a well established pattern of producing toy figures of many different types. In 1974, twenty years after their move, they decided the time was right to diversify.

They started to produce a line of toy buildings using the trade name Plasticobois. This was a major step that involved the production of a wide range of buildings – farms, garages, houses, and the like, together with buildings of the Wild West, and, of course, the castles and forts of the Middle Ages.

To the day they went out of business in 2003, their forts were basically the same as all of their competitors'. They were white throughout with the entrance at ground level, doing away with the need for a ramp. A piece of hardboard or similar material laid flat represented the ground and provided a base for the fort.

Starlux, however, brought a rationalization and modernization to the thinking about toy forts, which was necessary for manufacturing and economic reasons. In effect, they made only one model. This had a gateway in the middle, flanked by two equal circular towers, to which they attached different backings and roofing details for the different forts. This may not have been very exciting for the user, but it made a lot of sense in terms of mass production.

They started with three forts with two, three, and four towers, numbered rationally 1, 2, and 3. (This is a little reminiscent of the unknown manufacturer, whose production seems to provide the transition from La Hotte aux Jouets.) No.1 had crenellated towers and walls, while No.2 and No.3 had towers with conical roofs and crenellation confined to the walls and a square keep.

They clearly wanted to make an impression with this new product, so they made use of plastic details. It was introduced in the creation of a gateway and drawbridge, a square door, the conical roofs, and the crenellation. Everything else was made of wood, card, and some form of hardboard.

The new gateway was impressive. A sharply pointed head and a stone surround with a portcullis – regretfully non-operational. The side door was fairly simple, and the crenellation consisted of plastic "clip-on" merlons. The roofs were of a new design specific to Starlux, and only appear on circular towers without crenellation.

In addition, there was a baseboard with a slightly rough texture, colored green to represent grass, used for the fort to stand on. There was no river or moat, so the drawbridge was not so much a bridge as it was a strong door operated by chains. Vegetation on the walls was considered superfluous.

7-058 **Starlux**: *first version No.2 (Courtesy Marc Azzini)*
This image is notable for featuring the front arrangement with its entrance gateway flanked by two equal circular towers. This repetition of parts obviously made for easier mass production. It is standard throughout the range in all versions, except, much later, when a keep was substituted for one of the towers. The different forts were created by adding various backings and roofing details.
The 40mm figures of knights are by Wetthra, the Belgian manufacturer.

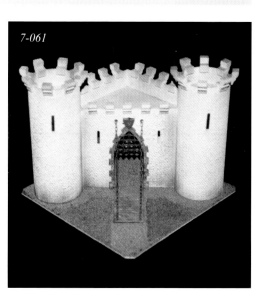

7-059 **Starlux**: second version No.3 (Courtesy Musée du Jouet, Brussels)

7-060 **Starlux**: second version No.4 (Courtesy Marc Azzini)

7-061 **Starlux**: first version No.1 (Courtesy Marc Azzini)

One can see the two towers flanking the gateway, which made up the front of all the forts. This repetition of parts obviously made for easier mass production. The vegetation on the towers is merely an airbrushed coating at the junction with the baseboard.

The No.1 fort to the right below (7-061) is in the classic first version style, except for the fancy landscaping that is visible on the base board. It was thought that this came with the second version, and is an example of Starlux's unpredictability.

The No.3 fort to the left above (7-059) is of the second version (see the structure over the gateway). It has the conical roofs that the No.4 fort does not, protecting the occupants from falling arrows. This makes it without doubt the most defensible of the forts in the series – that is with the exception of the side door. The merlons at the corners of the square tower are mostly missing.

The No.4 fort to the right above (7-060) is apparently better defended, but the men in the towers are vulnerable to attack with arrows because there are no roofs. The 40mm figures of knights are by Starlux.

There is some question in my mind as to the wisdom of having a side door. It would have made much more sense defensively if access to the large square tower had been from the inside only. The drawbridge, while having definite play value, is hardly necessary if you do not have to cross water to enter. However, apart from these, it appears to be eminently defensible.

STARLUX: First Version
1974

NO.	DESCRIPTION	DATE	DIMENSIONS	DISTINCTIVE FEATURES
1 (7-061)	**the first in the series** (identified by an example in the ownership below) eg: Marc Azzini, Jambes, B	1974	12¼"x12¼"x9¾" 310x310x250mm	• drawbridge on ground to gateway • two med towers flanking gateway • triangular fort behind • crenellated
2 (7-058)	**a second in the series** (identified by an example in the ownership below) eg: SOFIA Foundation, CY	1974	16½"x15½"x15" 420x395x380mm	• drawbridge on ground to gateway • two med towers flanking gateway • square fort behind w/lg circ tower • three plastic conical roofs
3	**a third in the series** (identified by an example in the ownership below) eg: Musée du Jouet, Bxl, B	1974	19½"x18½"x15" 495x470x380mm	• drawbridge on ground to gateway • two med towers flanking gateway • sq fort behind w/1 sq & 1 lg circ towers • circ towers w/roof - sq tower crenellated

Sometime later, they introduced a structure overhanging the gateway. This had a mono-pitched roof, and represented a new level of defense, with the possibility of dropping stones and boiling oil on people at the gate, while being protected by the roof from falling arrows. It was attached to their existing No.3 fort. In addition there was now a No.4 fort, which was the same as the No.3 with its new defense over the gateway, but fully crenellated without the conical roofs.

STARLUX: Second Version
c1975

NO.	DESCRIPTION	DATE	DIMENSIONS	DISTINCTIVE FEATURES
3 (7-059)	**a third in the series** (identified by an example in the ownership below) eg: Musée du Jouet, Bxl, B	c1975	19½"x18½"x15" 495x470x380mm	• db on ground to gate w/structure over • two med towers flanking gateway • sq fort behind w/1 sq & 1 lg circ towers • circ towers w/roof – sq tower crenellated
4 (7-060)	**the last in the series** (identified by an example in the ownership below) eg: Allen Hickling Toy Forts	c1975	19½"x18½"x9¾" 495x470x250mm	• db on ground to gate w/structure over • two med towers flanking gateway • sq fort behind w/1 sq & 1 lg circ towers • all towers crenellated – no roofs

There was also a revolution on the packaging front. I do not know what went before, but I guess it was the more or less standard brown cardboard sort of thing. Each fort now had a fancy white box with a full-color illustrative label of the fort on it. It really made the forts look quite special.

A major reshuffle took place in 1978, about four years after the initial launch, with the introduction of the third version. But with the exception of the No.3

and No.5 forts, which were completely new and came out at this time, there were in fact quite small changes.

They decided that people had to live in these forts as well as defend them. So, instead of arrow slits they put plastic windows high up on all their circular towers, looking forward.

The series also introduced the idea of landscaping. This merely showed a difference between the area one walked on (paths) and those on which the grass was allowed to grow. This feature seems to have been a bit erratic in its implementation, probably partly due to the fact that it did not wear too well.

7-062 **Starlux**: *third version No.1 (Courtesy Marc Azzini)*
This is one of the smallest of the third version, although the look-out tower may have come later. The improvements in these were very small. The windows high up on all of the circular towers are obvious, but there also appears to have been the development of landscaping on the baseboard in some cases, though not on this one with the lookout. The 40mm figures are by Starlux.

As far as I can make out, the new No.1 now had roofs on the two towers and had a small tower which acted as a look-out mounted at the rear. The No.2 and No.4 forts appear to have changed little except for the windows. I should point out, however, that some of the changes may have taken place a little later.

The No.3 fort was the same as the No.2, except that a square keep was substituted for one of the front towers. This made for a particularly vulnerable situation, with the rectangular door right beside the gateway.

STARLUX: Third Version
1978

NO.	DESCRIPTION	DATE	DIMENSIONS	DISTINCTIVE FEATURES
1 (7-062)	**the first in the series** (identified by an example in the ownership below) eg: Marc Azzini, Jambes, B	1978	12½"x12½"x10¼" 315x315x260mm	• drawbridge on ground to gateway • two med towers flanking gateway • triangular fort behind w/circular look-out • windows & two conical roofs
2 (7-063)	**the second in the series** (identified by an example in the ownership below) eg: Marc Azzini, Jambes, B	1978	15¾"x16½"x11¾" 400x420x300mm	• drawbridge on ground to gateway • two med towers flanking gateway • square fort behind w/lg circ tower • windows & three plastic conical roofs
3 (7-066)	**the third in the series** (identified by an example in the ownership below) eg: Alain Thomas, B	1978	19¾"x18¾"x13" 500x475x330mm	• drawbridge on ground to gateway • med tower & keep flanking gateway • one med circ towers • circ towers w/roofs- sq keep crenellated
4 (7-065)	**the fourth in the series** (identified by an example in the ownership below) eg: Marc Azzini, Jambes, B	1978	19¾"x18¾"x13" 500x475x330mm	• drawbridge on ground to gateway • two med towers flanking gateway • fort behind w/sq keep & 1 lg circ tower • all towers with roofs
5 (7-064)	**the last in the series** (identified by an example in the ownership below) eg: Alain Thomas, B	1978	19¾"x18¾"x13" 500x475x330mm	• drawbridge on ground to gateway • two med towers flanking gateway • sq fort behind w/1 sq & 1 lg circ towers • crenellated wall protecting door in tower

It appears to me that the introduction of variations was somewhat erratic during the next years. For example, I have seen a No.3 fort with the large square keep flanking the entrance. There were also several forts with odd pieces, which do not fit into any particular sequence.

The structures overhanging the entrances on Nos.3, 4, and 5 seem to have been discontinued, although there is some uncertainty about when this actually happened. At least it is known that the initial version had them.

One fort, which came out sometime about 1985, needs a mention here. It would seem to have appeared before the second version; it certainly had arrow slits rather than windows. However, its position relative to this and others is a bit of a mystery. Although it is somewhat like the No.4 second version, it had a regular circular tower instead of the large square keep at the back. There was no structure above the gate, as in some examples of the third version.

STARLUX: Second Series: Special
c1985

NO.	DESCRIPTION	DATE	DIMENSIONS	DISTINCTIVE FEATURES
unknown (7-067)	**one not in a the series** (identified by an example in the ownership below) eg: Allen Hickling Toy Forts	c1985	unknown	• drawbridge on ground to gateway • two medium towers flanking gateway • two medium circ towers at rear (one tall) • all towers supplied with roofs

Its "footprint" was noticeably different in that it splayed out at the back. Thus, it retained the same entry arrangement of the gateway flanked by two towers, while permitting a slightly larger fort. This was unlike any of the others.

The company finally went into liquidation in 2003.

7-063 **Starlux***: third version No.2 (Courtesy Marc Azzini)*
There is very little difference between this and the first series. The use of windows in place of arrow slits, a shortening of the other arrow slits, and the introduction of landscaping are everything. The figures are of British and French origin (Starlux).

7-064

1978-c.1985

7-065

7-066

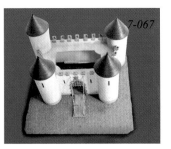

7-067

7-064 **Starlux**: *third version No.5 (Courtesy Alain Thomas)*
7-065 **Starlux**: *third version No.4 (Courtesy Marc Azzini)*
7-066 **Starlux**: *third version No.3 (Courtesy Alain Thomas)*
7-067 **Starlux**: *special (four circular towers)*
   These are three of the third version, and one special fort that came out later.
   The windows on all of the circular towers in the third version are obvious, as is the representation of landscaping on the baseboards. The structure over the gateway is present

on the Nos.3 and 5 (7-066 & 7-064) but is absent on the new No.4 (7-065). The new No.3 (7-066) is the only fort where Starlux departed from the two circular towers flanking the gateway, replacing it with the keep. On the No.5 (7-064), they finally got around to defending the door to the keep with a crenellated wall.
   The 40mm figures on all the castles on this page are of French (Starlux) origin.

c.1950-c.1980

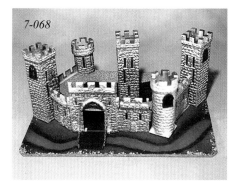

7-068

7-069

7-073

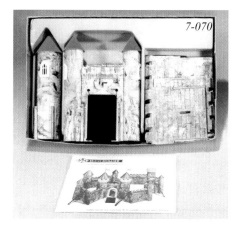

7-070

7-071

7-072

Various French Manufacturers

(7-068, 7-070, 7-071 & 7-072 courtesy Musée du Jouet, Bxl)
(7-069 & 7-073 courtesy Marc Azzini)

The fort at top left (7-068) is by JEM-MCB. The one at top center (7-069) is possibly by Clairbois; the 45mm figures are by Starlux. The left center and bottom right photos (7-070 and 7-072) show the pieces for constructing a castle (7-071) marketed by Marius Minaire under the name "Mon Carcassonne." The box is shown inside and out. The fort above (7-073) is by Clairbois, and is the chateau of Thierry La Frondre, a TV character from the 1960s; its figures are 54mm Deetail knights by Britains.

—BELGIUM—

Nazaire Beeusaert Started after the First World War

Nazaire Beeusaert set up his business in Deinze in 1921. They initially made horses to push along and to ride on, which varied in height from 20cm to 84cm. They were made out of cardboard and glue, and Nazaire Beeusaert became so proficient at it that he became known as the expert.

Later, at the beginning of the Second World War, the company turned its attention to small figures made out of composition. It made soldiers and animals, together with various small buildings – farms, zoos, etc. Nazaire Beeusaert died in 1965, and the company, now called simply Beeusaert, was taken on by his son Julien. It gradually left manufacturing behind and became a wholesale operation.

Beeusaert did not produce forts until about 1952. There are at least three types. Two of them are definitely by Beeusaert, and the third is highly likely to have been made by it as well.

There is the more military type, in which defensibility is key. The only color in them is the black and white of the buildings, the green grass and vegetation, and the blue of water.

The next type had similar construction, but on interesting bases – if there was one – with tunnels, caves, long winding ramps, etc. This was the fairy or princess castle with a myriad of towers with red and gold conical roofs, for which Nazaire Beeusaert made special fantasy figures.

The third type is the less militaristic chateau type. There is some small doubt concerning the manufacturer of these. They still have some of the features that make them fort-like, but they also have colorful roofs and habitable buildings. They were made after the death of Nazaire and included some elements of plastic.

NAZAIRE BEEUSAERT: More Militaristic Forts
1953 to c1970

NO.	DESCRIPTION	DATE	DIMENSIONS	DISTINCTIVE FEATURES
1452i	the smallest fort (identified by an example in the ownership below) eg: Luc van Wanzeele, B	1953	16¼"x8¾"x9" 410x220x230mm	• simple ramp to dbridge & gateway • two lg circ towers each side of gate • rectangular courtyard no buildings
1452ii	the smallest fort (identified by an example in the ownership below) eg: Marc Azzini, Jambes, B	c1956	11¾"x12¼"x8¼" 300x310x210mm	• simple ramp to dbridge & gateway • rectangular courtyard • no buildings no towers
1452iii	the smallest fort (identified by an example in the ownership below) eg: Luc van Wanzeele, B	1960	14¼"x11¾"x11" 360x300x280mm	• simple ramp to dbridge & gateway • rectangular courtyard no tower • one two-storey rectangular building
unknown	the second fort (identified by an example in the ownership below) eg: Marc Azzini, Jambes, B	c1955	14¼"x11¾"x7½" 360x300x290mm	• simple ramp to dbridge & gateway • courtyard with square main building
unknown (7-075)	the third fort (identified by an example in the ownership below) eg: Marc Azzini, Jambes, B	c1955	15¾"x10¼"x15" 400x260x380mm	• simple ramp to dbridge & gateway • gateway at right angles to front • courtyard with two circular towers
1453	the fourth fort (identified by an example in the ownership below) eg: Luc van Wanzeele, B	1955	15¾"x15"x14" 400x380x370mm	• simple ramp to dbridge & gateway • courtyard with high walls • one medium circ corner tower • 2-storey rectangular main building
1454 (7-077)	the fifth fort (identified by an example in the ownership below) eg: Marc Azzini, Jambes, B	c1955	19¾"x15¾"x15" 500x400x380mm	• simple ramp to dbridge & gateway • courtyard with high walls • one lg & 1 medium circ corner towers • 2-3 storey rectangular main building
1455	the sixth fort (identified by an example in the ownership below) eg: Marc Azzini, Jambes, B	c1955	19¾"x18"x15¾" 500x460x400mm	• simple ramp to dbridge & gateway • courtyard with high walls • two medium circular corner towers • 3-storey rectangular main building
1456 (7-076)	the seventh fort (identified by an example in the ownership below) eg: Marc Azzini, Jambes, B	c1955	23¾"x17"x19¼" 600x430x490mm	• simple ramp to dbridge & gateway • courtyard with high walls • one large & 1 tall med tower in court • 2-3 storey rectangular main building
1457 (7-074)	the eighth fort (identified by an example in the ownership below) eg: Musée du Jouet, Bxl, B	c1955	23¾"x17"x19¼" 600x430x490mm	• reentrant ramp to dbdge & gatehse • courtyard with high walls • one lg & 1 medium circ corner towers • 3-storey 2-level rect main building
1473	the largest fort (identified by an example in the ownership below) eg: Luc van Wanzeele, B	1966	26"x24¾"x22½" 660x620x570mm	• tall plastic base w/simple ramp to db • gatehse to courtyard with high walls • two tall medium circular corner towers • 2-storey 2-level rect main building

It seems that Beeusaert made four types of base on which the forts sat. They all had a wooden base board.

One was a quite rough affair made of cloth soaked in plaster of Paris or some similar material. The folds of the material provided a reasonable impression of rock. A second, which seems to have been used exclusively on the less militaristic forts and was an altogether smoother finish, something akin to the German plastic ones. The third type was basically wooden with *papier mâché* rock formations. Of the fourth type, in which the base was kept flat to give the impression of a lake, there is but one example.

The buildings were all made of thick cardboard, all in one piece, with the occasional exception of tall towers, which were made separately. This, of course, led to the merlons in the crenellation being vulnerable to becoming bent over.

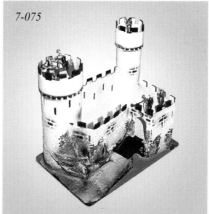

7-074 **Nazaire Beeusaert No.1457**: *most defensible fort (Courtesy Musée du Jouet, Brussels)*
7-075 **Nazaire Beeusaert**: *defensible fort (Courtesy Marc Azzini)*
7-076 **Nazaire Beeusaert No.1456**: *basic fort (Courtesy Marc Azzini)*
7-077 **Nazaire Beeusaert No.1454**: *defensible fort (Courtesy Marc Azzini)*
   These are all defensible military forts. They all have a simulation of rocky terrain made of cloth soaked in plaster of Paris or papier mâché, and they are all surrounded by water. They are also all on the small side, and I do not know if Nazaire Beeusaert made any larger ones. This may have been a limitation of the technology or a response to the market.

The only bits made of wood were the long horizontal members, such as behind the battlements for men to stand on and the circular shapes in the towers.

They were all given a coat of thick white paint, with windows, doors and stone details stenciled on in black. The vegetation and water were then spray painted around the bottom.

NAZAIRE BEEUSAERT: **Fairy/Princess Fort**
c1956 to c1960

NO.	DESCRIPTION	DATE	DIMENSIONS	DISTINCTIVE FEATURES
1461 (7-078)	**the smallest in this series** (identified by an example in the ownership below) eg: Musée du Jouet, Bxl, B	1956	11¾"x11¾"x17¾" 300x300x450mm	• shallow ramp to gateway w/two towers • court w/hi wall & two circ corner towers • main building w/four circ towers • all towers w/shallow conical roofs
1462	**the middle in this series** (identified by an example in the ownership below) eg: Luc van Wanzeele, B	1956	16½"x13¾"x23¾" 420x350x600mm	• base w/cave w/ramp to dbridge & gate • court w/hi wall & four circ corner towers • main building w/four circ towers • all towers w/shallow conical roofs
1463	**the largest in this series** (illustrated in Nazaire Beeusaert catalogue c1956) eg: no known example	1956	13¾"x15¾"x30¾" 350x400x780mm	• complex base w/ramp to dbridge & gate • court w/hi wall & 4 circ corner towers • solitary tower w/bridge to corner tower • bldg w/4 circ towers all w/conical roofs

NAZAIRE BEEUSAERT: **Less Militaristic Forts**
c1965 to c1975

NO.	DESCRIPTION	DATE	DIMENSIONS	DISTINCTIVE FEATURES
unknown	**the smallest fort** (identified by an example in the ownership below) eg: Musée du Jouet, Bxl, B	unknwn	unknown	• basic ramp to drawbridge to gateway • courtyard w/three circ corner towers • three-storey main building w/hi back wall
1471 (7-080)	**the second fort** (identified by an example in the ownership below) eg: Musée du Jouet, Bxl, B	c1965	17"x13¾"x14¼" 430x350x360mm	• basic ramp to drawbridge to gateway • courtyard w/sweeping semicircu;lar wall • one circular corner tower with roof • two-storey main building with roof
1471 (7-079)	**the second fort** (identified by an example in the ownership below) eg: Marc Azzini, Jambes, B	c1965	17"x13¾"x14¼" 430x350x360mm	• basic ramp to drawbridge to gateway • courtyard w/sweeping semicircu;lar wall • one circular corner tower • two-storey main building
unknown (7-081)	**the third fort** (identified by an example in the ownership below) eg: Musée du Jouet, Bxl, B	unknwn	unknown	• drawbridge over lake to gateway • court w/circ tower & two circ turrets • four-storey main building
unknown (7-082)	**the largest fort** (identified by an example in the ownership below) eg: Musée du Jouet, Bxl, B	unknwn	unknown	• reentrant ramp to db, gate & lower yard • rect & circ corner towers w/tunnel under • stair to upper yard two circ towers • four storey main building

7-078 Nazaire Beeusaert No.1461: *Fairy/Princess castle (Courtesy Musée du Jouet, Brussels)*
This has to be called a castle because of its character. It has all the trappings of the other forts, including a drawbridge, but it is considerably smaller. Presumably it was designed to satisfy young girls and fill that "fairy tale" gap in the market.

The clustered towers make for an air of fantasy. One does not have to have a particularly vivid imagination to see the princess locked in her room in one of the turrets, or the handsome prince charging up the stairs to save her. The gold roofs on the gateway towers seem to say it all.

Exactly how fairies come into it I am not sure. Maybe my informant got it wrong somehow. Of course, there are good and bad fairies, and maybe therein lies the explanation.

c.1960-c.1975

7-079

7-080

7-081

7-082

7-079 **Nazaire Beeusaert No.1471** *Chateau (Courtesy Marc Azzini)*
7-080 **Nazaire Beeusaert No.1471** *Chateau (with roofs) (Courtesy Musée du Jouet, Brussels)*
7-081 **Nazaire Beeusaert**: *Chateau in a lake (Courtesy Musée du Jouet, Brussels)*
7-082 **Nazaire Beeusaert**: *Large chateau (with railway tunnel) (Courtesy Musée du Jouet, Brussels)*

These forts are all from the less militaristic and defensible range of Nazaire Beeusaert.

The two forts in the top left (7-079 & 7-080) are on bases that appear to have been made in a mold, somewhat similar to those of Elastolin in the 1950s. It could be that the red roofs are not original, or they may have been been lost from the top left fort. The 40mm figures are by Merton of Germany.

The bottom left fort (7-081) is not a typical example in that the base board is larger and flatter than the norm and represents a lake. Note the colorful roofs.

The large fort above (7-082) is built on a wood carcass, making the railway tunnel possible, all covered in cloth and papier mâché for the effect of rocks. The steps to the upper level are not formed very well, which is a function of the cardboard material and the pressures of time in production.

An Unidentified but Prolific Belgian Manufacturer

This manufacturer is known to us only by the forts it made. If I know a little of Nazaire Beeusaert, then I know almost nothing of this one. Although there are plenty of examples of the forts, they bear no maker's name, no label, no number, or anything else which would give us a lead as to their identity.

It is even difficult to put a date on them as there are no catalogues, at least as far as I am aware. From the style of construction and a level of detail, at least for some of them, we can say that they were probably made in the period between the wars. This makes the dates from about 1930 until plastics became established, about 1965, the likely window of time during which they might have been produced.

There is one striking feature which is common to all of them, and that is the stylistic use of red bricks, which were stenciled on. These were put on quite liberally, in clusters of anywhere from six to fifteen. It is not clear whether they were meant to imply a rendering falling off in patches or something else. Perhaps they were just a means of getting color into the forts.

They are all made predominantly of wood, with a principal building piece – two basic types – set between a flanking square tower with a pyramidal roof and another flanking tower. In addition there are one or two medium-sized circular towers on the corners at the front.

The general appearance and painting is perhaps the most telling similarity between them. They are all basically white, with the red bricks, of course, and black stenciled windows and doors. There are details and highlighting in rust brown, and red roofs. All stand on a greenish box base with dry brush coloring.

UNIDENTIFIED MANUFACTURER
c1930 to c1965

NO.	DESCRIPTION	DATE	DIMENSIONS	DISTINCTIVE FEATURES
unknown (7-087)	**the smallest fort** (identified by an example in the ownership below) eg: Musée du Jouet, Bxl, B	unknwn	unknown	• double ramp to drawbridge & gateway • courtyard with main bldg to rear • one square & one circ flanking towers
unknown (7-088)	**the second fort** (identified by an example in the ownership below) eg: Musée du Jouet, Bxl, B	unknwn	unknown	• simple ramp to drawbridge & gateway • courtyard with one circular corner tower • main building to rear • one square & one circ flanking towers
unknown (7-089)	**the third fort** (identified by an example in the ownership below) eg: Marc Azzini, Jambes, B	unknwn	17½"x14¼"x15¼" 445x365x385mm	• double ramp to drawbridge & gateway • courtyard w/two circular corner towers • main building to rear w/long gallery over • 2 circ flanking towers 1 w/½-timbering

unknown	**the fourth fort** (identified by an example in the ownership below) eg: Musée du Jouet, Bxl, B	unknwn	unknown	• double ramp to drawbridge & gateway • courtyard w/2 sm circ corner towers • 3-arch main building (centre part) • two sq flanking towers one castellated
unknown (7-083)	**the fifth fort** (identified by an example in the ownership below) eg: Musée du Jouet, Bxl, B	unknwn	unknown	• double ramp to drawbridge & gateway • courtyard w/2 small circ corner towers • 3-arch main building (centre part) • two sq flanking towers one castellated
unknown (7-085)	**the sixth fort** (identified by an example in the ownership below) eg: Musée du Jouet, Bxl, B	unknwn	unknown	• simple ramp to drawbridge & gateway • courtyard w/1 med circ corner tower • central entrance tower on main bldg • one square & one circ flanking towers
unknown (7-084)	**the seventh fort** (identified by an example in the ownership below) eg: Musée du Jouet, Bxl, B	unknwn	unknown	• simple ramp to drawbridge & gatehouse • courtyard w/1 med circ corner tower • central entrance tower on main bldg • one square & one circ flanking towers
unknown (7-086)	**the largest fort** (identified by an example in the ownership below) eg: Musée du Jouet, Bxl, B	unknwn	unknown	• two reentrant ramps to db & gateway • courtyard w/2 med circ corner towers • three arch main building (centre part) • two sq flanking towers one crenellated

There is a sub-category that can be identified, which have a clear indication that they were made around the same time; they use of a shallow plinth for the box base to stand on. Also worth noting is the fact that the box base in question has vertical sides, unlike all the others, which have sloping sides. The forts also have half-timbered details. I have no idea when this was made in relation to the others.

UNIDENTIFIED MANUFACTURER: Forts with Plinths
c1930 to c1965

NO.	DESCRIPTION	DATE	DIMENSIONS	DISTINCTIVE FEATURES
unknown	**the first fort** (identified by an example in the ownership below) eg: Musée du Jouet, Bxl, B	unknwn	unknown	• box on plinth w/ramp to db & gateway • gateway to court w/one circ tower • main bldg w/central entrance tower • two flanking towers one sq & one circ
unknown (7-091)	**the first fort** (identified by an example in the ownership below) eg: Musée du Jouet, Bxl, B	unknwn	unknown	• box on plinth w/ramp to db & gatehse • gatehse to court w/one circ tower • main bldg w/central entrance tower • two flanking towers one sq & one circ
unknown (7-090)	**the second fort** (identified by an example in the ownership below) eg: Marc Azzini, Jambes, B	unknwn	23½"x17¾"x21¾" 600x450x550mm	• box on plinth w/ramp to db & gateway • gate w/tower to court w/two circ towers • main bldg w/3 arches & gallery over • two sq flanking towers one castellated
unknown	**the second fort** (identified by an example in the ownership below) eg: Musée du Jouet, Bxl, B	unknwn	unknown	• box on plinth w/ramp to db & gateway • gate w/tower to court w/one circ tower • main bldg w/3 arches & gallery over • two sq flanking towers one castellated

7-083

7-084

7-085

7-086

7-083 **Unidentified manufacturer**: *possibly early small version (Courtesy Musée du Jouet, Brussels)*
7-084 **Unidentified manufacturer**: *the regular version (Courtesy Musée du Jouet, Brussels)*
7-085 **Unidentified manufacturer**: *the regular version (Courtesy Musée du Jouet, Brussels)*
7-086 **Unidentified manufacturer**: *large possible transition version (Courtesy Musée du Jouet, Brussels)*

The possibly early version above (7-083) has a crude but interesting base. It is cut very severely and contains a roughly cut railway tunnel running underneath. The gateway is unusually plain and the archway looks quite unreal. The rest is however reasonable.

The possible transition version below right (7-086), is difficult to place in the overall scheme of things. One obvious difference is the two ramps, which are much more realistically cut, though the detail is similar to the possibly early version. The gateway is clearly better constructed and one can well imagine it in use. Thereafter everything is much the same except for the arches, which are more rounded, and the small penthouse above the door.

The two examples of the regular version, top center and right (7-084 and 7-085), are almost the same. There are many small differences, and a big difference between the gatehouse on the one and the gateway on the other. Apart from the different application of the stencils, the different treatment of the battlements above the center doors and the consequent prominence of the entrance tower in the version at the left (7-084) deserve a mention.

7-087

7-088

7-089

7-090

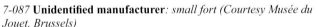

7-091

7-087 **Unidentified manufacturer**: *small fort (Courtesy Musée du Jouet, Brussels)*
7-088 **Unidentified manufacturer**: *small fort (Courtesy Musée du Jouet, Brussels)*
7-089 **Unidentified manufacturer**: *possible late version small fort (Courtesy Marc Azzini)*
7-090 **Unidentified manufacturer**: *large fort with plinth (Courtesy Marc Azzini)*
7-091 **Unidentified manufacturer**: *regular fort with plinth (Courtesy Musée du Jouet, Brussels)*

The three small forts (7-087 to 7-089) probably come from different periods. The most distinctive is the bottom version with its half-timbering and long gallery over the door, making it something like the one with a plinth (7-090).

Only the top example (7-087) has a more or less realistic gateway. This realism is rather let down by the low wall around the courtyard, which would have been difficult to defend. The others (7-088 & 7-089) have openings that are hardly convincing.

The fort at the bottom (7-089) is quite like those from the regular version, although it is difficult to understand the reasoning behind the truncated towers. This could also be said about the fort in the middle (7-088), which is even more truncated. It is the only one of the three to have a simple ramp.

The two large images (7-090 & 7-091) are from the series with a plinth. This plinth is really quite thin and is probably made of plywood. It stretches completely across the length of the fort and is painted blue at the ends, presumably to represent a moat or similar water.

The two box bases are relatively high, with the half-timbered one so high that the ramp becomes unreasonably steep. All the examples we have of these forts with a plinth have "wrap-around" battlements to the courtyard, bringing the corner tower and the gate inside. Apart from that, and a few extra roofs, they appear to differ little from those without a plinth. In the case of the center one (7-090), this can be attributed to the fact that the corner turret and the top of the tower possibly are from other forts.

7-092

7-093

7-094

7-095

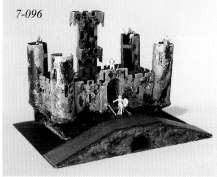

7-096

Various other Belgian Manufacturers
(All of these Courtesy Marc Azzini)

The fort in illustration 7-093 was the No.3 Fort manufactured by Verhelst and Linotte, based in Liège. It was produced about 1938. The fort is incomplete in that the central part of the main building at the back and a tower with two entrances located at the turn in the ramp are missing. It is made of wood and painted by hand. It is professionally done. The 40mm figures of knights are by Elastolin.

There is some uncertainty about the top left and top center forts, in that they may not have been made in Belgium. The one in illustration 7-092 is missing a tower, a gateway, and battlements around the courtyard. It carries the number 18 and is on the large side. The fort in illustration 7-094 is complete and carries the number 4-456; it is thought to have been made at the end of the Second World War. It also is made of wood painted with the aid of stencils. The standard-size knights are by Wetthra (Marcel Vergeylen) in Belgium.

There is no doubt about the two forts in illustration 7-095 and 7-096 – they were definitely made in Belgium, even if we do not know by whom. The fort in illustration 7-095 is made of cardboard with a wood box base, and was made in one piece – not to be taken apart. The fort in 7-096 is made of wood and cardboard, but is more fantastic in its detailing. It is strongly made and well painted by hand. The figures on both of these are standard size knights by Marx.

—DENMARK—

Dansk Legetøjsfabrik Was the Market Leader

Dansk Legetøjsfabrik (Danish Toy Factory) was started in Copenhagen in 1905. It was organized in the prisons by the Danish prison authorities, and intended to be a means of rehabilitation and a source of income for the organizers – not the prisoners.

The operation had a difficult beginning, when their salesman (a 24-year-old prisoner due for imminent release) disappeared with all the samples and was never heard from again. They had a good product, however, and, with no minimum wage to consider, they could hardly fail.

In 1916, the operation was restructured into a stock company, "A/S Dansk Legetøjsfabrik," under the directorship of Otto Larsen. This businessman led the company until his death in 1931, when his son took over, probably until the company was dissolved in 1971.

Their product range was wide from the outset, including horse-drawn vehicles, toy soldiers, guard houses, and dolls' furniture, as well as toy forts. Everything, with the exception of some soldiers, was made of wood and painted by hand.

Throughout the production, the prisoners worked in their cells, rather than in proper work areas. This meant, of course, that there was hardly any possibility of big tools, as you would find in a normal industrial operation. It also meant that there was little communication between them as they worked.

The forts made by the company were of many different sizes and shapes. The prisoners all worked to a basic design for the product they were working on, but each interpreted it in his own way. Consequently, we get forts that are almost the same, but different. For example, the largest, Fort No.41, which was to be made for the whole sixty-six year period of production, comes in a wide variety of forms.

DANSK LEGETØJSFABRIK
1905 to 1971

NO.	DESCRIPTION	DATE	DIMENSIONS	DISTINCTIVE FEATURES
unknown (7-098)	**a small fort–** (identified by an example in the ownership below) eg: Bertel Brunn, NY, US	unknwn	unknown	• ramp (missing) to drawbridge & gate • courtyard with main bldg to rear • two wings & two square flanking towers
unknown (7-097)	**a small fort–** (identified by an example in the ownership below) eg: Bertel Brunn, NY, US	unknwn	unknown	• simple ramp to drawbridge & gateway • courtyard with one squarer corner tower • 3-storey main building to rear • 1 square & 1 octagonal flanking towers

unknown (7-100)	**a small fort** (identified by an example in the ownership below) eg: SOFIA Foundation, CY	unknwn	14¼"x18"x8" 360x455x200mm	• central ramp to drawbridge & gateway • courtyard w/two cannon • main bldg to rear w/central clock tower • 2 square flanking towers
33 (7-099)	**a medium fort** (identified by an example in the ownership below) eg: Musée du Jouet, Bxl, B	unknwn	unknown	• simple ramp to drawbridge & gateway • lower courtyard w/two sq corner towers • ramp up to court w/circ corner tower • main bldg w/2 wings & sq corner tower
33	**a medium fort** (identified by an example in the ownership below) eg: Musée du Jouet, Bxl, B	unknwn	unknown	• simple ramp to drawbridge & gateway • lower court w/bldg & 2 sq corner towers • ramp to yard w/circ tower (missing) • main bldg w/2 wings & sq corner tower
unknown (7-101)	**a medium fort** (identified by an example in the ownership below) eg: de Nayer, B	unknwn	unknown	• simple ramp to drawbridge & gateway • courtyard w/one red top corner tower • 2-storey crenellated main bldg to rear • 2 square flanking towers
41 (7-105 (7-106)	**a large fort** (identified by an example in the ownership below) eg: SOFIA Foundation, CY	unknwn	25¾"x15"x18½" 655x380x470mm	• ramp to gate & court w/bldgs & tower • dbridge (missing) to gate to upper crtyd • circular corner tower & chapel (w tower) • main bldg w/2 sq flanking towers
41 (7-103)	**a large fort** (identified by an example in the ownership below) eg: de Nayer B	unknwn	unknown	• ramp to gate & crtyd w/bldgs & sq tower • db to upper court w/circ corner tower • chapel (w tower) & 2-storey main bldg • 2 square flanking towers
41 (7-104)	**a large fort** (identified by an example in the ownership below) eg: Musée du Jouet, Bxl, B	unknwn	unknown	• ramp to gate (missing) to court w/bldgs • w/corner tower & dbridge to upper court • circular corner tower & chapel (w tower) • main bldg w/two square flanking towers
41	**a large fort** (identified by an example in the ownership below) eg: de Nayer, B	unknwn	unknown	• ramp to gate & court w/bldgs & tower • db to upper court w/circ corner tower • chapel (w tower) & 2-storey main bldg • 2 square flanking towers
41 (7-102)	**a large fort** (identified by an example in the ownership below) eg: Allen Hickling Toy Forts	unkwnn	25¼"x13¾"x13¼" 640x350x335mm	• ramp to gate (missing) to court w/bldgs • w/corner tower & dbridge to upper court • circ corner tower & 2 sq flanking towers • missing chapel, main bldg & gateway

We can gain some insight into the age of a fort by its color scheme. In the early years, the colors, chosen by the prisoners themselves, were dark, grey, and gloomy, as a reflection of the surroundings and mood of the workers. However, as time progressed and the company prospered, the outside sales force was able to instigate a change to more cheerful colors.

There were other companies, for example Hedeboflid (Heathdweller Craft), producing forts in Denmark at the time, but they could hardly compete with Dansk Legetøjsfrabrik, with its almost unlimited free labor, and did not last long.

c.1920-1935

7-097

7-098

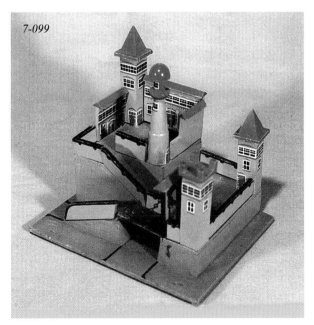

7-099

7-100

7-097 **Dansk Legetøjsfabrik (?)**: *small fort*
7-098 **Dansk Legetøjsfabrik**: *small fort*
7-099 **Dansk Legetøjsfabrik No.33**: *medium residential (?) fort (Courtesy Musée du Jouet, Brussels)*
7-100 **Dansk Legetøjsfabrik**: *small fort*

The three forts at the top are typical of the smaller ones Dansk Legetøjsfabrik manufactured. Without catalogues, it is impossible to say when they were produced. The white and grey forts (7-098 & 7-100) are really quite alike in size and style, but the grey fort (7-100) appears to have been made more recently. The white fort (7-098) is missing its ramp and drawbridge. The red brick fort (7-097) may not be by Dansk Legetøjsfrabrik.

The medium residential (?) fort to the left (7-099) is No.33. It is beautifully painted, which indicates that it was an earlier version, presumably made soon after the call went out for brighter forts. The layout is reminiscent of Carl Weber and others in Germany about 1910, who made forts in very similar form, but in a very different architectural style. The positions and types of building are remarkably similar. The fenestration, in particular, is a clue to the age. It is clearly not medieval, and is of a modern style typical of the Bauhaus in the 1930s.

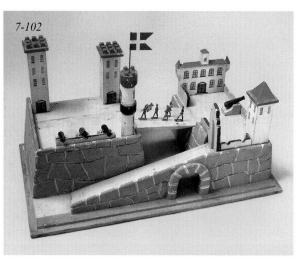

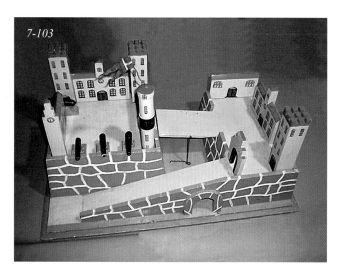

7-101 **Dansk Legetøjsfabrik**: *medium fort*
7-102 **Dansk Legetøjsfabrik No.41**: *large fort*
7-103 **Dansk Legetøjsfabrik No.41**: *large fort*
7-104 **Dansk Legetøjsfabrik No.41**: *large fort (Courtesy Musée du Jouet, Brussels)*

The medium fort above (7-101) is a more usual design than the Fort No.33 (7-099) on the previous page. Though the painting of the windows implies an early version, the fenestration around the tops of the towers seems to contradict this. One is tempted to question the base, which seems to have been stripped, leaving no trace of the "stone" finish. My guess is that it was about 1925.

The other three forts are all versions of No.41, which demonstrate how the prisoners had their own variations on a theme. They were made somewhat later, as evidenced by the brighter colors that were demanded by the sales force. Also, the painting lacks the finesse of the earlier forts. For example, the depiction of the big stones making up the base is not so well defined. The incision became weaker over time, and in some cases it was omitted altogether and just painted on. The building pieces are more or less the same as the earlier forts, and in the same location; the overall size is comparable.

The upper right fort (7-103) is complete (some pieces are misplaced). The fort to its left (7-102) is missing the chapel, the main building, a secondary building, and the gateway at the top of the drawbridge. The fort below (7-104) is more or less complete; it has a gateway missing from the top of the ramp and its drawbridge chains have gone.

7-105

7-106

7 105 **Dansk Legetøjsfabrik No.41**: *large fort*
7-106 **Dansk Legetøjsfabrik No.41**: *main courtyard showing the cannon & label*

This is an early version of No.41, which was manufactured throughout the production life of the company – a period of about sixty-five years. Its somber colors reflected the feelings of the prisoners; it was only after goading by the sales staff that lighter and brighter colors became the order of the day.

The precision of the wood cutting, the assembly of the buildings, and the wonderful painting of the windows, clocks, and bell pull are typical of the early period. The stained glass windows in the chapel are particularly worthy of note. The only really toy-like part of the fort is in the crenellation on the top of the towers, which is just not deep enough.

The condition of the fort is really very good, given its age, but the drawbridge and its chains are missing. Interestingly, two windows on the tower nearest the camera, which would have been visible on the face to the front, have been erased. Also there are a couple of pieces of the plinth missing.

The label pasted in the middle of the courtyard (7-106), was introduced by Otto Larsen, who was the first director. There were several versions of it, but they all retained the basic design of crossed Danish flags with a wooden horse in front of them. The cannon, which can also be seen in this view, are also beautifully made – all of wood, which was the custom in the prisons.

7-107

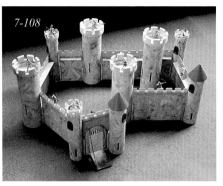

7-108

7-109

7-110

7-111

Various Other European Manufacturers

(7-108 courtesy Musée du Jouet, Bxl)

Here is a selection of forts from other countries in Europe. There is no doubt that forts were manufactured in one form or another all over the world; unfortunately, I do not know them. These are a few that I have come across.

The top left fort (7-107) comes from Spain. It certainly displays a Moorish sort of detailing, which would be appropriate. Quite apart from some ingenious ways of coupling the pieces together using wood brackets, which I have not come across elsewhere, it is really quite unlike any other. It is difficult to put a date on it; the paint style seems reasonably modern, which probably makes it after the 1939-45 war.

The two in the middle (7-108 & 7-109) are made of injection-molded plastic, which means they could not have been made until after 1960. The one at the top (7-108) also comes from Spain and is of modular design that can be assembled in a number of ways. The one below (7-109) was manufactured by Tibado in Italy. It is, in fact, almost a direct copy of the Cherilea Medieval Castle made in Britain. Whether this was by accident or design is not known.

The top right fort (7-110) originated in Sweden. It is so well made that one is tempted to think that it was not manufactured at all. It is of modular design so that the pieces can be put on anywhere within reason. The ramp and gateway, however, are fixed, and the front wall looks like a neat unit. The pieces are made of fairly large bits of wood and are really quite heavy, so that shooting at it with the average toy gun is likely to have little effect.

The bottom right fort (7-111) was manufactured in Russia, probably in about 1985. It is made of relatively thin corrugated cardboard and demonstrates a fine degree of ingenuity and imagination. No glue was used in its assembly, yet it stands remarkably firm.

EIGHT

FINAL THOUGHTS

When I started this book, so long ago I can scarcely remember it, I think I had the idea of getting a load off my mind – and a number of people off my back! These people said that I owed it to the collecting world – what a thought! It is true that, over the years, I have picked up much information about the subject, and it would be a pity if it all just disappeared with me. Maybe they were right, so, many years later, here it is.

In retrospect, rather than a stimulating read from start to finish, this has turned out to be more of a reference book or a browsing piece. I am not unhappy about that, because the subject is fragmented by the scarcity of information in many cases. In fact, this may be considered a strength by the many and various potential readers, all of whom have an interest in the subject, but many of whom come to it with different needs.

The three chapters on specific manufacturers are as complete as I could make them. Of course, not all forts are covered, but many are via the illustrations or the spreadsheets. In the other three chapters, which are geographically based, the forts were selected on the basis of those about which I had information. All of them are included on this simple criterion, rather than some personal assessment of their relative importance.

When it comes to drawing conclusions from it all, I find it really difficult. There is no basis for comparison, because each fort is assessed on its own merits, and only rarely relative to others. I think it is wise not to say anything specific and to avoid conclusions, which can only be drawn in general terms in any case. For example, for the first fifty years of manufacture, the only manufacturers came from Germany. The only comparisons that can be drawn are concerned with the decline in their grip on the market and the relative increase of manufacturers in other countries, all of which is pretty obvious – and boring.

I am sure there are enormous gaps in my account of the story. Also, I am sure, there are many mistakes. But there is this other role that my book may take on – the role of trail-blazer. Now that I have broken the ice, so to speak, maybe it will give impetus to others to take up the story – to fill the gaps and correct the inaccuracies. But why stop there? I know there is so much more to learn, both in depth and breadth. It is a very large subject; about that there is no doubt. So let's go folks! Let's do it!

BIBLIOGRAPHY

Ackerman, Evelyn. *The Genius of Moritz Gottschalk.* (Annapolis, MD: Gold Horse Publishing, 1994).

Azzini, Marc. "Les Chateaux Forts: De (speelgoed-) Kastelen en Burchten." In: *Le Petit Soldat – Het Soldaatje.* (St Servais, BE. ASBL, 2001)

_____. "Les Chateaux Forts: De (speelgoed-) Kastelen en Burchten" (continued). In: *Le Petit Soldat – Het Soldaatje.* (St Servais, BE. ASBL, 2001)

_____. "Les Chateaux Forts de l'Erzgebirge; Part 1." In: *Le Petit Soldat – Het Soldaatje No.29.* (St Servais, BE. ASBL, 2008)

_____. "Les Chateaux Forts de l'Erzgebirge; Part 2." In: *Le Petit Soldat – Het Soldaatje No.30.* (St Servais, BE. ASBL, 2008)

Bachmann, Manfred, *Das Waldkirchner Spielzeugmusterbuch* (Edition Leipzig, 1978).

Broquet, Patrick. "Décors en Boîtes à Rabat: les Bon Dufour n'en sont pas!" In *Collectioneur & Chineur, No. 194.* (Fontainebleu, France, 2015)

Cieslik, Marianne, and Jürgen Cieslik. *Moritz Gottschalk 1892–1931.* (Baden-Baden, DE: Verlag Marianne Cieslik, 2000).

Cooper, Patty, and Dian Zillner. *Toy Buildings 1880–1980.* (Atglen, PA: Schiffer Publishing Ltd., 2000).

Fawdry, Marguerite. *British Tin Toys.* (London, UK: New Cavendish Books Ltd., 1990).

Fritzsch, Karl Ewald, and Manfred Bachmann. *An Illustrated History of German Toys.* (New York, NY: Hastings House Inc., 1978).

Herman, Paul. *Le Jouet en Belgique.* (Bruxelles, B: Rossel Edition, I984).

Hickling, Allen. "A Toy Fort Anomaly." In: *The Tri-ang Telegraph, Number TT16.* (Sale, UK: The Tri-ang Society, 2003.

_____. "Balmoral Castle: a Moko Toy." In: *Old Toy Soldier, Volume 23, Number 1.* (Oak Park, IL: OTSN Inc., 1999).

_____. "BINBAK Follow Up." In: *Old Toy Soldier, Volume 29, Number 4.* (Pittsburgh, PA: OTS., 2005). Plastic Warrior, 2004

_____. "Burleytoys' Buster Fort No.1." In: *Old Toy Soldier, Volume 22, Number 2.* (Oak Park, IL: OTSN Inc., 1998).

_____. "Chad Valley Toy Fort: Size No.1." In: *Old Toy Soldier, Volume 22, Number 3.* (Oak Park, IL: OTSN Inc., 1998).

_____. "Elf into Joy: Toy Forts Made by the Hall Family." In: *Old Toy Soldier, Volume 31, Number 3.* (Pittsburgh, PA: OTS., 2007).

_____. "From Dollhouse to 'Fortress:' the Military Aspect of Moritz Gottschalk's Toy World, Part 1." In: *Old Toy Soldier, Volume 25, Number 1.* (Oak Park, IL: OTSN Inc., 2001).

_____. "From Dollhouse to 'Fortress:' the Military Aspect of Moritz Gottschalk's Toy World, Part 2." In: *Old Toy Soldier, Volume 25, Number 2.* (Oak Park, IL: OTSN Inc., 2001).

_____. "From Dollhouse to 'Fortress:' the Military Aspect of Moritz Gottschalk's Toy World, Part 3." In: *Old Toy Soldier, Volume 25, Number 4.* (Pittsburgh, PA: OTS., 2001).

_____. "From Dollhouse to 'Fortress:' the Military Aspect of Moritz Gottschalk's Toy World, Part 4." In: *Old Toy Soldier, Volume 27, Number 2.* (Pittsburgh, PA: OTS., 2003).

_____. "Great Minds Think Alike or Tri-ang -v- Elastolin." In: *Old Toy Soldier, Volume 33, Number 4.* (Pittsburgh, PA: OTS., 2009).

_____. "Jack Binns and Bill Baker were BINBAK." In: *Old Toy Soldier, Volume 28, Number 4.* (Pittsburgh, PA: OTS., 2004).

_____. "Mr Kleemann's Legacy: the Original (History)." In: *Plastic Warrior, Number 101.* (Woking, Surrey. Plastic Warrior, 2004).

_____. "Mr Kleemann's Legacy: the Original (Design)." In: *Plastic Warrior, Number 102.* (Woking, Surrey. Plastic Warrior, 2004).

_____. "Mr Kleemann's Legacy: Copies and Derivatives." In: *Plastic Warrior, Number 103.* (Woking, Surrey. Plastic Warrior, 2004).

_____. "Snow Castles in the Playroom." In: *Old Toy Soldier, Volume 23, Number 4.* (Oak Park, IL: OTSN Inc., 1999).

_____. "Sod's Law: A Snow Castles Round-up." In: *Old Toy Soldier, Volume 24, Number 4.* (Oak Park, IL: OTSN Inc., 2000).

_____. "The Lines Bros.' New Toy Forts: 1939." In: *The Tri-ang Telegraph, Number TT36*. (Sale, UK: The Tri-ang Society, 2010.

_____. "The Siege of Sebastopol: a Classic Three-in-One Toy Based on the Historical Event." In: *Old Toy Soldier, Volume 24, Number 2*. (Oak Park, IL: OTSN Inc., 2000).

_____. "Tri-ang Forts." In: *The Tri-ang Telegraph, Numbers R005 & R006*. (Sale, UK: The Tri-ang Society, 2000.

_____. "Tri-ang Fort No.1." In: *Old Toy Soldier, Volume 22, Number 4*. (Oak Park, IL: OTSN Inc., 1998).

_____. "Tri-ang's Harlech Castle: the Story in Two Scenarios." In: *Old Toy Soldier, Volume 23, Number 2*. (Oak Park, IL: OTSN Inc., 1999).

_____. "'You Build It': a Short History of UBILDA Toy Forts." In: *Toy Soldier Parade, Volume 2, Issue 2*. (London, UK: Yesteryear Publishing Ltd., 1992).

Hossann, Jean-Pierre. "Les Châteaux Forts – à l'Assaut de Leurs Secrets!". In: *Collectionneur & Chineur No.147*. (Fontainebleau, France: 2013).

Kurtz, Henry I., and Burtt R. Ehrlich. *The Art of the Toy Soldier*. (London, UK: New Cavendish Books Ltd., 1987).

Legrand, Marc. "La Représentation du Château Fort dans les Jouets." Thesis in pursuit of a Masters Degree in the Department of Archeology and the History of Art, Catholic University of Louvain, Belgium, 2009.

Lines, Richard. "Introduction." In: *Tri-ang Toys 1937/38*. (London, UK.: New Cavendish Books Ltd., 1988).

Müller, Peter. "Von Spielburgen in Kinderzimmern." In: *Figuren Magazin Special, Burgen und Kastelle*. (Berlin, DE. Verlag *Figuren Magazin*, 2003).

_____ "Burgen der Hausser-Nachtkriegsära Teil 1: Burgen – mit Burgteilen aus Holz-Pappe und Kunststoffhügel." In: *Figuren Magazin Special, Burgen und Kastelle*. (Berlin, DE. Verlag *Figuren Magazin*, 2003).

_____. "Burgen der Hausser-Nachtkriegsära Teil 2: Burgen mit Burgteilen aus Kunststoff und Kunststoffhügel." In: *Figuren Magazin Special, Burgen und Kastelle*. (Berlin, DE. Verlag *Figuren Magazin*, 2003).

_____. "Burgen der Hausser-Nachtkriegsära Teil 3: Die Kastelle." In: *Figuren Magazin Special, Burgen und Kastelle*. (Berlin, DE. Verlag *Figuren Magazin*, 2003).

_____. "Burgen der Hausser-Nachtkriegsära Teil 4: Die tiefgezogenen Burgen." In: *Figuren Magazin Special, Burgen und Kastelle*. (Berlin, DE. Verlag *Figuren Magazin*, 2003).

_____. "Burgen der Hausser-Nachtkriegsära Teil 5: Einige wichtige Ergänzungen." In: *Figuren Magazin Special, Burgen und Kastelle*. (Berlin, DE. Verlag *Figuren Magazin*, 2003).

_____. "Bastionen – die neuen Befestigungsanlagen." In: *Figuren Magazin Special, Burgen und Kastelle*. (Berlin, DE. Verlag *Figuren Magazin*, 2003).

Parry-Crooke, Charlotte. *Mr. Gamage's Great Toy Bazaar 1902-1906*. (New York, NY: Hasting House Publishers Inc., 1982).

Pietruschka, Andreas. "Der König von Kreuzberg." In: *Figuren Magazin Special, Burgen und Kastelle*. (Berlin, DE. Verlag *Figuren Magazin*, 2003).

_____. "LINEOL Burgen." In: *Figuren Magazin Special, Burgen und Kastelle*. (Berlin, DE. Verlag *Figuren Magazin*, 2003).

_____. "ELASTOLIN – Burgen aus Masse." In: *Figuren Magazin Special, Burgen und Kastelle*. (Berlin, DE. Verlag *Figuren Magazin*, 2003).

_____. "ELASTOLIN – Burgen aus Holz." In: *Figuren Magazin Special, Burgen und Kastelle*. (Berlin, DE. Verlag *Figuren Magazin*, 2003).

_____. "Eine seltene ELASTOLIN-Ritterburg." In: *Figuren Magazin Special, Burgen und Kastelle*. (Berlin, DE. Verlag *Figuren Magazin*, 2003).

Polaine, Reggie, and David Hawkins. *The War Toys 1*. (London, UK: New Cavendish Books Ltd., 1991).

Ristau, Malte. "Burgen passend zu 7cm-Figuren." In: *Figuren Magazin Special, Burgen und Kastelle*. (Berlin, DE.

Van Wanzeele, Luc. *Nazaire Beeusaert: A History of a Toy Factory*. (BE. Luc Van Wazeele, 2009)

Verlag *Figuren Magazin*, 2003).

INDEX